Mastering LOB Development for Silverlight 5: A Case Study in Action

Develop a full LOB Silverlight 5 application from scratch with the help of expert advice and an accompanying case study

Braulio Díez Botella

José Fernando Almoguera

Pablo Núñez

Sebastian Stehle

Rocío Serrano Rudilla

Reyes García Rosado

[PACKT] enterprise
PUBLISHING
professional expertise distilled

BIRMINGHAM - MUMBAI

Mastering LOB Development for Silverlight 5: A Case Study in Action

Copyright © 2012 Packt Publishing

First published: February 2012

Production Reference: 1170212

Published by Packt Publishing Ltd.
Livery Place
35 Livery Street
Birmingham B3 2PB, UK.

ISBN 978-1-84968-354-8

www.packtpub.com

Cover Image by Antonio J. Nebro (antonio@lcc.uma.es)

Credits

Authors

Braulio Díez Botella

José Fernando Almoguera

Pablo Núñez

Sebastian Stehle

Rocío Serrano Rudilla

Reyes García Rosado

Reviewers

Kevin DeRudder

Alex Golesh

Carlos Hernández

Tarkan Karadayi

Jose Luis Latorre

Porter Steven

Davide Trotta

Acquisition Editor

Stephanie Moss

Lead Technical Editor

Hyacintha D'Souza

Technical Editors

Joyslita D'Souza

Veronica Fernandes

Unnati Shah

Copy Editors

Leonard D'Silva

Laxmi Subramanian

Project Coordinator

Leena Purkait

Proof readers

Mario Cecere

Bernadette Watkins

Indexers

Hemangini Bari

Tejal Daruwale

Graphics

Valentina D'Silva

Manu Joseph

Production Coordinator

Prachali Bhiwandkar

Cover Work

Prachali Bhiwandkar

Foreword

Line of Business applications. Think about this term for a moment—Line of Business. Yes, *Business*. Business means change. Changes are happening faster than we usually think it is possible. How can we deal with it? With the right set of knowledge and tools, of course!

Business, nowadays, is more demanding than ever, but so are the technologies we have in hand. We have moved away from the times when a fully-featured desktop application was enough. Now, we want to be able to work from anywhere—from any place on Earth, by any means—let it be our office computer (PC or Mac), our netbook at home, our mobile, or tablet on the plane. This is how RIA applications emerged. This book is about how to get started, with developing RIA applications using one particular set of technologies—those in the Microsoft domain, namely, Silverlight, WCF RIA Services, and other frameworks and tools around them.

Back in 2007, when the first pre-release bits of Silverlight were introduced, there weren't many ways to build fully-featured and always-connected applications. JavaScript was one of the options. It had been out there for a long, time and, although it could help you build magnificent applications, it didn't come far when talking about robust, highly-maintainable, change-resistant, and easy to get started code. Its support for different browsers was not a pretty story. The pre-release version of Silverlight was rather limited, but even then people started to see big potential in it to target media and business applications. The potential turned out to be real, when a year and a half later, the Redmond campus released the First Official Release of the plugin, which had .NET Framework support called Silverlight 2. Developers were excited, and this is how things got to work. The whole community was pushing hard; .NET developers were finally able to start writing applications that could work everywhere. The Silverlight release cycle period is an unbelievable nine months. That means every nine months, the community was getting a new version! Silverlight 3 came packed with lots of features enabling the development of Line of Business applications. Everyone was wowed, as to how quickly Microsoft got their product ready for the enterprise and some big players, such as banks, started paying attention.

Thanks to the great support, both from the community and Microsoft, Silverlight emerged a real business-oriented platform. A lot of open source projects popped up—MVVM Light Toolkit (by Laurent Bugnion, see *Chapter 4, Architecture*), Prism (by Microsoft Patterns & Practices), MEF (later included in the .NET Framework version 4, see *Chapter 4, Architecture*), WCF RIA Services (see *Chapter 5, RIA Services Data Access*), and enabled rapid development of strong and well-architected applications. At least two web communities (one Microsoft, Silverlight.net and another independent, SilverlightShow.net), focused entirely on Silverlight, starting right from the birth of the plugin and covering every little piece of the framework with news, articles, and video tutorials, both contributing solely to the evolution and adoption
of Silverlight as the platform for the development of Line of Business applications.

Microsoft continued their work on the platform and released Silverlight 4, a version I like to refer to as business-feature complete. With that release, Microsoft enabled us to do whatever we needed, to satisfy business requirements. From then on, only a few things could be done better, and that is exactly what happened with the latest fifth release.

Now both, the JavaScript and Silverlight world has evolved to a point where you can accomplish astonishing things in very little time. But even with the latest powerful JavaScript frameworks such as jQuery, Knockout, Kendo UI, and many more, we still struggle to create well-performing and easily-maintainable Line of Business applications. While it is easy to use JavaScript for lots of different types of applications, Silverlight remains the platform to go with, when you are looking for a business-class environment.

Starting from the fundamental *Create Project*, to architecting your application, this book guides you through all the major steps and dives into details of creating Line of Business applications that are resistant to change. Give yourself a jump start and ride the wave of exciting and continuously changing world business applications.

Emil Stoychev
Co-founder, SilverlightShow.net

About the Authors

Braulio Díez Botella is a Software Developer specializing in Microsoft technologies. He has more than 15 years of experience working on international projects. He is a Silverlight MVP, freelance Developer, Technical Writer, Trainer, and Speaker.

José Fernando Almoguera has over seven years of experience in software development and the IT industry. He works as a consultant specializing in LOB development using Microsoft technologies (Silverlight and ASP.NET). Besides that, José works as a Trainer and a Technical Writer for sites such as SilverlightShow and DNM+.

> I would like to thank my family who have been positive and unconditional supporters, especially my parents, because they always believed in me. I would also like to thank my colleagues who have provided invaluable opportunities for me to expand my knowledge and boost my career.

Pablo Núñez is a Developer with more than 10 years of experience in Microsoft technologies. He has worked on Line of Business applications for important sectors such as automotive, telephony, textile, and logistics. Pablo has experience with web and desktop technologies, which ultimately converge on Silverlight. In addition, Pablo works as a Trainer and is an active member on the MS communities.

Sebastian Stehle is a Software Engineer from Germany. He is an enthusiastic Silverlight Developer and the author of the ImageTools library and Co-founder of the SilverDiagram group. He is also interested in game development and service-oriented architecture.

Rocío Serrano Rudilla is a freelance English/Spanish Scientific-Technical Translator, Software Localizer, Linguist, and Proofreader. She has worked as a Translator and Editor for Custom PC Spain, as well as for other relevant magazines and websites. Her main areas of expertise are in IT (hardware, software, networking, video conferencing, Internet, and so on), marketing and communication, and biomedics/pharmaceutical fields.

She also collaborates with several translation agencies and direct clients (mainly IT companies).

> To Miguel, for his enormous patience and, above all, his essential support.

Reyes García Rosado is very experienced as a Multidisciplinary Consultant. Lately, she is devoted to teaching and writing technical articles.

About the Reviewers

Kevin DeRudder is a Web Developer working for several big companies. He is also a Lecturer in the Technical University of West Flanders, where he teaches frontend web development techniques such as Silverlight, Mobile development, HTML 5, and so on, to future web developers.

Kevin is also heavily involved in several communities such as the Belgian Silverlight User Group and some web communities.

Alex Golesh, Microsoft Most Valuable Professional (MVP) , is a Senior Architect and a Silverlight Leader at Sela Group. He is an international expert in Silverlight, WPF, Windows Phone 7, and XNA. Alex is currently consulting for various enterprises in Israel and worldwide, architecting and developing RIA and mobile solutions. He has been developing training samples and courses for various product groups in Microsoft (Redmond). He conducts lectures and workshops and leads projects all around the world in the fields of RIA, Smart Client, and Windows Phone 7.

Interesting facts:

- MVP in Silverlight
- One of the top Silverlight experts
- Conducted WPF and Silverlight training in India, Sweden, and Poland as a part of the Metro Program (Microsoft Early Adopter program)
- "Top Trainer" of Silverlight in Metro program, FY09
- Author of Sela courses that are available on the MS Learning Courseware Library such as Silverlight 2.0 for Developers (50145), Upgrade to Silverlight 3, Silverlight 3 Introduction, and Silverlight 3 Advanced
- Speaker at Tech-Ed Israel 2008, 2010, Tech-Ed South Africa 2008, Microsoft Dev Academy III, IV, PDC 2010 workshop and numerous Microsoft Developer Days/Open Houses

- Participated in a Microsoft/SAP joint project as a Senior Software Developer from Microsoft Consulting Services
- Presented a session at PDC 2010 Workshop about XNA Game development for Windows Phone 7
- Examples of projects that he developed/was a part of the development team:
    - Silverlight TreeView (http://silverlighttreeview.codeplex.com/)
    - Silverlight String-To-PathGeometry Converter (http://stringtopathgeometry.codeplex.com/)
    - Silverlight Hebrew & Arabic Language Support (http://silverlightrtl.codeplex.com/)
    - Silverlight and WPF game development for Microsoft DPE — a game that demonstrates the concepts and best practices in Silverlight and WPF game development
    - Windows Phone 7 Training kit labs (http://msdn.microsoft.com/en-us/wp7trainingcourse.aspx)
    - APP HUB (http://create.msdn.com/en-US/education/)

Mr. Golesh has his own blog (http://blogs.microsoft.co.il/blogs/alex_golesh/), where he constantly writes about interesting topics in Silverlight and Windows Phone 7 development.

> I would like to thank my wife and daughter for having so much patience and supporting me while working on this book and my other projects.

Carlos Hernández is an experienced Silverlight developer, a technology that fascinates him and which he has followed since Silverlight 3. Carlos is a Microsoft Certified Technology Specialist (MCTS) in Silverlight 4 and has four years of experience in .NET development.

Currently he works at SolidQ in several projects related to Silverlight, WPF, Windows Phone 7, and Windows Azure platform.

> I am very thankful to the author for sharing this experience with me and for teaching me a lot of useful things about this technology and this profession.

Tarkan Karadayi has been a professional Software Developer for over 12 years. He has a Masters in Computer Science and is currently working as a Lead Developer.

I would like to thank my wife Anna, my three sons Taran, Kyle, and Ryan, and my parents for their love and support.

Jose Luis Latorre is a Microsoft Silverlight MVP (Most Valuable Professional), Toastmasters Competent Communicator, STEP member, Writer, and Trainer, who is deeply involved with technical communities through his collaboration with INETA Europe, Barcelona Developers, and DEVITUG UK user groups.

He is strongly focused on XAML technologies and user interfaces design and development, focused mostly in presentation layer technologies such as Silverlight, WP7, WPF, and Windows 8. He has written several articles on these topics.

He is the founder of Brainsiders, a Microsoft Partner which is dedicated to provide services of consulting, design, and development of user interfaces and RIA solutions for mobile, desktop, and web platforms. It also provides training solutions.

Davide Trotta was born in Turin (Italy) in 1980. Since childhood, he had the opportunity to work closely with computers, as his father worked for a major company that made computers. By the age of 15 years, he entered the programming world. At 19, his first job was a contract for a company in the financial sector, whose job included the development of web pages (ASP 3.0). In .NET Framework, Davide realized its potential and has followed all its changes, working as a freelancer and finding complex projects based on that technology.

In the last two years, he worked in the production of desktop/RIA/mobile, exploiting the world of WPF/Silverlight. He has worked for large local and international systems integrators companies such as Altran, Atos Origin, and Delta3.

Thank you for your support, Simone Agostini and Silvia Albanesi.

www.PacktPub.com

Support files, eBooks, discount offers and more

You might want to visit www.PacktPub.com for support files and downloads related to your book.

Did you know that Packt offers eBook versions of every book published, with PDF and ePub files available? You can upgrade to the eBook version at www.PacktPub.com and as a print book customer, you are entitled to a discount on the eBook copy. Get in touch with us at service@packtpub.com for more details.

At www.PacktPub.com, you can also read a collection of free technical articles, sign up for a range of free newsletters and receive exclusive discounts and offers on Packt books and eBooks.

http://PacktLib.PacktPub.com

Do you need instant solutions to your IT questions? PacktLib is Packt's online digital book library. Here, you can access, read and search across Packt's entire library of books.

Why Subscribe?

- Fully searchable across every book published by Packt
- Copy and paste, print and bookmark content
- On demand and accessible via web browser

Free Access for Packt account holders

If you have an account with Packt at www.PacktPub.com, you can use this to access PacktLib today and view nine entirely free books. Simply use your login credentials for immediate access.

Instant Updates on New Packt Books

Get notified! Find out when new books are published by following @PacktEnterprise on Twitter, or the *Packt Enterprise* Facebook page.

To Antonio Nebro, great lecturer, passionate for technology and even better Sushiman.

Braulio Díez Botella

To my parents, because they always believe in me. I love you

José Fernando Almoguera

To my wife Patricia and my kids Julia, Marcos and Claudia, thanks for your support and the patience you had when I was writing this book

Pablo Núñez

To my two lovely sons Nacho and Sergio

Reyes García Rosado

Table of Contents

Preface

Management applications, also known as **Line of Business (LOB)** applications, constitute a great piece of the pie, that is the software development market. Until a few years ago, a management application used to be implemented as a desktop app. However, this approach has some drawbacks, as globalization pushes us to implement information systems that support remote access via a standard web browser.

Targeting an LOB application to run on a web platform adds greater complexity to such a development, bearing in mind the fact that the Web was not conceived to host applications which need heavy interaction with the user. Derived from this necessity, the term **Rich Internet Application (RIA)** emerged. RIAs are web applications that are used in a similar way to desktop applications.

Silverlight 5 is Microsoft's commitment to the implementation of RIA, which will allows us, among other things:

- To implement an application from beginning to end with powerful languages (C#, VB.NET, and so on), with no more of JavaScript
- To implement advanced UI (XAML markup language)
- To work with professional data access (WCF, RIA Services, Entity Framework, and so on)
- To decouple designer and developer roles
- To have the user able to install the application as if it was a desktop one

LOB application case study: applying what we have learned

With the purpose of applying theoretical concepts, the contents of this book are accompanied by the implementation of an LOB application. In this case, it is an application intended for office space reservations. We have chosen this kind of application, as it includes the following features:

- It contains master-detail relationships.

- It's implemented as a real project, using best practices (MVVM pattern based, unit testing, and so on). It allows us to implement a standard management application interface, as well as a more advanced one (Bing Maps integration).

- It incorporates user roles (administrator/average user).

At the end of every chapter, we will implement the most significant parts of this app. You can see a map of the site we are going to create in the following figure:

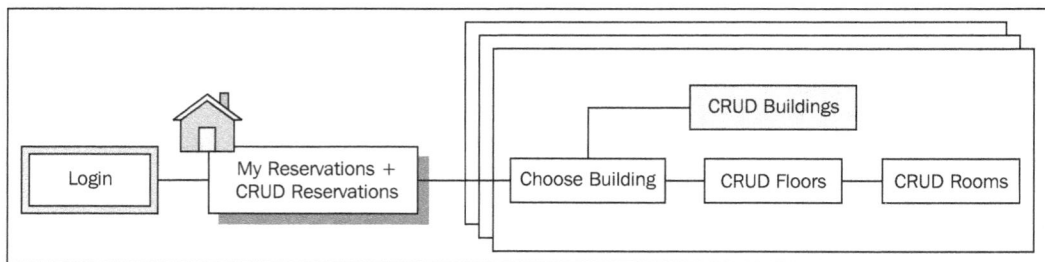

The details of every window can be seen in the following screenshots:

- My reservations and CRUD (Create, Read, Update, and Delete) reservations:

- Choose building:

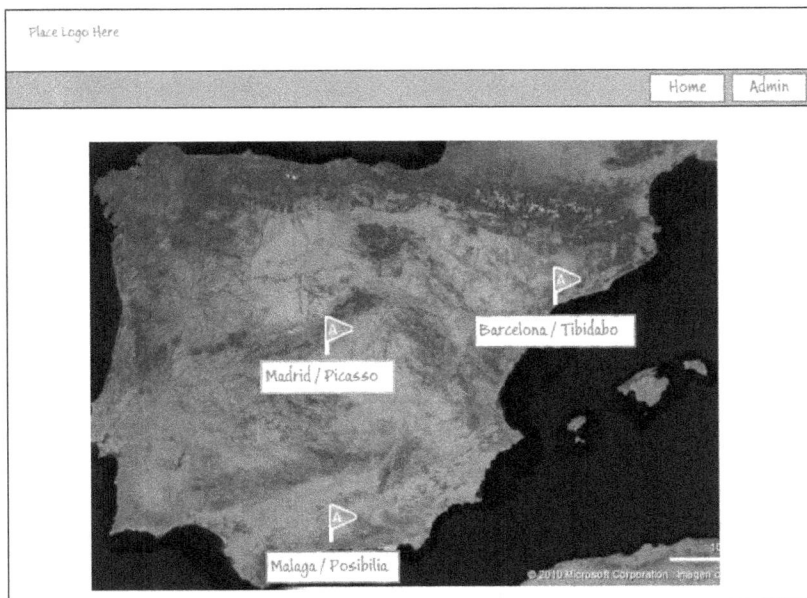

- CRUD floors:

Place Logo Here

| | Home | Admin |

Building:

Floor	Rooms
First floor	Gibralfaro Catedral Alcazaba
Second floor	Cantarrijan
Third floor	Bajondillo Sohail

Floor TextBox

Room	Capacity	Facilities
Gibralfaro	10	Spider
Catedral	40	Projector Video
Alcazaba	5	Spider

Edit Rooms

New Save Delete

- CRUD rooms:

```
CRUD Rooms                                                              ⊠

  Basic Text

  ┌──────────────────────┬──────────────┬────────────────────────┐
  │ Room                 │ Capacity     │ Facilities             │
  ├──────────────────────┼──────────────┼────────────────────────┤
  │ Gibralfaro           │ 10           │ Spider                 │
  │ Catedral             │ 40           │ Projector Video        │
  │ Alcazaba             │ 5            │ Spider                 │
  └──────────────────────┴──────────────┴────────────────────────┘


  ┌────────────────────────────────────────────────────────────────┐
  │  Name  [Gibralfaro                    ]    Capacity  [ 10 ]      │
  │  Facilities                                                      │
  │  ┌──────────────────────────────────────────────────────────┐   │
  │  │                                                          │   │
  │  │                                                          │   │
  │  └──────────────────────────────────────────────────────────┘   │
  └────────────────────────────────────────────────────────────────┘
                           [  New  ]  [  Save  ]  [  Delete  ]
```

The application prototype is available for download at www.packtpub.com.

What this book covers

Chapter 1, Express Introduction to Silverlight, introduces the basic concepts for those who have not previously worked with this technology. In case you have experience with Silverlight, you can skip this chapter or read it as reinforcement.

Chapter 2, Forms and Browsing, explains how the standard line of a business user interface is implemented in Silverlight (views, child windows, and navigation framework).

Chapter 3, Data Binding, explains how data binding works (a connection between the UI controls and data objects), allowing us to decouple the presentation layer of the business layer (data, validations, and so on).

Chapter 4, Architecture, explains how to define an architecture for our application. For this reason, we will cover a series of patterns, as well as their application in Silverlight (MVVM, MVVM Light Toolkit, MEF, and so on).

Chapter 5, RIA Services Data Access, explains how to interact with databases, via technologies such as WCF, RIA Services, and ADO.NET Entity Framework.

Chapter 6, Out of Browser (OOB) Applications, explains how to install our own application on our client's desktop, and even ask the user for elevated permissions in order to communicate via COM or P/Invoke with other components.

Chapter 7, Testing your LOB Application, explains how to implement automatic unit testing and UI testing.

Chapter 8, Error Control, explains how to deal with server communication errors and application execution errors.

Chapter 9, Integration with other Web Applications, explains how to integrate a Silverlight component in an existing web application and how to establish communication between JavaScript and Silverlight.

Chapter 10, Consuming Web Services, explains how to integrate WCF Web Services in our application.

Chapter 11, Security, explains how to deal with security regarding:

- Application: Those aspects which make a Silverlight application secure so as to run in a web client
- Communications: What should be done to secure our communications
- Authentication/Authorization: How can a login page and authentication /authorization levels be added to a Silverlight application

What you need for this book

In order to compile and run the sample code included in this book, you will need to install:

- Visual Studio 2010
- Visual Studio 2010 SP1
- Silverlight 5 Tool for Visual Studio 2010 SP1

Who this book is for

This book is aimed at:

- Developers who have previously worked with Silverlight
- Web developers who have some knowledge of Line of Business applications
- Software architects who want to learn how to define an LOB architecture for a Silverlight-based development and how to solve common LOB challenges

If you already have a firm grasp of Silverlight development and are keen to advance your specialist knowledge of Line of Business (LOB) application development, then *Mastering LOB Development for Silverlight 5: A Case Study in Action* is for you.

If you are a developer with experience with other technologies, you may also find this book useful.

Conventions

In this book, you will find a number of styles of text that distinguish between different kinds of information. Here are some examples of these styles, and an explanation of their meaning.

Code words in text are shown as follows: "We can include other contexts through the use of the `include` directive."

A block of code is set as follows:

```
<StackPanel
  Grid.Row="2"
  Orientation="Horizontal" HorizontalAlignment="Right">
  <Button Content="New"
    Width="60" Height="30"/>
  <Button Content="Save"
    Margin="5,0,0,0"
    Width="60" Height="30"/>
  <Button Content="Delete"
    Margin="5,0,0,0"
    Width="60" Height="30"/>
</StackPanel>
```

When we wish to draw your attention to a particular part of a code block, the relevant lines or items are set in bold:

```
Grid x:Name="LayoutRoot" Background="White">
  <TextBlock Text="Hello World!" FontSize="20"/>
</Grid>
```

Any command-line input or output is written as follows:

```
install-package Moq
```

New terms and **important words** are shown in bold. Words that you see on the screen, in menus or dialog boxes for example, appear in the text like this: "For **Comments** textbox to occupy all of the grid width, we add a property called ColSpan".

> Warnings or important notes appear in a box like this.

> Tips and tricks appear like this.

Reader feedback

Feedback from our readers is always welcome. Let us know what you think about this book—what you liked or may have disliked. Reader feedback is important for us to develop titles that you really get the most out of.

To send us general feedback, simply send an e-mail to feedback@packtpub.com, and mention the book title through the subject of your message.

If there is a topic that you have expertise in and you are interested in either writing or contributing to a book, see our author guide on www.packtpub.com/authors.

Customer support

Now that you are the proud owner of a Packt book, we have a number of things to help you to get the most from your purchase.

Downloading the example code

You can download the example code files for all Packt books you have purchased from your account at http://www.packtpub.com. If you purchased this book elsewhere, you can visit http://www.packtpub.com/support and register to have the files e-mailed directly to you.

Errata

Although we have taken every care to ensure the accuracy of our content, mistakes do happen. If you find a mistake in one of our books—maybe a mistake in the text or the code—we would be grateful if you would report this to us. By doing so, you can save other readers from frustration and help us improve subsequent versions of this book. If you find any errata, please report them by visiting http://www.packtpub.com/support, selecting your book, clicking on the **errata submission form** link, and entering the details of your errata. Once your errata are verified, your submission will be accepted and the errata will be uploaded to our website, or added to any list of existing errata, under the Errata section of that title.

Piracy

Piracy of copyright material on the Internet is an ongoing problem across all media. At Packt, we take the protection of our copyright and licenses very seriously. If you come across any illegal copies of our works, in any form, on the Internet, please provide us with the location address or website name immediately so that we can pursue a remedy.

Please contact us at copyright@packtpub.com with a link to the suspected pirated material.

We appreciate your help in protecting our authors, and our ability to bring you valuable content.

Questions

You can contact us at questions@packtpub.com if you are having a problem with any aspect of the book, and we will do our best to address it.

1
Express Introduction to Silverlight

Nowadays, starting a web development poses a considerable challenge, since clients have got used to having powerful desktop-based interfaces at their disposal, which can also be delivered in record time. If we focus on Line of Business (LOB) applications, we find the additional challenge which is the fact that our apps have to be ready for massive changes, taking into account tight deadlines without sacrificing stability. All of us have suffered that "little last-minute change". Everybody has heard things like, "We got to change the way in which discounts for purchases are managed. This could be ready in just five minutes, couldn't it?"

To overcome such situations, web developers can make use of a combination of ASP. NET (webforms or MVC), HTML, JavaScript, AJAX, and the more advanced HTML 5 and jQuery.

Nevertheless, when we implement LOB applications we often find that:

- We have to struggle in order to make our pages consistent in different browsers; even in different versions of the same browser.

- Our developers have to learn a language to develop client side, and another one to develop the server side.

- JavaScript is a polemic language — love it or hate it. For some developers it is not object-oriented (although it has OO capabilities) and is an interpreted language. One only has to forget to add a semicolon, or introduce a syntax error when typing a command, and our application may produce an execution time error.

- HTML 5 only works in updated browsers. Could you imagine yourself telling your client something like, "Well, what you have to do is install the latest version of Chrome or IE on your 1,000 PCs. This is also applicable to your associate companies."

- We have to mix business and presentation logic. We try to avoid going to the server, for instance, to make validations which do not require reading a database. That is to say, we mix the reading of an input or an HTML ComboBox with the realization of validations. For example, if the user chooses more than four high-end products and is a premium client, we can enable a special 10 percent discount. This causes serious trouble when changes are required in the page layout, even if they are insignificant.

Introduction to Silverlight

Microsoft has published a plugin called Silverlight (the word *plugin* reminds us of Flash, one of the most accepted plugin-based technologies) which allows us to encode with sturdy, compiled languages (such as C# and VB.NET). This plugin incorporates a lite version, that is the .NET Framework, which offers us the possibility to take advantage of everything offered at the client side while implementing a new markup language called XAML. The advantages of using Silverlight are as follows:

- Our applications are sturdier; for example, allowing us to implement automatic unit testing at the client side.

- We can decouple business presentation and implement an architecture at the client side.

- We can decouple roles. While a designer can deal with presentation, we as developers are able to focus on the business of building the application.

- Our application is more scalable (we free up resources on the server) and we do not depend on tricks to maintain application status.

- We can have a standard XAML implemented the same way in every single browser. No more headaches such as, "it looks good in IE6 but not in IE7, or Firefox, and so on".

In addition, Silverlight is multi-platform (for example, Windows or Mac) and multi-device (computers, mobile devices with Symbian or WP7 support, for instance, among others).

Installation

In this book, we are going to deal with Silverlight 5. The tool that Microsoft recommends for development is Visual Studio 2010. Therefore, we will have to install the following software:

- Visual Studio 2010 (if you do not have a commercial license, you can download the express version available at `http://www.microsoft.com/express/downloads/#2010-Visual-CS`)

- Visual Studio 2010 SP1 at `http://www.microsoft.com/download/en/details.aspx?id=23691`
- Microsoft Silverlight 5 Tools for Visual Studio 2010 at `http://www.microsoft.com/download/en/details.aspx?id=23887`

All of these individual links are available at `http://www.silverlight.NET/getstarted/`.

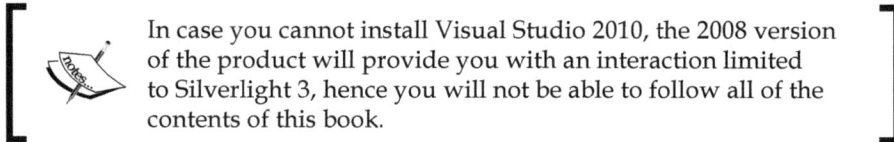

> In case you cannot install Visual Studio 2010, the 2008 version of the product will provide you with an interaction limited to Silverlight 3, hence you will not be able to follow all of the contents of this book.

Silverlight architecture

Silverlight is a plugin installed in web browsers in a quick and clean way similar to Flash. That is, Flash is in a controlled environment, and applications run under a sandbox environment.

As for the architecture, if we compare it to a standard web application, we can substitute XAML for HTML, C# or VB.NET for JavaScript, and so on. We can also make use of a reduced version of the .NET Framework as shown in the following figure:

<XAML>	• Markup language created from scratch • Designed to build UI • Just one standard
.NET Code	• Clear separation between UI definition (XAML) from execution/business logic • Powerful client-side and compiled languages (C# or VB.NET, among others) • We can use the same language in client and in server side
SL.NET Framework	• Light version of .NET Framework (it weighs 4 MB) • Multiplatform • It offers most of the potential of .NET Framework, all available client side • Advanced user controls, WCF, LINQ, and so on

The plugin is about 4 MB in size and does not depend on the desktop version of Microsoft .NET Framework.

All this is fine but there a few questions to be answered such as how is the Silverlight application installed on a server? How is it executed on a client machine? Let's see how it works:

- When we build a Silverlight project, an XAP file is generated (Silverlight can also be configured to generate several files).

- This file is just a ZIP file with all the necessary assemblies and resources to execute the application.

- This XAP file is stored on our web server.

- In an HTML page, we reference it using an OBJECT tag.

- When the user navigates to that page, the XAP file of the application is downloaded and unzipped. Then, the application starting point is sought and the application is executed.

Application execution takes place in a controlled **sandbox** environment, so a malicious developer cannot format the client's HDD (in some cases, user confirmation is required to interact with the hardware, otherwise interaction is simply denied to the application).

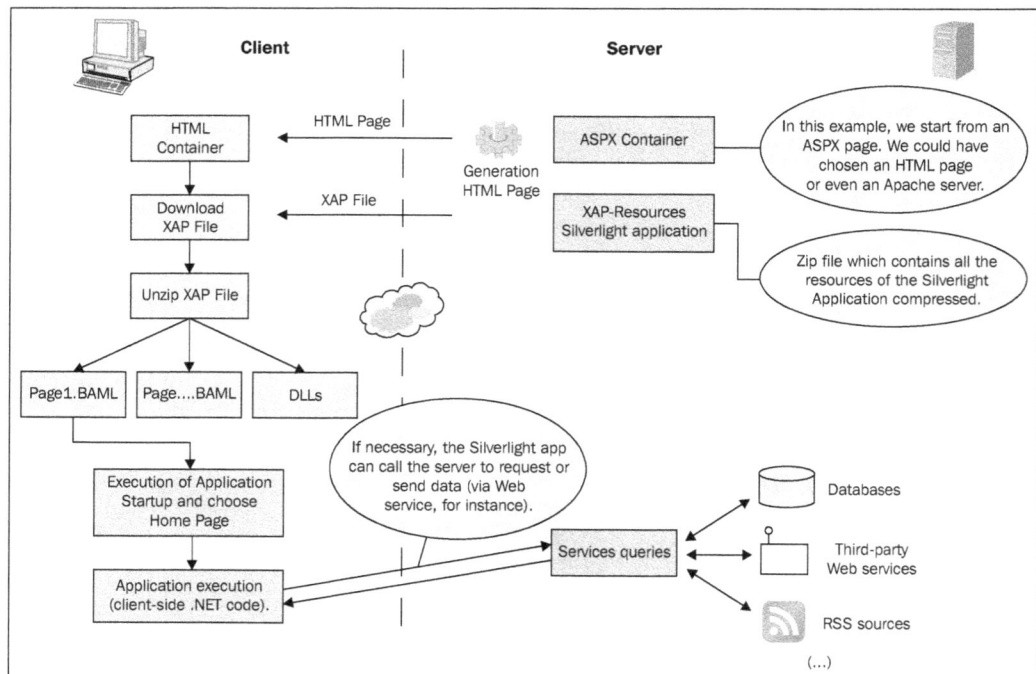

To get a better idea of how it works, let's compare an HTML web application with a Silverlight one:

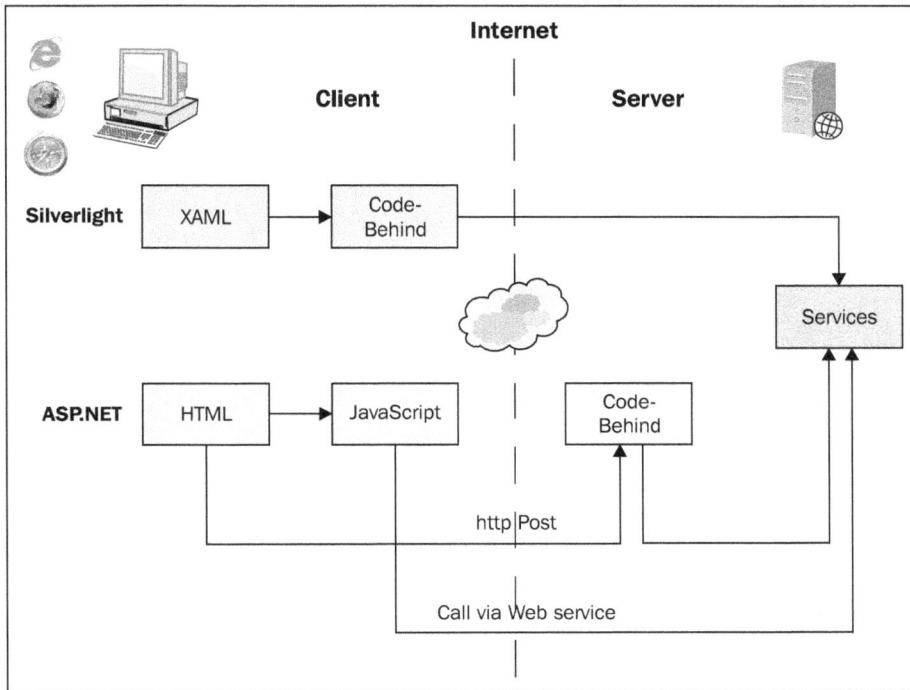

Creating the Hello World project

Now that we have our development environment ready, we will create our first Silverlight project. Of course, it will be the classic Hello World. On this occasion, we will use the example to learn:

- How to create a new project
- How to encode directly into the markup language
- How to drag elements from the Toolbox palette and configure them using Properties
- How to respond to an event and call a Code-Behind method

Creating a new project

Let's open Visual Studio and start creating the app:

1. To create a new project, we must launch Visual Studio. Select **File | New Project** and choose the **Silverlight Application** option:

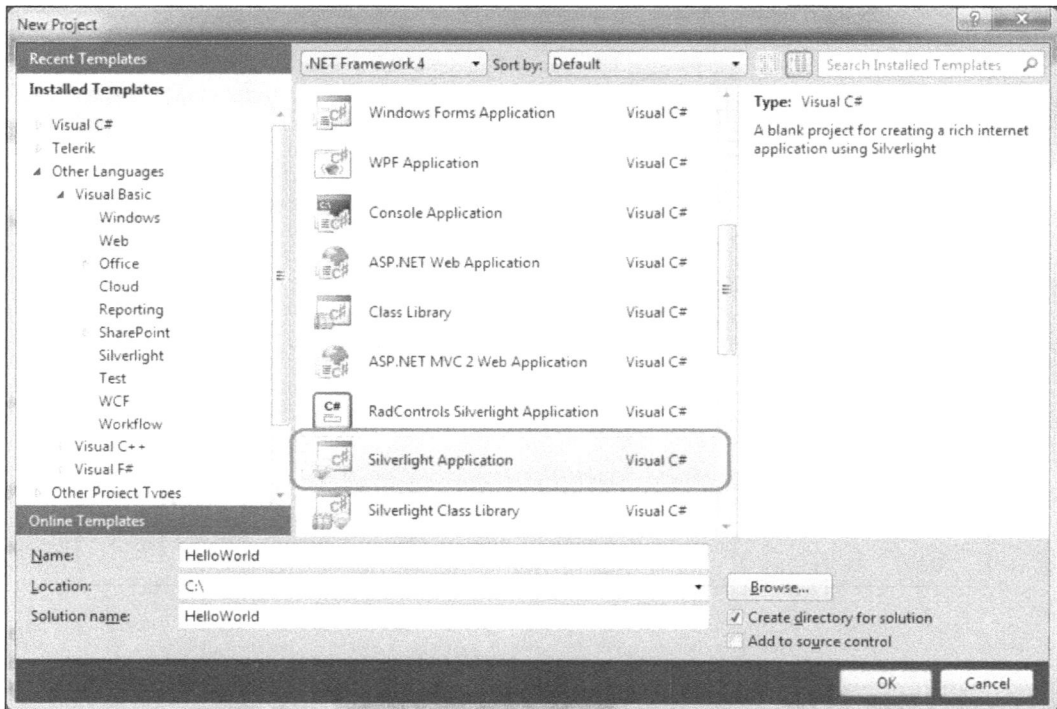

2. Once the route and type of project has been chosen, a dialog will appear, asking us if we want to create a web project to host our Silverlight application.

3. Click on **OK** (a Silverlight application needs a web page which instantiates it with an OBJECT tag).

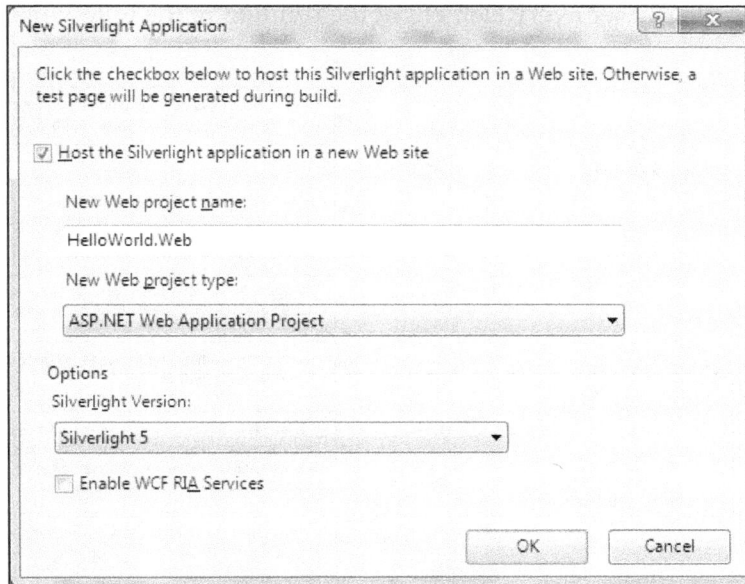

```
New Silverlight Application                              [?] [X]

Click the checkbox below to host this Silverlight application in a Web site. Otherwise, a
test page will be generated during build.

[✓] Host the Silverlight application in a new Web site

    New Web project name:

    HelloWorld.Web

    New Web project type:

    ASP.NET Web Application Project                    ▼

Options
Silverlight Version:

ASP.NET Web Application Project                        ▼
Silverlight 5                                         ▼

[ ] Enable WCF RIA Services

                                    OK            Cancel
```

We now have the solution created. It consists of two projects:

*   Silverlight project: The wizard creates an entry point (.app file) and a default page (MainPage). In the default MainPage, we can see the layout definition (MainPage.xaml) and its associated Code-Behind (mainpage.cs). It is advisable to remember that this Code-Behind is executed at the client side and not at the server side.

- Web project: This simply consists of an ASP.NET page and an HTML page to try our Silverlight application.

We can clearly see every element of the solution in the following figure:

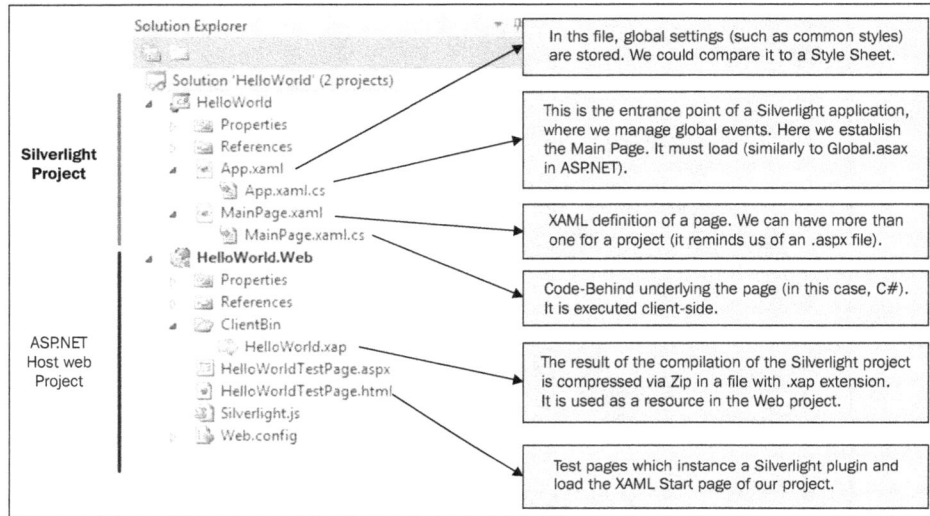

Coding directly into the markup language

In this section, we will add our first Silverlight controls, encoding them directly into the markup language. We will see next how to carry out the same operation via drag-and-drop:

1. Open the file `MainPage.xaml`.

2. Add a text block containing the expression Hello World. To do this, we will enter the following code:

```
<Grid x:Name="LayoutRoot" Background="White">
  <TextBlock Text="Hello World!" FontSize="20"/>
</Grid>
```

Downloading the example code

You can download the example code files for all Packt books you have purchased from your account at http://www.packtpub. com. If you purchased this book elsewhere, you can visit http://www.packtpub.com/support and register to have the files e-mailed directly to you.

3. We must build the project and execute the example by clicking on the play icon.

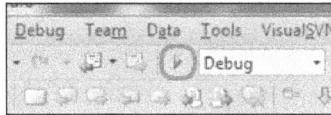

4. We can now see our first Silverlight application in action!

Dragging-and-dropping controls

It is highly recommended that you have a good knowledge of the XAML markup language and some experience practicing it. Nevertheless, if you intend to make a rapid prototype or just need to begin developing immediately, you can use the drag-and-drop controls from the toolbar directly in to the form (as in a WinForms application).

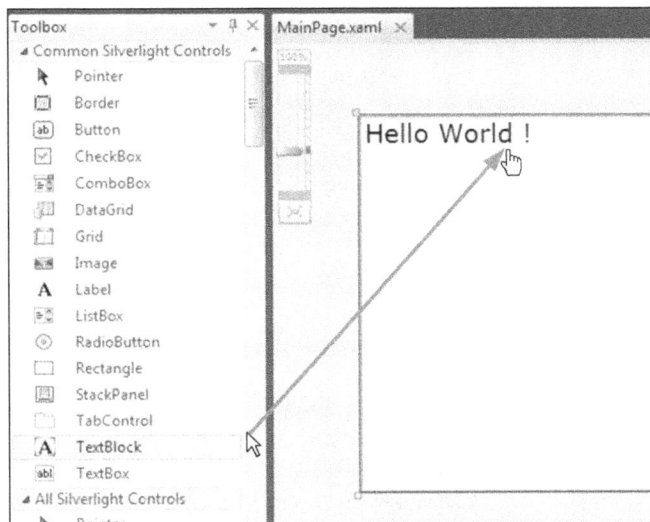

You can also edit the features of a control by accessing the **Properties** window as shown in the following screenshot:

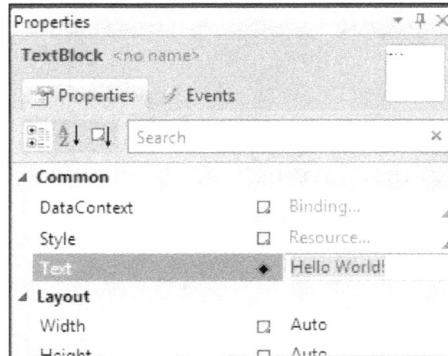

In order to achieve a higher control over the windows layout (with the aim to, for example, achieve an optimal disposition of the controls in different resolutions), we suggest learning the XAML markup language or using Expression Blend, which is a tool for designers (and developers).

Interacting with Code-Behind

In the following example, we will allow the user to change the message **Hello World!** to one of their choice. Starting from the previous example, we will follow the given steps:

1. Open the `mainpage.xaml` file.

2. Replace the XAML code inserted in the previous example by the one highlighted as follows (we have added an additional textbox, a button, and identifiers for the controls).

```
<Grid x:Name="LayoutRoot" Background="White">
  <StackPanel Orientation="Vertical">
  <TextBlock x:Name="tbLabel"
  Text="Hello World!"
  FontSize="20"/>
            <StackPanel Orientation="Horizontal">
                <TextBlock
                    Text="New Text:"
                    FontSize="16"/>
                <TextBox
                    x:Name="txInput"
                    Width="120"/>
```

```
            <Button Content="Change"/>
         </StackPanel>
      </StackPanel>
   </Grid>
```

3. When we build and execute the project, we realize that our window now has the aspect as shown in the following screenshot:

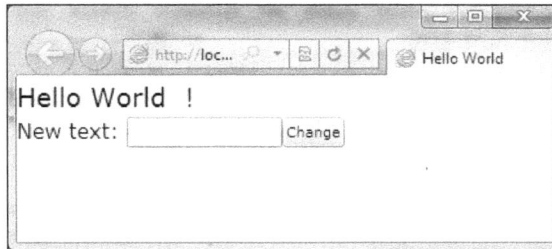

4. Next, we must implement the response to the `Click` event of the **Change** button.

5. Hook to the `Click` event directly in the XAML file. As soon as we start typing, IntelliSense (Microsoft's implementation of autocompletion) will ask us if we want to create the method (hitting *Enter* or *Tab* would create the method with the default name or with the name of the control after selecting a `Click` event).

6. Execute the same operation from the **Properties** panel (or by directly double-clicking on the button control):

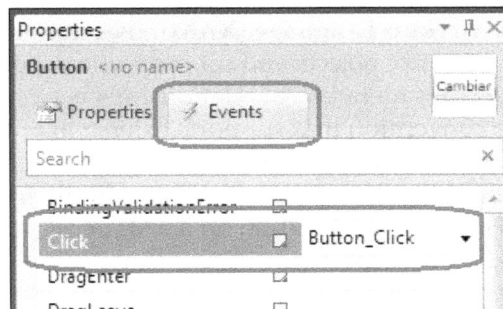

7. As a result, XAML will look as follows:

```
<Button Content="Change" Click="Button_Click"/>
```

8. In Code-Behind, in the method invoked by the `Click` event, we must add a line of code, which transfers the text content entered by the user to the tag where we showed 'Hello World'.

```
private void Button_Click(object sender, RoutedEventArgs e)
{
    tbLabel.Text = txInput.Text;
}
```

9. When we execute, we will be able to enter a new text that substitutes 'Hello World'.

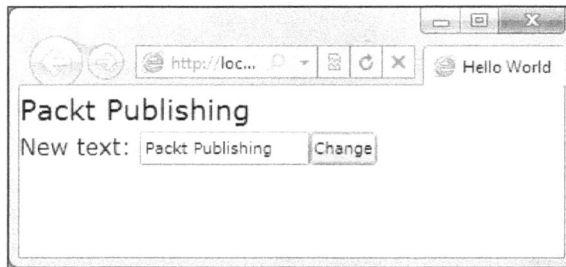

XAML basic concepts

Now that we have taken our first steps with Silverlight, let's have a quick introduction to some basic concepts in XAML.

What is XAML?

Extensible Application Markup Language (**XAML**) is a declarative language. Specifically, XAML can initialize objects and set properties of objects, using a language structure that shows hierarchical relationships between multiple objects, and uses a backing type convention that supports extension of types. You can create visible user interface (UI) elements in the declarative XAML markup. You can then use a separate Code-Behind file to respond to events and manipulate the objects you declare in XAML (For more information on XAML, you can take a look at http://msdn.microsoft.com/en-us/library/cc189036(v=vs.95).aspx).

The advantages of XAML when compared to HTML are as follows:

- XAML is a modern language, adapted to the current needs of users and implemented from scratch (whereas HTML suffers from organic growth)
- We have only one way to implement it, which avoids us headaches derived from the problems of adaptation with different browsers and their versions
- There is a clear differentiation between declarative (XAML) and business logic/code parts (.cs Code-Behind)

The best you can do is try it and see for yourself.

Basic elements for layout definition

When you work with HTML, you build the basic visual structure of a page by using tables or divs (in more modern browsers, you can use a canvas as well). In Silverlight 5 we have three basic elements: Canvas, StackPanel, and Grid.

Canvas

This layout control permits us to place Child controls in coordinates relative to the canvas parent (taking into account that the upper-left corner of the canvas is the (0,0) coordinate) X, Y, Z (Z for the zIndex). It is perfect for the implementation of drawing applications or those devoted to diagram management.

In the following code you can see an example where a rectangle and an ellipse are drawn:

```
<Canvas>
  <Rectangle
    Canvas.Top="25" Canvas.Left="50"
    Fill="Blue" Width="70"
    Height="80" StrokeThickness="3" Stroke="Black" />
  <Ellipse
    Canvas.Top="50" Canvas.Left="80"
    Fill="Yellow" Width="120"
    Height="80" StrokeThickness="3" Stroke="Black"
  />
</Canvas>
```

Canvas.Top and Canvas.Left are attached properties. Such properties allow a child element to store a value associated with a property defined on an ancestor element.

The result is as shown in the following screenshot:

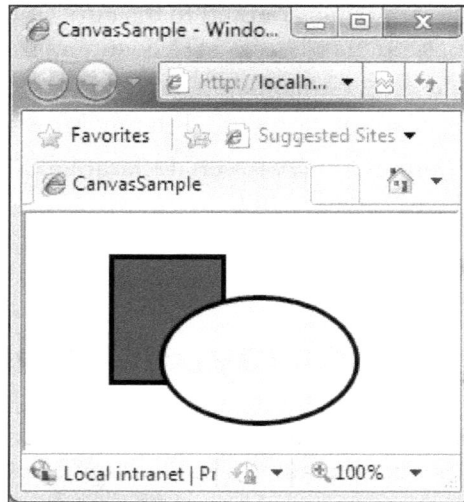

StackPanel

The StackPanel control allows us to pile up child controls in horizontal or vertical rows. We can nest several StackPanel controls. This combination makes it possible to implement complex layouts, as shown in the following code and the resulting screenshot:

```
<StackPanel Orientation="Vertical" HorizontalAlignment="Center">
  <Image Source="./images/Hydrangeas.jpg" Height="200" Margin="5"/>
  <StackPanel Orientation="Horizontal">
    <Image Source="./images/Chrysanthemum.jpg" Height="100"
      Margin="5"/>
    <Image Source="./images/Hydrangeas.jpg" Height="100" Margin="5"/>
    <Image Source="./images/Jellyfish.jpg" Height="100" Margin="5"/>
  </StackPanel>
</StackPanel>
```

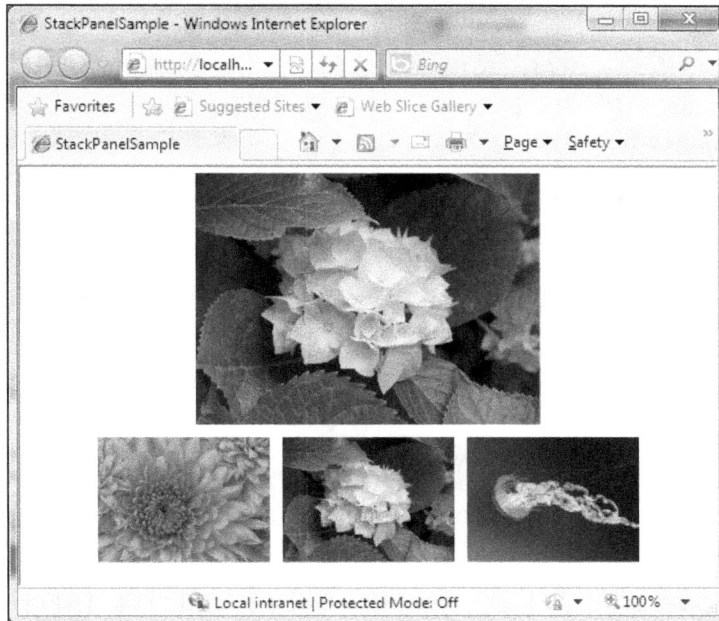

Grid

A grid permits us to place content in rows and columns. The concept is similar to an HTML table, but much more evolved. Before you start adding controls to the grid, you need to specify its layout. This is done with the `Grid.RowDefinitions` and `Grid.ColumnDefinitions` collection.

To set the position of the element inside the grid, we use the attached properties `Grid.Row` and `Grid.Column`. The first position starts at `0`. To establish the width or height of a given row or column, we can use a fixed pixel width/height. Let the layout manager autoadjust the size to the space available (auto), or provide a given width/height based on percentages instead of pixels.

```
<Grid x:Name="LayoutRoot" Background="White">
  <Grid.RowDefinitions>
    <RowDefinition Height="100"/>
    <RowDefinition Height="100"/>
  </Grid.RowDefinitions>
  <Grid.ColumnDefinitions>
    <ColumnDefinition Width="150"/>
```

```xml
    <ColumnDefinition Width="90"/>
    <ColumnDefinition Width="*"/>
</Grid.ColumnDefinitions>

<Image Source="./images/Desert.jpg"
  Height="100" Margin="5"
Grid.Row="0" Grid.Column="0"/>
<TextBlock Text="Desert"
  Grid.Row="0" Grid.Column="1"/>
<TextBlock Text="Geographical area whose average annual
  precipitation is less than 250 millimeters (10 in) per year."
  Grid.Row="0"
  Grid.Column="2"
  TextWrapping="Wrap"
/>

<Image Source="./images/Tulips.jpg"
  Height="100" Margin="5"
  Grid.Row="1" Grid.Column="0"/>
<TextBlock Text="Tulip"
  Grid.Row="1"
Grid.Column="1"/>
<TextBlock Text="Perennial, bulbous plant which belongs to the
family Liliaceae."
  Grid.Row="1"
  Grid.Column="2"
  TextWrapping="Wrap"
/>
</Grid>
```

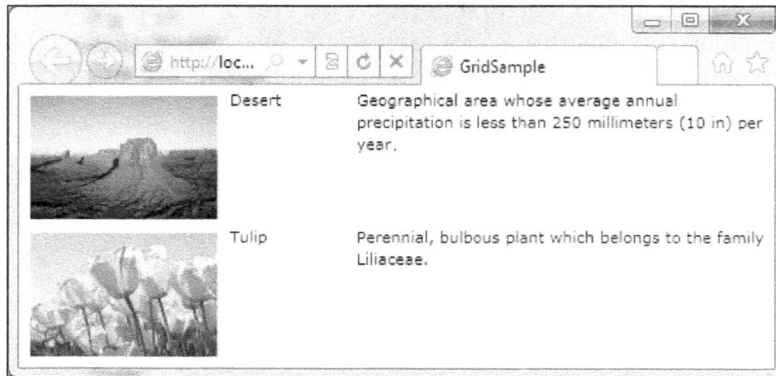

Controls

Silverlight offers us a series of user controls, which are available in the Toolbox palette. The most common ones are shown in the following screenshot:

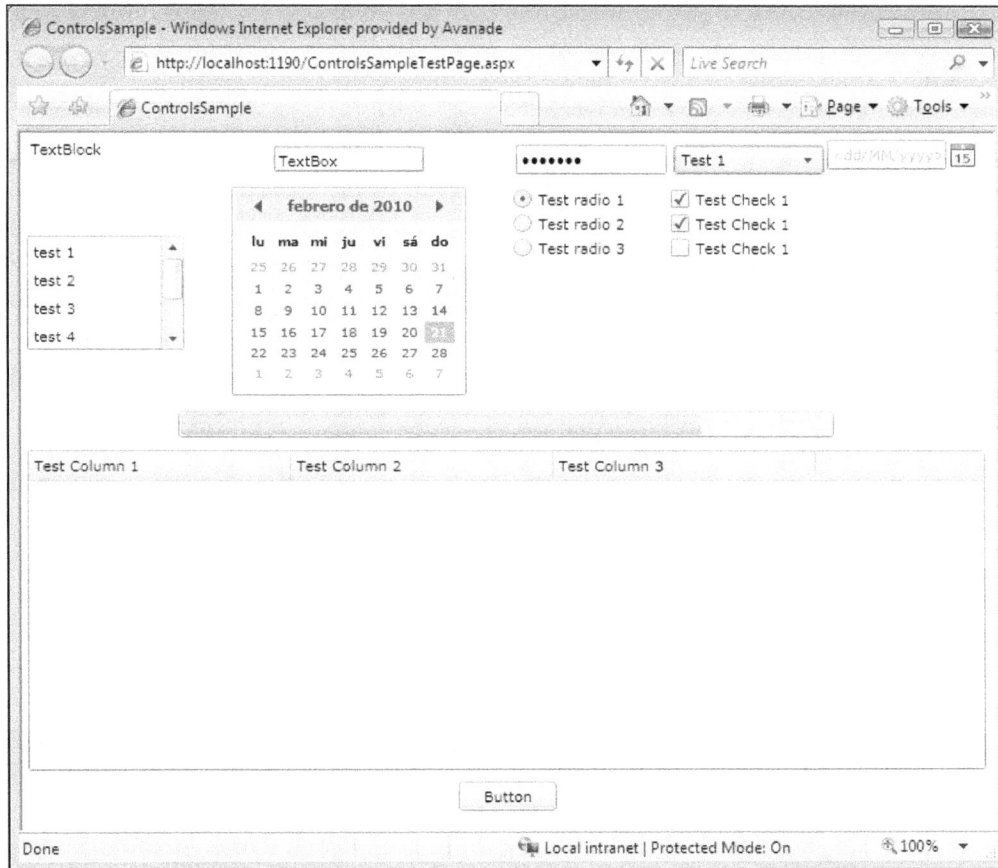

You can find additional controls (for free) in the Silverlight Toolkit (`http://silverlight.codeplex.com/`). There are plenty of commercial libraries available.

LOB application case study: applying what we have learned

Now we will lay out the main window of our application:

Place Logo Here

| Home | Admin |

City	Building	Room	Date	Start	End	Comments
London	Plantation Palace	Green	29/09/20	10:00	11:00	Weekly progress meeting
Paris	Eurocon	Manuelle	01/10/20	10:00	11:00	Weekly progress meeting
Malaga	Picasso	Room 221	05/10/20	13:00	14:00	Product presentation
Munich	Sky	Planck	15/10/20	10:00	11:00	Weekly progress meeting

Country [　　　∨]　　City [　　　∨]　　Building [　　　∨]

Date Reservation [29/09/2010]　Start Time [10:00]　Duration [1]　Room [　　∨]

Comments

[　　　　　　　　　　　　　　　　　　　　　　]

| New | Save | Delete |

This window lets the user see the meeting room reservations which are already made, as well as edit them, or create new ones.

First, we must create a new project, and then edit the XAML code of the MainPage file.

We must now define three rows to the grid layout container:

1. One of them will contain a `DataGrid` control, which shows the list of reservations assigned to our account.

2. Another one will allow us to edit/create a particular reservation.

3. The last one will contain the buttons that will permit us to execute commands such as **New**, **Save**, and **Delete**.

The resulting user control includes the grid and rows created:

```xml
<UserControl x:Class="ReservationLayout.MainPage"
  xmlns="http://schemas.microsoft.com/winfx/2006/xaml/presentation"
  xmlns:x="http://schemas.microsoft.com/winfx/2006/xaml"
  xmlns:d="http://schemas.microsoft.com/expression/blend/2008"
  xmlns:mc="http://schemas.openxmlformats.org/markup-
    compatibility/2006"
  mc:Ignorable="d"
  d:DesignHeight="300" d:DesignWidth="400">

  <Grid x:Name="LayoutRoot" Background="White">
    <Grid.RowDefinitions>
      <RowDefinition Height="300"/>
      <RowDefinition Height="300"/>
      <RowDefinition Height="90"/>
    </Grid.RowDefinitions>
  </Grid>

</UserControl>
```

Next, we must add a DataGrid control to the layout and indicate the row in which its parent container will be assigned:

```xml
<UserControl
  x:Class="ReservationLayout.MainPage"
  xmlns="http://schemas.microsoft.com/winfx/2006/xaml/presentation"
  xmlns:x="http://schemas.microsoft.com/winfx/2006/xaml"
  xmlns:d="http://schemas.microsoft.com/expression/blend/2008"
  xmlns:mc="http://schemas.openxmlformats.org/
    markup-compatibility/2006"
  xmlns:sdk="http://schemas.microsoft.com/winfx/2006/xaml/
    presentation/sdk"
  mc:Ignorable="d"
  d:DesignHeight="300" d:DesignWidth="400">

  <Grid x:Name="LayoutRoot" Background="White">
    <Grid.RowDefinitions>
      <RowDefinition Height="200"/>
      <RowDefinition Height="150"/>
      <RowDefinition Height="90"/>
    </Grid.RowDefinitions>

    <sdk:DataGrid Grid.Row="0"/>
  </Grid>
</UserControl>
```

> The easiest way to insert `DataGrid` control is by dragging it directly from the **Toolbox** window in Visual Studio and then dropping it in our layout (it adds all the necessary references for us). After that, we only have to jump to the XAML of the application and define the row and/or column where we want it to appear.

If we execute the application, the result is not very appealing. We will only see a white rectangle that represents the `DataGrid` control. We will learn how to manage this control in subsequent chapters. For now, we will add some column definitions to make it look more similar to the following example screen.

To make it easier, we have to select the **DataGrid** object and use the **Properties** tab.

1. On the one hand, we disable auto-generation of columns.

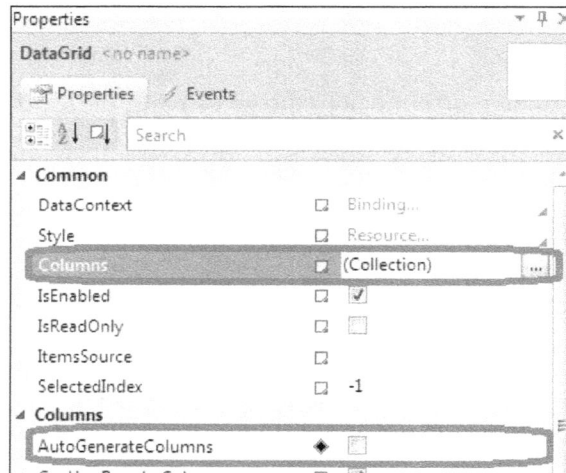

2. On the other hand, we will define the columns manually, clicking on the property **Columns**.

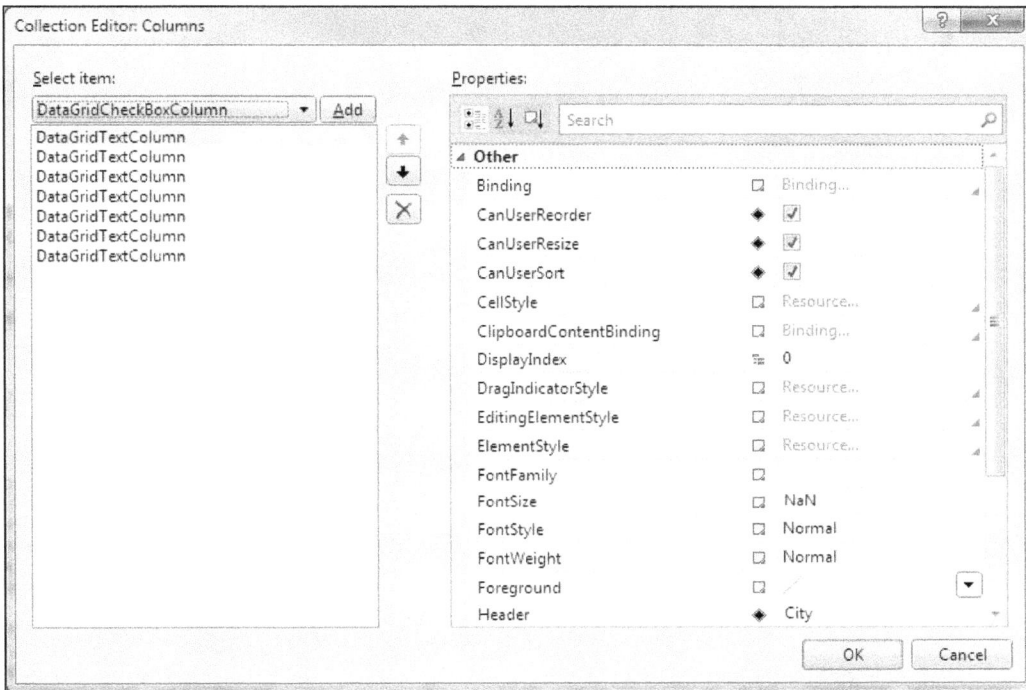

The following is the XAML that we get:

```xaml
<sdk:DataGrid Grid.Row="0" AutoGenerateColumns="False">
  <sdk:DataGrid.Columns>
    <sdk:DataGridTextColumn
      CanUserReorder="True"
      CanUserResize="True"
      CanUserSort="True"
      Header="City"
      Width="Auto"
    />
    <sdk:DataGridTextColumn
      CanUserReorder="True"
      CanUserResize="True"
      CanUserSort="True"
      Header="Building"
      Width="Auto"
    />
```

```
        <sdk:DataGridTextColumn
          CanUserReorder="True"
          CanUserResize="True"
          CanUserSort="True"
          Header="Room"
          Width="Auto"
        />
        <sdk:DataGridTextColumn
          CanUserReorder="True"
          CanUserResize="True"
          CanUserSort="True"
          Header="Date"
          Width="Auto"
        />
        <sdk:DataGridTextColumn
          CanUserReorder="True"
          CanUserResize="True"
          CanUserSort="True"
          Header="Start"
          Width="Auto"
        />
        <sdk:DataGridTextColumn
          CanUserReorder="True"
          CanUserResize="True"
          CanUserSort="True"
          Header="End"
          Width="Auto"
        />
        <sdk:DataGridTextColumn
          CanUserReorder="True"
          CanUserResize="True"
          CanUserSort="True"
          Header="Comments"
          Width="*"
        />
      </sdk:DataGrid.Columns>
    </sdk:DataGrid>
```

Let's take a look at the final result:

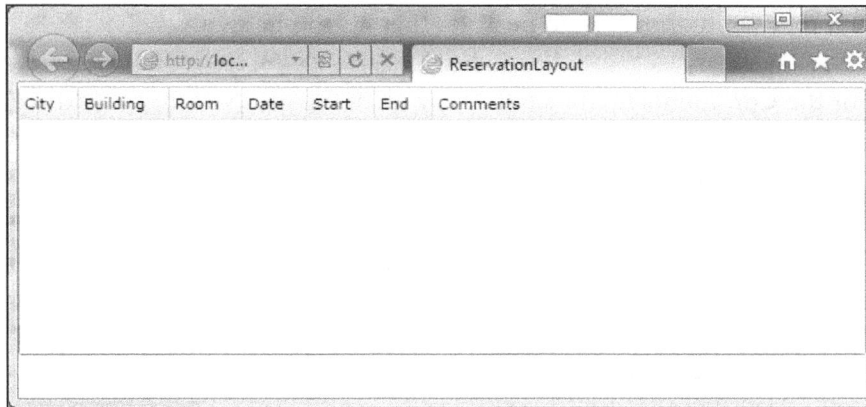

We now move to the detailed area. The easiest thing to do here will be to design the page using Expression Blend or Visual Studio. We will use the knowledge acquired in this chapter to design the window manually using grid control. To do this, we must define the following area of rows and columns:

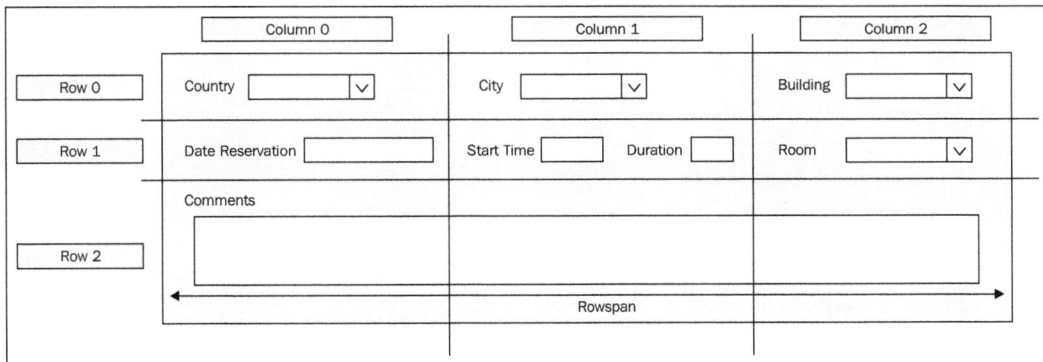

The generated XAML can be seen in the code that follows. A few things should be taken care of. They are:

- The grid container which we insert is inside the parent layout grid
- We use `Margin` properties to assign space between grid rows, as well as between labels and controls

- To lay out labels and controls, we will use a `StackPanel` control and adjust the `orientation` property, setting it to vertical or horizontal, as applicable (another valid approach to position them is to play with each `Margin` property of each control, this margin being related to its container cell)
- For the **Comments** textbox to occupy all of the grid width, we add a property called `ColSpan`

```
<Grid Grid.Row="1" HorizontalAlignment="Center" MinWidth="670"
  Margin="5">
  <Grid.RowDefinitions>
    <RowDefinition Height="25"/>
    <RowDefinition Height="30"/>
    <RowDefinition Height="80"/>
  </Grid.RowDefinitions>
  <Grid.ColumnDefinitions>
    <ColumnDefinition Width="200"/>
    <ColumnDefinition Width="250"/>
    <ColumnDefinition Width="220"/>
  </Grid.ColumnDefinitions>

  <StackPanel
    Orientation="Horizontal"
    Grid.Row="0"
    Grid.Column="0">
    <TextBlock
      Text="Country"
      Margin="0,5,5,0"/>
    <ComboBox Width="143"/>
  </StackPanel>

  <StackPanel
    Orientation="Horizontal"
    Grid.Row="0"
    Grid.Column="1">
    <TextBlock
      Text="City"
      Margin="0,5,5,0"
    />
    <ComboBox Width="221"/>
  </StackPanel>

  <StackPanel
    Orientation="Horizontal"
```

```
    Grid.Row="0"
    Grid.Column="2">
    <TextBlock
      Text="Building"
      Margin="0,5,5,0"/>
    <ComboBox Width="100"/>
</StackPanel>

<StackPanel
    Orientation="Horizontal"
    Grid.Row="1"
    Grid.Column="0"
    Margin="0,5,0,0"
    >
    <TextBlock
    Text="Date Reservation" Margin="0,5,5,0"
    />
     <TextBox Width="90"/>
</StackPanel>

<StackPanel
    Orientation="Horizontal"
    Grid.Row="1"
    Grid.Column="1"
    Margin="0,5,0,0"
    >
    <TextBlock
      Text="Start Time"
      Margin="0,5,5,0"
    />
    <TextBox Width="70"/>
    <TextBlock
      Text="Duration"
      Margin="0,5,5,0"
    />
    <TextBox Width="61"/>
</StackPanel>

<StackPanel
    Orientation="Horizontal"
    Grid.Row="1"
    Grid.Column="2"
    Margin="0,5,0,0"
    >
```

```
      <TextBlock
        Text="Room"
        Margin="0,5,5,0"/>
      <ComboBox Width="113"/>
    </StackPanel>

    <StackPanel
      Orientation="Vertical"
      HorizontalAlignment="Left"
      Grid.Row="3"
      Grid.Column="0" Grid.ColumnSpan="3"
      Margin="0,5,0,0"
      >
      <TextBlock
        Text="Comments"
        Margin="0,5,5,0"/>
      <TextBox
        Width="599"
        Height="50"/>
    </StackPanel>

  </Grid>
```

The result of the page layout is as follows:

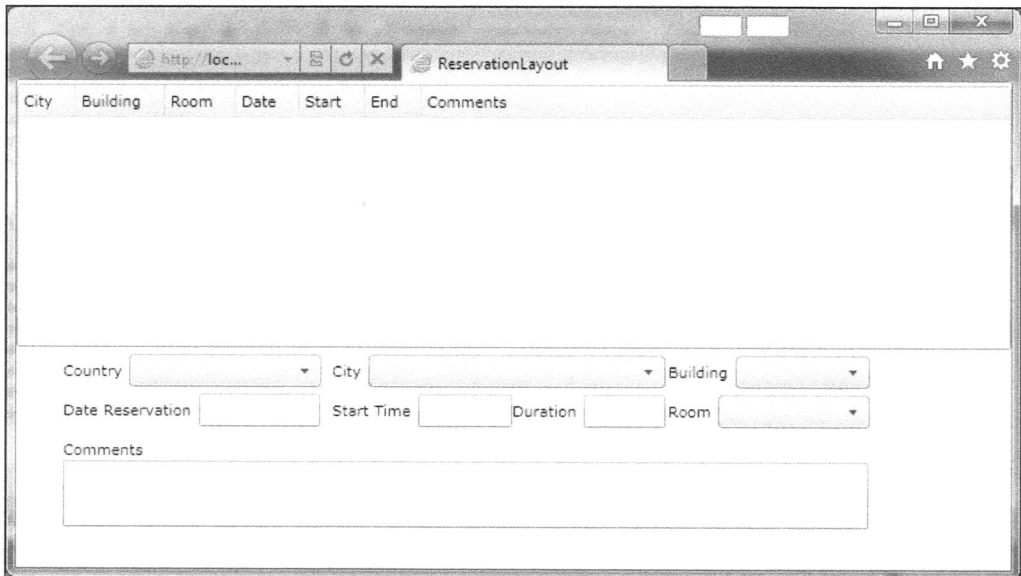

We will add the control panel in the lower part of the window to complete the layout. We will use a `StackPanel` container with horizontal orientation to do so.

```
<StackPanel
  Grid.Row="2"
  Orientation="Horizontal" HorizontalAlignment="Right">
  <Button Content="New"
    Width="60" Height="30"/>
  <Button Content="Save"
    Margin="5,0,0,0"
    Width="60" Height="30"/>
  <Button Content="Delete"
    Margin="5,0,0,0"
    Width="60" Height="30"/>
</StackPanel>
```

We have now laid out our window as shown in the following screenshot:

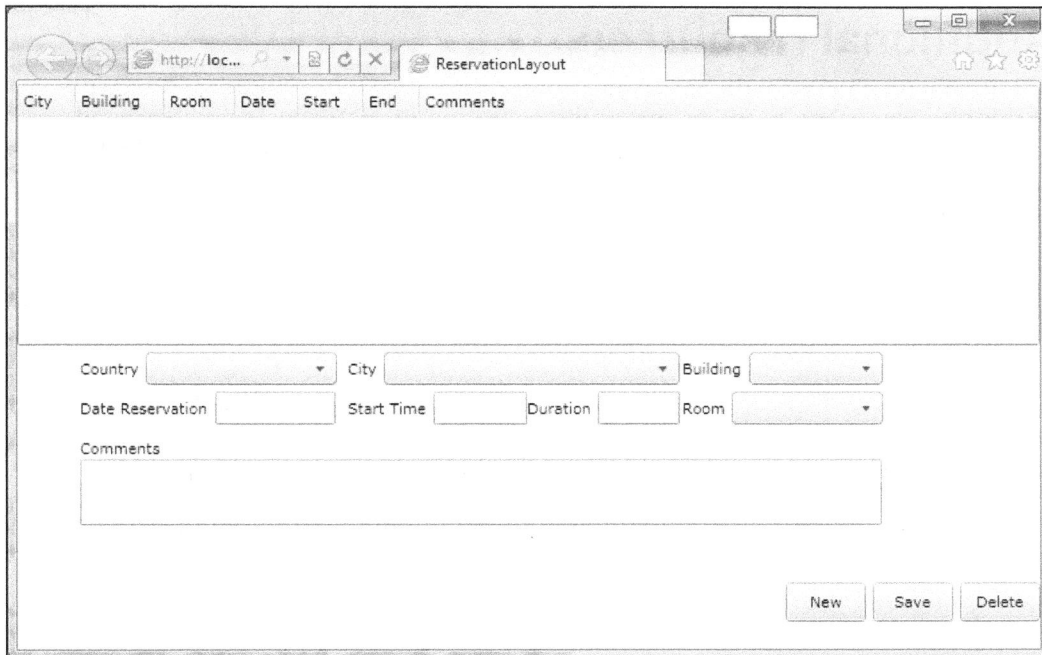

Summary

In this chapter, we have assimilated the fundamentals of Silverlight architecture, installed the necessary tools, implemented the classic 'Hello World' project, and learned some basic concepts related to XAML.

The main points to be remembered are as follows:

- Silverlight provides us with a very powerful development framework
- Silverlight allows us to develop with .NET client-side coding
- Even though we can lay out windows via drag-and-drop, it is crucial to know the basics of XAML

In the next chapter, we will begin with some concepts concerning management applications. Similarly, we will learn how to add windows and dialogs, as well as how to implement navigation between those windows.

Additional resources

If you haven't worked with Silverlight before, you probably couldn't get enough of this chapter. If you want to further increase your knowledge, we recommend *Microsoft Silverlight 4 Business Application Development: Beginner's Guide*, *Albert Cameron* and *Frank LaVigne*, *Packt Publishing*. Likewise, you can find more information at the following sites:

- XAML Silverlight Quick Start:

  ```
  http://www.silverlight.NET/learn/quickstarts/xaml
  ```

- Build your First Silverlight app:

  ```
  http://www.silverlight.net/learn/overview/getting-started/
  getting-started-with-silverlight
  ```

- Getting Started with Silverlight Development (8 part tutorial):

  ```
  http://timheuer.com/blog/articles/getting-started-with-
  silverlight-development.aspx
  ```

2
Forms and Browsing

The aim of this book is that you, the reader, become capable of implementing your own Silverlight application. You may be getting an idea of the controls you need and how many screens your application will contain.

In this chapter, you will learn the features that Silverlight offers for large-scale application layout (UserControls, Page, ChildWindow, Navigation Framework), as well as the mechanism which Silverlight provides for browsing between the different pages the application may have.

Controls definitions

Most management applications base their User Interface (UI) on **forms**. However, each technology names them in its own way (forms, views, windows). Let us begin by defining the elements Silverlight offers and their description:

Control	Description
Container	It allows us to host other controls within itself. All controls mentioned in the table are **Containers**.
UserControl	We can define content on it.
Page	It inherits from UserControl and adds functionalities which permit a better integration with the Windows Navigation Framework in Silverlight.
Popup	It also depends on UserControl. It is shown above all Silverlight controls.
ContentControl	It represents a control with a single piece of content.
ChildWindow	It is a specialization of Popup control. It is used to show modal dialogs.

[
ContentControl is beyond this book's contents. Nevertheless, you can find a good introductory article at: `http://www.mostlydevelopers.com/mostlydevelopers/blog/post/2009/03/30/Silverlight-Custom-Content-Control.aspx`
]

To understand better, we can take a look at the hierarchy tree in the following figure:

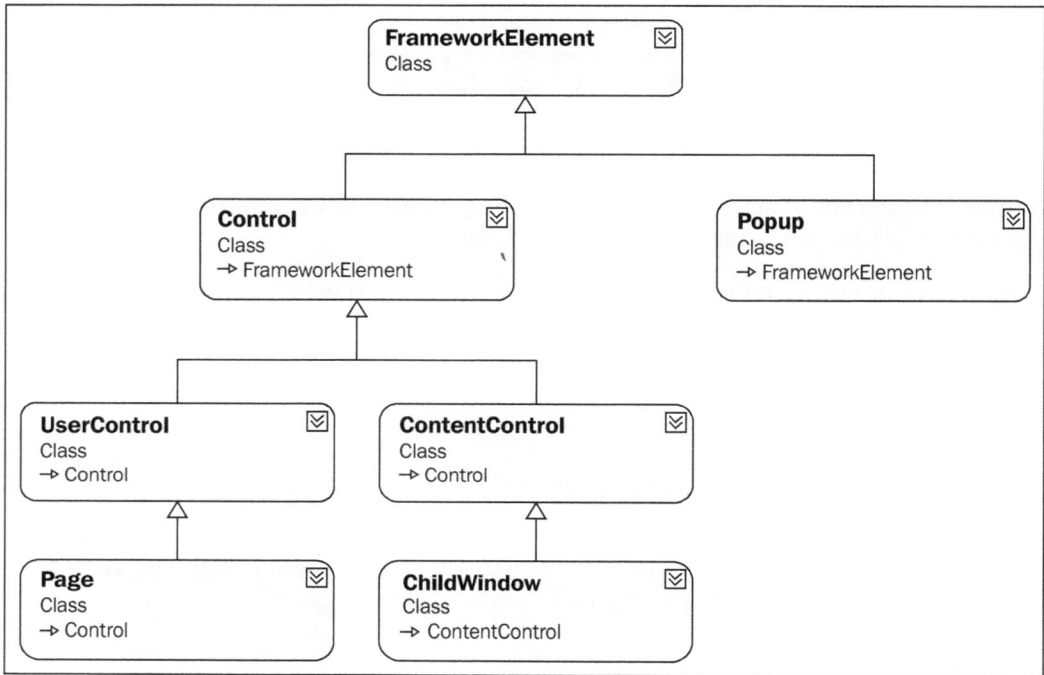

Creating windows and controls

At most times, when we develop an application, it is not possible to fit all the content in just one page. Even if we were able to do so, sometimes it is preferable to divide the content in several parts and group areas by functionality or reusability. On other occasions, we may need other windows, such as modal dialogs, to show other information to the user. Finally, we should not forget that the application may get bigger and we could need more pages for all of its functionality.

UserControl

Let us begin by talking about the most versatile and easiest control to use, UserControl.

It consists of two parts, Interface definition (XAML) and Code (Code-Behind).

In a new Project, the main page inherits from this control.

We can use both to create a form and a user control. When we create user controls, we encapsulate some of the functionality of our application so as to instantiate this control in other places without replicating code.

Example of UserControl

Let us pose a simple example where we will see how to create a UserControl and instantiate it declaratively (XAML) and from code (Code-Behind). The application will show a form where the user will be able to enter their name and address. The form will be encapsulated in a UserControl, and this will be instantiated by the Page.

Hands on! We will start from a Silverlight blank project (created in the same way we showed in the previous chapter). The name of this new project will be **Chapter2. Sample.Forms**, as shown in the following screenshot:

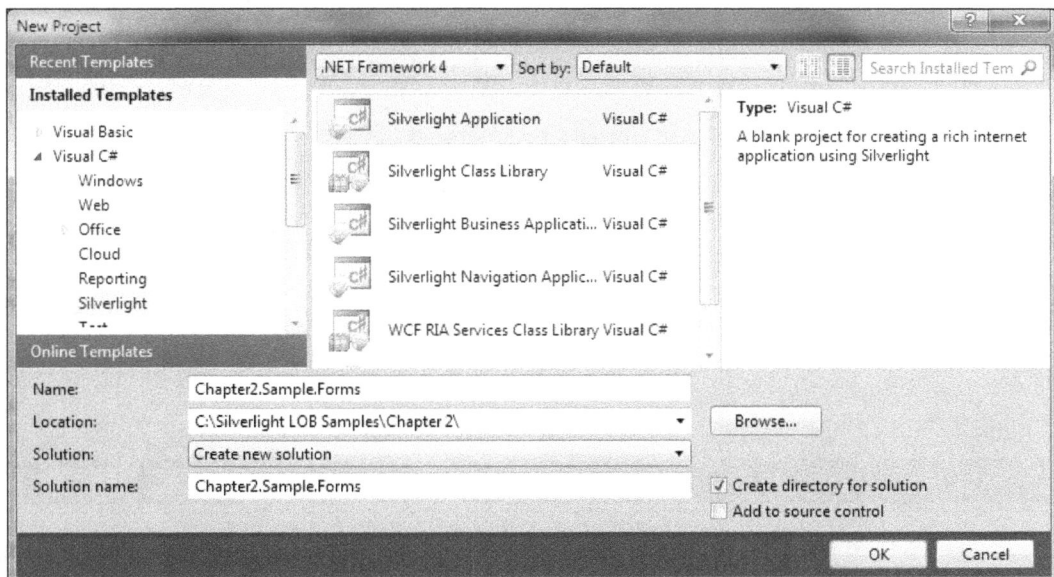

1. Add a new **Views** folder, which will help us make the code a little bit tidier. We will add UserControl views (or other pages, if necessary) to this folder.

2. In this folder, right-click and choose **Add | New Item** on the **Context** menu, as shown in the following screenshot:

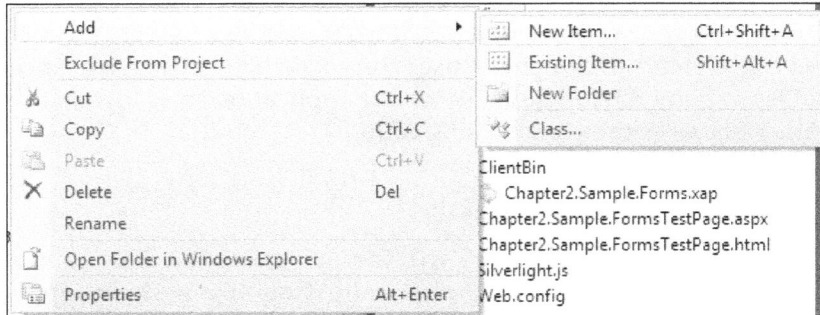

Add	▶	New Item...	Ctrl+Shift+A
Exclude From Project		Existing Item...	Shift+Alt+A
✂ Cut	Ctrl+X	New Folder	
Copy	Ctrl+C	Class...	
Paste	Ctrl+V	ClientBin	
✕ Delete	Del	Chapter2.Sample.Forms.xap	
Rename		Chapter2.Sample.FormsTestPage.aspx	
Open Folder in Windows Explorer		Chapter2.Sample.FormsTestPage.html	
Properties	Alt+Enter	Silverlight.js	
		Web.config	

3. Select the option **Silverlight User Control** and give it a name (for example, **MyControlUCView**), as shown in the next screenshot:

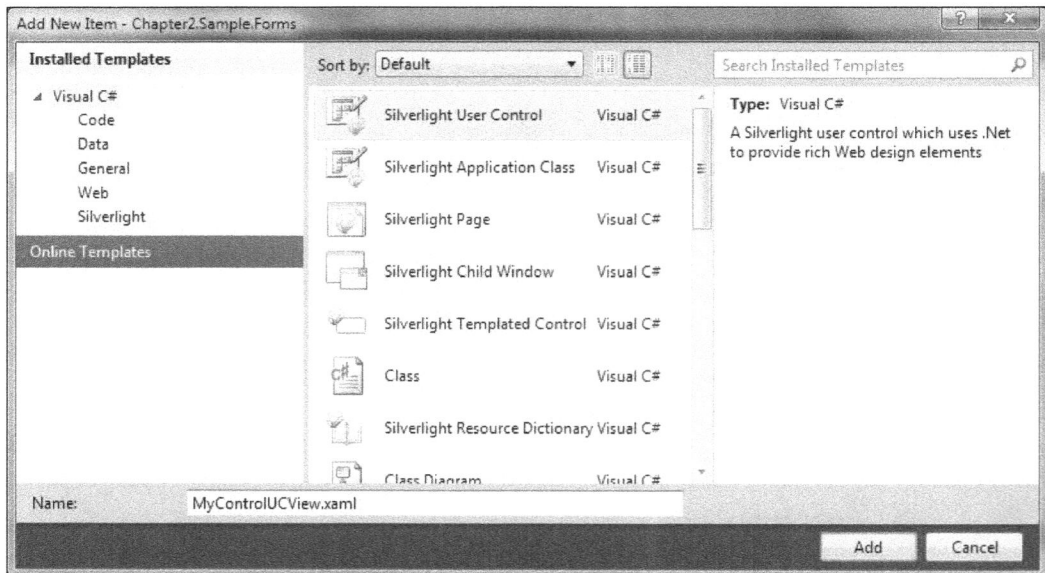

4. When the UserControl is created, lay out the form that we have defined within the control. To do so, define a Grid layout container and insert the corresponding controls. The final aspect of the layout we want to build is similar to the following screenshot:

5. Open the `MyControlUCView.XAML` file and insert the following code:

```xml
<Grid Margin="10">
  <Grid.RowDefinitions>
    <RowDefinition Height="30"/>
    <RowDefinition Height="30"/>
    <RowDefinition Height="30"/>
  </Grid.RowDefinitions>
  <Grid.ColumnDefinitions>
    <ColumnDefinition Width="80"/>
    <ColumnDefinition Width="*" />
  </Grid.ColumnDefinitions>
  <TextBlock Text="Name: "
    VerticalAlignment="Center"/>
  <TextBox x:Name="txtName" Grid.Row="0" Grid.Column="1"
    Width="200" Height="25" HorizontalAlignment="Left"/>
  <TextBlock Text="Mail Address: " VerticalAlignment="Center"
    Grid.Row="1" Grid.Column="0"/>
  <TextBox x:Name="txtAddress" Grid.Row="1" Grid.Column="1"
    Width="200" Height="25" HorizontalAlignment="Left"/>
  <TextBlock Text="Country: " VerticalAlignment="Center"
    Grid.Row="2" Grid.Column="0"/>
  <ComboBox x:Name="ddlCountry" Grid.Row="2" Grid.Column="1"
    Width="200" Height="25" HorizontalAlignment="Left">
    <ComboBoxItem Content="Spain"/>
    <ComboBoxItem Content="Germany"/>
    <ComboBoxItem Content="Italy"/>
    <ComboBoxItem Content="France"/>
    <ComboBoxItem Content="EEUU"/>
  </ComboBox>
</Grid>
```

This is the way the code is instantiated declaratively.

6. Open the file `MainPage.XAML` and add the following statements:

```
<UserControl x:Class="Chapter2.Sample.Forms.MainPage"
xmlns="http://schemas.microsoft.com/winfx/2006/xaml/
  presentation"
xmlns:x="http://schemas.microsoft.com/winfx/2006/xaml"
xmlns:d="http://schemas.microsoft.com/expression/blend/2008"
xmlns:mc="http://schemas.openxmlformats.org/markup-
  compatibility/2006"
xmlns:MyControls="clr-namespace:
  Chapter2.Sample.Forms.Views;assembly=Chapter2.Sample.Forms"
mc:Ignorable="d"
d:DesignHeight="300" d:DesignWidth="400">
```

Thereby, a namespace is added, which references the assembly in which the control was created (in our example, the main project one).

If we break down the chain which defines namespace, we can see four parts:

*   `Xmlns`: It indicates that we are adding a namespace: XML NameSpace.
*   `Mycontrols`: It is the name which comes after the character ":". It assigns a descriptive name to the namespace, in a way in which we can reference the controls easily.
*   `clr-namespace:Chapter2.Sample.Forms.Views`: It indicates the namespace which contains the elements we want available.
*   `assembly=Chapter2.Sample.Forms`: This indicates the assembly in which the namespace we are adding is defined. In our example, it is optional that the namespace which we are referring is in the same assembly as the page.

We are ready to instantiate the control. In order to do this, we add the control within the main layout element. The right way is `namespace:control`.

```
<StackPanel x:Name="LayoutRoot" Background="White"
Orientation="Vertical"
  Margin="10" >
  <MyControls:MyControlUCViewx:Name="myControl">
  </MyControls:MyControlUCView>
</StackPanel>
```

When we execute this, we see the control is instantiated.

Instantiating the control from code (Code-Behind)

Before going to the code file, we need to add a button to the page. At the click of this button, we can add a new instance of our UserControl.

To do this, open the `MainPage.XAML` file and add the following code, which defines a button in our main layout.

```
<StackPanel x:Name="LayoutRoot" Background="White"
Orientation="Vertical"
  Margin="10">
  <Button x:Name="btnAddUserControl" Content="Add Control" Width="100"
    Height="30" Click="btnAddUserControl_Click"/>
</StackPanel>
```

When we observe the XAML code which defines the button, we see it specifies a function to manage the action when the user clicks. Instead of copying the code, if we write it manually and we write `Click`, Visual Studio brings us the possibility of creating an event handler automatically (we only need to press *Tab* or *Enter* once, and the pop-up helper window is displayed) as shown in the following figure:

```
<Button x:Name="btnShowDialog" Content="Show Dialog" Width="100" Height="30" Click="|></Button>
                                                                        <New Event Handler>
```

> Another way of adding an event handler is to use the Visual Studio Design Properties (you have to click on the **Events** tab and then double-click on the **Click Event** property).

Now, we can navigate to the implementation of the event handler by right-clicking on the event and choosing **Navigate to Event Handler**. Let's add few lines of code to create a new instance of the control `MyControlUCView` and add it to the object collection in the main layout container:

```
private void btnAddUserControl_Click(object sender, RoutedEventArgs e)
{
  //Create a new Instance of our User Control
  MyControlUCView myUC = new MyControlUCView();
  //Add the control to the Container of our MainPage
  LayoutRoot.Children.Add(myUC);
}
```

If we copy the code, the compiler will show an error, as it will not find the definition for `MyControlUCView`, because it is located in a different namespace. We must add a reference to it via the `using` clause in the following manner:

```
using Chapter2.Sample.Forms.Views;
```

When we execute the previous code, we will be able to see how it instantiates and also shows the control when we press the button.

> If we instantiate a definite object in a different namespace, we will have to import it, either by defining a new xmlns:name in the XAML file or via the using clause, if it comes from the Code-Behind code file.

Page control

Page control is a specialization of UserControl. It includes functionality to integrate with the Silverlight Navigation Framework. Since it is a control which inherits from UserControl, it is a container element. We will use this control to create an application with several pages, if we are going to make use of the Navigation Framework.

Page control offers functionality to make use of navigation history, **NavigationService** (going backwards or forwards in the history), and events where we can control every single state of the navigation process. We will go deeper into these points in this chapter devoted to Navigation Framework.

It is a fundamental control for developing management applications.

To create a new page, click **Add New Item** and choose the option **Silverlight Page**, as shown in the following screenshot:

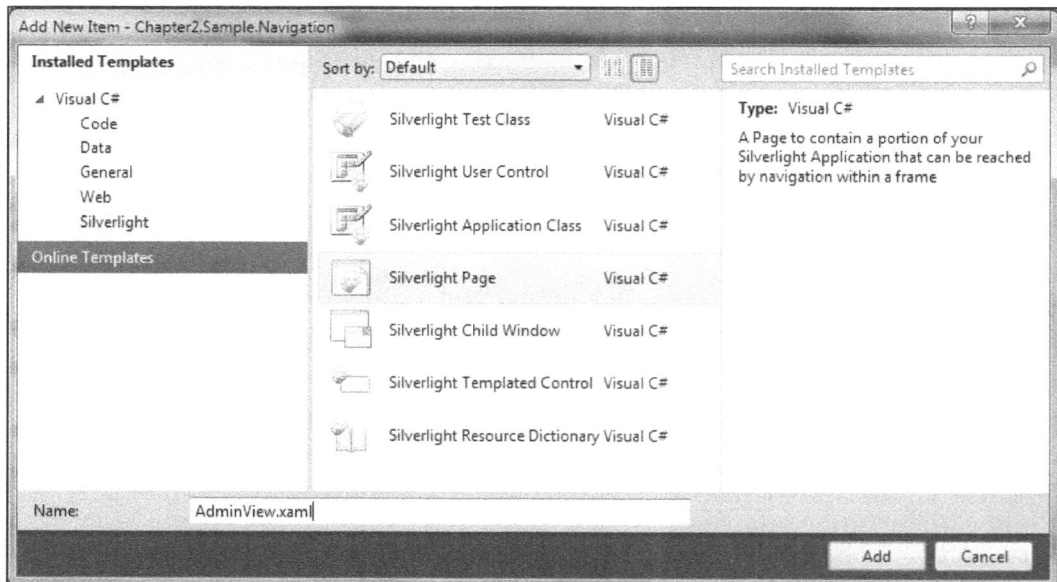

Creating modal dialogs

Modal dialogs are also common components in LOB (Line Of Business) applications and management applications. That is to say, a pop-up window that blocks the rest of the application appears. Once the user has completed the pertinent application, he or she can close it and the application unblocks.

ChildWindow is the implementation of a modal dialog in Silverlight.

Example of modal dialogs

We will continue with the previous example, now adding a ChildWindow control. Also, we will make the modal window host the same content as the main window, adding the UserControl we previously created. Finally, we will communicate with the main page using the modal control. To do so, we will copy the values we entered in the form of the modal window to the form of the main page, as shown in the following screenshot:

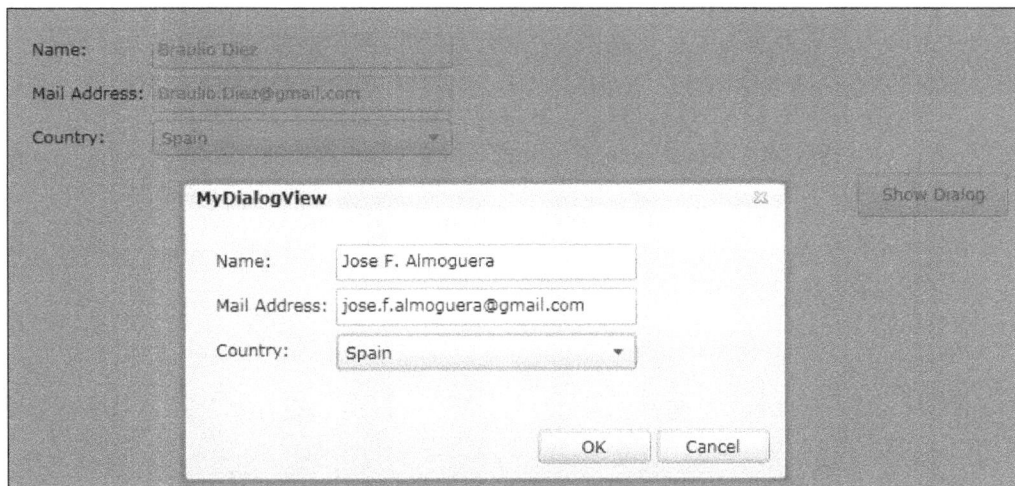

To create a ChildWindow, carry out the following steps:

1. On the **Views** folder, right-click and select **Add | New Item**.

2.   Choose the option **Silverlight Child Window** and name it **MyDialogView**, as shown in the next screenshot:

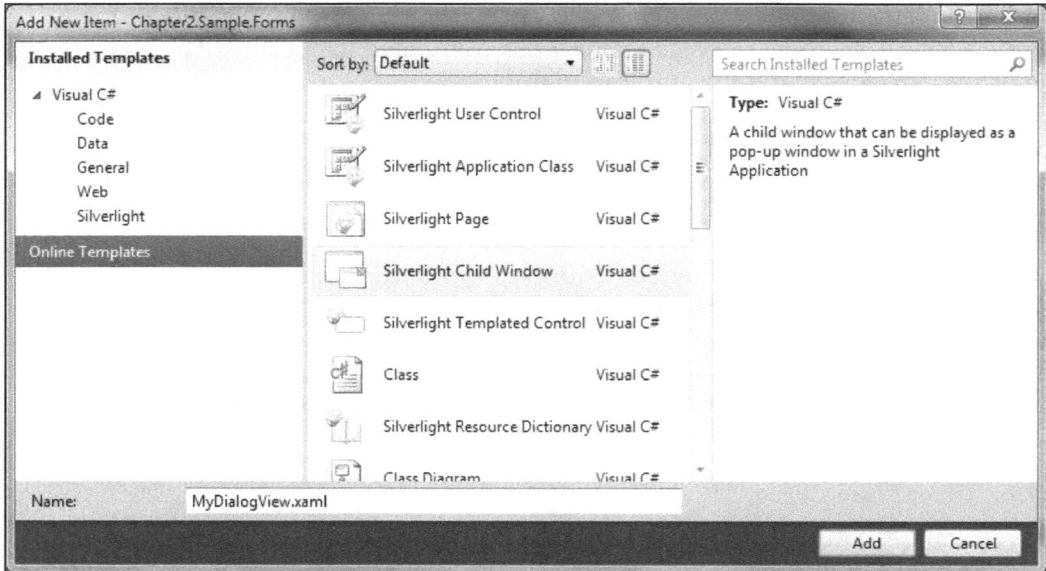

3.   Once the project is created, open `MyDialogView.XAML` and add the following content to customize it. We will also use the UserControl, created in the previous section, to display within the modal dialog. We will proceed as we did in the previous example. The final result will look similar to the following screenshot:

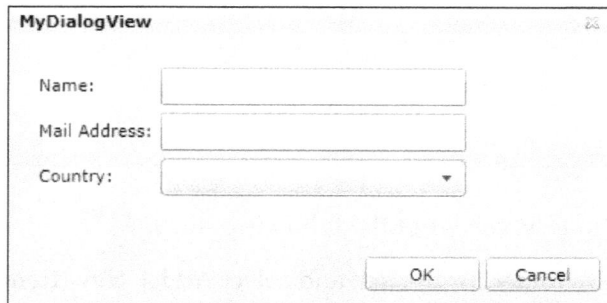

4. First, add the namespace where the UserControl is located and then reference both using the following lines of code:

```
<controls:ChildWindow
  x:Class="Chapter2.Sample.Forms.Views.MyDialogView"
  xmlns=http://schemas.microsoft.com/winfx/2006/xaml/presentation
  xmlns:x="http://schemas.microsoft.com/winfx/2006/xaml"
  xmlns:controls="clr-namespace:System.Windows.Controls;
    assembly=System.Windows.Controls"
  xmlns:MyControls="clr-namespace:Chapter2.Sample.Forms.Views"
  Width="400" Height="200" Title="MyDialogView">
  <Grid x:Name="LayoutRoot" Margin="2">
    <Grid.RowDefinitions>
      <RowDefinition />
      <RowDefinition Height="Auto" />
    </Grid.RowDefinitions>
    <MyControls:MyControlUCView x:Name="myControl"/>
    <Button x:Name="CancelButton" Content="Cancel"
      Click="CancelButton_Click" Width="75" Height="23"
      HorizontalAlignment="Right" Margin="0,12,0,0"
      Grid.Row="1"/>
    <Button x:Name="OKButton" Content="OK"
      Click="OKButton_Click" Width="75" Height="23"
      HorizontalAlignment="Right" Margin="0,12,79,0"
      Grid.Row="1" />
  </Grid>
</controls:ChildWindow>
```

5. In the Code-Behind file, let's add public properties to store the name, address, and country ID that the user is going to type in the dialog:

```
public partial class MyDialogView : ChildWindow
{
  public string MyName { get; set; }
  public string MyAddress { get; set; }
  public int MyCountry { get; set; }
}
```

6. In the `handler` function of the **OK** button, collect the values of the form shown in the modal dialog, copy them to the properties defined in the previous step, and set the dialog result to `true` to indicate that the user clicks the **OK** button using the following lines of code:

```
private void OKButton_Click(object sender, RoutedEventArgs e)
{
  MyName = myControl.txtName.Text;
  MyAddress = myControl.txtAddress.Text;
  MyCountry = myControl.ddlCountry.SelectedIndex;
  this.DialogResult = true;
}
```

Once we have defined our `ChildWindow`, we still need a few actions to display it:

1. In the **MainPage** page, add a `btnShowDialog` button. When we click the button, the Modal window is displayed.

2. To do so, associate a handler with the `Click` event. For this example, we will not need the code we previously added to insert objects in the form from the Code-Behind. We can comment on that code, as shown in the following code:

```
<UserControl x:Class="Chapter2.Sample.Forms.MainPage"
  xmlns="http://schemas.microsoft.com/winfx/2006/xaml/
    presentation"
  xmlns:x="http://schemas.microsoft.com/winfx/2006/xaml"
  xmlns:d="http://schemas.microsoft.com/expression/blend/2008"
  xmlns:mc="http://schemas.openxmlformats.org/markup-
    compatibility/2006"
  xmlns:MyControls="clr-namespace:Chapter2.Sample.Forms.Views"
  mc:Ignorable="d"
  d:DesignHeight="300"
  d:DesignWidth="400">
  <StackPanel x:Name="LayoutRoot" Background="White"
    Orientation="Vertical" Margin="10" >
    <MyControls:MyControlUCView x:Name="myControl"/>
    <!--<Button x:Name="btnAddUserControl" Content="Add Control"
      Width="100" Height="30" Click="btnAddUserControl_Click"/>-->
    <Button x:Name="btnShowDialog" Content="Show Dialog"
      Width="100" Height="30" Click="btnShowDialog_Click"/>
  </StackPanel>
</UserControl>
```

3. In the Code-Behind, in response to the `Click` event, we instantiate the control `MyDialogView`, show it via the method `Show()`, and link to the ChildWindow `Closed` event, using the following code:

```
private void btnShowDialog_Click(object sender, RoutedEventArgs e)
{
  MyDialogView childwindow = new MyDialogView(myControl);
  childwindow.Closed += new
    System.EventHandler(childwindow_Closed);
  childwindow.Show();
}
```

4. In the `Closed` event handler, we check if the `DialogResult` is `true` (not cancelled) and collect the values to display them on the main page by including the following code:

```
void childwindow_Closed(object sender, System.EventArgs e)
{
  MyDialogView dlg = sender as MyDialogView;
  if(dlg.DialogResult == true)
  {
    myControl.txtName.Text = dlg.MyName;
    myControl.txtAddress.Text = dlg.MyAddress;
    myControl.ddlCountry.SelectedIndex = dlg.MyCountry;
  }
}
```

Let us execute our example and see that when we press the button, the modal dialog appears. If we fill in the controls and click **OK**, we will see how the values are copied and the Modal window is closed.

Navigation

Navigation between windows and pages is a crucial point, both in web and desktop applications. If you are an experienced developer, you may remember those times when the event of a button was directly associated with instantiation and the call of a `window` `show` method. Nowadays, the tendency is to decouple navigation and windows along with using a Navigation Framework.

Navigating the Web

For those coming from web development using **iFrames,** the idea will sound familiar (better still, the Silverlight Navigation Framework integrates flawlessly in our Silverlight developments). Imagine a web application in which the header, which contains a navigation menu, is fixed. Finally, let us imagine that every menu option makes the content of our application (the page) change. However, what really happens is that it loads another page in the central iFrame in the backend. Roughly speaking, this is the Navigation Framework.

Another viewpoint (that of an ASP.NET developer) is thinking that we have a MasterPage and several pages associated with it. Silverlight, nevertheless, goes a step beyond, as one of our pages could contain another navigation control.

Let us have a look at the draft of a hypothetical application. The following screenshot displays a sample application that includes a menu and an area for content to be added. The content may differ according to the options selected from the menu:

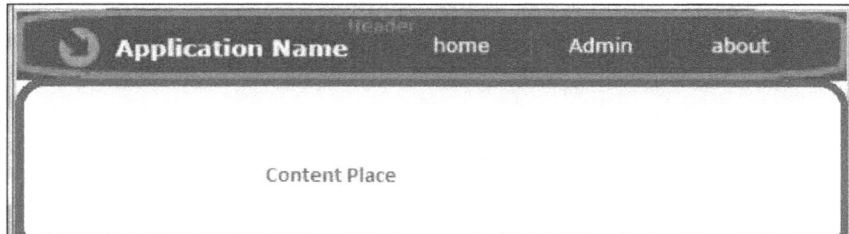

We can identify two areas:

- One in the previous part, which contains a menu and whose content is fixed.
- Another one which occupies the greatest part of our application. It changes according to the option chosen in the menu. This was an iFrame, which contains another HTML page.

Silverlight Navigation Framework

Navigation Framework is defined as navigation architecture between the pages of a Silverlight application.

Until version 2 (The Silverlight Navigation Framework was introduced in version 3), the main options to lay out an application with several windows were the following:

- Defining UserControls for every page of the application and show/hide them manually, depending on the status of the application.
- Having several HTML container pages, with each one of them having a Silverlight object instantiated.

We wouldn't recommend the second option, since it implies an extra communication system, different XAP modules, and we don't find any advantage versus the first.

With the appearance of Navigation Framework, we are able to centralize navigation automatically from a single point. Navigation between pages is quite clean, thanks to the use of friendly URLs such as `http://www.albloguera.com/Silverlight.html#home`.

In this way, we are able to tell the application what we want to display.

Integrating Navigation Framework in the browser

Navigation Framework allows us to make use of the navigation history. This means that if we click **Forward** and **Back**, the application uses the navigation history and loads the page which it has indicated. This is not the only good feature. The navigation route can also show, apart from the page, parameters which initialize the application one way or another. In order to allow a Silverlight application to make use of the history, the page where the Silverlight object is instantiated must contain an iFrame object with the following name:

```
<iframe id="_sl_historyFrame"
    style="visibility:hidden;height:0px;width:0px;border:0px"></iframe>
```

An application created with the Navigation Template adds this iFrame by default. Finally, we would like to point out that we can disable the navigation history for everything that has taken place outside the application. That is, the Silverlight application will not register anything about the navigation that the user does outside. For example, if the user goes to another page, the navigation history of the application will not take that into account. In this respect, we must add the following property to iFrame:

```
<iframe id="_sl_historyFrame"
    style="visibility:hidden;height:0px;width:0px;border:0px"
    JournalOwnership="OwnsJournal">
```

Once we have gotten an idea of what navigation between different parts of an application is, let us go deeper into the UriMapper concepts.

UriMapper

We could think of UriMapper as the navigation control centre of our application. Here, we define the links or pages of the application (real URI) and assign it a friendly name (URI shown), so that the user does not see the physical address of the page shown, but a name describing it (for those coming from the ASP.NET MVC background, this concept will be quite familiar).

URI	URI shown	Real URI
Uri = "/Home" MappedUri = "/Views/Home.xaml"	/Home	/Views/Home.xaml
Uri = "/{page}" MappedUri = "/Views/{page}Page.xaml"	/About	/Views/AboutPage.xaml
Uri = "/Product/{category}" MappedUri = "/ContosoShop/Product.xaml? category ={category}"	/Product/bikes	/ContosoShop/Product.xamlñ?category=bikes

We can see several examples of URI mappings in the following table:

We can observe in the table that URIs do not have to define a fixed physical address, but they can define a flexible behavior, depending on the URI. To define a segment of the URI as a variable, we must add the value in braces; it will be later replaced in the real URI. This is quite useful for parameter passing in the URI.

Frame

This is the container of the application. For those who are familiar with ASP.NET, it is similar to the ContentPlaceHolder. For older users, it is the central iFrame. It is in charge of navigation and shows the different pages of the application.

```
<navigation:Frame x:Name="ContentFrame" Style="{StaticResource
  ContentFrameStyle}" Source="/Home" Navigated="ContentFrame_
Navigated"
  NavigationFailed="ContentFrame_NavigationFailed">
  <navigation:Frame.UriMapper>
    <uriMapper:UriMapper>
      <uriMapper:UriMapping Uri="" MappedUri="/Views/Home.xaml"/>
      <uriMapper:UriMapping Uri="/{pageName}"
        MappedUri="/Views/{pageName}.xaml"/>
    </uriMapper:UriMapper>
  </navigation:Frame.UriMapper>
</navigation:Frame>
```

Creating a sample Navigation Application

Now that we have identified the main points of the Navigation Framework, we will begin by creating a sample from the beginning.

We will create an application which makes use of the Silverlight Navigation functionality, showing how we can control the navigation status when it begins or ends. Also, we will learn how to pass parameters via URI.

1. To create a new project, go to **New Project** and choose a **Silverlight Navigation Application** project.

2. Give the project a name and click **Ok**.

3. Later, we will be asked if we want to create a project for hosting the Silverlight application. For convenience, choose to create an **ASP.NET Web Application** project.

4. After clicking **OK**, Visual Studio applies the Template associated with this kind of project. It generates a structure depending on the solution to locate an area for page definition at first sight, as shown in the following screenshot.

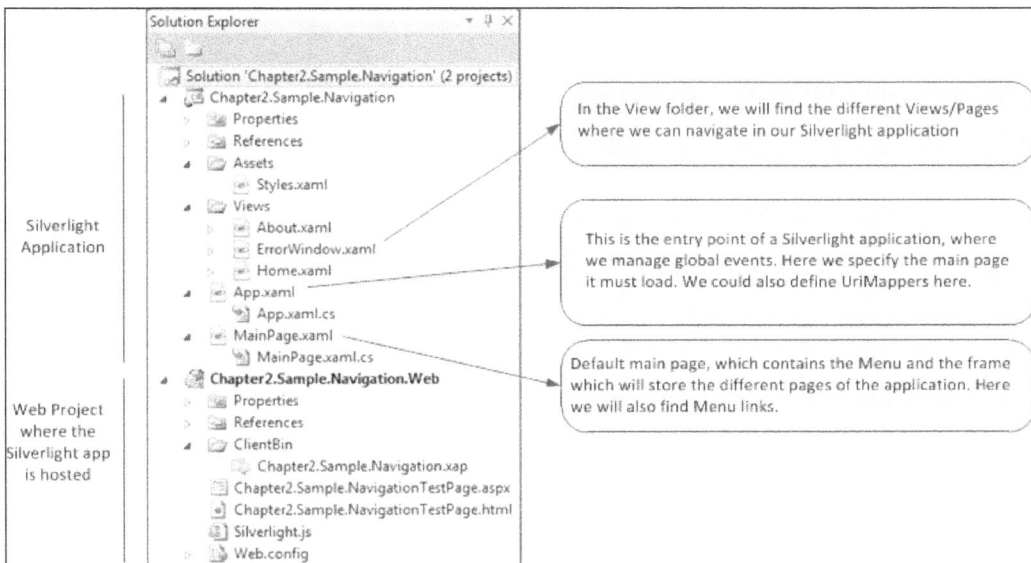

- ○ **Main Page**: If we observe it, we can see that it has created a main page (`MainPage.XAML`). This page also contains the Navigation controls (and UriMappers). Here, we can also find the menu links.

- ○ **App.xaml**: In this file, we define the application styles (we could add URIMappers here as well).

- ○ **App.cs**: This is the application entry point.

- ○ **Page container area**: It creates a **Views** folder and here we add the new pages our application needs. By default, we will find two sample pages, Home.xaml and About.xaml. A ChildWindow control has also been added to the **Views** folder in order to show the possible errors that the application may generate. ErrorWindow.xaml.

Finally, we can see the web project upon which the Silverlight application will be executed.

Adding a new page

We will add a new page to our project and also create the resulting option in the Navigation menu, which will allow us to display it.

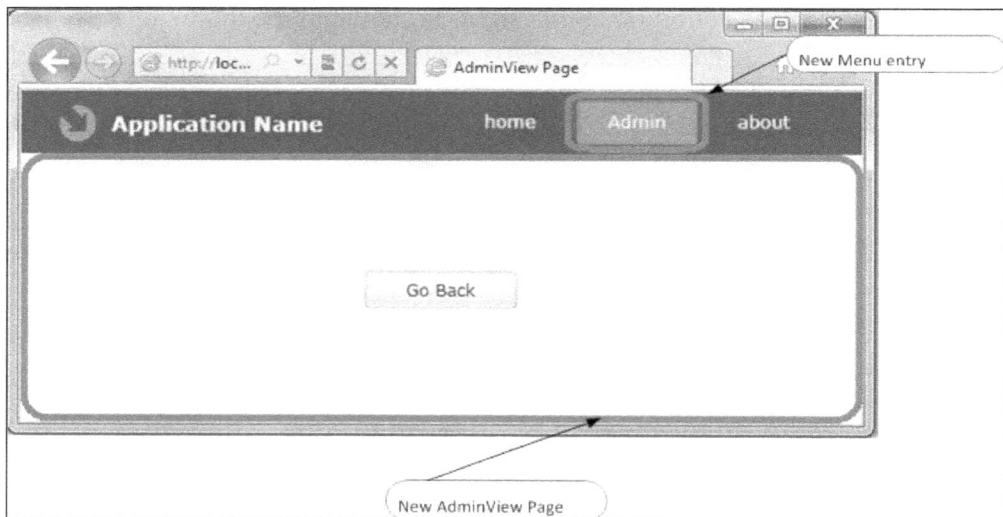

1. On the **Views** folder, add a new **Silverlight Page** item.

2. Name it AdminView.XAML.

   If we execute the application at this point, we will see that there is no link to the new page. To get one, we need to modify the MainPage.XAML page, by adding a new UriMapper that identifies the AdminView.XAML page in the following manner:

```
<uriMapper:UriMapper>
  <uriMapper:UriMapping Uri="" MappedUri="/Views/Home.xaml"/>
  <uriMapper:UriMapping Uri="/{pageName}"
    MappedUri="/Views/{pageName}.xaml"/>
  <uriMapper:UriMapping Uri="/{pageName}"
    MappedUri="/Views/{pageName}View.xaml"/>
</uriMapper:UriMapper>
```

- ° Conventionally, when identifying interface objects, we will rename the pages Home.XAML and About.XAML to HomeView.XAML and AboutView.XAML respectively (we should not forget to rename classes). Thus it is clear that the second UriMapper is superfluous; if we execute the application right now, the error "Home Page is not found" would occur (it is configured by default), as displayed in the following screenshot. The application matches the Home URI with the second UriMapper and does not find the /Views/Home.XAML URI.

> Interface Object Name: It is a good practice to name the interface objects with the suffix "View" in order to identify them clearly.

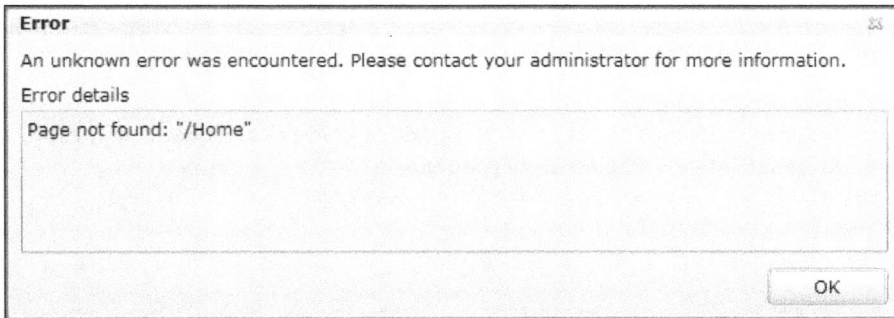

```
Error                                                            ⋈
An unknown error was encountered. Please contact your administrator for more information.
Error details
┌────────────────────────────────────────────────────────────────┐
│ Page not found: "/Home"                                         │
│                                                                  │
│                                                                  │
│                                                                  │
└────────────────────────────────────────────────────────────────┘
                                                      ┌──────────┐
                                                      │    OK    │
                                                      └──────────┘
```

3. We must delete the second URI of the collection because the UriMapper cannot map the /home URI to the Home.xaml now, because the Navigation Framework takes the first entry in the URI collection that matches with the specified URI, as shown in the UriMapper code.

4. Then execute the application again.

So where should you click to go to the new page?

We are still to enter another menu entry.

1. To do so, add a new **HyperLinkButton** control to the `MainPage.XAML` page and establish the `NavigateUri` property to the `Admin` value as shown in the following code:

2. Let us execute the application again.

```
<StackPanel x:Name="LinksStackPanel" Style="{StaticResource
  LinksStackPanelStyle}">
  <HyperlinkButton x:Name="Link1" Style="{StaticResource
    LinkStyle}" NavigateUri="/Home" TargetName="ContentFrame"
    Content="home"/>
  <Rectangle x:Name="Divider2" Style="{StaticResource
    DividerStyle}"/>
  <HyperlinkButton x:Name="Link3"          Style="{StaticResource
    LinkStyle}" NavigateUri="/Admin" TargetName="ContentFrame"
    Content="Admin"/>
  <Rectangle x:Name="Divider1" Style="{StaticResource
    DividerStyle}"/>
  <HyperlinkButton x:Name="Link2" Style="{StaticResource
    LinkStyle}" NavigateUri="/About" TargetName="ContentFrame"
    Content="about"/>
</StackPanel>
```

This is how our UriMapper will look:

```
<uriMapper:UriMapper>
  <uriMapper:UriMapping Uri="" MappedUri="/Views/HomeView.xaml"/>
  <uriMapper:UriMapping Uri="/{pageName}"
    MappedUri="/Views/{pageName}View.xaml"/>
</uriMapper:UriMapper>
```

Navigation control services

Navigation control offers methods to navigate and navigation control events.

The following are the methods:

*   **GoBack**: It goes back to the page previously visited.
*   **GoForward:** It goes a page forward in the navigation history.
*   **Navigate**: It goes to the indicated page.
*   **Refresh**: Reloads the current page.
*   **StopLoading**: Cancels any asynchronous navigation actions that haven't been processed yet.

Following are the Events:

- **Navigated**: This occurs when the navigation to a particular page has ended.
- **Navigating:** This occurs when the navigation to a particular page is about to begin.

To put this functionality into practice, we will add a button to the **AdminView** page. At the click of this button, we will be able to navigate to the last visited page.

1. Begin by adding a button definition in the XAML file.

2. We will establish, as we saw previously, a manager for the `Click` event.

```
<Grid x:Name="LayoutRoot">
  <Button x:Name="btnGoBack"
    Width="100"
    Height="25"
    Content="Go Back"
    Click="btnGoBack_Click">
  </Button>
</Grid>
```

3. We must add the `Click` event manager with the following code:

```
private void btnGoBack_Click(object sender, RoutedEventArgs e)
{
  if (this.NavigationService.CanGoBack)
    //go to the previous page in the history
    this.NavigationService.GoBack();
}
```

4. We can also intercept the exact moment in which navigation occurs. To see how it works, we must subscribe to the `Navigating` event and a message that indicates the page being navigated is shown. We do this on the `Frame` control of the `MainPage.XAML` page, similar to the following code:

```
<navigation:Frame x:Name="ContentFrame" Style="{StaticResource
  ContentFrameStyle}" Source="/Home"
  Navigated="ContentFrame_Navigated"
  NavigationFailed="ContentFrame_NavigationFailed"
Navigating="ContentFrame_Navigating">
```

5. Lastly, add the following code to the Code-Behind, so that it displays a message with the information of the page that is being navigated.

```
private void ContentFrame_Navigating(object sender,
  NavigatingCancelEventArgs e)
{
  MessageBox.Show("You are navigating to " + e.Uri, "Information",
    MessageBoxButton.OK);
}
```

URI parameters

Similar to a web application, we can pass parameters between the different websites via URI.

We will add a new `UriMapper` for the **Admin** page to receive a parameter in this manner.

UriMappers will look similar to the following block of code:

```
<uriMapper:UriMapping Uri="" MappedUri="/Views/HomeView.xaml"/>
<uriMapper:UriMapping Uri="/Admin/{userName}"
  MappedUri="/Views/adminView.xaml?userName={userName}"/>
<uriMapper:UriMapping Uri="/{pageName}"
  MappedUri="/Views/{pageName}View.xaml"/>
</uriMapper:UriMapper>
```

Now we will add a button to the Home page with a handler for the Click event, which is used to navigate to the Admin page, and also adds a parameter to the URI. The code in Code-Behind will look similar to the following:

```
private void btnGoAdminAsAdmin_Click(object sender, RoutedEventArgs e)
{
  this.NavigationService.Navigate(new Uri("/Admin/{jose.f.almoguera}",
    UriKind.RelativeOrAbsolute));
}
```

Finally, we must control the existence of any parameter in the URI of the **Admin** page.

Go to the Code-Behind of the **Admin** page and complete the function `OnNavigatedTo` with the following code. This shows a message if the URI contains a parameter named `userName`, when navigating to this page.

```
// Executes when the user navigates to this page.
protected override void OnNavigatedTo(NavigationEventArgs e)
{
  //Check if URI contains a parameter named "userName"
  if (this.NavigationContext.QueryString.ContainsKey("userName"))
    MessageBox.Show("You are " +
      this.NavigationContext.QueryString["userName"]);
}
```

If we execute the application right now and click on the **Go to Admin** page as Admin, we will obtain the following message sequence:

1. **You are navigating to /Home**

2. **{click on Go To Admin Page As Admin} You are navigating to /admin{jose.f.almoguera}**

3. **You are {jose.f.almoguera}**, as shown in the following screenshot:

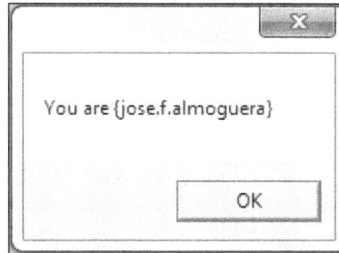

Deep Linking

In a **Rich Internet Application (RIA)** – Silverlight, Flex – it is quite common that the URL reflects an application's web direction (that is, a global direction), which remains unchanged through its whole life. Now, with the Navigation Framework, the term **Deep Linking** can be understood. We can define Deep Linking as a URL, which clearly defines a place within a website – URI. The URL contains the entire information defining the target.

> You can find a more in-depth definition about deep linking here:
> `http://en.wikipedia.org/wiki/Deep_linking`

Thanks to the Navigation Framework, we can access a particular section of a specific page or content within the application. It allows us to use Deep Linking in our application. However, thanks to the use of parameters in the URI, we can access a particular status too. As an illustration, we can mention a link to a book within a particular library:

`http://www.mylibrary.com/#seebook?bookId=5`

- First, the place we want to go to or the action we want to do must be specified. In this case, we want to view a book, so we must go to the **see book** page.

- Once in the selected place, we have to indicate that we want to see the book with `ID=5`.

We have already seen an example of this while dealing with URI parameters when we implemented the Navigation Framework sample.

LOB application case study: applying what we have learnt

To apply what we have learnt so far, we will create the navigation for our application. In this example, we will create three pages for navigation and a modal dialog to edit rooms. The flowchart will look like the following diagram:

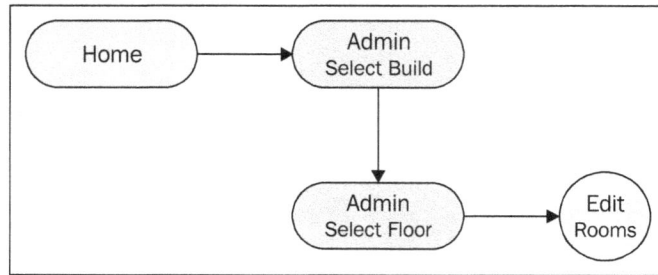

1. Let us begin by creating a new navigation project, as we have learnt in this chapter. The project will be named `ReservationNavigation`. We will later add the following elements in the `Views` folder:

    °   **MapView**: Object of the type `Page`. We will be able to navigate to this page via the general menu of the application. It will show a map on which to choose a building to edit.

    °   **AdminView**: Object of the type `Page`. We will be able to navigate to this page from the **MapView** page after choosing a building.

    °   **AdminEditionView**: Object of the type `ChildWindow`. This modal window will show a form with the necessary fields to edit/add/delete a room in a building.

2. Once we have added these two pages and the modal window; modify the UriMapper in order to add the new navigation possibilities of our application. For this example, we will generate the UriMapper as a resource and move it to the `app.xaml` file, using the following code. We will assign the `uriMapper` key.

```
<Application x:Class="ReservationNavigation.App"
  xmlns="http://schemas.microsoft.com/winfx/2006/xaml/
    presentation"
  xmlns:uriMapper="clr-namespace:System.Windows.Navigation;
    assembly=System.Windows.Controls.Navigation"
```

```
    xmlns:x="http://schemas.microsoft.com/winfx/2006/xaml">
    <Application.Resources>
      <ResourceDictionary>
        <uriMapper:UriMapper x:Key="uriMapper">
          <uriMapper:UriMapping Uri="" MappedUri="/Views/Home.xaml"/>
          <uriMapper:UriMapping Uri="/Admin/{buildId}"
            MappedUri="/Views/AdminView.xaml?buildId={buildId}"/>
          <uriMapper:UriMapping Uri="/Admin"
            MappedUri="/Views/MapView.xaml"/>
          <uriMapper:UriMapping Uri="/{pageName}"
            MappedUri="/Views/{pageName}.xaml"/>
        </uriMapper:UriMapper>
        <ResourceDictionary.MergedDictionaries>
          <ResourceDictionary Source="Assets/Styles.xaml"/>
        </ResourceDictionary.MergedDictionaries>
      </ResourceDictionary>
    </Application.Resources>
  </Application>
```

> Resources are a powerful, easy, and elegant way to define
> objects and styles, which can be used in different parts of the
> application, apart from allowing for a cleaner code. We can
> have different resource files and later unite name-value pairs
> in a dictionary within the app.xaml file.

3. Now we can clean the XAML code within the MainPage.XAML, which defines navigation control.

4. We have eliminated the UriMapper, which the MainPage.XAML contained, and have established it as a property, as shown in the following code:

```
<navigation:Frame x:Name="ContentFrame" Style="{StaticResource
  ContentFrameStyle}" Source="/Home"
  Navigated="ContentFrame_Navigated"
  NavigationFailed="ContentFrame_NavigationFailed"
  UriMapper="{StaticResource uriMapper}"/>
```

5. Finally, we will add the new entries to the navigation menu. In our example, there will be only one, namely, the **Admin** option.

```
<Border x:Name="LinksBorder" Style="{StaticResource
  LinksBorderStyle}">
  <StackPanel x:Name="LinksStackPanel" Style="{StaticResource
    LinksStackPanelStyle}">
    <HyperlinkButton x:Name="Link1" Style="{StaticResource
      LinkStyle}" NavigateUri="/Home" TargetName="ContentFrame"
      Content="home"/>
```

```
        <Rectangle x:Name="Divider1" Style="{StaticResource
          DividerStyle}"/>
        <HyperlinkButton x:Name="Link3" Style="{StaticResource
          LinkStyle}" NavigateUri="/Admin" TargetName="ContentFrame"
          Content="admin"/>
        <Rectangle x:Name="Divider2" Style="{StaticResource
          DividerStyle}"/>
        <HyperlinkButton x:Name="Link2" Style="{StaticResource
          LinkStyle}" NavigateUri="/About" TargetName="ContentFrame"
          Content="about"/>
      </StackPanel>
  </Border>
```

If we executed it right now, the page would look similar to the following screenshot:

MapView.XAML page

This page is transparent for the user, that is, the user can only see an administration page. Before getting to it, the user will stop at the **MapView** page to choose a building to administrate, similar to the following screenshot. The page shows an image with a map and several links to click. Later, after selecting a venue, the application will navigate to the administration page.

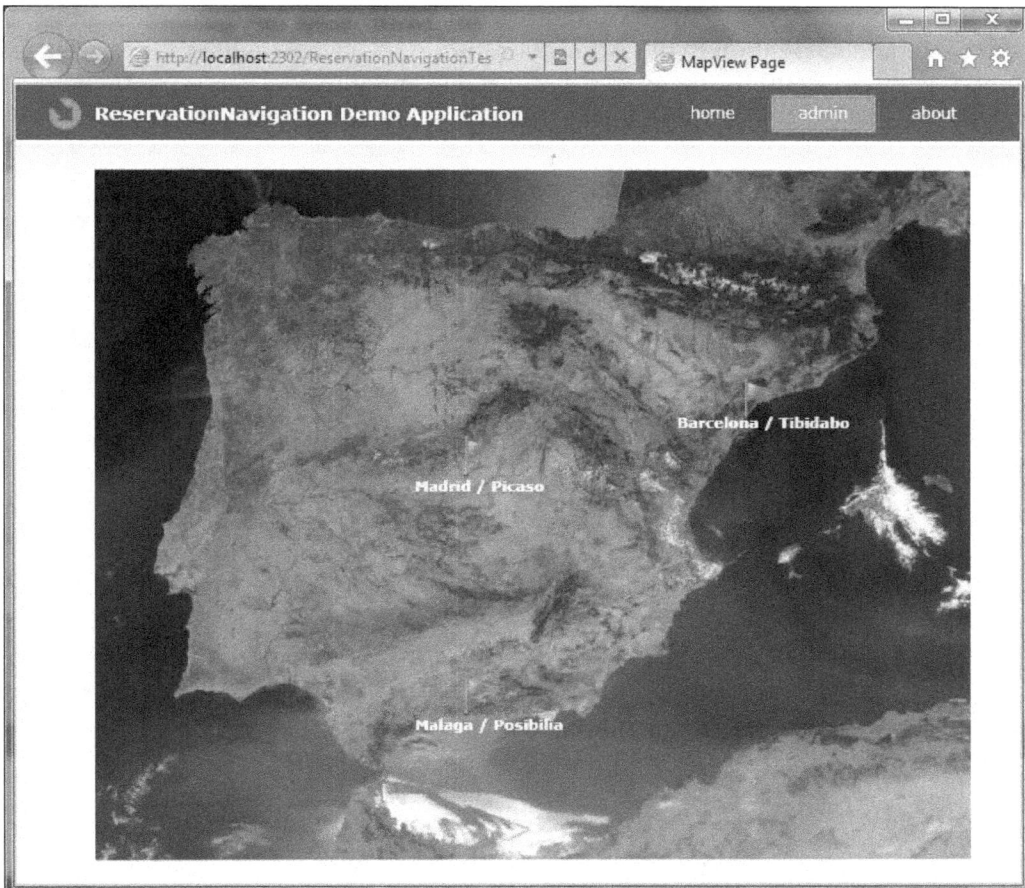

All the XAML code in this page can be found within the example in this chapter. Roughly speaking, it is a **Canvas** object containing several **Image** objects: one for the map and the other three for the flags.

The flags (and labels) have a manager associated for the `MouseLeftButtonDown` event to initiate navigation to the **Administration** page. Before calling the `Navigate` method, we will obtain the name of the selected element to add it as a parameter to the URI.

```
/// <summary>
/// Take the name of the link selected
/// and navigate to the admin page
/// </summary>
private void imgMadrid_MouseLeftButtonDown(object sender,
  MouseButtonEventArgs e)
{
  // var to store the name of the link clicked
  string target = "";
  //Depending on the object's type we do the cast
  if (sender.GetType() == typeof(Label))
  {
    Label lbl = (Label)sender;
    target = lbl.Name.Substring(3);
  }
  else
  {
    Image img = (Image)sender;
    target = lbl.Name.Substring(3);
  }
 //Navigate to the Admin page adding a parameter
 //to the URL to identify the building selected
  this.NavigationService.Navigate(new Uri("/Admin/" + target,
    UriKind.RelativeOrAbsolute));
}
```

AdminView.XAML Page

In this page, we can administrate the available rooms in the different buildings. For the layout, we will use Grid and StackPanel (see the following diagram). We will also add the following objects:

- **DataGrid**: One to show the floors and the general view of the building, and a second one connected (master/detail), which shows the different rooms defined in the selected floor.

- **Button**: Several buttons to add, delete, or edit the floors of the building. We also find an **Edit** button, which will open the modal window to edit a floor.

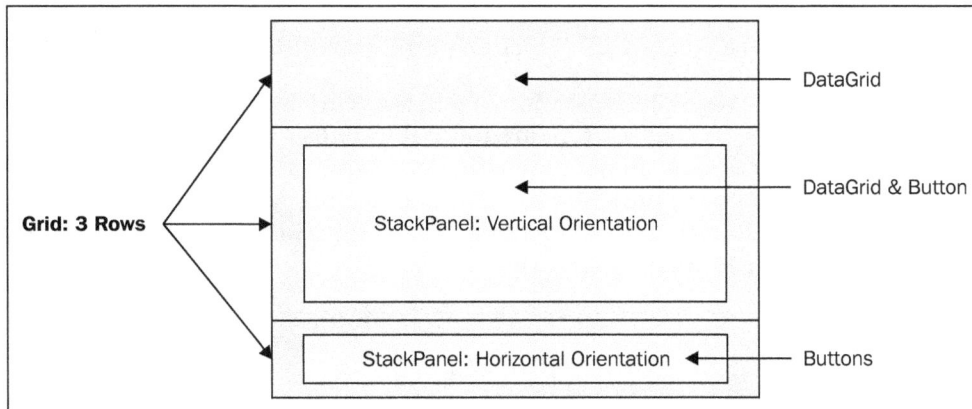

Let us lay out the page and give it an aspect similar to the following screenshot, that is, the **AdminView** page (we learned how to achieve this in the previous chapter):

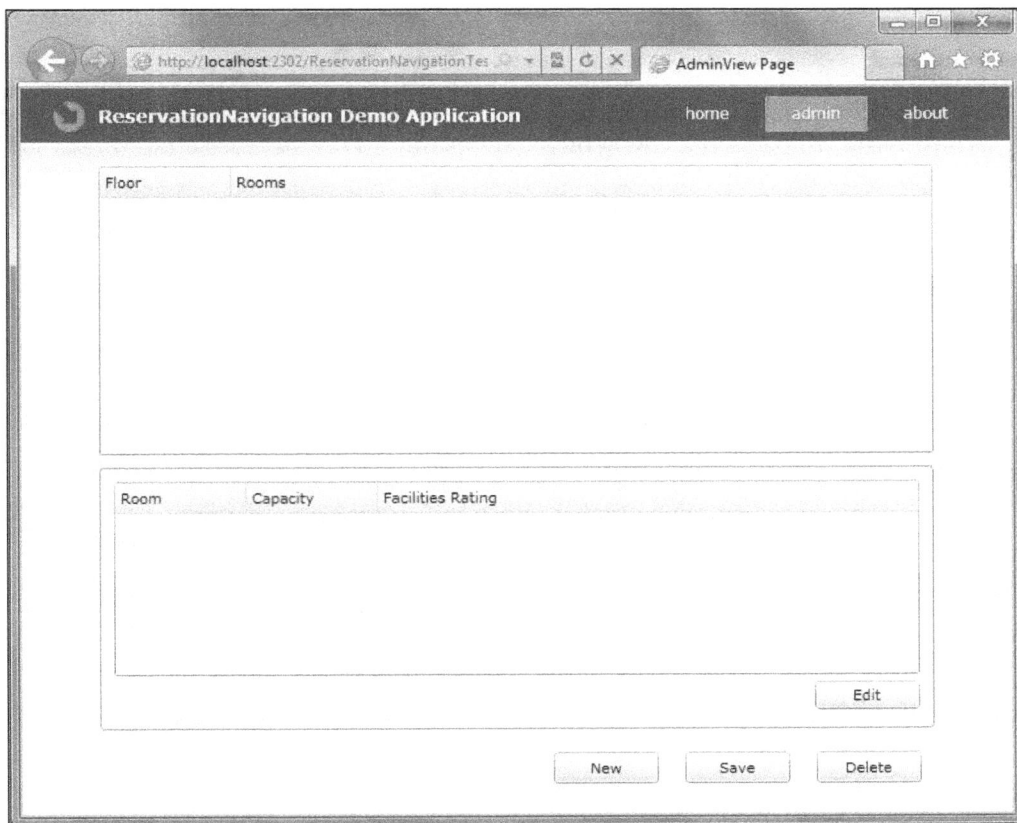

The XAML code of the page `AdminView.xaml` can be seen by downloading the examples in *Chapter 2* (see *Source Code* section at the end of the book).

If we take a look at the navigation menu, we will see there is no selected option, and it is caused by the code in charge of maintaining the status of the different menu options. We have two options in the menu, namely, **home** and **admin** (let us omit the option **about**). However, the same status in the control panel is defined by two different pages, namely, `MapView` and `AdminView`. The buttons and the respective URI's are shown in the following diagram:

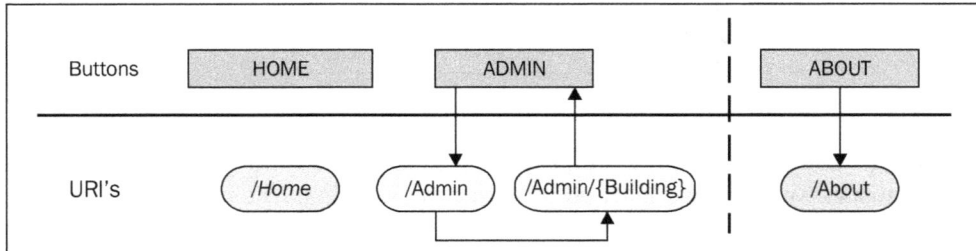

The problem is that the URI defined in the `HyperLinkButton` and the URI to which we are navigating to are being compared. When we select a building and navigate to the **Administration** page, the URI which defines our target includes a parameter and makes it different from the URI defined in the `HyperLinkbutton` as target. To solve this, we can include the following code:

```
// After the Frame navigates, ensure the HyperlinkButton
// representing the current page is selected
private void ContentFrame_Navigated(object sender, NavigationEventArgs
e)
{
  foreach (UIElement child in LinksStackPanel.Children)
  {
    HyperlinkButton hb = child as HyperlinkButton;
    if (hb != null && hb.NavigateUri != null)
    {
      // We have to check if the URI we are navigating
      // is equal that the HyperLinkButton defines, or
      // it is contained in it.Remember that we have 2
      // pages for only one name. The difference is the
      // parameter of the build selected.
      if(hb.NavigateUri.ToString().Equals(e.Uri.ToString()) ||
        e.Uri.ToString().Contains(hb.NavigateUri.ToString()))
```

```
        {
          VisualStateManager.GoToState(hb, "ActiveLink", true);
        }
        else
        {
          VisualStateManager.GoToState(hb, "InactiveLink", true);
        }
      }
    }
  }
```

The code controlling the status of the Navigation buttons can be found in the Code-Behind of `MainPage.xaml`.

Modal AdminEditionView.xaml dialog

If the user clicks **Edit**, which is located just below the **DataGrid** showing the rooms, a modal dialog, similar to the following screenshot, will open:

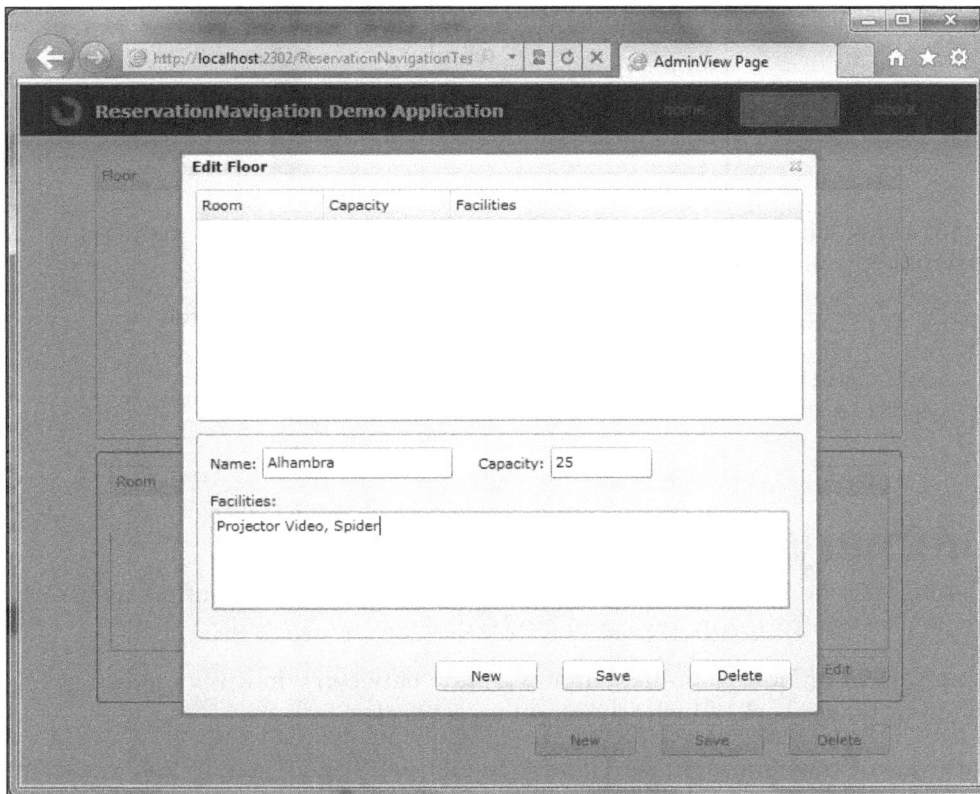

The layout of this window is very similar to the one created in the `AdminView.xaml` page. You can see all the code in the final example.

To open this window, we must add the manager of the `Click` event to the **Edit** button. There are two quick ways to add the code required for this action, both in the XAML file and the Code-Behind file.

- Double-click on the button in the **Layout** view in Visual Studio.
- Through the **Properties** window of the editor, we must select the button in the **Layout** view, open the **Properties** view, and select the **Events** tab. Here we can see all the events that the object can manage. Now we must double-click on the event we want to implement and the code required to manage the event will automatically be created.

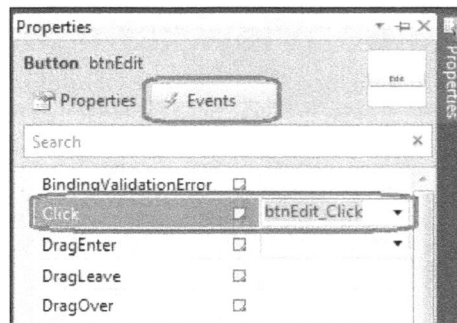

The only thing left to do now is to fill in the code for the event for it to open the modal dialog when we click it.

```
private void btnEdit_Click(object sender, RoutedEventArgs e)
{
  AdminEditionView theChild = new AdminEditionView();
  theChild.Show();
}
```

Summary

In this chapter, we have covered the basic element that Silverlight offers us in order to create user controls, windows, and modal dialogs.

We have also seen how to implement navigation between windows via the Navigation Framework, which Silverlight incorporates.

We now know how to mount the UI layer in our web application. In the next chapter, we will learn how to bind the UI controls with the data of our application.

Additional resources

- MSDN

  `http://msdn.microsoft.com/en-us/library/cc838245(v=vs.95).aspx`

- Tim Heuer: Here we can find many entries with Navigation Framework examples and other information. If you like Silverlight, Tim's site must be one of our bedside readings on this topic.

  `http://timheuer.com/blog/archive/2009/04/06/Silverlight-3-navigation-behavior-customization.aspx`

- SilverlightShow: We cannot help mentioning this reference site, where we can find tutorials and examples on this topic as well as others.

  `http://www.Silverlightshow.net/items/The-Silverlight-3-Navigation-Framework.aspx`

3
Data Binding

The concept of **Data Binding** is not something new in the development of LOB applications, and can be defined as the action of *tying* data to the interface.

Another way to understand data binding is the way in which data is presented to the user, as well as how they interact with that data. The key concept to understand here is how data is presented to the user once it has been obtained. Similarly, we can apply it the other way around. That is, once the user has established the data, we can decide how to store that data in our entities. In this process, we can differentiate two objects, first, the object that defines the link and second, the object Data.

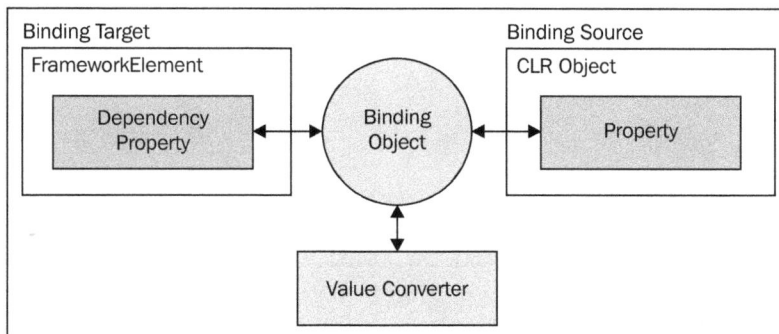

As an illustration, we can mention the typical **Recordset**, which probably sounds familiar to many users and may throw some light on the subject. We can say that data binding in Silverlight is a recordset, but with a firewall between the application and the database, since the connection between both is not a direct one.

An added value of data binding in Silverlight—in comparison to an ASP.NET application — is that binding remains *alive* and the term **Postback** does not make sense in this type of application. In Silverlight, when we have actions that have to be executed on the server side, we only need to send data, and we only receive data as response, so the page is not repainted, we just have to set new values. The development of a Silverlight application has a great similarity to the development of a desktop application, than a web application, purely due the fact that we do not have to maintain the application status after any postback (it does not exist) and we program the same way as we do in a WPF/Winforms application.

Understanding DataSource

Let us begin with a simple instance where we will make use of the main concepts related to data binding, and how data is bound to controls in a declarative way. Similar to the previous chapters, we will create a brand new Silverlight project called, in this case, MyFirstDataBinding. We will create a translator of the message "Hello World" into different languages. A ComboBox control will show the available languages, and a textbox will show the result. We will establish binding in a declarative way.

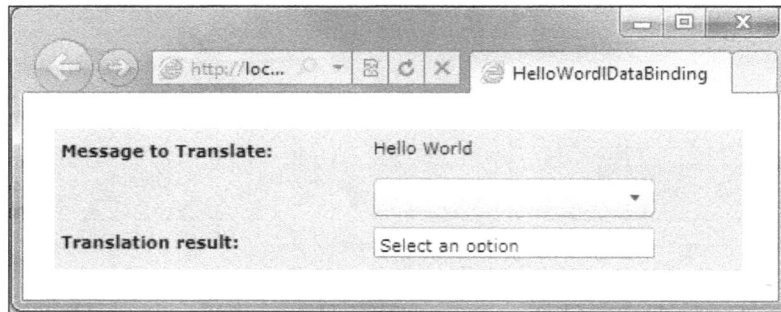

We start by adding content to the MainPage.xaml file so that it has the aspect in the previous screenshot with the following code snippet:

```xml
<Grid x:Name="LayoutRoot" VerticalAlignment="top"
  HorizontalAlignment="Left" Margin="20"
  Background="#FFCFCFD0" Width="440" Height="100">
  <Grid.RowDefinitions>
    <RowDefinition Height="30" />
    <RowDefinition Height="30" />
    <RowDefinition Height="30" />
  </Grid.RowDefinitions>
  <Grid.ColumnDefinitions>
```

```
            <ColumnDefinition Width="200"/>
            <ColumnDefinition Width="210"/>
        </Grid.ColumnDefinitions>
        <TextBlock Text="Message to Translate: " Grid.Row="0" Grid.
          Column="0" FontWeight="Bold" VerticalAlignment="Center"
          Margin="4,0"/>
        <TextBlock Name="lblMessage" Width="180"
          Text="{Binding Path=MessageLabel}"
          HorizontalAlignment="Left" Margin="4,0"
          Height="20" Grid.Row="0" Grid.Column="1"
          Grid.ColumnSpan="2"/>
        <TextBlock Name="lblLanguages"
          Text="{Binding  Path=Items.Count, ElementName=cbMessages}"
          Width="180" HorizontalAlignment="Left" Margin="4,0" Height="20"
            Grid.Row="1" Grid.Column="0" Grid.ColumnSpan="2"/>
        <ComboBox Name="cbMessages" Grid.Row="1" Grid.Column="1"
          Grid.ColumnSpan="2" Height="25" Width="180"
          HorizontalAlignment="left" Margin="4,0"
          ItemsSource="{Binding MessagesList}"
          SelectedValuePath="MessageCode"
          DisplayMemberPath="Language"
          SelectedValue="{Binding MessageSelected, Mode=TwoWay}"/>
        <TextBlock Text="Translation result: " FontWeight="Bold" Grid.Row="2"
          Grid.Column="0" VerticalAlignment="Center" Margin="4,0"/>
        <TextBox Name="txtMesage"
          Text="{Binding MessageSelected}"
          Grid.Row="2" Grid.Column="1" HorizontalAlignment="Left"
            VerticalAlignment="Center" Width="180" Height="20" Margin="4,0"/>
    </Grid>
```

Let's first go through this sequence step by step. If we pay attention to the code, we can identify some keywords, which are part of the XAML extensions for data binding, such as the following::

- **Path**: When we establish a data binding, we indicate a path to a datasource, and this results in an object property.

- **Mode**: Data flow can be unidirectional or bidirectional.

- **ItemsSource**: It specifies the origin of data in a control of the type `ItemsControl` (ComboBox, ListBox, and similar).

Path

By means of the Path property, we specify the property of the source object on which we want to establish binding.

```
<TextBlock Name="lblMessage"
    Text="{Binding Path=MessageLabel}"/>
```

Using the word Path is optional, we can just name the property of the object datasource, provided that this is the first property we specify in the binding.

```
<TextBlock Name="lblMessage"
    Text="{Binding Messagelabel}"
    Width="180" HorizontalAlignment="Left" Margin="4,0" Height="20"
    Grid.Row="0" Grid.Column="1" Grid.ColumnSpan="2"/>
```

Binding sources

When we create a new binding between a control property and the property of a datasource, we have to specify that source. In Silverlight, this source can be established in four different ways, or rather, data can come from four different sources:

- **Implicit DataContext**: This is the easiest path, and consists of specifying nothing. We simply leave the datasource as the *DataContext*, which the control includes by default.

- **ElementName**: It is used when we want to establish the properties of another control as the datasource. In this case, we enter the name of the control bound as value of the property, ElementName. The following code will show the control ComboBox as the datasource. We will take the number of options it shows, as a value:

```
<TextBlock Name="lblLanguages"
    Text="{Binding Path=Items.Count,ElementName=cbMessages}"
    Width="180" HorizontalAlignment="Left" Margin="4,0"
    Height="20" Grid.Row="1" Grid.Column="0"
    Grid.ColumnSpan="2"/>
```

- **Source**: It is used to establish a resource defined in the ResourceDictionary as a datasource. We will come back to this later, nevertheless, we will now mention some related concepts, such as a ViewModel object, to familiarize you with.

```
<Grid.Resources>
  <src:Customers x:Key="Languages"/>
</Grid.Resources>
<TextBlock Name="lblLanguages"
  Text="{Binding Path=Items.Count,Source= Languages}"
/>
```

- **RelativeSource**: With this kind of source, we can establish the object RelativeSource Self as DataSource, being able to bind it with another object property. This kind of DataSource also allows us to establish as source of binding an object, which is part of the Template where the object is defined, such as *RelativeSource Parent Template*.

```
<TextBlock Name="lblLang"
  Text="{Binding Path=Name,
  RelativeSource={RelativeSource Self}"/>
```

DataContext

Going back to our example, we have decided to take the easiest path and not establish any DataSource over the controls and let the DataContext of the page provide a source for the data. This sounds great, but surely you are wondering whether you will have to establish a value for the DataContext. The answer is yes; in our example, we will do it from the Code-Behind in the following manner:

```
public MainPage()
{
  InitializeComponent();
  this.DataContext = this;
}
```

In this way, we are offering a global DataSource for the page, since we are establishing a DataContext in the Page control. This is done in a way that those controls, under the tree of the Page control, will share the same source.

What this means is that the DataContext is inherited downstream over all the controls, which hang under the tree defining the page. This can be extrapolated to all container controls. That is, we could have a page with a Grid and a StackPanel, and establish a DataContext for the Grid and another one for the StackPanel, in a way that the DataSource for the controls in each container will be different.

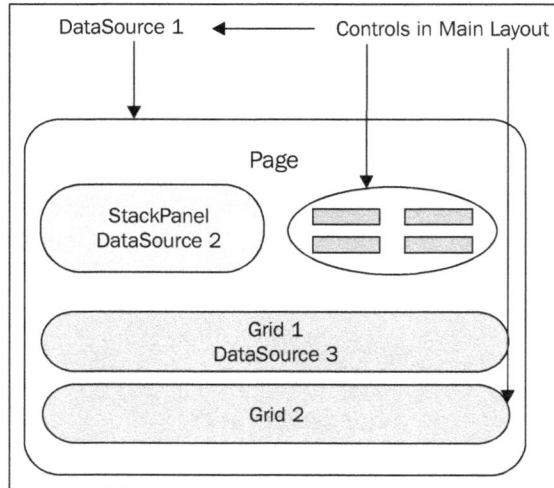

Now, we will add some properties to the `MainPage` class to consume them from the interface. Use the following code:

```
public partial class MainPage : UserControl
{
  private string _messageSelected = "Select an option";
  public ObservableCollection<MessageEntity> MessagesList{get;set;}
  public String MessageLabel{get;set;}
  public String MessageSelected
  {
    get {
      int number;
      if (Int32.TryParse(_messageSelected, out number))
        return MessagesList[number].MessageValue;
      return _messageSelected;
    }
    set
    {
      _messageSelected = value;
    }
  }
}
```

```
public MainPage()
{
  InitializeComponent();
  MessagesList = new ObservableCollection<MessageEntity>();
  MessageLabel = "Hello World";
  MessagesList.Add(new MessageEntity() { MessageCode = 0,
    Language="English", MessageValue = "Hello World" });
  MessagesList.Add(new MessageEntity() { MessageCode = 1,
    Language = "Italian", MessageValue = "Ciao Mondo" });
  MessagesList.Add(new MessageEntity() { MessageCode = 2,
    Language = "French", MessageValue = "Bonjour le monde" });
  MessagesList.Add(new MessageEntity() { MessageCode = 3,
    Language = "German", MessageValue = "Hallo Welt" });
  MessagesList.Add(new MessageEntity() { MessageCode = 4,
    Language = "Spanish", MessageValue = "Hola Mundo" });
  this.DataContext = this;
  }
}

public class MessageEntity
{
  public int MessageCode { get; set; }
  public string MessageValue { get; set; }
  public string Language { get; set; }
}
```

The code is simple; what we have done is simply define public properties and establish initial values in the constructor. We have also created an entity class MessageEntity with three properties. This class will establish the options of the ComboBox and return the translated message.

Change notifications

If we execute the application right now, we will see that the ComboBox shows data, the initial message **Hello World** is displayed, and the number of available languages in the ComboBox appears. All control values have been bound in a declarative way and show data. Nevertheless, when you choose an option, you may expect that the message **Hello World** would to be translated into the chosen language. But this has not happened.

We still have to add the magic touch to the application, particularly to the class which provides data. To do so, the class MainPage.xaml.cs has to implement the interface INotifyPropertyChanged (this interface implementation makes more sense in a ViewModel class, as it will be seen later).

By implementing it, we obtain an event in charge of notifying when a property suffers a change, both in the view (data target) and their source. To make our class implement this interface, you will need to enter the following code:

```
using System.ComponentModel;
public partial class MainPage : UserControl, INotifyPropertyChanged
{
  public event PropertyChangedEventHandler PropertyChanged;
  private void OnPropertyChanged(string p)
  {
    if (PropertyChanged != null)
    {
      PropertyChanged(this, new PropertyChangedEventArgs(p));
    }
  }
  . . .
  . . .
}
```

We have added the OnPropertyChanged function to centralize the place from which the notification event is launched. The event receives an object PropertyChangeEventArgs as the parameter, with the name of the property that causes notification.

Now, you just have to modify the properties previously defined for them to make use of the new functionality using the following code:

```
private ObservableCollection<MessageEntity> _messageList =
  new ObservableCollection<MessageEntity>();
private string _messageLabel = "Hello World";
private string _messageSelected = "Select an option";
public ObservableCollection<MessageEntity> MessagesList
{
  get
  {
    return _messageList;
  }
  set
  {
    _messageList = value;
    OnPropertyChanged("MessagesList");
  }
}

public String MessageLabel
```

```
{
  get
  {
    return _messageLabel;
  }
  set
  {
    _messageLabel = value;
    OnPropertyChanged("MessageLabel");
  }
}

public String MessageSelected
{
  get
  {
    int number;
    if (Int32.TryParse(_messageSelected, out number))
      return MessagesList[number].MessageValue;
    return _messageSelected;
  }
  set
  {
    _messageSelected = value;
    OnPropertyChanged("MessageSelected");
  }
}
```

As you can see, we invoke the function, which generates the notification event in every Properties Set.

Data binding modes

So far, we have defined the datasource and target. Now, we will define how data can flow between the source and the target, that is, datasource and controls. To do so, there are three options in Silverlight:

- **OneWay**: Data flows from the datasource to the target property of the control. This is the default mode if we do not specify any other.
- **TwoWay**: In this case, data flows in both directions. Changes in source are shown in the interface, and changes in the interface are notified to the origin object, so that this takes into account the new value.
- **OneTime**: Data flows from the source to the target only once, when the interface is generated.

In our example, we have established a binding using TwoWay mode on the
SelectedValue property of the ComboBox, which stores the option selected
by the user. The following figure shows how it works:

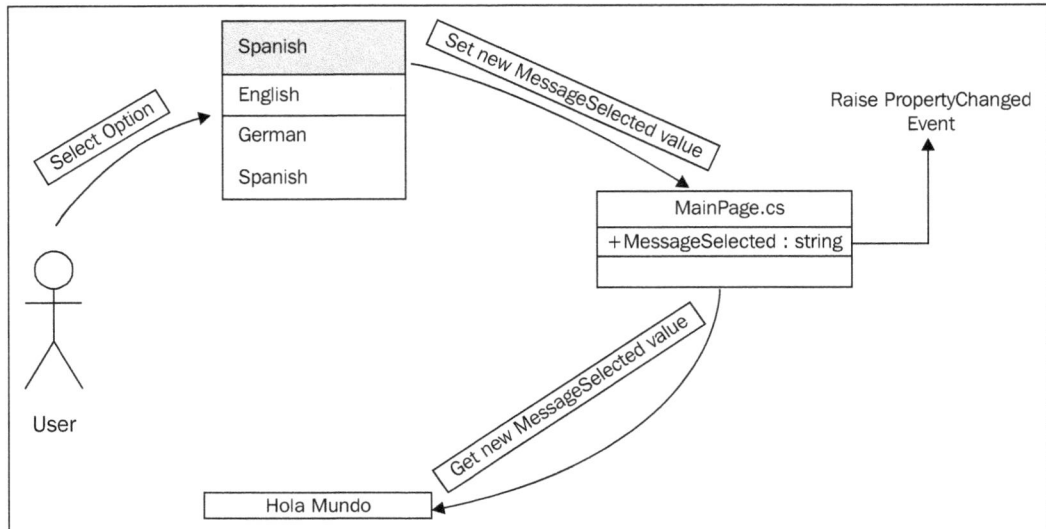

The user selects an option in the languages ComboBox, changes the value in the
SelectedValue property, as it has a binding in TwoWay Mode, and causes the
launch of the PropertyChanged event on the datasource property MessageSelected.
The textbox, bound to the MessageSelected property, is subscribed to the
notification of value changes on it, so it makes the control request for the new value.
The following code is used for TwoWay mode:

```
<ComboBox Name="cbMessages" Grid.Row="1" Grid.Column="1"
    id.ColumnSpan="2" Height="25" Width="180" HorizontalAlignment="left"
    Margin="4,0"ItemsSource="{Binding MessagesList}"
    SelectedValuePath="MessageCode" DisplayMemberPath="Language"
    SelectedValue="{Binding MessageSelected,Mode=TwoWay}"
/>
<TextBox Name="txtMesage"
    Text="{Binding MessageSelected}"
    Grid.Row="2" Grid.Column="1" HorizontalAlignment="Left"
    VerticalAlignment="Center" Width="180" Height="20" Margin="4,0"
/>
```

Introducing the ViewModel

Although we will go deeper into patterns in the following chapters, we can complete the theoretical concepts related to data binding by introducing the ViewModel.

In this chapter's introduction, we dealt with two objects that were part of data binding in Silverlight. We will particularly focus on the object which binds View and Model.

> **ViewModel** can be defined as the binding object or communication channel between the interface and the data model.

A ViewModel object shows properties which act as datasource for an interface. When we associate a ViewModel object to an interface, we are indicating the interface where it can pick up the data that its controls are binding. In other words, we are establishing DataContext (as we saw previously).

When we define a ViewModel class, we are specifying a combination of public properties with the necessary information to feed the view. We will also find that the handlers of the events are generated when the user interacts with the interface controls, such as clicking on a button. Finally, it is the element which accesses the data model. The goal is that the Code-Behind associated to each view is left empty.

You will see this in a new example.

ViewModel example

We will create a form which calculates all purchases made by a company during the first quarter of a year. The example will show three textboxes for each month, and **TextBlock** will show the final result.

We will create a new Silverlight project named INotifyMonths.

1. Let us begin by giving content to the MainPage page, so that it looks similar to the following screenshot:

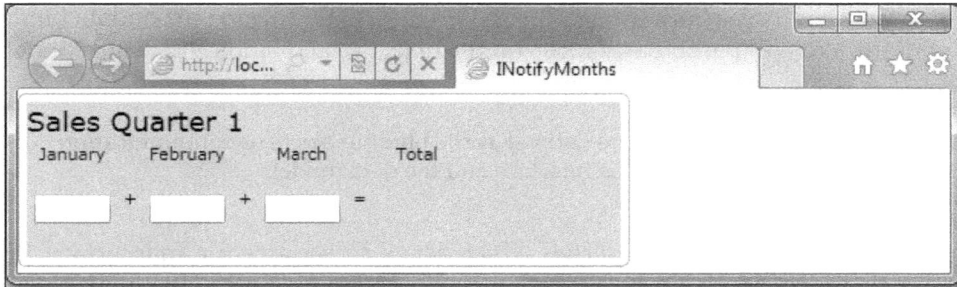

2. Once the interface is implemented, add a new class to your project. Right-click on the Silverlight project and choose the option **Add New Class**.

3. Name it NotifyMonthsViewMode.cs.

4. Then, implement the INotifyPropertyChanged interface as in the previous example.

5. Also, add the OnPropertyChanged function, as shown in the following code:

```
namespace INotifiyMonths
{
  public class NotifyMonthsViewModel:INotifyPropertyChanged
  {
    public event PropertyChangedEventHandler PropertyChanged;
    private void OnPropertyChanged(string p)
    {
      if (PropertyChanged != null)
        PropertyChanged(this, new PropertyChangedEventArgs(p));
    }
  }
}
```

6. It will be complete by adding Properties, one for each month and another one for the final result. Following code shows the property definition for January:

```
int _january = 0;
public int January
{
  get
  {
```

```
        return _january;
    }
    set
    {
      if (_january != value)
      {
        _january = value;
        OnPropertyChanged("January");
        OnPropertyChanged("Total");
      }
    }
}
```

7. Add two more properties, one for February and another for March.

8. Finally, add a read-only property which returns the addition of the other three. As you could see in the previous code, when the value of a month is modified, it provokes a notification about the Total property to update the result shown to the user.

```
public int Total
{
  get
  {
    return January + February + March;
  }
}
```

Once this is done, our ViewModel class will be ready. Now, let us bind it to the interface. To do so, we have to define a new resource in our page with an instance of the ViewModel.

1. First, add a namespace to the assembly containing ViewModel and give it a name.

```
<UserControl
  x:Class="INotifiyMonths.MainPage"
  xmlns="http://schemas.microsoft.com/winfx/2006/xaml/
    presentation"
  xmlns:x="http://schemas.microsoft.com/winfx/2006/xaml"
  xmlns:d="http://schemas.microsoft.com/expression/blend/2008"
  xmlns:mc="http://schemas.openxmlformats.org/markup-
    compatibility/2006"
  xmlns:localViewModel="clr-namespace:INotifiyMonths"
  mc:Ignorable="d"
  Height="117" Width="400">
```

2. Then, add a resource to the `UserControl` resources dictionary with an instance of the `NotifyMonthViewModel`.

```
<UserControl.Resources>
  <localViewModel:NotifyMonthsViewModel x:Key="theViewModel">
  </localViewModel:NotifyMonthsViewModel>
</UserControl.Resources>
```

3. Finally, establish a DataContext in the page and the necessary bindings on the text controls. If you pay attention to the following source code, you will realize the datasource on the `DataContext` property of the `Border` control, which is the control located up in the page control tree.

```
<Border BorderBrush="Gray" BorderThickness="1" CornerRadius="5"
  Padding="5" DataContext="{Binding Source={StaticResource
  theViewModel}}">
  <StackPanel Orientation="Vertical" Background="#FFCEB6B6">
    <TextBlock Text="Sales Quarter 1" FontSize="18"/>
    <Grid>
      <Grid.RowDefinitions>
        <RowDefinition Height="30"/>
        <RowDefinition Height="30"/>
      </Grid.RowDefinitions>
      <Grid.ColumnDefinitions>
      </Grid.ColumnDefinitions>
      <TextBlock Text="January" Grid.Column="0" Grid.Row="0"
        HorizontalAlignment="Center"/>
      <TextBlock Text="February" Grid.Column="2" Grid.Row="0"
        HorizontalAlignment="Center"/>
      <TextBlock Text="March" Grid.Column="4" Grid.Row="0"
        HorizontalAlignment="Center"/>
      <TextBlock Text="Total" Grid.Column="6" Grid.Row="0"
        HorizontalAlignment="Center"/>
      <TextBox
        Text="{Binding January, Mode=TwoWay}"
        Grid.Column="0" Grid.Row="1" Height="20"
          HorizontalAlignment="Center" Width="50"/>
      <TextBlock Text="+" Grid.Column="1" Grid.Row="1"
        HorizontalAlignment="Center" />
      <TextBox Text="{Binding February, Mode=TwoWay}"
        Grid.Column="2" Grid.Row="1" Height="20"
        HorizontalAlignment="Center" Width="50"/>
```

```
    <TextBlock Text="+" Grid.Column="3" Grid.Row="1"
        HorizontalAlignment="Center"/>
    <TextBox Text="{Binding March, Mode=TwoWay}" Grid.Column="4"
        Grid.Row="1" Height="20" HorizontalAlignment="Center"
        Width="50"/>
    <TextBlock Text="=" Grid.Column="5" Grid.Row="1"
        HorizontalAlignment="Center"/>
    <TextBlock Text="{Binding Total, Mode=OneWay}"
        Grid.Column="6" Grid.Row="1" Height="20"
        HorizontalAlignment="Center" Width="50"/>
    </Grid>
  </StackPanel>

</Border>
```

You can see that the binding is established in TwoWay mode for those controls that have to notify the `ViewModel` object (the DataSource) that the user has made a change (textboxes), and OneWay for those that are read-only in the `ViewModel` properties (text block for the final result).

Dependency properties

We have already used dependency properties, but without knowing that those properties on which we were establishing a data binding were somewhat special. From the LOB point of view, dependency properties allow us to establish their value in a declarative way and are capable of notifying a change in them. Also, they can establish data binding, so that they are able to propagate a change notification between properties.

> Dependency properties is the way to show properties in the UserControls which are generated and establish values on them, creating a communication channel between properties.

Let us see an instance. We will modify the first example we posed in this chapter, for it to show the result of the translation in a UserControl:

1. Create a new project named `HelloWorldDP` and copy the content we had in the original sample (XAML and Code-Behind). The finished result can be seen in the following screenshot:

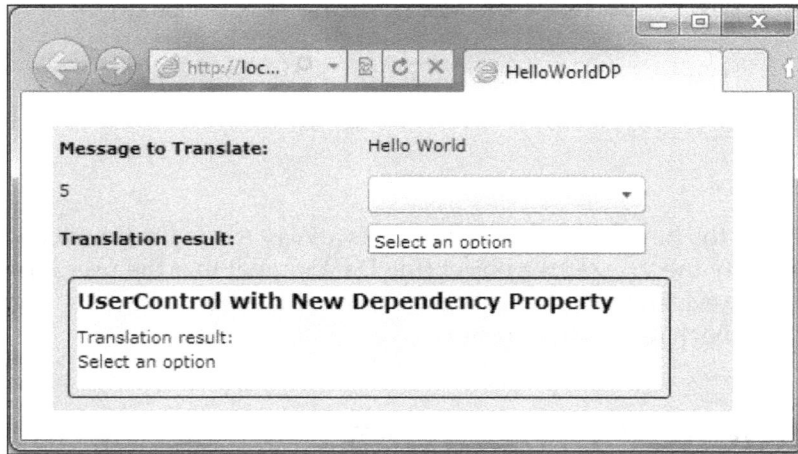

2. Once you've added the content of the previous sample, add a UserControl named `TranslationResultUC` to the Silverlight project, with a text block to show the translation result. This will be the content of the `TranslationResultUC.xaml` file:

```
<UserControl x:Class="HelloWorldDP.TranslationResultUC"
  xmlns="http://schemas.microsoft.com/winfx/2006/xaml/
    presentation"
  xmlns:x="http://schemas.microsoft.com/winfx/2006/xaml"
  xmlns:d="http://schemas.microsoft.com/expression/blend/2008"
  xmlns:mc="http://schemas.openxmlformats.org/markup-
    compatibility/2006"
  mc:Ignorable="d" d:DesignHeight="78">
  <Border BorderBrush="Black" BorderThickness="1" CornerRadius="3"
    Margin="10">
    <StackPanel x:Name="LayoutRoot" Background="Beige" Height="80"
      VerticalAlignment="Top" Margin="5">
      <TextBlock FontWeight="ExtraBold" Text="UserControl with New
        Dependency Property" FontSize="14" Height="26"/>
      <TextBlock Text="Translation result: "/>
      <Border Background="Yellow" Width="150"
        HorizontalAlignment="Left" Height="25">
        <TextBlock Name="txtResult" Text="{Binding Result}"
```

```
            Height="25"/>
        </Border>
      </StackPanel>
    </Border>
  </UserControl>
```

3. Now, it is time to generate the dependency property in the Code-Behind file. Let's look at the file content:

```
public partial class TranslationResultUC : UserControl
{
  public TranslationResultUC()
  {
    InitializeComponent();
  }
  public string TranslationResult
  {
    get { return (string)GetValue(TranslationResultProperty); }
    set { SetValue(TranslationResultProperty, value); }
  }
  public static readonly DependencyProperty
    TranslationResultProperty =
    DependencyProperty.Register("TranslationResult",
    typeof(string), typeof(TranslationResultUC), new
    PropertyMetadata(string.Empty, new
    PropertyChangedCallback(OnTranslationChanged)));
  private static void OnTranslationChanged(DependencyObject d,
    DependencyPropertyChangedEventArgs e)
  {
    TranslationResultUC control = d as TranslationResultUC;
    control.txtResult.Text = e.NewValue as string;
  }
}
```

This may go some way beyond the scope of the chapter, but it is beneficial to go a little deeper into the three parts that define the property.

1. The property itself accesses the value with its get and set. In this case, it must be noticed that the value is not accessed directly, but via the mechanism of the system in charge of handling dependency properties to establish and obtain values, through the methods GetValue and SetValue, as shown in the following code:

```
public string TranslationResult
{
  get {return (string)GetValue(TranslationResultProperty);}
  set {SetValue(TranslationResultProperty, value);}
}
```

2. The property registers in the system which handles Dependency properties. To do this, we use the static method `DependencyProperty.Register`. This method uses four parameters such as property name, property type, the type of object which contains the property, and a mechanism to establish a default value and the operations, which become necessary when the property value changes, as shown in the following code snippet:

```
public static readonly DependencyProperty
TranslationResultProperty =
    DependencyProperty.Register(
        // The Name of the property
        "TranslationResult",
        //the type of the property
        typeof(string),
        // the type of object where the property is
        typeof(TranslationResultUC),
        // the metadata which define a default value
        // and callback for changes
        new PropertyMetadata(string.Empty,
                new PropertyChangedCallback(OnTranslationChanged))
    );
```

3. Finally, the function implements the actions to be performed when the property content changes. This is optional, because it will not always be necessary. A default value is also specified.

```
/// <summary>
/// What have to do when the value changes
/// </summary>
private static void OnTranslationChanged(DependencyObject d,
    DependencyPropertyChangedEventArgs e)
{
    TranslationResultUC control = d as TranslationResultUC;
    control.txtResult.Text = e.NewValue as string;
}
```

At this point, you will have all the necessary tools to create your `DependencyProperty`. Now we can make use of it by performing the following steps:

1. Open the `MainPage.xaml` file, where the UserControl `TranslationResultUC` will be added, and create a binding between the `TranslationResult` dependency property and the `MessageSelected` property of the DataContext.

2. The first thing to do is add a new namespace to the `MainPage.xaml` file using the following line of code:

```
xmlns:localUC="clr-namespace:HelloWorldDP"
```

3. Then you can add the control to your page. A new row has been added to the grid where the control will be added. Once the UserControl is in the page, establish a binding in the `TranslationResult` DependencyProperty.

```
<localUC:TranslationResultUC Grid.Column="0" Grid.Row="3"
  Grid.ColumnSpan="2" TranslationResult="{Binding
  MessageSelected}">
</localUC:TranslationResultUC>
```

The result is similar to the following screenshot:

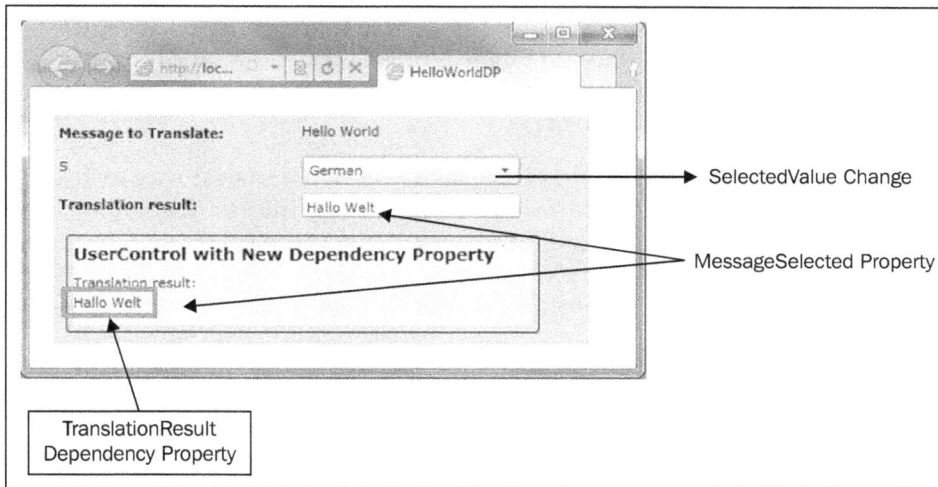

Data binding from Code-Behind

Although the most common thing is to establish declarative data binding, we can also do this via code from the Code-Behind file using the following lines of code:

```
Binding binding = new Binding("MyValue");
binding.Mode = BindingMode.TwoWay;
txMyValueOneTime.SetBinding(TextBox.TextProperty, binding);
```

With this code, a new object of the `Binding` class is created, indicating the name of the DataSource property to which it will be bound. Then, we establish the sort of binding, for instance, TwoWay. To finish, we indicate the link between the desired property (`TextProperty`, in this case) and the defined `Binding` object. This will be the declarative equivalent to the previous source code, as shown in the following line of code:

```
<TextBox Width="100" x:Name="txMyValueOneTime" Text="{Binding MyValue,
    Mode=TwoWay}" />
```

Adding validations

An important aspect of developing LOB applications is the validation of the data entered by the user. There is no need to say that those validations we are about to see, are client-side. So it will be necessary to validate them again, once the data gets server-side. Remember that, although Silverlight is .NET and a sandbox within our browser, it is exposed to hacking by advanced users. That said, we will see two ways to add validations in Silverlight forms.

Implementing the **IDataErrorInfo** interface is probably the easiest way to add validation in applications. This interface is not new for Winform developers, as we have had it at our disposal since Framework 1. Nevertheless, from Silverlight 4 onwards, we have been able to make use of it. It is really easy to add validations to our applications thanks to this technique. We will use a new example to see how validations work.

Let us create a new Silverlight application called `FormValidation`, where we will ask the user for their name, e-mail, and age, validating data with certain restrictions.

- The field **Name** is required and has to begin in capital letters.
- **Email** field is not compulsory, but if it is entered, it needs a valid format.
- Finally, **Age** field is not compulsory either. Yet if it is completed, it has to contain only numerical characters.

The aim is to have a form similar to the following screenshot:

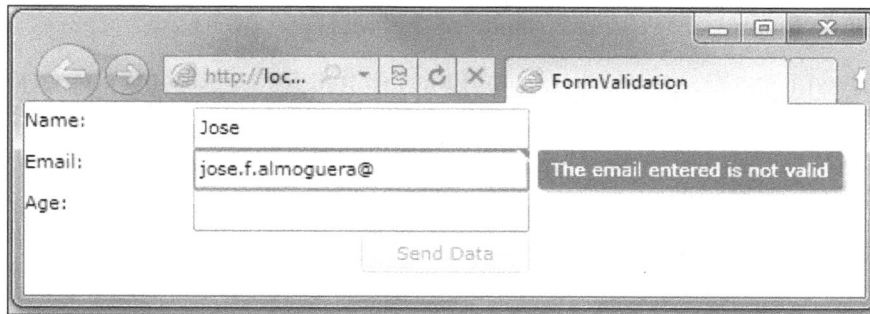

The **Email** field is surrounded by a red border and a tooltip appears on the right side, indicating that the value entered is not valid. The visualization or error notification to the user is automatic in Silverlight. To take advantage, it is necessary to establish the `ValidateOnDataError` property as `true`, and the system will show an error message if, after changing the value on the dependency property where we are applying the binding, it has some validation rules defined, and any of them notifies that the validation failed.

```
<TextBox Name="txtname" Grid.Row="0" Grid.Column="1" Text="{Binding
    Name, Mode=TwoWay, NotifyOnValidationError=True,
    ValidatesOnDataErrors=True}"/>
```

Add three text fields as we did in the previous source code, establishing binding f or each one of them.

As we said before, so as to use this validation mode we have to implement the `IDataErrorInfo` interface. While doing this, we have to define two members in the class:

- **Property Error**: This is not used unless we want to return an error that is common for all of the properties of the object.

- **Index (or rules collection)**: Index is that on which we will define rules for the properties that we want to validate.

Now, it is time to implement INotifyPropertyChanged and IDataErrorInfo interfaces on the Code-Behind of our page (optionally, we can create a ViewModel object, define its properties, and implement the interfaces on it).

Create three properties (Name, Email, and Age) so that they notify the changes on them as you learned in previous chapters, using the following code:

```
public partial class MainPage : UserControl, IDataErrorInfo,
INotifyPropertyChanged
{
  public string Name
  {
    get
    {
      return _name;
    }
    set
    {
      if (_name == value)
        return;
      _name = value;
      OnPropertyChanged("Name");
    }
  }
}
```

Then, add validation rules in the index that has to be implemented in the IDataErrorInfo interface as the following code:

```
#region IDataErrorInfo Members
public string Error
{
  get { return null; }
}
public string this[string columnName]
{
  get
  {
    // Boolean flag property
    DataIsOk = ValidateAll();
    if (columnName == "Name")
    {
      return ValidateName();
    }
```

```
    if (columnName == "Email")
    {
      return ValidateEmail();
    }
    if (columnName == "Age")
    {
      return ValidateAge();
    }
    return null;
  }
}
#endregion
```

Depending on the property that has been modified, validation will be executed in one field or another. The last field modified will be the only one validated, so there could be errors in other fields of the form.

In the following code, notice that we can have a set of rules for each property and they will be executed sequentially. That is, the user will be notified at only one validation rule that is, the first one containing errors. For instance, the Name field has two rules associated, but the user will only be notified that the second validation rule is failing provided that the first one is accomplished.

```
private bool ValidateAll()
{
  return (ValidateAge()==null && ValidateEmail()==null &&
    ValidateName()==null);
}

private string ValidateName()
{
  if (string.IsNullOrEmpty(txtname.Text))
    return "The Field Name can't be in blank";
  if (txtname.Text[0] != txtname.Text.ToUpper()[0])
    return "The first char must be in capital";
  return null;
}

private string ValidateEmail()
{
  if (string.IsNullOrEmpty(txtEmail.Text))
    return null;
  string expression = @"^[a-zA-Z][\w\.-]*[a-zA-Z0-9]@[a-zA-Z0-9][\w\.-
    ]*[a-zA-Z0-9]\.[a-zA-Z][a-zA-Z\.]*[a-zA-Z]$";
```

```
    if (!Regex.IsMatch(txtEmail.Text, expression))
    {
      return "The email entered is not valid";
    }
    return null;
}

private string ValidateAge()
{
  if (string.IsNullOrEmpty(txtAge.Text))
    return null;
    string expression = @"^[0-9]*$";
  if (!Regex.IsMatch(txtAge.Text, expression))
  {
    return "Only numbers allowed";
  }
  return null;
}
```

BindingValidationError

Looking at our previous XAML code, you will realize that the NotifyOnValidationError property has been established as true. By enabling this property, we are indicating that if an error is produced in the field, a notification event is launched. We can deal with it in any other element in the hierarchy level that is superior to the control enabling it. In our example, we will capture this event in the Grid where the form is constructed, so that we can centralize all form data. To do so, we will define a handler for the BindingValidationError event, as shown in the following code:

```
<Grid x:Name="LayoutRoot" Background="White"
  BindingValidationError="LayoutRoot_BindingValidationError">
  <Button Name="btnSendData" Grid.Row="3" Grid.Column="1"
    Content="Send Data" Width="100" HorizontalAlignment="Right"
    IsEnabled="{Binding DataIsOk}"/>
</Grid>
```

Here, the handler defined is in charge of enabling/disabling the **Send Data** button depending on whether there are errors in the form or not. To achieve this, and as you can see in the previous source code, the value of the IsEnabled dependency property of the Button control, has been established through a binding, which will change from True to False on the basis of form errors.

```
private void LayoutRoot_BindingValidationError(object sender,
   ValidationErrorEventArgs e)
{
   //when the event is raised we disabled the button
   if (e.Action != ValidationErrorEventAction.Removed)
     DataIsOk = false;
}
```

DataAnnotations

Another way to add validations in form data is via **DataAnnotation**. In this case, validation rules are defined by adding attributes to object properties. Their operation, unlike those seen above, is based on the launch of exceptions when a validation rule is not accomplished. We will perform these validations using our previous example. It is a good idea to create a copy of that solution and modify just the necessary sections.

To begin with, let us add the reference in the **System.ComponentModel. DataAnnotations** library in our Silverlight project, as shown in the following screenshot:

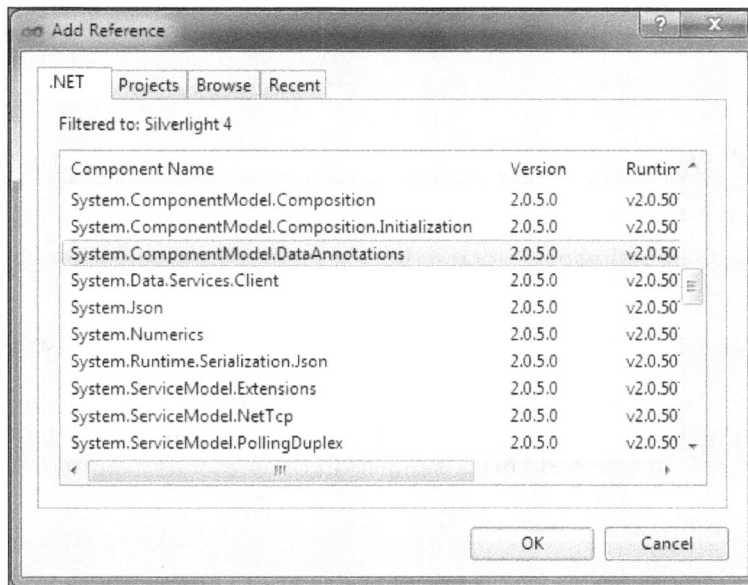

Delete references to the `IDataErrorInfo` interface and those elements required by it. Validations have to be defined again, but now we will define them in the properties header.

```
[Required(ErrorMessage = "The Field Name can't be in blank")]
[RegularExpression("^[A-Z][a-zA-Z]*$",ErrorMessage="The first char
must be in capital")]
public string TheName
{
  get
  {
    return _name;
  }
  set
  {
    if (_name == value)
      return;
    Validator.ValidateProperty(value, new ValidationContext(this,
      null, null) { MemberName = "TheName" });
    _name = value;
    //Activate button if all the validations are corrects
    ValidateAll();
    OnPropertyChanged("TheName");
  }
}
```

Two new attributes have been added to the header of `TheName` property:

- `[Required()]`: Here, we mark the value as required `[Required()]`.

- `[RegularExpression ()]`: It defines a regular expression to validate the entry.

In both attributes, we specify the message that will be displayed in case of error.

In `set`, we have called the `ValidateProperty` method of the `Validator` object, with the name of the property to be validated. This will launch an exception if an error occurs. The rest of the `set` code is the same as in the previous example.

The difference is that we have to check the rest of form fields in order to activate the **Send Data** button. This action will be performed in the `ValidateAll()` method.

```
/// <summary>
/// Activate Send button if all validation return true
private void ValidateAll()
{
  if (Validator.TryValidateProperty(TheName, new
ValidationContext(this,
    null, null) { MemberName = "TheName" },null) &&
    Validator.TryValidateProperty(Email, new ValidationContext(this,
    null, null) { MemberName = "Email" },null) &&
    Validator.TryValidateProperty(Age, new ValidationContext(this,
null,
    null) { MemberName = "Age" },null))
    DataIsOk = true;
}
```

The final aspect in the second example is similar to the previous one.

Finally, we will learn what Converters are and how they are defined.

Converters

Most of the time, when data is shown to the user, there are aspects or values, which are not clear or intuitive enough for them. A way to solve this problem is by changing the format or making a conversion before binding. To do so, Silverlight offers an interface which allows us to perform this action.

> If you need to make simple formatting (for example, displaying a Date or Time), StringFormat can be directly used on the XAML (this was introduced in Silverlight 4). For more information, please visit `http://bit.ly/jMBtDp`.

IValueConverter

When this interface is implemented, we obtain the following functions:

- **Convert**: This function prepares the data, obtained from the DataSource, to display it in the view.
- **ConvertBack**: This one is in charge of making the opposite change, it gets the data ready from the view to store in the source.

We will generate an instance to convert the numerical value provided by a property, to an image. The final result will appear similar to the following screenshot. In order to do so, we will create a new Silverlight project called `GenderConverter`.

Add a new class to our solution, name it `GenderImgConvert`, and implement the `IValueConverter` interface. Then copy the following source code:

```
public class GenderImgConverter : IValueConverter
{
  /// <summary>
  /// We convert the source value (integer)
  /// in the source path of an Image
  /// </summary>
  public object Convert(object value, Type targetType, object parameter,
    CultureInfo culture)
  {
    int? genderId = (int?)value;
    string imagePath = "Images/";
    if (genderId.HasValue)
    {
      switch (genderId)
      {
        case 1:imagePath += "woman.png";
          break;
        case 2:imagePath += "man.png";
          break;
      }
    }
    else{
      imagePath += "";
    }
    return imagePath;
  }
```

```
/// <summary>
/// No convert back, in one-way mode
/// </summary>
public object ConvertBack(object value, Type targetType, object
  parameter, CultureInfo culture)
{
  return null;
}
}
```

The code is simple and plainly returns an image path on the basis of the entry value. The following is the XAML code:

```xml
<UserControl x:Class="GenderConverter.MainPage"
  xmlns="http://schemas.microsoft.com/winfx/2006/xaml/presentation"
  xmlns:x="http://schemas.microsoft.com/winfx/2006/xaml"
  xmlns:d="http://schemas.microsoft.com/expression/blend/2008"
  xmlns:mc="http://schemas.openxmlformats.org/markup-
compatibility/2006"
  xmlns:LocalConverters="clr-namespace:GenderConverter"
  mc:Ignorable="d"
  d:DesignHeight="60" d:DesignWidth="400">
  <UserControl.Resources>
    <LocalConverters:GenderImgConverter x:Key="TypeGenderConverter"/>
  </UserControl.Resources>
  <Grid x:Name="LayoutRoot" Height="50" Width="144" Background="Beige">
    <Grid.RowDefinitions>
      <RowDefinition></RowDefinition>
      <RowDefinition></RowDefinition>
    </Grid.RowDefinitions>
    <Grid.ColumnDefinitions>
      <ColumnDefinition Width="100"/>
      <ColumnDefinition Width="40"/>
    </Grid.ColumnDefinitions>
    <TextBlock Text="Gender (Female):" Grid.Column="0" Grid.Row="0"/>
    <Image x:Name="imgGenderMale" HorizontalAlignment="Left" Grid.
Row="0"
      Grid.Column="1" VerticalAlignment="Center" Source="{Binding
      GenderFemale,
      Converter={StaticResource TypeGenderConverter},
      Mode=OneWay}" Width="20" Height="20"/>
    <TextBlock Text="Gender (Male):" Grid.Column="0" Grid.Row="1"/>
    <Image x:Name="imgGenderFemale" HorizontalAlignment="Left"
      Grid.Row="1"     Grid.Column="1" VerticalAlignment="Center"
      Source="{Binding GenderMale, Converter={StaticResource
      TypeGenderConverter}, Mode=OneWay}" Width="20" Height="20"/>
  </Grid>
</UserControl>
```

Now, let's check the steps to consume the converter and add some sample data in the `MainPage` Code-Behind:

1. First, add a `namespace` in the assembly of this Silverlight project.

2. Then, add an instance of the `GenderImgConverter` class as page resource.

3. After that, specify the source of the image, taking two properties that are already defined in the page's Code-Behind as source.

4. Finally, establish the Converter you want to apply in the binding. In this case, it will be the resource defined previously. The following code is the Code-Behind:

```
public partial class MainPage : UserControl
{
  public int GenderFemale
  {
    get { return 1; }
  }
  public int GenderMale
  {
    get { return 2; }
  }
  public MainPage()
  {
    InitializeComponent();
    this.DataContext = this;
  }
}
```

LOB application case study: applying what we have learned

We will pick up the project from where we left in the previous chapter, in order to give it controls. We can generate a copy if we want to keep it as we left it for further revisions.

We will continue working upon the `Management` page. Our goal will be to load the grid with the floors of the selected building and also load the grill that shows each floor's rooms. These two grids will be bound in a master/detail relationship. On the other hand, we can add, modify, and delete rooms through the modal dialog we have, in order to do so.

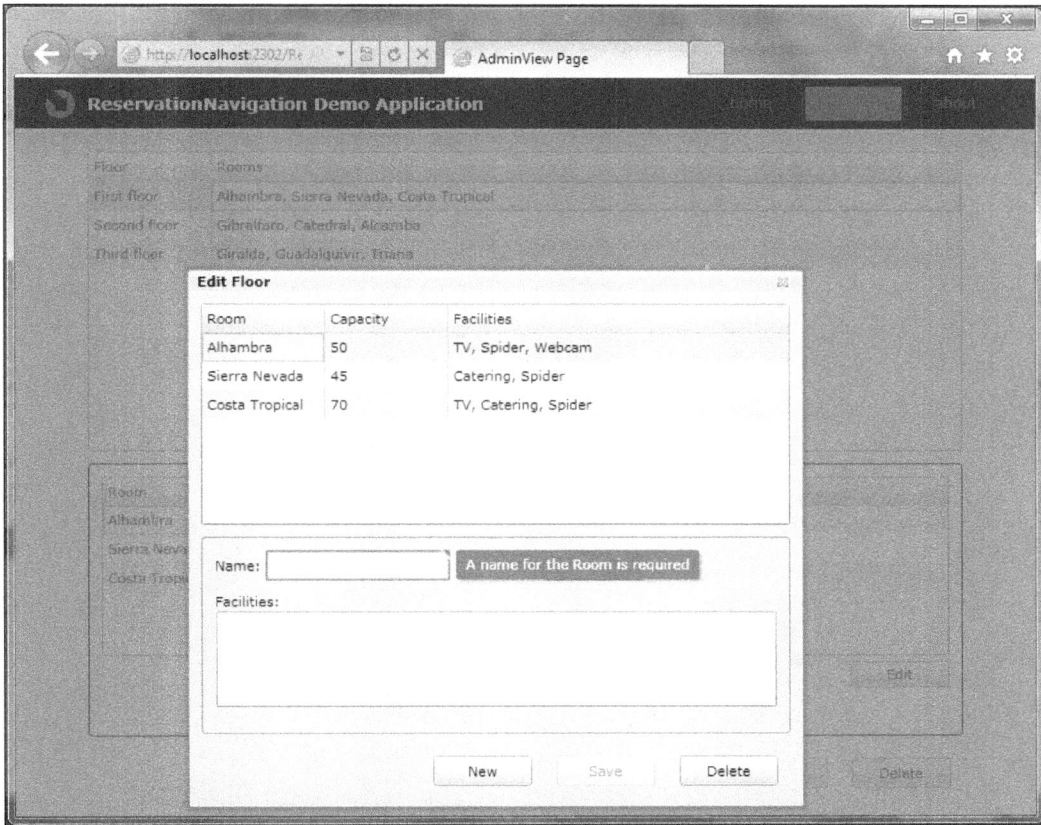

First of all, we will see the new elements added to the Visual Studio solution.

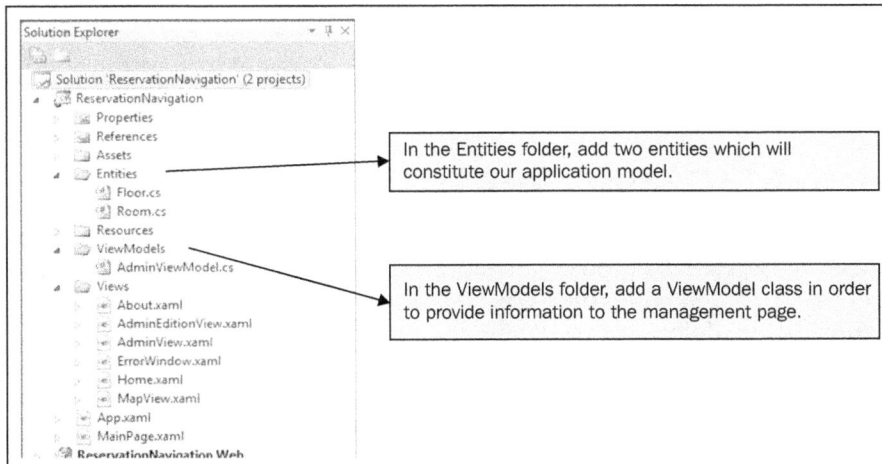

In the Entities folder, add two entities which will constitute our application model.

In the ViewModels folder, add a ViewModel class in order to provide information to the management page.

As you can see from the previous screenshot, two Entity classes have been added to model the Management page, as well as a ViewModel class in charge of providing data, managing actions on the interface, and storing the data for the management page.

Entity classes

We need to create two classes to define our data model, one to define Rooms and another one to define Floors. You can see their properties in the following screenshot:

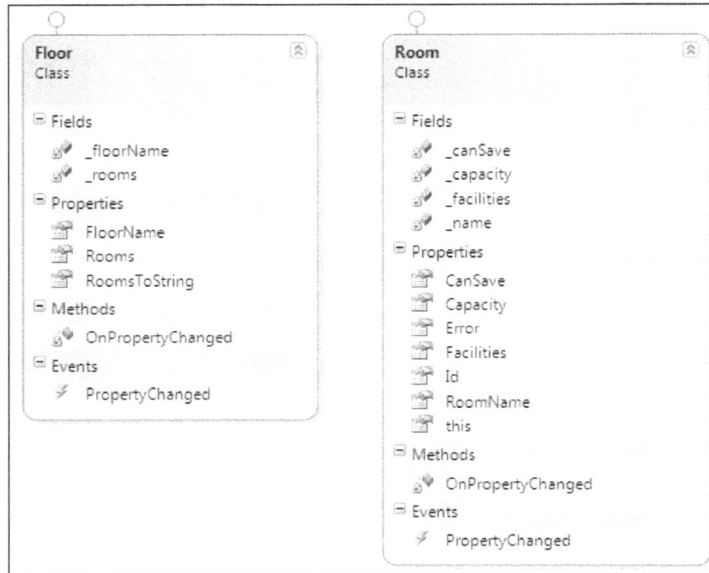

We will begin by adding these elements and defining properties as we previously did in the chapter. We will also implement the INotifyPropertyChanged interface at the same time that we launch the PropertyChanged event in every Properties setters of the entities.

ObservableCollection

The Floor entity has a Rooms property. It is a collection of the **ObservableCollection** type of Rooms entities. This type of collection is special because it implements the INotifyCollectionChanged interface, so that whenever the content of the collection changes (by adding, deleting a new element, or updating the collection), the CollectionChanged event will be launched. In this way, if any property of this type is bound to any data container control, the content will be refreshed automatically after adding or removing items from it. See the following code to know how the Rooms Property is defined:

```
public ObservableCollection<Room> Rooms
{
  get { return _rooms; }
  set
  {
    _rooms = value;
    OnPropertyChanged("Rooms");
  }
}
```

We have implemented the `IDataErrorInfo` interface in the `Room` class, and added a validation rule on the **RoomName** field to make it a required field. This class also has a **CanSave** property, which enables or disables the **Save** button if all the entity validation rules are accomplished.

AdminViewModel object

In this class, we define those properties, which will act as datasources for the bindings established on page controls. An instance of this class could be DataContext. Let us go deeper into its content.

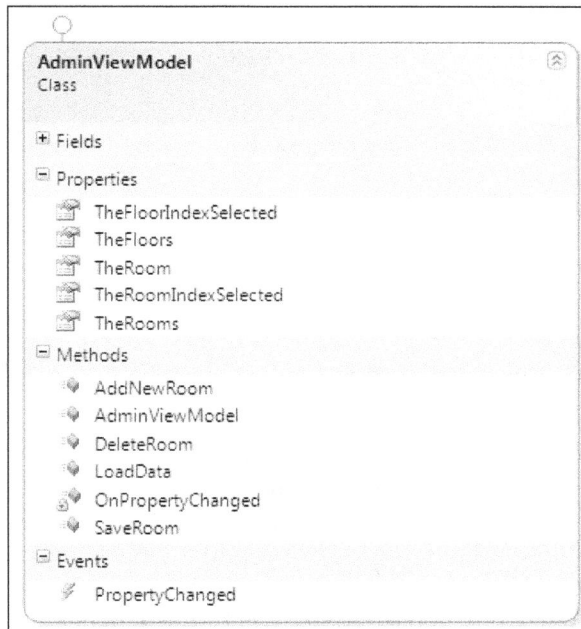

To define the instance of the ViewModel object declaratively from the XAML file, in the `AdminView.xaml` page, the following are the steps that are to be carried out:

1. First, add a namespace in the assembly that contains the class.

2. Second, create a new resource with it.

3. Third, establish the DataContext of the container object, which is located higher in the page hierarchy, as shown in the following code:

```
<navigation:Page x:Class="ReservationNavigation.Views.AdminView"
  xmlns="http://schemas.microsoft.com/winfx/2006/xaml/
    presentation"
  xmlns:x="http://schemas.microsoft.com/winfx/2006/xaml"
  xmlns:d="http://schemas.microsoft.com/expression/blend/2008"
  xmlns:mc="http://schemas.openxmlformats.org/markup-
    compatibility/2006"
  mc:Ignorable="d"
  xmlns:navigation="clr-
    namespace:System.Windows.Controls;assembly=
    System.Windows.Controls.Navigation"
  xmlns:localViewModels="clr-
    namespace:ReservationNavigation.ViewModels"
  Title="AdminView Page"
  xmlns:sdk="http://schemas.microsoft.com/winfx/2006/xaml/
    presentation/sdk">
  <UserControl.Resources>
    <localViewModels:AdminViewModel x:Key="TheAdminViewModel"/>
  </UserControl.Resources>
  <Grid x:Name="LayoutRoot" DataContext="{Binding
    Source={StaticResource TheAdminViewModel}}">
  (...)
```

The ViewModel properties are:

- **TheFloors**: This property is the datasource of the grid showing the building floors.

- **TheFloorIndexSelected**: When a floor is selected, the selected object index is stored so as to sync the Floors grid with the Rooms grid. They show a master/detail behavior. When this value is established, the event `PropertyChanged` is launched not on the **TheFloorIndex** property, but on the **TheRooms** property. The goal is that the grid showing rooms, understands that the selected room has been changed and, consequently, the rooms it needs to display are different. These properties are defined similar to the following code:

```
///<summary>
///Get & Set the index of the selected floor
///</summary>
public int TheFloorIndexSelected
{
  get { return _theFloorIndexSelected; }
  set
  {
    if (value >= 0)
    {
      _theFloorIndexSelected = value;
      ///We notify to the view that the user changed the
      // selected Floor, so it needs to reload the
      ///Rooms Grid
      OnPropertyChanged("TheRooms");
    }
  }
}

///<summary>
///Return the rooms of the selected floor
///</summary>
public ObservableCollection<Room> TheRooms
{
  get
  {
    return TheFloors[_theFloorIndexSelected].Rooms;
  }
}
```

- **TheRooms**: This property is the DataSource of the second grid and shows the rooms that are located in a particular floor.

- **TheRoomIndexSelected**: This property works similar to **TheFloorIndexSelected**, but its task is to identify the selected room. It provokes the `PropertyChanged` event on **TheRoom** property instead of invoking itself. It must be taken into account that, when we select a room, we create a new `Room` object to unbind the edition of a room from the entity showing data on the grid until the **Save** button is pressed. Otherwise, data will be updated in the grid at the same time we are updating fields in the form.

- **TheRoom**: This property is in charge of storing the room, which is being edited or added. These properties are defined in the following code:

```
private int _theRoomIndexSelected = -1;
/// <summary>
/// Get & Set the index of the selected room
/// When it changes, the "TheRoom" PropertyChanges
/// is notified to show the new data
/// </summary>
public int TheRoomIndexSelected
{
  get { return _theFloorIndexSelected; }
  set
  {
    if (value >= 0 && value <= TheRooms.Count-1)
    {
      _theRoomIndexSelected = value;
      _theRoom = new Room();
      _theRoom.Id = TheRooms[_theRoomIndexSelected].Id;
      _theRoom.RoomName =
        TheRooms[_theRoomIndexSelected].RoomName;
      _theRoom.Capacity =
        TheRooms[_theRoomIndexSelected].Capacity;
      _theRoom.Facilities =
        TheRooms[_theRoomIndexSelected].Facilities;
      OnPropertyChanged("TheRoom");
    }
  }
}
```

The ViewModel public methods are:

- **AddNewRoom**: This method will be executed when clicking the **New** button. It will create a new Room object and establish it in the **TheRoom** property.

- **SaveRoom**: This is associated to the Click event on the **Save** button, and will insert a new room or modify an existing one depending on the ID property of the Room object. If the ID value is 0, the Room object is new, so the action to perform will be insertion.

- **DeleteRoom**: It will delete the selected object from the **Rooms** list on the **TheRooms** property.

- **LoadData**: This method will be called from the view, with the parameter of the chosen city. Here, data load will be simulated, generating **Floor** and **Room** entities. These properties are defined in the following code:

```
/// <summary>
/// Insert the Room if its Id is 0,
/// otherwise update it
/// </summary>
public void SaveRoom()
{
  if (TheRoom.Id == 0)
  {
    TheRoom.Id = _lastRoomId+1;
    _lastRoomId++;
    TheRooms.Add(TheRoom);
  }
  else
  {
    // we are updating an existing item.
    // we overwrite the previous value.
    TheRooms[_theRoomIndexSelected] = TheRoom;
  }
  //Clean the form
  TheRoom = new Room();
  ObservableCollection<Floor> _theFloorsBK = TheFloors;
  TheFloors = null;
  TheFloors = _theFloorsBK;;
}

public void DeleteRoom()
{
  //check if any room selected
  if (_theRoomIndexSelected >= 0)
  {
    //and if there is any content
    if (TheRooms.Count > 0)
      TheRooms.RemoveAt(_theRoomIndexSelected);
    //Clean the form
    TheRoom = new Room();
    ObservableCollection<Floor> _theFloorsBK = TheFloors;
    TheFloors = null;
    TheFloors = _theFloorsBK;;
  }
}
```

The other objects are:

- **AdminView.xaml.cs**: From the Code-Behind of the Page view, we will pick the parameter identifying the chosen city from the URI, to pass it to the `ViewModel`, which will change the data related to it. In this class, we will also add DataContext to the modal dialog, just before displaying it using the following code:

```
protected override void OnNavigatedTo(NavigationEventArgs e)
{
  ((AdminViewModel)LayoutRoot.DataContext).LoadData(
    NavigationContext.QueryString["buildId"]);
}

private void btnEdit_Click(object sender, RoutedEventArgs e)
{
  AdminEditionView theChild = new AdminEditionView();
  theChild.DataContext = LayoutRoot.DataContext;
  theChild.Show();
}
```

- **AdminEditionView.xaml.cs**: From the Code-Behind of this view, we will merely call the `ViewModel` public methods, to perform the desired actions, as shown in the following code:

```
private void btnNew_Click(object sender, RoutedEventArgs e)
{
  ((AdminViewModel)this.DataContext).AddNewRoom();
}

private void btnSave_Click(object sender, RoutedEventArgs e)
{
  ((AdminViewModel)this.DataContext).SaveRoom();
}

private void btnDelete_Click(object sender, RoutedEventArgs e)
{
  ((AdminViewModel)this.DataContext).DeleteRoom();
}
```

Data binding

Data will be bound, establishing the datasource for the `DataGrid` in the `ItemSource` property and in all its columns. To do so, the property containing the value to display has to be chosen. We can also see how we have activated a validation notification on the **Name** field of a room. Finally, we can also check how the **Save** button is enabled on the basis of a property in the following code:

```
<sdk:DataGrid Grid.Row="0" AutoGenerateColumns="False" Name="gwRooms"
  ItemsSource="{Binding TheRooms}"
  SelectedIndex="{Binding TheRoomIndexSelected,Mode=TwoWay}" >
  <sdk:DataGrid.Columns>
    <sdk:DataGridTextColumn CanUserReorder="True" IsReadOnly="True"
      CanUserResize="True" CanUserSort="True" Header="Room" Width="100"
      Binding="{Binding RoomName}"/>
    <sdk:DataGridTextColumn CanUserReorder="True" IsReadOnly="True"
      CanUserResize="True" CanUserSort="True" Header="Capacity"
      Width="100" Binding="{Binding Capacity}"/>
    <sdk:DataGridTextColumn CanUserReorder="True" IsReadOnly="True"
      CanUserResize="True" CanUserSort="True" Header="Facilities"
      Width="*" Binding="{Binding Facilities}"/>
  </sdk:DataGrid.Columns>
</sdk:DataGrid>
<Border  Grid.Row="1" BorderThickness="1" Padding="10"
  BorderBrush="Gray"
  Margin="0,10" CornerRadius="3">
  <StackPanel Orientation="Vertical">
    <StackPanel Orientation="Horizontal">
      <TextBlock Text="Name: " VerticalAlignment="Center"/>
      <TextBox x:Name="txtRoomName" Width="150" Height="25"
        Text="{Binding TheRoom.RoomName,Mode=TwoWay,
        ValidatesOnDataErrors=True}"/>
      <TextBlock Name="lblCapacity" Text="Capacity: "
        VerticalAlignment="Center" Margin="20,0,0,0"/>
      <TextBox x:Name="txtCapacity" Width="80" Height="25"
        Text="{Binding TheRoom.Capacity,Mode=TwoWay}"/>
    </StackPanel>
    <TextBlock Text="Facilities: " VerticalAlignment="Center"
      Margin="0,10,0,0"/>
    <TextBox x:Name="txtFacilities" Height="80" Width="455"
      Text="{Binding TheRoom.Facilities,Mode=TwoWay}"/>
  </StackPanel>
</Border>
```

```
<StackPanel Orientation="Horizontal" Grid.Row="2"
  HorizontalAlignment="Right">
  <Button x:Name="btnNew" Width="80" Content="New" Height="25"
    Margin="10,0" Click="btnNew_Click"/>
  <Button x:Name="btnSave" Width="80" Content="Save" Height="25"
    Margin="10,0" Click="btnSave_Click"
    IsEnabled="{Binding TheRoom.CanSave}"/>
  <Button x:Name="btnDelete" Width="80" Content="Delete"
    Height="25" Margin="10,0" Click="btnDelete_Click"/>
</StackPanel>
```

Summary

In this chapter, we have dealt with what is probably the most important aspect related to LOB applications development, data binding in form controls. We have also discovered the flexibility that Silverlight offers in order to perform these tasks declaratively, without forgetting that they can also be carried out from Code-Behind. We have learned how to generate validations in controls and how to fulfill data conversions. Last but not least, we introduced the ViewModel concept, which will be explained in detail in the following chapter, when defining **Model View ViewModel** pattern (**MVVM**).

Now that we have covered the basics, in the next chapter, we will learn how to structure and design our application in a robust manner. Also, the MVVM pattern and the MVVM Light toolkit library will be covered in detail, as well as how to decouple modules using MEF.

Additional resources

- IDataErrorInfo in MSDN:

  http://msdn.microsoft.com/en-us/library/system.componentmodel.idataerrorinfo(v=vs.95).aspx

  http://msdn.microsoft.com/en-us/library/system.componentmodel.idataerrorinfo(v=vs.95).aspx

- Silverlight Data Binding in Silverlight.NET:

  http://www.silverlight.net/learn/tutorials/silverlight-4/silverlight-data-binding/

  http://www.silverlight.net/learn/tutorials/silverlight-4/silverlight-data-binding/

- Validation and Bindings tutorial by John Papa:

  ```
  http://channel9.msdn.com/learn/courses/Silverlight4/NewFea-
  tures/DataValidation
  ```

  ```
  http://channel9.msdn.com/learn/courses/Silverlight4/
  NewFeatures/DataValidation
  ```

- Debugging Data Binding:

  ```
  http://blogs.msdn.com/b/wpfsldesigner/archive/2010/06/30/debug-
  ging-data-bindings-in-a-wpf-or-silverlight-application.aspx
  ```

  ```
  http://blogs.msdn.com/b/wpfsldesigner/archive/2010/06/30/
  debugging-data-bindings-in-a-wpf-or-silverlight-application.aspx
  ```

4
Architecture

The development of business applications is similar to a building construction. If we put bricks and cement mortar together without following a well-defined pattern, we will move forward quickly but, sooner or later, we will face serious problems, and eventually the building may have to be evacuated.

In this chapter, we will show you how to build solid applications using the recommended pattern for Silverlight and WPF that is, MVVM. For its implementation, we will use the well-known library MVVM Light Toolkit (available at `http://mvvmlight.codeplex.com/`). Finally, we will see how to decouple the different modules of our application via **Managed Extensibility Framework (MEF)**.

Patterns

When developing business applications, it is normal to face considerable pressure to meet tight deadlines, as well as ever-changing functionalities. Our typical first reaction is to begin coding without having a pre-established design or plan. Although this approach normally bears fruit, it leads to the following situations:

- Something that should have been a "disposable" prototype is gradually provided with more and more functionality and ends up being the final application
- As the system grows, it gets more difficult to test the application, because the modules are coupled and they cannot be tested separately
- We find everything mixed and a simple change in the UI forces us to modify code in the business logic or data

All these reasons justify a greater investment of time in the design of the application architecture.

> When is it worth using the "Code-Behind" approach?
>
> When we are just developing some proof of concept or a quick prototype and we know that its code won't be reused for the rest of the scenarios, it is always better to debug and test first than to debug later.

First, we have to structure the application based upon a design pattern. If you already have experience in this area, you may be asked how to implement well-known patterns, such as **Model View Controller (MVC)** or **Model View Presenter (MVP)** for Silverlight or WPF applications. We will choose **Model View ViewModel (MVVM)**.

> Design pattern is just a solution (best practices) for a known problem. To begin with, a good reference can be found at: http://en.wikipedia.org/wiki/Design_patterns_book.

MVVM pattern

Model View ViewModel (MVVM) is an architectural pattern inspired by the Presentation Model design pattern designed by Martin Fowler (one of the greatest experts in the agile software development and object-oriented programming). It is the de facto standard for Silverlight and WPF. So why choose this pattern and not a different one? The answer is because it naturally adapts to the data binding mechanism of Silverlight, allowing us to explore all its capacities.

Let us begin by dissecting the pattern, where we can find the following layers:

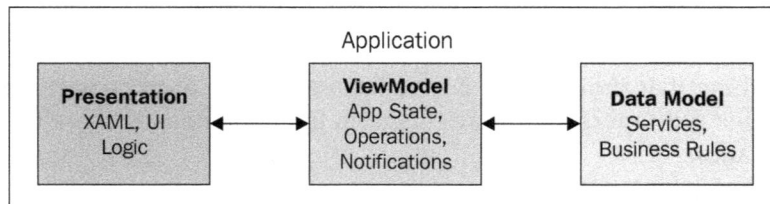

- **Presentation**: It defines the UI layout. The Code-Behind of every page only needs to contain code in charge of managing certain aspects of the UI.

- **ViewModel**: It stores the state of the application and defines operations and notifications to the **Presentation** layer.

- **Data Model**: It interacts with services and defines business rules.

How do these layers interact with each other? Let's take a look at the following figure:

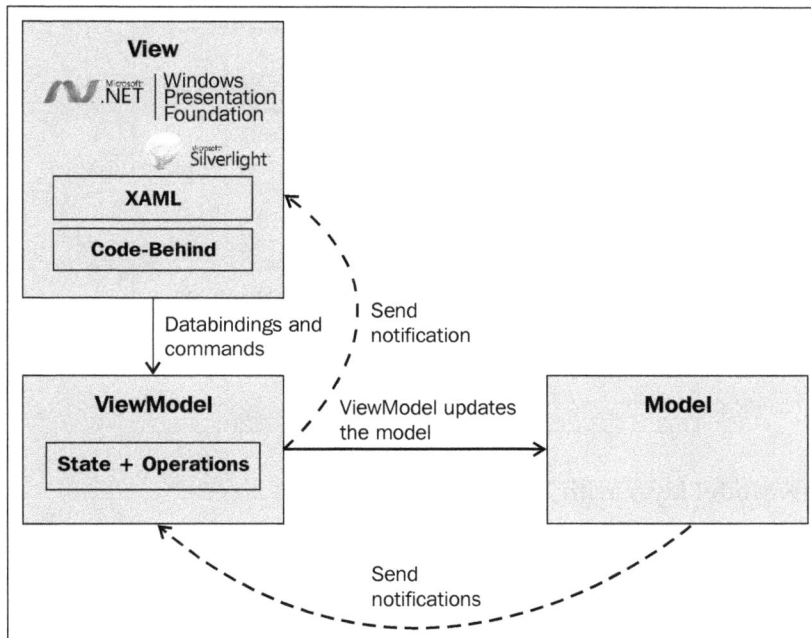

Let's take a look at how these layers interact with each other:

- **View** layer with the **ViewModel** layer:
    - ○ The view controls are bound to **ViewModel** properties, usually in a declarative way. For example, we can bind a TextBox to the Name property in a field of the client file, which we have in the **ViewModel**.

- ○ **ViewModel** shows a series of commands, such as **save changes to the database**. The **Presentation** layer associates them with certain controls in order to allow the user to carry these operations. For instance, the user can press a button to save changes and this button links to the `Save` command in the **ViewModel**. We must also highlight the separation of concerns. In a normal scenario, we bind a button to the `Click` event; in this case, we will link it to the action `SaveClientFile`.

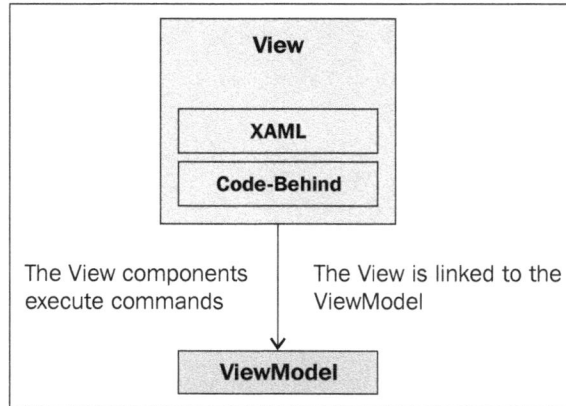

- **ViewModel** layer with **View** layer and **Model** layer:
    - ○ **ViewModel** asks for data or upgrades
    - ○ **Model** processes petitions, and when they are ready, notifies **ViewModel** about the results (the **Model** lives on the client side and makes calls to the server side to retrieve or update information)
    - ○ **ViewModel** notifies **View** layer through data binding

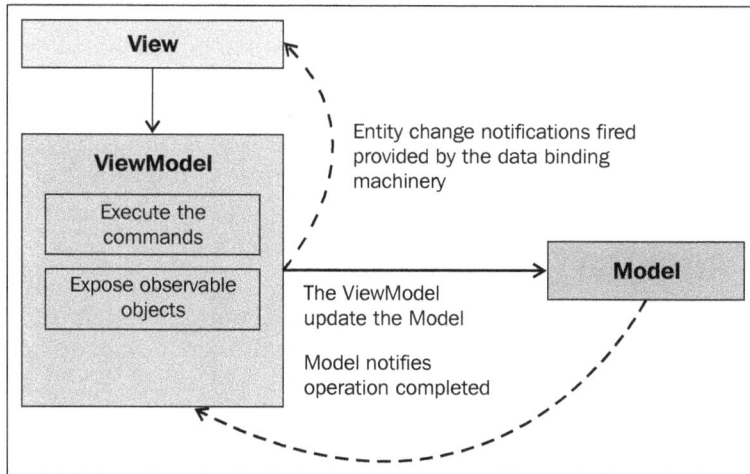

Creating an MVVM-based sample application

Most of the time when we develop an application, it is not possible to fit all the content in just one page. We in fact prefer to divide its content in several parts and group areas by functionality or reusability. So no more theory! We will now apply the concepts we have learned. To do so, we will implement a development, which allows us to search on Twitter. Its aspect can be seen in the following figure:

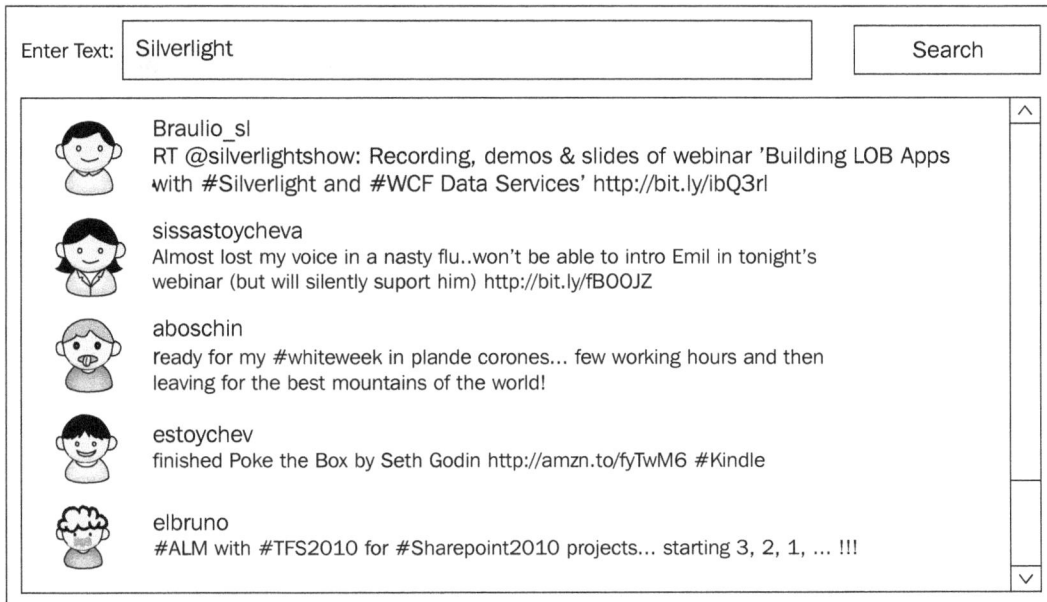

> To search on Twitter, we have adapted a library based on the example Twitter Search Monitor that can be found in Silverlight .NET (http://www.silverlight.net/learn/).

Its operation is quite easy. The user enters a search string, and as a result obtains the first 50 tweets, which satisfy these search terms.

How do we fit this into MVVM? Let's take a look:

- **Model**: It is in charge of making petitions to Twitter about entries which match the search string, and notify **ViewModel** when they are available
- **ViewModel:**
    - Properties:
    - **Search string**: The text string that has to be searched
    - **Tweet results**: The list with the results of the search for tweets
    - Commands:
    - **Search**: It executes the search for tweets containing the value indicated in the **Search string**
- **View**:
    - It links a Textbox control to the **Search string** field of the **ViewModel**
    - It links a ContentTemplate to the tweet list
    - It links the Search command of the **ViewModel** to a button

The following figure summarizes the properties/command and **ViewModel** interaction.

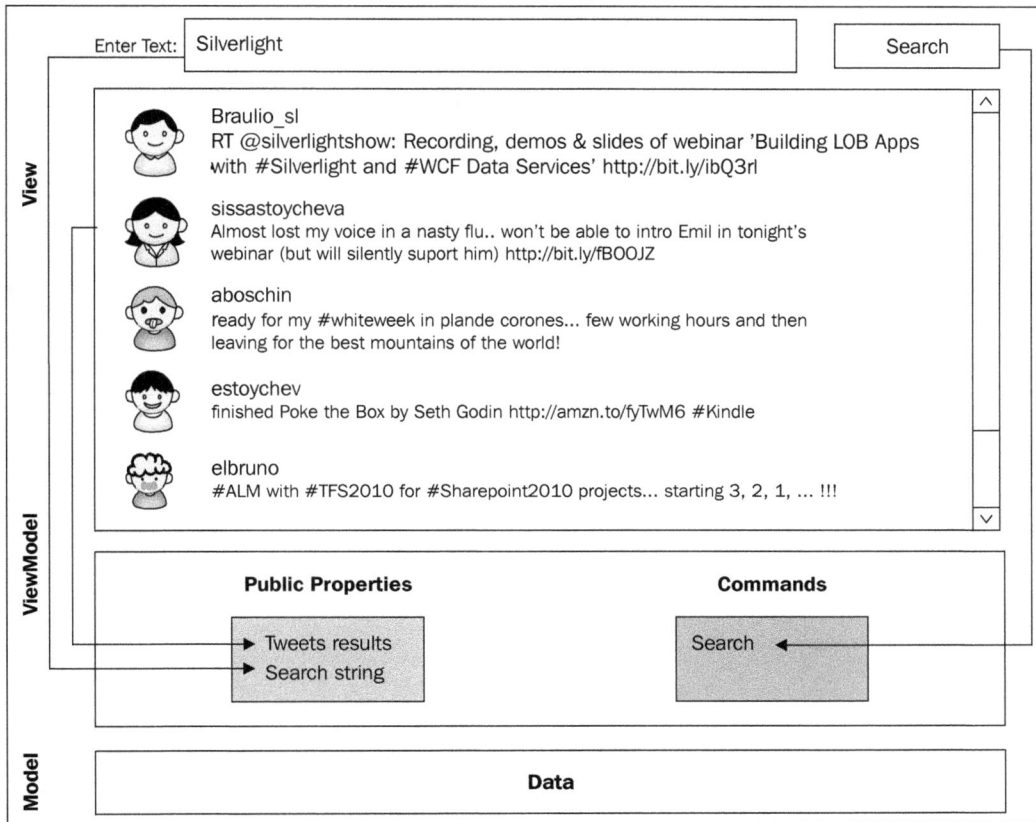

The detailed example can be found at www.packtpub.com. Now, let's summarize all the necessary steps to create it.

Creating the project structure

First, when creating the project framework, it is possible to separate each part of the project and make the application easier to maintain. Later on, we will deal with more advanced forms of structuring a solution.

Choose **Blank Solution** to create a new solution called MyTweet.

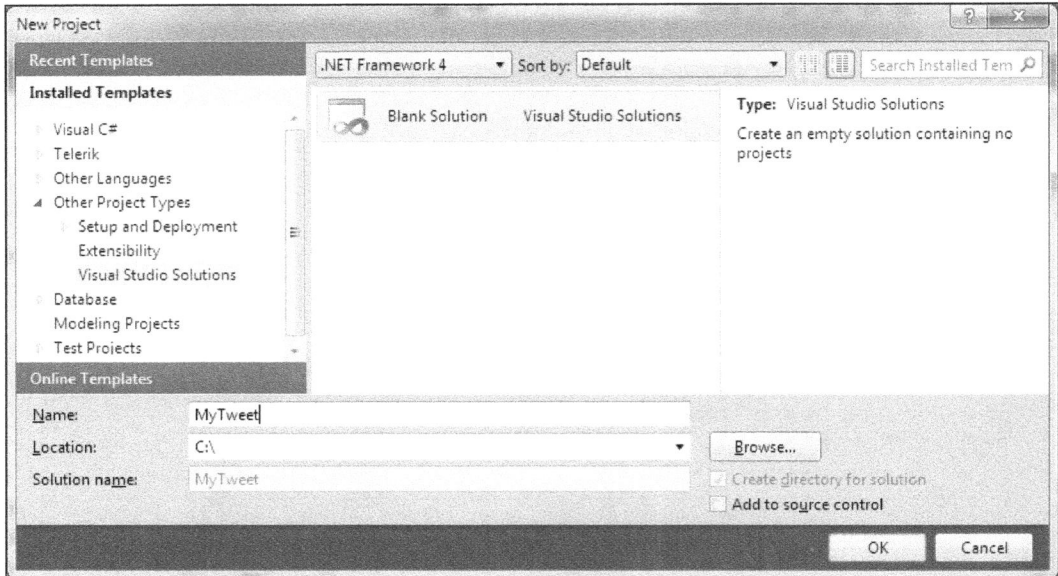

In this solution, create the following projects:

- MyTweet.Views:
  - ° Add a new project. To do so, place the mouse on the solution, right-click and, in the **Context** menu, choose **Add | New Project...**

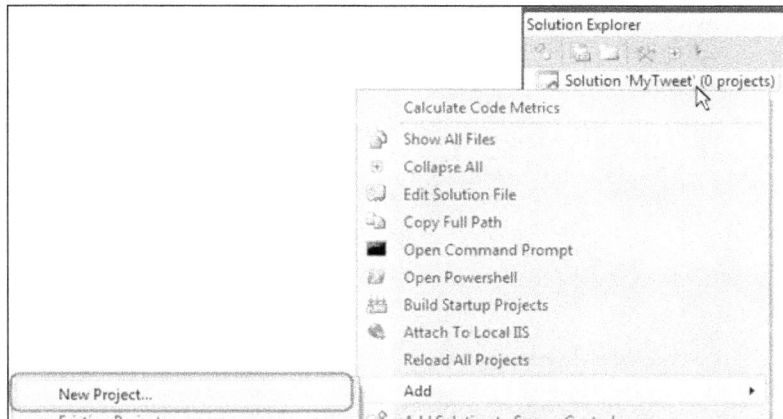

° Choose **Silverlight Application** and name it MyTweet.Views:

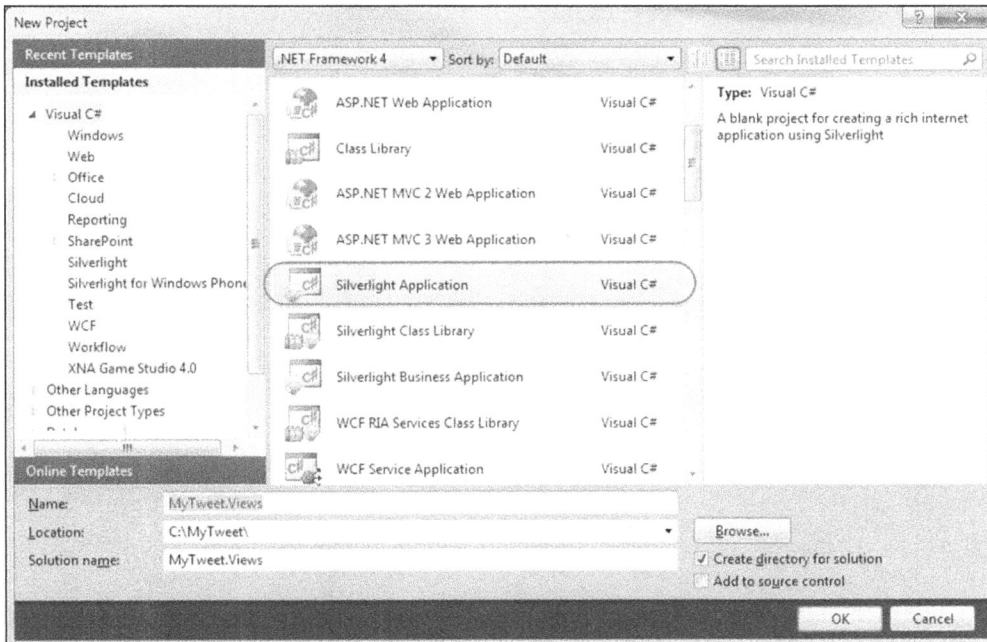

° In the next dialogue, indicate it has a web project associated

° Add a folder called **Views** and place the view created in the project in this folder:

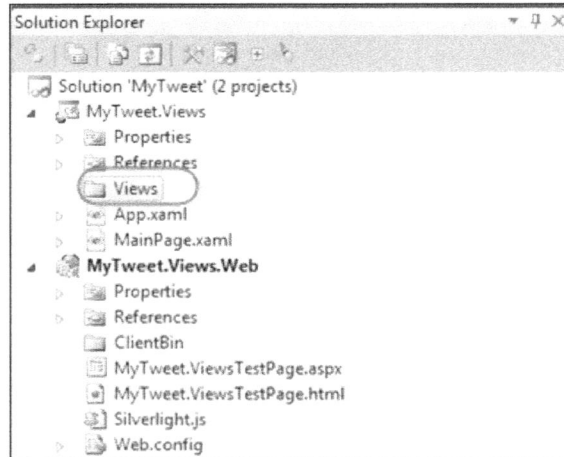

° The main window and its view will be stored in this application

• `MyTweet.ViewModel:`

° Create a new project in **Silverlight Class Library** called **MyTweet. ViewModel**:

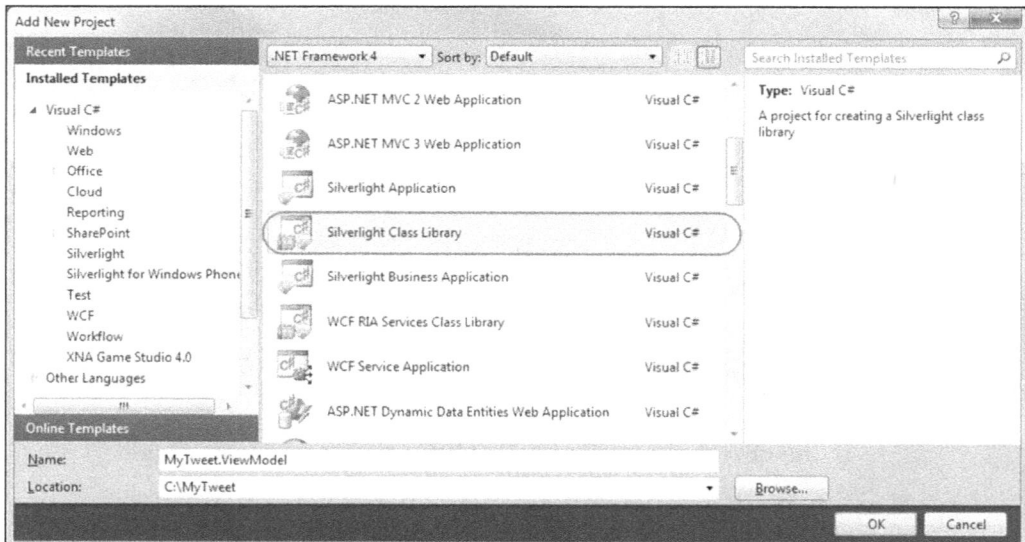

- In this project, we will create the ViewModel associated with the view previously created

- We will add a reference to third-party libraries (binary files and source code are available at `www.packtpub.com`):

  - `RIATec.Libs.TweetAPI`

  - `RIATec.Libs.TweetAPI.Entities`

- **MyTweet.Model:**

  - It is a Silverlight library.

  - We will define the application model. This will be the layer interacting with the library, also in charge of the search petitions on Twitter.

  - Create a project of the class library (as shown previously, in relation to ViewModel) and name it `MyTweetModel`.

  - Then, add the references to the DLLs:

    - `RIATec.Libs.TweetAPI.dll`

    - `RIATec.Libs.TweetAPI.Entities.dll`

  - These libraries allow us to make search petitions asynchronously, and give us back, in the form of an event, the list of tweets related to that search.

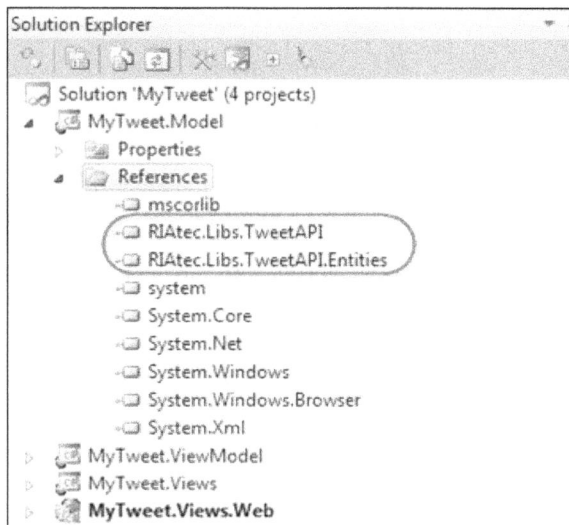

Coding the project

Now that we have built the structure, we will begin coding. To do so, we will begin from the Model, so as to continue with the ViewModel and end with the View.

MyTweet.Model

We will wrap up our library of tweet petition and expose it in our Model project (later, we will see how to decouple from this library).

We will assume that libraries have been already added.

The operations we will perform against the Model are usually asynchronous — that is to say, we make a petition and, when it is completed, an event is launched and picked up by the upper layers (ViewModel). In our case, we will have to launch an event containing the list of tweets. To achieve this goal, let us define an argument class:

1. Right-click on the project and choose **Add | Class** on the contextual menu.

2. Name this new class `ResponseTweetSearchArgs`. We will be able to couple in it the event we define:

```
using System;
using System.Collections.ObjectModel;
using RIAtec.Libs.TweetAPI.Entities;
namespace MyTweet.Model
{
  public class ResponseTweetSearchArgs : EventArgs
  {
    public ObservableCollection<SearchResult> searchResults;
  }
}
```

> Why use an `ObservableCollection` instead of a List? `ObservableCollection` works in a similar way to `INotifyProperty`; in this case the UI gets notified when an element is added or removed from the collection.

3. Create a new class (**Add | Class**) that we will name `Model`.

4. Define a tweet petition and subscribe the library event indicating the petition has been completed:

```
using System;
using RIAtec.Libs.TweetAPI;
namespace MyTweet.Model
```

```
{
  public class TweetModel
  {
    Search _searchAPI;
    // Instatiate the search API and hook to the completed event
    //of the SearchForTweet async call
    public TweetModel()
    {
      _searchAPI = new Search();
      _searchAPI.SearchForTweetCompleted += new
        EventHandler<RIAtec.Libs.TweetAPI.Entities.Events.
        ServiceResponseSearchTweetsArgs>
        (_searchAPI_SearchForTweetCompleted);
    }
    // This event will be fired once we get the callback from the
    //tweet library
    public event EventHandler<ResponseTweetSearchArgs>
      TweetSearchCompleted;

    // Helper method to fire the event
    private void OnTweetSearchCompleted(ResponseTweetSearchArgs e)
    {
      EventHandler<ResponseTweetSearchArgs> eventHandler =
        TweetSearchCompleted;
      if (eventHandler != null)
      {
        eventHandler(this, e);
      }
    }
  }
}
```

5. Within the `TweetModel` class, we will define the public method that will allow us to make an asynchronous call for the tweet petition:

```
public void TweetSearchAsync(string substringToFind)
{
  // Retrieve the first 50 results of the search.
  // This method is asynchronous, once we get the
  // response and notification will be fired.
  _searchAPI.SearchForTweetsAsync(substringToFind, 0);
}
```

6. When the petition has completed, we fire our own event. This will be picked by an upper layer (the associated ViewModel):

```
void _searchAPI_SearchForTweetCompleted(object sender,
  RIAtec.Libs.TweetAPI.Entities.Events.
  ServiceResponseSearchTweetsArgs e)
{
  ResponseTweetSearchArgs responseArgs = new
    ResponseTweetSearchArgs();
  // Call succeeded?
  if (e.Result ==
    RIAtec.Libs.TweetAPI.Entities.Events.
    ServiceResponseType.Succeeded)
  {
    // Add to the response event the list of tweets
    responseArgs.searchResults = e.searchResults;
  }
  // Fire this event (the ViewModel will be listening)
  OnTweetSearchCompleted(responseArgs);
}
```

MyTweet.ViewModel

In this layer, we are going to expose the functionality that will fire the tweets search and the collection that will be exposed to the view (tweets collection).

1. We will begin by adding the references (**Add | References**) to our model, **MyTweet.Model**, and to the Twitter entities we will use:

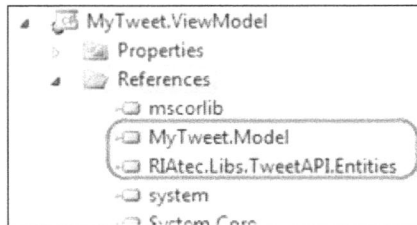

2. Create a class called SearchViewModel (**Add | New Class**) and implement the support to the interface:

```
using System.ComponentModel;
namespace MyTweet.ViewModel
{
  public class SearchViewModel : INotifyPropertyChanged
  {
    // Usually implement this on a base class
```

```
      #region INotifyPropertyChanged Members
      public event PropertyChangedEventHandler PropertyChanged;
      private void OnPropertyChanged(string propertyName)
      {
        if (PropertyChanged != null)
        PropertyChanged(this, new
          PropertyChangedEventArgs(propertyName));
      }
      #endregion
    }
}
```

3. Create a member variable which will instantiate the model previously defined (we will see how to do this without coupling in subsequent chapters):

```
using MyTweet.Model;
namespace MyTweet.ViewModel
{
  public class SearchViewModel : INotifyPropertyChanged
    {
    #region fields
    private TweetModel _model = new TweetModel();
    #endregion
  }
}
```

> INotifyPropertyChanged is covered in detail in *Chapter 3, Data Binding.*

4. Add a property of the string type, which contains the text string we have to search for:

```
public string SearchText
{
  get { return _searchText; }
  set
  {
    if (_searchText != value)
    {
      _searchText = value;
      // To notify any UI element bound to this property
      RaisePropertyChanged("SearchText");
    }
  }
}
```

5. Add a collection containing the tweet search results:

```
private ObservableCollection<SearchResult> _members = new
  ObservableCollection<SearchResult>();
public ObservableCollection<SearchResult> Members
{
  get { return _members; }
  set
  {
    _members = value;
    RaisePropertyChanged("Members");
  }
}
```

6. Add a public method, which will fire the search (**Important**: This should be exposed as a command. We will see how to do this in the following section):

```
public void ExecuteSearch()
{
  _model.TweetSearchAsync(SearchText);
}
```

7. Subscribe to the event of the Model, which will indicate to us when the result of the search has been retrieved, and assign the result to the property of the results already defined:

```
public SearchViewModel()
{
  _model.TweetSearchCompleted += new
    EventHandler<ResponseTweetSearchArgs>
    (_model_TweetSearchCompleted);
}
void _model_TweetSearchCompleted(object sender,
  ResponseTweetSearchArgs e)
{
  Members = e.searchResults;
}
```

MyTweet.View

In the **View** layer, create an interface so that the user can interact with the logic defined in the **ViewModel**:

1. We will begin by adding references to our ViewModel, **MyTweet. ViewModel**.

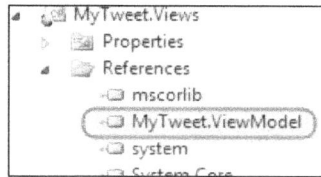

2. Now, create a folder called **Views** (**Add | New Folder**) and add a Silverlight Page Control type called **SearchView** (**Add | New Item**):

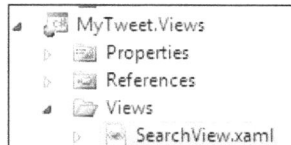

3. The next step will consist in the creation of the XAML page layout. In order to do this, we can choose among the tools Expression Blend, Visual Studio (layout), or just XAML. It is intended to get the following result:

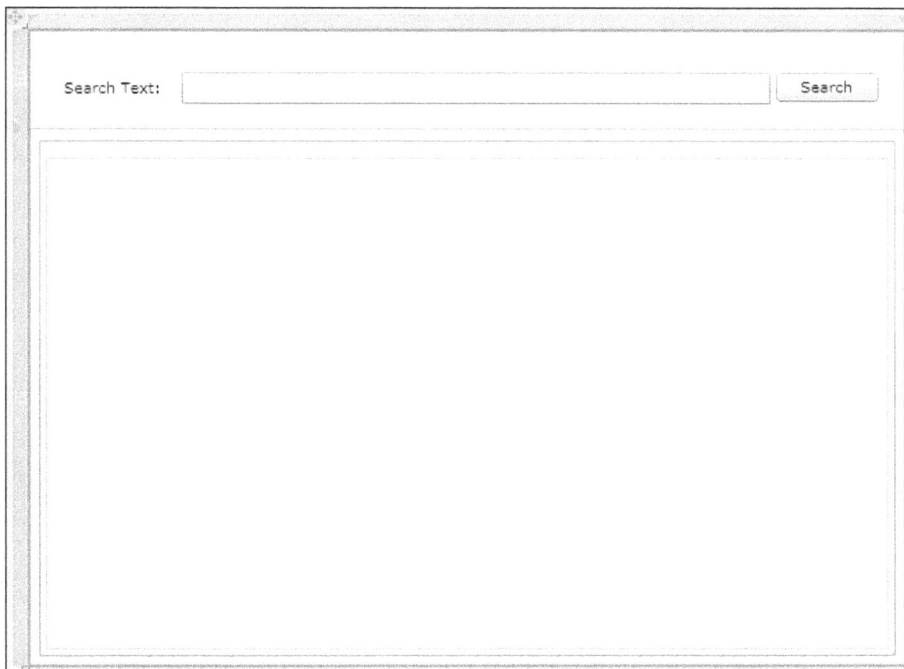

4. In our case, we will structure the page in the following way:

    ◦ Define the main layout on the basis of a grid control.

    ◦ Define two rows:

        ◦ One row will have fixed height and we will establish the search box on it

        ◦ The other one makes use of the remaining space and uses it to show the search results box

    ◦ To show the results:

        ◦ Use a control of `ScrollViewer` type

        ◦ Define a data template to represent all the elements in the results list

    ◦ When binding data, assign the ViewModel in the XAML as design `DataContext`. This permits data binding from Visual Studio properties (see *Chapter 3, Data Binding* to learn more).

    ◦ Bind the **Search** textbox to the `Search` property defined in the ViewModel, together with the list of results to the `ScrollView` control (we will define the details for every field in the data template).

The following is the XAML that is generated (simplified for the sake of readability):

```
<!-- Header, referencing tweet view model, plus defining -->
<!-- design DataContext -->
<navigation:Page
  x:Class="MyTweet.Views.Views.SearchView"
  (...)
  xmlns:d="http://schemas.microsoft.com/expression/blend/2008"
  xmlns:mc="http://schemas.openxmlformats.org/markup-
    compatibility/2006"
  mc:Ignorable="d"
  xmlns:vm="clr-
    namespace:MyTweet.ViewModel;assembly=MyTweet.ViewModel"
  d:DataContext="{d:DesignInstance IsDesignTimeCreatable=False,
    Type=vm:SearchViewModel}"
  Title="SearchView Page">

  <navigation:Page.Resources>
    <!-- Here we define the layout of a single search result -->
    <!-- Picture + Author + Message + Pub Date-->
```

```xml
<DataTemplate x:Key="SearchResultsTemplate">
  <Grid Margin="4,0,4,8"
    d:DesignWidth="446"
    d:DesignHeight="68">
    <Grid.ColumnDefinitions>
      <ColumnDefinition Width="Auto" />
      <ColumnDefinition Width="*" />
    </Grid.ColumnDefinitions>
    <Border VerticalAlignment="Top"
      Margin="8" Padding="2"
      Background="White">
      <Image Width="40" Height="40"
        Source="{Binding Path=Avatar, Mode=OneWay}"/>
    </Border>

    <StackPanel Grid.Column="1"
      VerticalAlignment="Top"
      Margin="0,4,0,0">
      <TextBlock x:Name="AuthorName"
        FontWeight="Bold"
        Text="{Binding Path=Author, Mode=OneWay}" />
      <Grid Margin="0,6,0,0">
        <Grid.RowDefinitions>
        <RowDefinition Height="Auto" />
        <RowDefinition Height="2" />
        <RowDefinition Height="Auto" />
        </Grid.RowDefinitions>
        <TextBlock x:Name="TweetMessage"
          Text="{Binding Path=Tweet, Mode=OneWay}"
          TextWrapping="Wrap" />
        <TextBlock x:Name="PublishDateLabel"
          Text="{Binding Path=PublishDate, StringFormat='dd-MMM-
            yyyy hh:mm tt'}"
          Grid.Row="2"  />
      </Grid>
    </StackPanel>
  </Grid>
</DataTemplate>
</navigation:Page.Resources>

<!-- We define two rows, first (fix height) one search area,-->
<!-- second one results pane-->
```

```xml
<Grid x:Name="LayoutRoot" Background="White">
  <Grid.RowDefinitions>
    <RowDefinition Height="75"/>
    <RowDefinition Height="*"/>
  </Grid.RowDefinitions>
  <TextBlock HorizontalAlignment="Left"
    Margin="26,36,0,22"
    TextWrapping="Wrap"
    Text="Search Text:"
    d:LayoutOverrides="Height"
VerticalAlignment="Top"/>
  <!-- Bind the textBox to the SearchText ViewModel property -->
  <TextBox Margin="112,32,99,0" TextWrapping="Wrap"
    Text="{Binding Path=SearchText, Mode=TwoWay}"
    d:LayoutOverrides="Width, HorizontalMargin"
    VerticalAlignment="Top" />
  <Button Content="Search"
    HorizontalAlignment="Right"
    Margin="0,32,20,20"
    Width="75"
    d:LayoutOverrides="Height"
    VerticalAlignment="Top" />

  <ScrollViewer HorizontalScrollBarVisibility="Disabled"
    VerticalScrollBarVisibility="Auto"
    Margin="8" Grid.Row="1">
  <!-- Bind the item's control to the -->
  <!-- SearchResults ViewModel -->
  <!-- ObservableCollection.The item -->
  <!-- layout is defined in the -->
  <!-- SearchResults Template-->
  <ItemsControl x:Name="SearchResults"
    Margin="0,8,0,0"
    Grid.Row="1"
    ItemTemplate="{StaticResource SearchResultsTemplate}"
    ItemsSource="{Binding Path=Members}" />
  </ScrollViewer>
</Grid>
</navigation:Page>
```

The page layout is now ready. We add the page to the main page of the application (`MainPage.XAML`):

```
<UserControl x:Class="MyTweet.Views.MainPage"
  (...)
  xmlns:vi="clr-namespace:MyTweet.Views.Views"
  d:DesignHeight="300" d:DesignWidth="400">

  <Grid x:Name="LayoutRoot" Background="White">
    <vi:SearchView/>
  </Grid>
</UserControl>
```

Let us now focus on the Code-Behind of the page:

1. Bind `DataContext` on the constructor (we will see a cleaner form to do this in the following section):

```
public SearchView()
{
  InitializeComponent();

  this.DataContext = new SearchViewModel();
}
```

2. Going back to XAML, subscribe to the `Click` event in the `Search` button:

```
<Button Content="Search"
  Click="Button_Click"
  (...)
/>
```

3. We launch the code in the Code-Behind to search:

```
private void Button_Click(object sender, RoutedEventArgs e)
{
  SearchViewModel svm = this.DataContext as SearchViewModel;
  svm.ExecuteSearch();
}
```

We are done! Once the search is completed, the property containing the results collection gets updated and, automatically, it is notified to the associated UI control, which is also updated. The following is the final result:

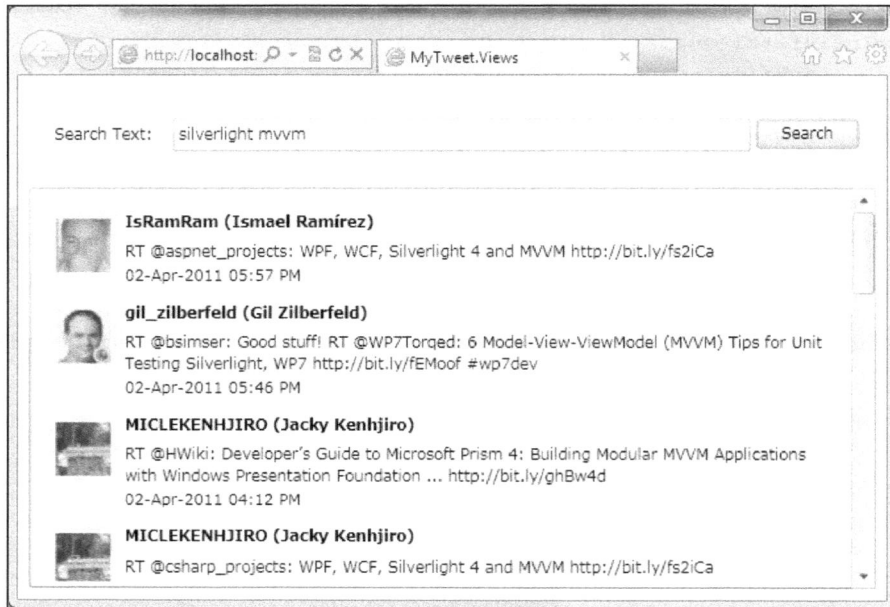

This is an interesting example where we will apply the MVVM pattern. Nevertheless, there are certain topics which are still pending:

- When implementing a ViewModel, we have to add "boilerplate code". That is to say, we have to inherit from `INotifyPropertyChange` and implement the interface. Wouldn't it be better to have a base class at our disposal from which to inherit?

- The code we implement when the click event is fired is partially implemented in the Code-Behind of the view (code in the Code-Behind cannot be unit tested). Isn't there a better way to do this? Yes, there is. We can make use of commands, binding the command event of the button directly to a method implemented in the ViewModel. In this case, we face a situation, which is very similar to the one in the previous section. Isn't there a class already constituted, which helps us to implement commands?

- One of the advantages of MVVM is the "separation of concerns" between Vista and ViewModel, allowing us to make automatic unit tests on the ViewModel and avoid couplings between different views. Nevertheless, what happens if we have to communicate to other views? And if we need to show a `Messagebox` from the ViewModel?

- What happens if we want to try our logic implemented in the ViewModel, abstracting from what has already been implemented in the Model?

- How can we substitute a sample model for our own model and implement unit tests on the ViewModel?

We could create our own libraries to cover this functionality, but there are excellent libraries, which help us to avoid implementing them. In the following sections, we will show how to work with MVVM Light Toolkit and MEF.

MVVM Light Toolkit

MVVM is a set of libraries which make our task easier when dealing with the MVVM pattern. They are available at `http://mvvmlight.codeplex.com/`.

When dealing with MVVM libraries and frameworks, some fears arise. Among others, we can mention the following: "Shall I redo my application?" "Do I need to comply with the templates and structures given by the Framework?" The answer is no. Even if Light Toolkit includes a series of project templates, nothing prevents us from "picking cherries" in relation to functionalities and incorporating them to our own project, minimizing the impact upon our application.

How can Light Toolkit be incorporated to our project? Just by downloading these libraries and adding the following references to the project:

- `Galasoft.MvvmLight.SL4`:
  - It implements a ViewModel base (`ViewModelBase`)
  - It implements support to commands (`RelayCommand`)
  - It implements support for message publishing and subscribing (`Messenger`)

- `GalaSoft.MvvmLightExtras`:
  - It implements `EventToCommand`, a class which allows us to bind events such as `Page Load` to commands in our ViewModel
  - `DispatcherHelper`, help the class to update and make safe calls to the UI thread from a worker thread

In this book, we will cover the basic elements of the library. For further information, visit `http://www.galasoft.ch/mvvm/`.

ViewModelBase

The base class we missed for our ViewModel implements the
INotifyPropertyChanged interface for us. To use it, we only have to:

1. Add the MVVM Light Toolkit library (Galasoft.MvvmLight) to the
   using namespace and make our ViewModel (MyViewModel) inherit from
   ViewModelBase:

   ```
   using GalaSoft.MvvmLight;

   namespace INotifiy_Months
   {
     public class ViewModel : ViewModelBase
     {
       (...)
     }
     (...)
   }
   ```

2. Add RaisePropertyChanged to the properties we implement, together with
   the name of the property (this method is implemented in the base class,
   ViewModelBase):

   ```
   string _clientName;
   public string ClientName
   {
     get
     {
       return _clientName;
     }

     set
     {
       if (_clientName != value)
       {
         _clientName = value;

         RaisePropertyChanged("ClientName");
       }
     }
   }
   ```

RelayCommand

This class implements the `ICommand` interface for us. It allows us to bind a `RelayCommand` defined in our ViewModel with a button click. Thanks to this, we can:

- Execute code belonging to our ViewModel (without having to delegate on view's Code-Behind events).

- Define whether or not the command is enabled directly from the ViewModel. For example, if all the required data is not filled, the command `Save` will not be executed.

In order to understand how this is applied, let us see how it works by implementing a basic sample based on MVVM. We will create an application that links together two strings of text when clicking on a button. The button which launches the `Concatenate` command will only be enabled if the two strings of text that have to be linked are not empty. We will follow the given steps:

1. Create a ViewModel. It will expose the two strings that have to be concatenated (`FirstName`, `LastName`) as properties, as well as the resulting string (`FullName`). We will also inherit our ViewModel from `ViewModelBase`:

```
private string _firstName;
public string FirstName
{
    get
    {
        return _firstName;
    }

    set
    {
        _firstName = value;
        RaisePropertyChanged("FirstName");
    }
}

private string _lastName;
public string LastName
{
    get
    {
        return _lastName;
    }

    set
    {
        _lastName = value;
```

```
                RaisePropertyChanged("LastName");
        }
    }

    string _fullName;

    public string FullName
    {
        get
        {
            return _fullName;
        }

        set
        {
            _fullName = value;
            RaisePropertyChanged("FullName");

        }
    }
```

2. Now, define the command of the `RelayCommand` type that is in charge of the concatenate operation:

```
private RelayCommand _concatCommand;

public RelayCommand ConcatCommand
{
  get
  {
    if (_concatCommand == null)
    {
      _concatCommand = new RelayCommand(() =>
      // Lambda expression, when the user clicks on
      // the button this code will be executed
      {
        FullName = _firstName + " " + _lastName;
      },
      // Lambda expression: Disable this command if
      // the search text is empty
      (() => (!string.IsNullOrEmpty(FirstName) &&
        !string.IsNullOrEmpty(LastName)))
      );
    }

    return _concatCommand;
  }
}
```

3. At this point, we are almost done. We only need to indicate where it is necessary to reassess the condition, which enables or disables the command. To do this, we add the call `RaiseCanExecuteChanged` to the set accessors of the `FirstName` and `LastName` properties:

```
private string _firstName;
public string FirstName
{
  get
  {
    return _firstName;
  }

  set
  {
    _firstName = value;
    RaisePropertyChanged("FirstName");
    // Need to recalc the can execute of the search button
    // command
    ConcatCommand.RaiseCanExecuteChanged();
  }
}
```

4. Now, let us create the view layout, which will look similar to the following screenshot:

5. Define the necessary bindings for the textboxes in the XAML and associate `ConcatCommand` to the **Concat** button:

```
<UserControl x:Class="CommandSample.MainPage"
xmlns="http://schemas.microsoft.com/winfx/2006/xaml/presentation"
xmlns:x="http://schemas.microsoft.com/winfx/2006/xaml"
```

```
xmlns:d="http://schemas.microsoft.com/expression/blend/2008"
xmlns:mc="http://schemas.openxmlformats.org/markup-
compatibility/2006"
mc:Ignorable="d"
d:DesignHeight="192" d:DesignWidth="400">

  <Grid x:Name="LayoutRoot" Background="White">
    <TextBlock Height="23" HorizontalAlignment="Left"
      Margin="30,40,0,0" x:Name="textBlock1"
      VerticalAlignment="Top"
      Text="FirstLastName" />
    <TextBlock Height="23" HorizontalAlignment="Left"
      Margin="30,66,0,0"
      x:Name="textBlock2"
      VerticalAlignment="Top"
      Text="LastName" />
    <TextBox Margin="104,36,36,0" TextWrapping="Wrap"
      VerticalAlignment="Top"
      Text="{Binding Path=FirstName,
      Mode=TwoWay}"/>
    <TextBox Margin="104,66,36,0"
      TextWrapping="Wrap"
      VerticalAlignment="Top"
      Text="{Binding Path=LastName, Mode=TwoWay}"/>
    <Button Content="Concat" Margin="30,99,36,0"
      VerticalAlignment="Top"
      Command="{Binding Path=ConcatCommand}"/>
    <TextBlock Margin="30,137,36,27" TextWrapping="Wrap"
      Text="{Binding Path=FullName}"
      FontSize="24" Foreground="# FF282A2F"/>
  </Grid>
</UserControl>
```

6. In the Code-Behind of the page, associate the ViewModel already created as DataContext:

```
public partial class MainPage : UserControl
{
  public MainPage()
  {
    InitializeComponent();

    DataContext = new ViewModel();
  }
}
```

Messenger

A `Messenger` class allows us to establish communication in an application. That is, we can send messages from any point of the application and have recipients on the alert subscribed to them. These messages can contain additional information, including complex types.

Messenger is the Light Toolkit solution to the following:

- Allowing the ViewModel to perform an operation related to UI without mixing presentation code. For example, showing a MessageBox or a modal dialogue.
- Communicating two ViewModels without referencing each other.

Let us see how this works with an easy-to-follow example of an application showing two views. In the first one, the user enters a text that has to be sent to other views. The process of sending occurs via a message containing that text. In the second view, the application is awaiting the receipt of that message in order to display it:

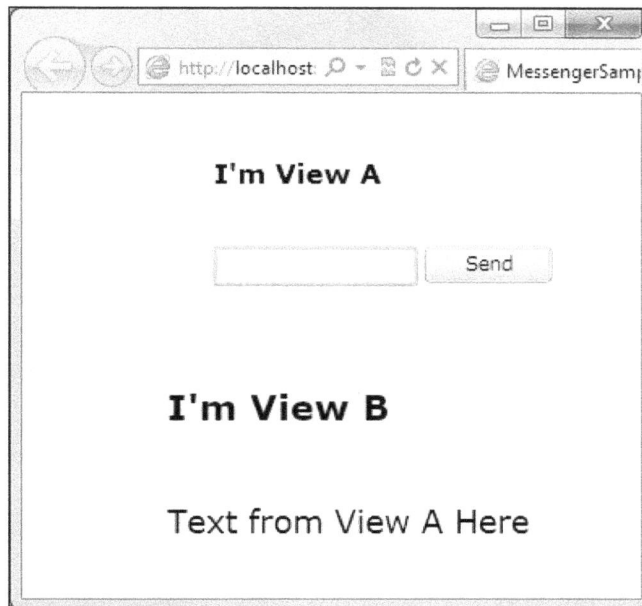

We will now focus on the message definition and the Code-Behind of the two views (please enter www.packtpub.com to download the sample):

1. First, we have to define a class for the message, MyTextMessage, which inherits from GenericMessage:

```
using GalaSoft.MvvmLight.Messaging;

namespace MessengerSample
{
  public class MyTextMessage : GenericMessage<string>
  {

    public MyTextMessage(string textToDisplay)
    : base(textToDisplay)
    {
      if (textToDisplay == null)
      {
        throw new ArgumentNullException("textToDisplay");
      }
    }

  }
}
```

2. In **View A**, when the user presses the **Send** button, the message is sent, including the text entered in the textbox:

```
private void Button_Click(object sender, RoutedEventArgs e)
{
  Messenger.Default.Send(new MyTextMessage(txText.Text));
}
```

3. In **View B**, we subscribe to that message and, as soon as it is received, the text is shown in a TextBlock control:

```
public ViewB()
{
  InitializeComponent();

  Messenger.Default.Register<MyTextMessage>(this,
  OnNewTextArrived);

}

public void OnNewTextArrived(MyTextMessage message)
{
  tbMyText.Text = message.Content;
}
```

You can find more details on the use of Messenger in the *LOB application case study: applying what we have learned* section in this chapter.

Managed Extensibilty Framework (MEF)

When implementing a Silverlight application, some doubts, such as the following can arise:

- How can the different modules be decoupled? Is there an easy way to replace modules, keeping interdependence? Moreover, it would be interesting to replace modules with others containing hardcoded data, so as to perform unitary tests easily.

- It would be great for my application to be extensible, and even better if third-party developers could couple their developments to my project easily.

- I would like to control the size of the application XAP and load modules on demand.

It is possible to implement our own functionality in order to give support to these points, but it is not always practical (similar to what happened when analysing MVVM Light Toolkit). There are libraries and frameworks such as **MEF**, which already cover these features.

> **Managed Extensibility Framework (MEF)** offers discovery and composition capabilities, which we can make use of in order to load application extensions (load application modules on demand).

MEF definitions

Let us now see a series of definitions, which will lead us to manage MEF more easily. In the following figure, you can see the structure of MEF:

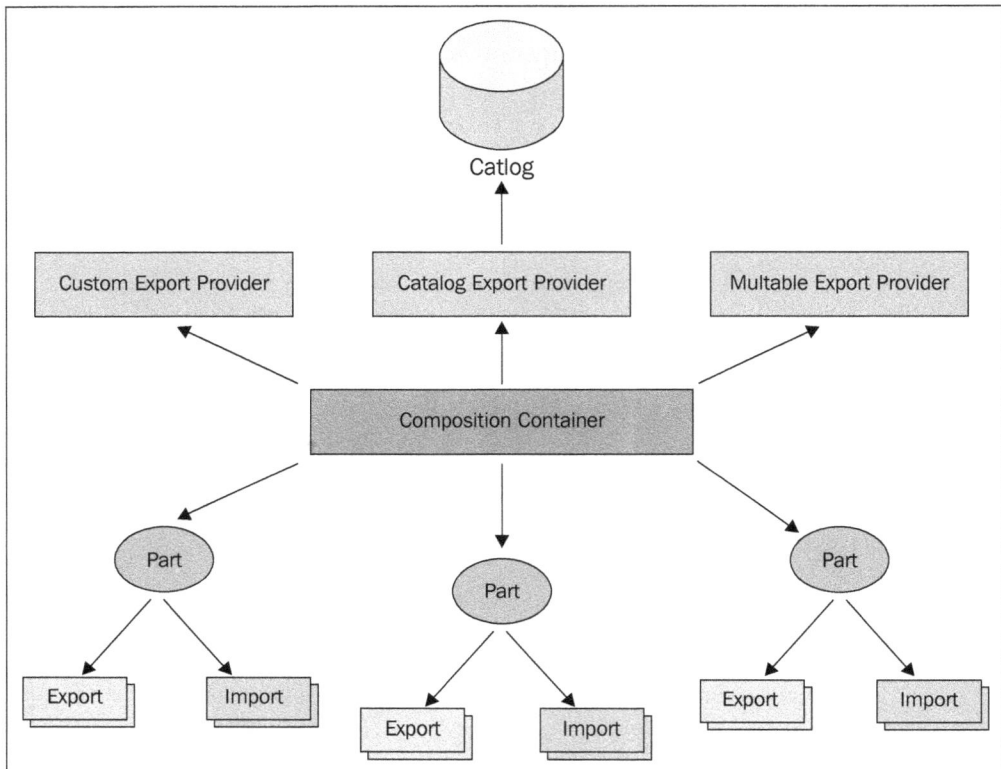

Composable part: A **Part** gives services to other parts at the same time that it consumes them. They can have different origins. For example, the application or a call to a service.

Export: This is a service exposed by a **Part**. For example, an editor for Visual Studio IDE (in this case, the Visual Studio IDE would import this particular editor).

Import: This is a service consumed by a **Part**.

Contracts: It identifies an **Import** or an **Export**. That is, it acts as the glue between them.

Composition Container: MEF is in charge of composing parts (in other words, mapping between **Import** and **Export** and creating the appropriate instances).

Export Providers: It returns all **Export** that accomplishes an **Import** definition. In this chapter, we will make use of **CatalogExportProvider**, which extracts the parts from a given **catalog**.

Catalogs: They allow us to discover parts dynamically. **Catalogs** allow applications to consume exports that have self-registered themselves via the **Export** attribute in an easy way. MEF provides us with a series of catalogs already implemented (for example, **Assembly Catalog**, **Directory Catalog,** or **AgreggateCatalog** among others).

Parts and contracts

Let us see how the different parts relate to each other through a practical example. Imagine we have an application based on MVVM:

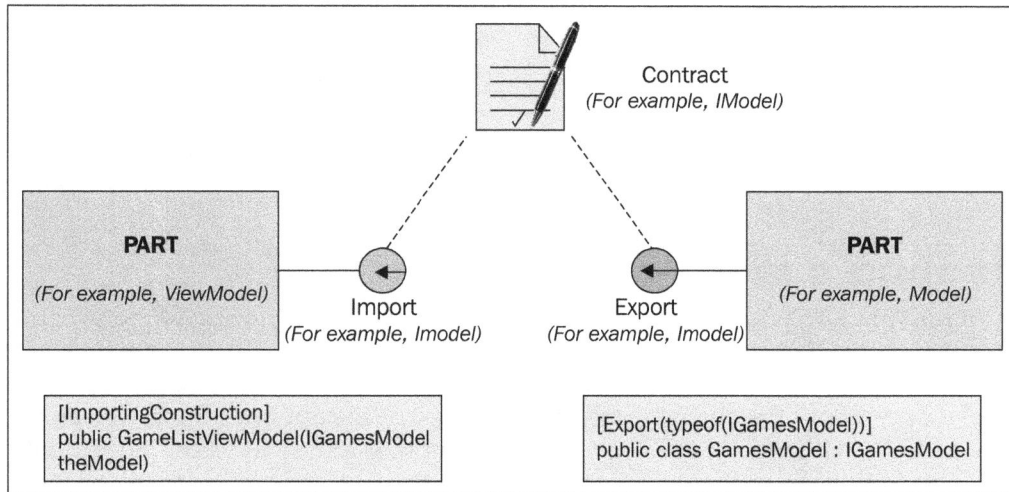

- Define the operations which the Model has to accomplish on an interface called `IMyModel`. This interface is the contract.

- Create a class calling `MyModel`, which implements the `IMyModel` interface, and export it with MEF. To do so, add the `Export` annotation to the class header.

- Create the `ViewModel` class (`MyViewModel`) and, in the constructor header, indicate that it is a necessary part, which implements `IMyModel` (that is, we need to import `IMymodel`).

Composition

Now that the parts, contracts, and relations (imports and exports) have been established, we have to link everything together when the application is executed. To do so, we will only have to indicate MEF to perform the operation calling `SatisfyImports`. This method will search exports and imports on all the assemblies and will match them.

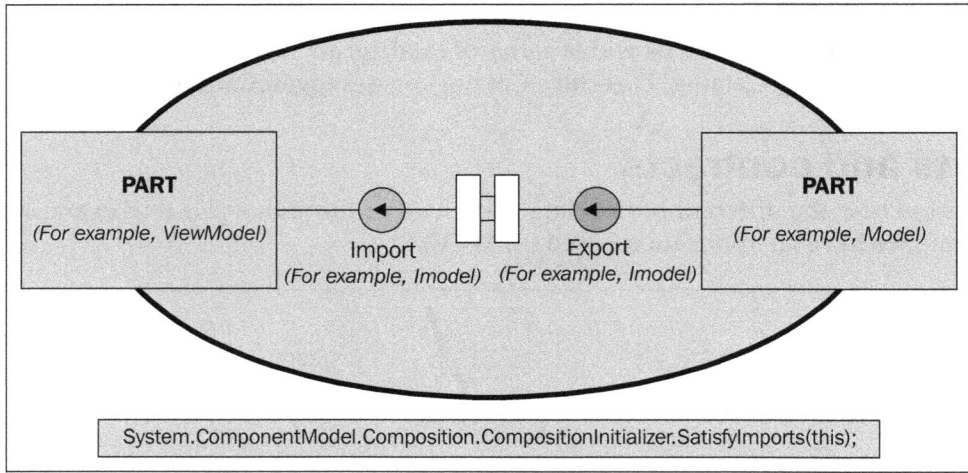

Creating a mock model using MEF

To put into practice what we have learned, we have done refactoring of the tweets browser previously created (it is available at www.packtpub.com). Our aim here is to be able to decouple the implementation of its contract model. This makes it possible to replace it without the changes impacting the rest of the application, as well as to create a model with mock data so as to implement unit tests against the ViewModel layer. This is all done without the need to have a physical connection to the service (for further information on this topic, see *Chapter 7, Testing your LOB Application*).

Now, we will see a summary of the steps we have to follow for refactoring:

1. Create a new project (**Add | New Project | Silverlight Class Library**) called **MyTweet.Model.Contracts**.

2. To make it simpler, we will add a reference to the DLL of the Twitter browser called **RIAtec.Libs.TweetAPI.Entities**. It would have been perfect to define our entities and events so that they do not depend on any third-party library:

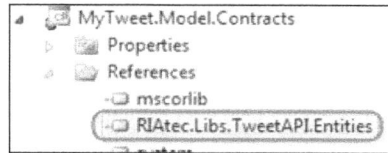

3. Move the `ResponseTweetSearchArgs` class defined in the Model to our new contracts project:

```
using System;
using System.Collections.ObjectModel;
using RIAtec.Libs.TweetAPI.Entities;

namespace MyTweet.Model.Contracts
{
  public class ResponseTweetSearchArgs : EventArgs
  {
    public ObservableCollection<SearchResult> searchResults;
  }
}
```

4. Add an interface (**Add | New Class**) to this project that will be called `IModel`. Define the operations and events that will be exposed to the ViewModel in this project:

```
using System;

namespace MyTweet.Model.Contracts
{
  public interface IModel
  {
    void TweetSearchAsync(string substringToFind);

    // This event will be fired once we get the callback
    //from the tweet library
    event EventHandler<ResponseTweetSearchArgs>
    TweetSearchCompleted;

  }
}
```

5. Go to **MyTweet.Model** project now and add the reference to the **MyTweet. Model.Contracts** project (**Add Reference**):

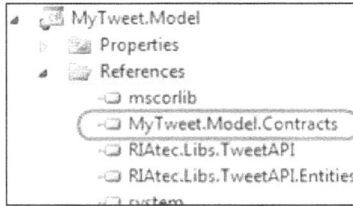

6. Make the `TweetModel` class inherit from the `IModel` interface (in this case, all the `IModel` methods are already implemented):

```
(...)
using MyTweet.Model.Contracts;

namespace MyTweet.Model
{
  public class TweetModel : IModel
  {
    (...)
  }
(...)
}
```

7. Add support to MEF. We intend to export our `Model`, therefore, we should not leave the **MyTweet.Model** project.

8. Add the reference to the **System.ComponentModel.Composition** assembly. To do so, go to **Add | New Reference** and then select **.NET Assemblies**.

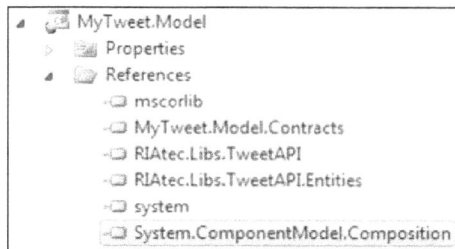

9. Mark the Model as exportable with the `IModel` contract:

```
using System.ComponentModel.Composition;

namespace MyTweet.Model
{
  [Export(typeof(IModel))]
  public class TweetModel : IModel

  (…)
}
```

Now, let us move to the ViewModel.

10. Eliminate the reference to the model implementation and replace it with the reference to the project containing the model contract. That is, we change **MyTweet.Model** to **MyTweet.Model.Contracts** (**Add | New Reference | Project**):

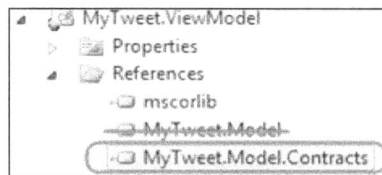

11. As in the previous example, add the libraries for MEF support: **System. ComponentModel.Composition** and **System.ComponentModel. CompositionInitialization**:

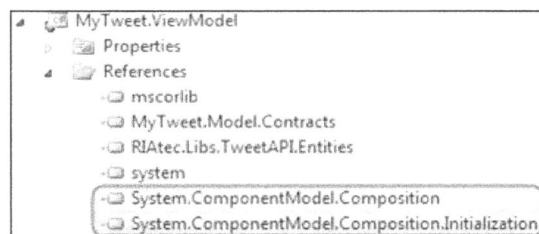

12. In our `SearchViewModel` class, remove the `using` in the model implementation and add that of the contract (`using MyTweet.Model. Contracts`).

On the other hand, the `_model` member variable now becomes a variable of the `IModel` type:

```
using MyTweet.Model.Contracts;

namespace MyTweet.ViewModel
{
  public class SearchViewModel : INotifyPropertyChanged
  {
    #region fields

    private IModel _model;

    #endregion
    (...)
  }
(...)
}
```

13. On the `ViewModel` constructor, indicate that MEF is in charge of searching for the implementation for this interface:

```
[ImportingConstructor]
public SearchViewModel(IModel model)
{
  _model = model;
  _model.TweetSearchCompleted += new EventHandler
    <ResponseTweetSearchArgs>(_model_TweetSearchCompleted);
}
```

14. To expose the ViewModel with the View, an interface could also be defined. However, as Shawn Wildermuth points out (see links at the end of the chapter), it is not worthwhile to build interfaces, since the dependence between View and ViewModel is not strict (declarative binding). Instead, we define a class of constants that identify the ViewModel:

   ° We will define this class in a library project that will be named **Common (Add New Project | Silverlight Class Library)**. It will be referenced in the ViewModel project, **MyTweet.ViewModel** and in the View project, **MyTweets.View**. Thanks to this, if we want to create a sample ViewModel, we will not need to add a reference to **MyTweetViewModel**.

◦ Also, add a class called `ViewModelTypes` (**Add | New Class**):

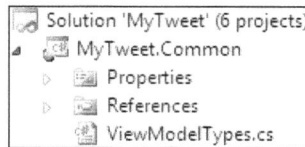

◦ With the aim of identifying the different ViewModels, this new class will contain a text string to identify each ViewModel belonging to the application:

```
/// <summary>
/// Contains constants to identify view models, when they are
/// imported using MEF.
/// </summary>
public class ViewModelTypes
{
  /// <summary>
  /// Identifies the SearchViewModel.
  /// </summary>
  public const string SearchViewModel = "SearchViewModel";
}
```

15. Back to ViewModel, add the Export. As identifier, we will use our class of constants:

```
[Export(ViewModelTypes.SearchViewModel)]
public class SearchViewModel : INotifyPropertyChanged
```

16. Now, let us focus on the view.

17. Add the reference to the common library that has just been created. Also, include the libraries for MEF support (in this case, they are **System. ComponentModel.Composition** and **System.ComponentModel. Composition.Initialization**). The last one allows us to call the method so that it launches the matching between contracts and parts:

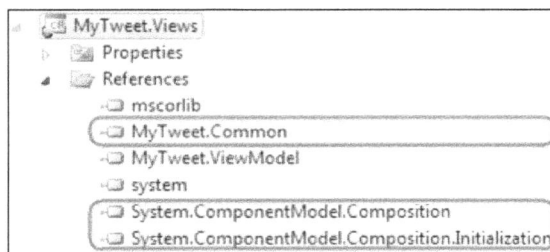

18. Continuing with references, up to this point we have always added references to the contracts project. Now it is time to add the ViewModel and Model implementations, `MyTweet.ViewModel` and `MyTweet.Model`, respectively. This will allow MEF to find the implementations that match the corresponding contracts. It also makes it possible to have the rest of the modules decoupled from the implementation, since they only depend on the defined contract:

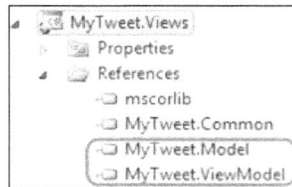

19. Remove the line where we instantiated the ViewModel from the view constructor:

```
public SearchView()
{
    InitializeComponent();

    this.DataContext = new SearchViewModel();
}
```

20. Then, define a property which assigns the ViewModel to the `DataContext`, adding the `Import` annotation, which shows how to import the ViewModel. Therefore, when the ViewModel is instantiated, the set accessor of the property will be triggered and the ViewModel will be assigned as view context:

```
using MyTweet.Common;

namespace MyTweet.Views.Views
{
    public partial class SearchView : Page
    {
        public SearchView()
        {
            InitializeComponent();
        }

        /// <summary>
        /// Sets the view model for this view using MEF.
        /// </summary>
```

```
/// <value>The view model.</value>
[Import(ViewModelTypes.SearchViewModel)]
public object ViewModel
{
  set
  {
    DataContext = value;
  }
  get
  {
    return DataContext;
  }
}
(...)
..}
}
```

21. In the view constructor, make a MEF call, CompositionInitializer. SatisfyImports(this), to match between imports and exports:

```
public SearchView()
{
  InitializeComponent();
  CompositionInitializer.SatisfyImports(this);
}
```

We are done! What are the advantages of the additional work we have done? The modules get decoupled, which means the following:

- To replace the implementation of a module with another one, we would only have to implement a new library with classes that accomplished those defined in the contracts. In other words, this change would not have any impact on other modules.

- If we want to perform unit tests (we will deal with them in depth in *Chapter 7, Testing your LOB Application*), we could, for instance, replace the Model layer with a Mock (a class with sample data). Thus, we will only have to worry about the fact that the Mock may implement the IModel contract.

In relation to the way in which we have referenced the implementations of contracts in the View project, we could have opted for a dynamic way of replacing modules — that is by wrapping them in XAP files and downloading them on demand. For further information, please visit http://codebetter.com/glennblock/2010/03/08/building-hello-mef-part-iv-deploymentcatalog/. This approach can be useful for breaking the XAP into several modules and reducing its size and load time. Also, it allows our application to be extensible through plugins.

Solution and folder structure

In this section, we will deal with how to structure our project with respect to physical and solution folders to name our projects, so that they help us to identify them quickly.

At the beginning of a small project, this point may not have much importance, but as it evolves, a bad folder structure or name convention can cause management difficulties (not to mention if the project is medium-sized or even larger).

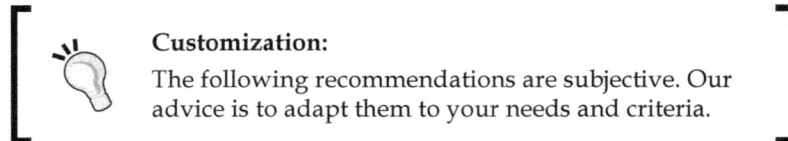

> **Customization:**
> The following recommendations are subjective. Our advice is to adapt them to your needs and criteria.

It's now time to define every item:

- **Folder**: It is a directory we create in our hard disk drive.
- **Solution**: It is created with Visual Studio and embraces several projects.
- **Solution folder**: Inside a solution, we can create several solution folders, which help us to structure them. They are logical, that is, they are not physically created as a directory on our HDD.
- **Project**: A Visual Studio project contains the code and resources we need. It can be Web or Silverlight, type library or application, and so on.
- **Project folder**: Within a project, we can also define subfolders that will make the task of structuring it easier. These are physical. In other words, when we create them, the corresponding subdirectories are also created in our HDD.

In order to define our structure, we are going to base it upon the following sample criteria:

- Our company is called RIATec
- The project we are going to create is called TweetSearch
- We are going to create a library of our own, so as to manage TweetSearch, as we intend to reuse this library in future projects
- We are going to use third-party libraries from Galasoft (MVVM Light Toolkit)

To begin with, define the folder structure that will be used. The first level would be as follows:

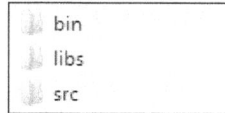

```
bin
libs
src
```

- **bin**: This is the place for the results of building all our projects (binary). Therefore, if we need to add a reference to a project that is not present in our solution, there is only a path to add it, that is the `bin` folder. To make this step effective, we will have to change the `Output Directory` property and make it point to the new `bin` folder in every Visual Studio project we create.

- **libs:** In this folder, we must copy all third-party DLLs, which we intend to use (for instance, those of MVVM Light Toolkit by Galasoft). Thereby, all our projects that need to add third-party references will take them from just one place and this helps to avoid problems. Another advantage is that we can see which third-party DLLs we are using.

- **src**: In this folder, we will group solutions, projects, and source code. That is to say, everything in this folder is our own creation.

  In this `src` folder, we must create a second level. Every folder in this level will take a prefix composed of our company name, followed by a dot. In our example, we will have the following:

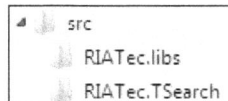

```
src
  RIATec.libs
  RIATec.TSearch
```

  - ° `CompanyName.Libs`: In our example, this would be **RIATec.Libs**. Here, we will add solutions and library projects, which we want to create and probably reuse in other projects. In this case, we will create the library project with our tweet browser. This allows us to have all our own libraries grouped together in a clear way, and be able to reuse them in subsequent projects.

  - ° `CompanyName.ProjectName`: In this example, it is called **RIATec. TSearch**. All the functionalities that depend on our project `TweetSearch` are stored here and are not easily reusable. As in the previous point, the main advantage is that functionalities are grouped together and we are able to find everything quickly.

> Short names: In our example, we have decided to shorten names (`TweetSearch` to `TSearch`) to avoid problems with routes whose length is over 255 characters.

Now, let's focus on how to create the main solution.

The easiest way to begin is from a blank solution (**Blank Solution**), which we can shape without tying ourselves to pre-established names and projects. We will call it `RIATec.TSearch`. The solution will be stored in this folder:

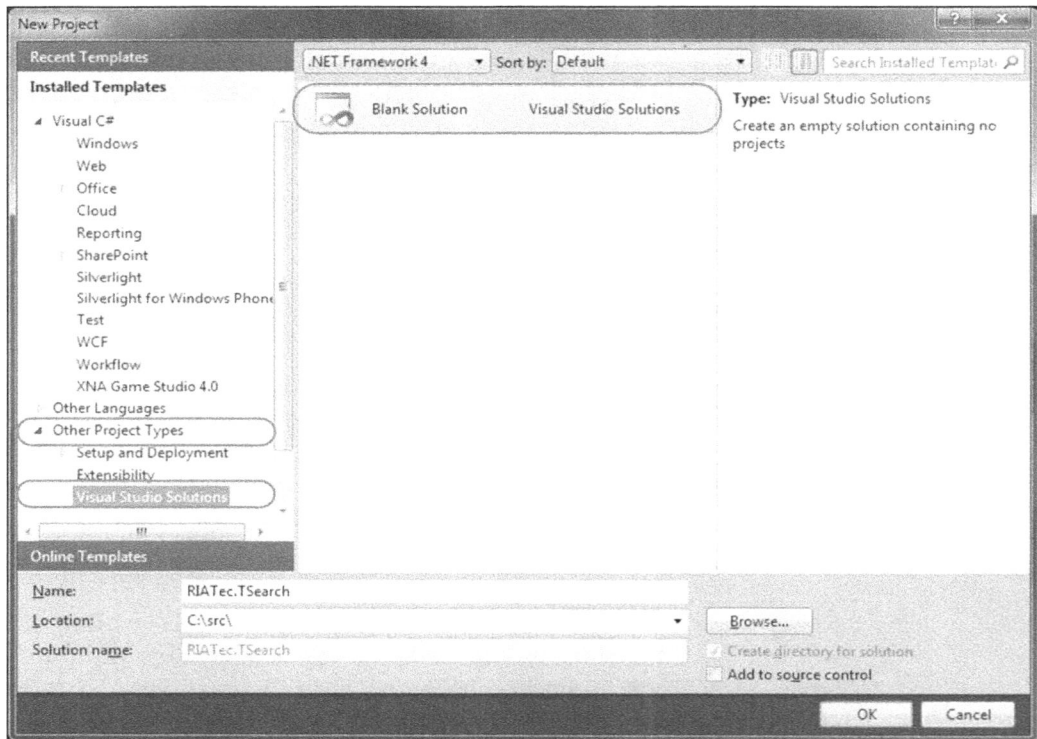

Then, create a series of solution folders that will help to structure our solution. To do so, right-click and choose the option **Add** from the contextual menu. Then, select **New Solution Folder**:

New Project...		Add	▸
Existing Project...		Add Solution to Source Control...	
New Web Site...		Paste	Ctrl+V
Existing Web Site...		Rename	
New Item...	Ctrl+Shift+A	Open Folder in Windows Explorer	
Existing Item...	Shift+Alt+A	Properties	Alt+Enter
New Solution Folder		Add Solution to Subversion	

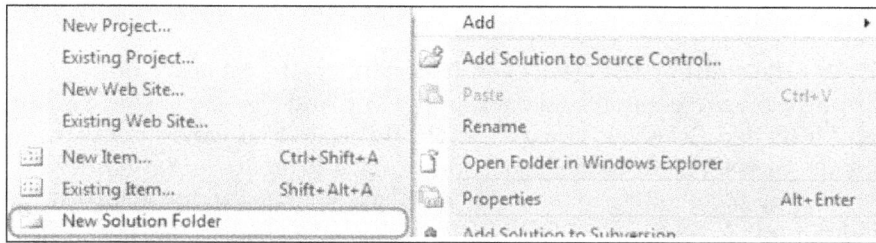

Create the following solution folders:

- **Common**: Here, the projects containing common dependencies are added. For example, the definitions of the messages we make.

- **Model**: In this solution, there will be those projects related to the model (contracts, implementation of the model, and mock of the model if it is necessary).

- **Modules**: It includes the different modules in which the application is divided.

- **Tests**: Under this solution, we can add the **TestRunners** (simple apps, which allow us to try a particular functionality manually). Here, unit tests projects will also be included (see *Chapter 7*, *Testing your LOB Application*).

- **Server**: Here, projects which have to be executed at the server-side are created. For instance, the project which will host our Silverlight application.

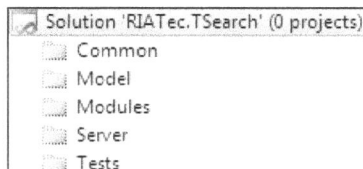

```
Solution 'RIATec.TSearch' (0 projects)
    Common
    Model
    Modules
    Server
    Tests
```

Separate the view in an independent solution:

Another interesting option is to separate the project(s) containing the View layer in a different solution. Therefore, a graphic designer will have clearly enough field where s/he must work. Moreover, the **View** layer could also be changed for another one so as to use it in a different platform and reuse all business and data-related modules.

Let's now create the following projects:

1. Under the solution root (**RIATec.TSearch**), create the entry point. This is the application project that will contain the app and the MainPage. This project will be called (**RIATec.TSearch.Shell**). Indicate that we do not want to create an associated web project. Our goal is to create it in the following step, indicating localization and names more appropriate to the structure that is being built.

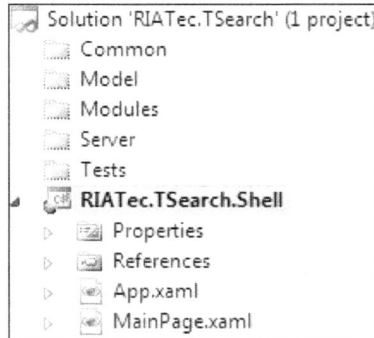

2. Next, create the web project, which will host the Silverlight application. For that, we need to create a web project under the solution folder called **Server**. The best way to do this is right-clicking on this solution folder and selecting **Add** and **New Project** in the contextual menu. Choose the **Web** template and the **ASP.NET Web application** option in the dialogue that appears then. This project will be called **SW.TSearch.Server.Web**. As it can be seen, the name of the **Server** folder has been included in the solution folder:

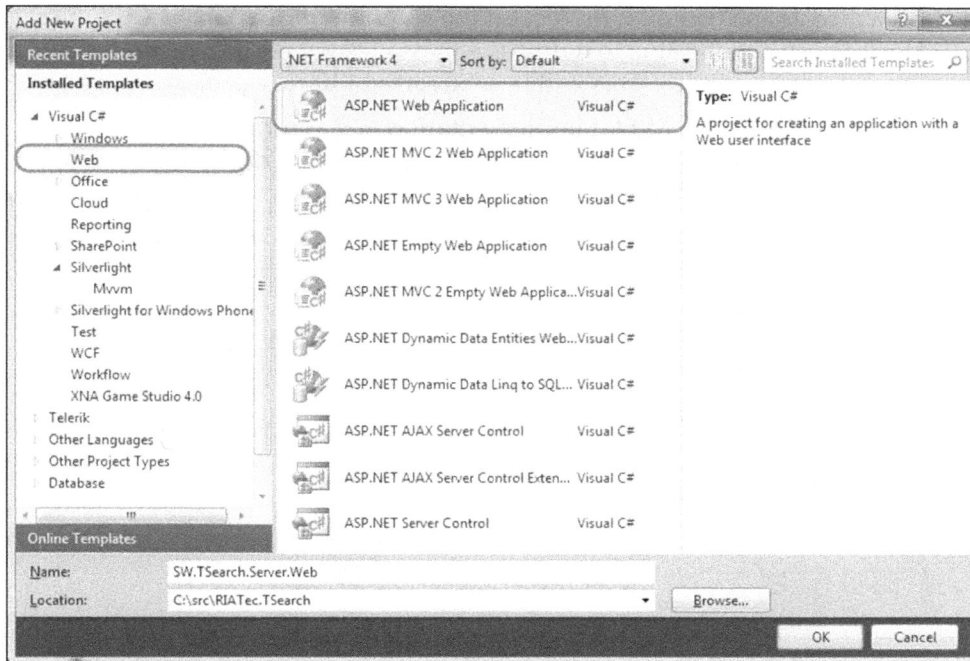

3. Right-click on the new project we have created, select **Properties** and, on the **Silverlight Applications** tab, press the button **Add...** to indicate we want to bind a new web project, **RIATec.TSearch.Shell**:

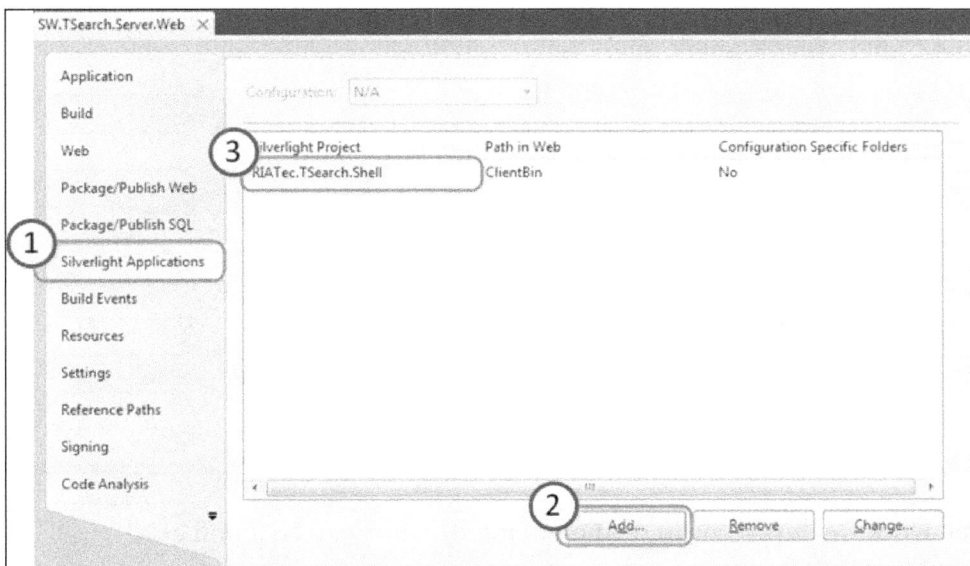

4. Now, create the common project on the solution folder named **Common**. Here, we should be able to define the messages we need to communicate to the different modules. This will be a Silverlight library project.

5. The project with the Model implementation and contracts will go to the solution folder called **Model**. This will also be a Silverlight library project.

6. The projects with the implementation of every model will go in the **Modules** folder. In our case, we will have a module to search and display tweets.

7. The final solution is illustrated in the following screenshot:

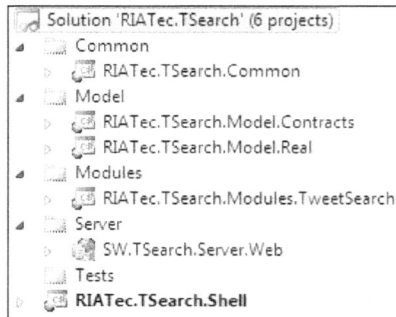

8. Finally, we just need to see how to redirect a project output to the **Bin** root folder we have already defined. We will see how to do this using the `Shell` project. Click on the `Shell` project's properties; then choose the **Build** tab and indicate a relative path for the **Output path**, such as **..\..\..\bin**:

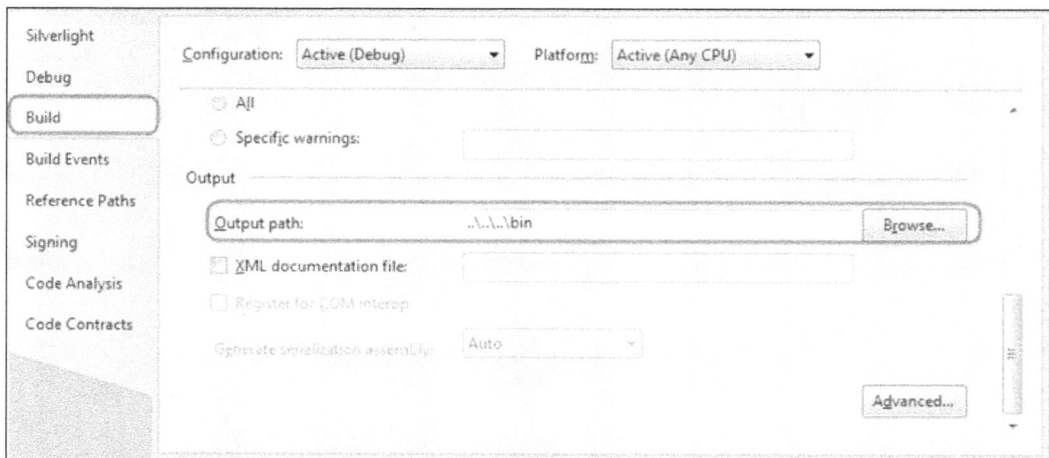

All the work we have done in relation to the structure can be found at www.packtpub.com.

LOB application case study: applying what we have learned

Let us apply what we have learned thanks to our sample application. To do so, we will first build the adequate structure for the project and then implement the MVVM pattern on it. Instead of just sticking to the structure, the first page of the application (`MyBookings`) has been implemented by using a mock data module. In the next chapter, the real RIA Services layer will substitute for the layer mentioned previously.

We have made some changes (refactoring) to adapt to the defined pattern and the structures. Some of the changes are as follows:

- Changes in the structure of the solution (which reflects full names, introduces solution folders, and so on)
- A new library has been introduced to adapt Silverlight navigation framework to the MVVM pattern (navigation now becomes ViewModel's responsibility)
- Floor and room administration windows have been unified in order to take advantage of and show how to edit inline in a `DataGrid`

Project structure

Let's start by reviewing the physical project structure, then the solution, solution folders, and the application project naming convention.

Folder structure

The first level of folders have been created:

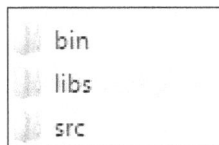

```
bin
libs
src
```

Under the `src` folder, two levels have to be distinguished:

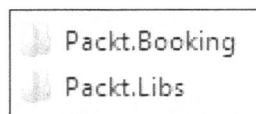

```
Packt.Booking
Packt.Libs
```

1. The first one is for the mail application, **Packt.Booking**.

2. The second one is for those libraries that are likely to be reusable in other projects, **Packt.Libs**.

Regarding names, we have chosen the following:

- **Packt.Booking** (follows the format *CompanyName.ApplicationName*)
- **Packt.Libs** (follows the format *CompanyName.Libraries*)

Main solution structure

Let us analyze the main solution. It can be found at `src\PacktBooking\PackBooking.sln`.

As shown in the following screenshot, the first level contains four solution folders (**Common, Model, Modules,** and **Server**) and an entry project (**Packt.Booking.Shell**):

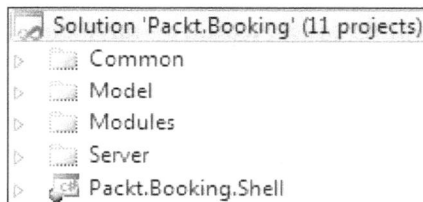

When looking at the second level, we find the following:

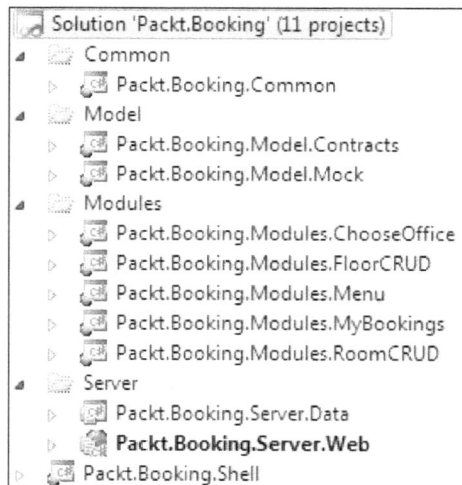

- **Common**: Classes and common components that are specific to the application (for example, message definition):
  - ○ **Packt.Booking.Common**: It contains converters, entities, messages, navigation help, resources, and styles.
- **Model**: Under this folder, we find everything related to the application model:
  - ○ **Packt.Booking.Model.Contracts**: Interface defining model operations.
  - ○ **Pactk.Bookings.Model.Mock**: Implementation of a mock model (using sample data, it simulates the real model by implementing the interface defined in the contracts project).
- **Modules**: Our decision has been to break every window in a module (every project of this type includes the associated View and ViewModel):
  - ○ **Packt.Booking.Modules.ChooseOffice**: Window where the building we want to edit is chosen.
  - ○ **Packt.Bookings.Modules.FloorsCRUD**: Windows which allow floors edition as well as rooms edition in a building.
  - ○ **Packt.Bookings.Modules.Menu**: This window implements the navigation menu of the application.
  - ○ **Packt.Bookings.Modules.MyBookings**: It allows a user to manage his/her reservations.
- **Server**: Here, those non-Silverlight projects executed on the server are stored:
  - ○ **Packt.Bookings.Server.Data**: In this project, the technology accessing our data source (seen in *Chapter 5, RIA Services Data Access*) is implemented.
  - ○ **Packt.Bookings.Server.Web**: In this project, we will have the website acting as host for our Silverlight application. In addition, we will expose services to interact with the data source defined in the previous project.

The way in which View, ViewModel, and Model are bound is the same as we used when building the example of the Twitter reader, based on interfaces and MEF.

Libraries

Let's review our own reusable libraries that we have built for the project.

Packt.Libs.Navigation

As in the previous chapter, Silverlight incorporates a very powerful navigation framework that also integrates with the history of different web browsers, and also allows to pass parameters via query string. How is this integrated with MVVM? After a first analysis, we have the following answers:

- Framework is integrated on the View level

- Decisions such as checking if we can navigate away from the actual view (for instance, if there are changes pending to save) or if we can navigate to a given view (for example, if the user has permissions) belong to the ViewModel layer

- If the URL contains parameters, the ideal solution will be that the ViewModel could process it without the intervention of View

What are the possible solutions?

1. It could be possible to use Light Toolkit Messenger to send messages when we want to initialize ViewModel or check if we can leave the current page. Even though this solution is valid for MVVM, it can be a little cumbersome to implement and maintain.

2. Another possible approach to the problem may be the transference of the Navigation Framework instance in execution to the ViewModel from the Code-Behind. This may cause two issues. The first one, although not so serious, means that we are introducing code in the View; the second one implies that we are making our ViewModel depend on a UI element and this increases the difficulty of implementing automatic unit tests.

3. Finally, working upon it a little more, it could be possible to encapsulate a framework functionality in an interface, which is non-dependent on implementation details, and assign it to the ViewModel declaratively through a Silverlight Behavior. In this way, we avoid the implementation of code in the Code-Behind, and the ViewModel is consequently not bound to any UI element (in order to make unit tests, a mock could be developed to implement the navigation interface that substitutes for the Navigation Framework interface).

Due to its elegance and simplicity, we have opted for the third solution. As a starting point, we have taken Robert Garfoot's (Microsoft application development consultant) implementation (`http://bit.ly/bg7Lg7`) and we have added support to establish the home page, as well as the access to the query string parameters, from the ViewModel.

Because of space limitations, we will just mention how to use the library. In case you are interested in knowing how it works internally, you can check the following URL: `http://bit.ly/cH3FfZ`.

The navigation solution we have built contains three projects:

1. `Packt.Libs.Navigation.Contracts`: It contains the definition of the navigation interface (agnostic implementation), as well as interfaces for the ViewModels to implement and obtain support to navigation.

2. `Packt.Libs.Navigation`: The particular implementation to support Silverlight Navigation Framework.

3. `TestRunner.App`: A simple example of how to consume this library is based upon the Navigation Framework sample that can be found in Silverlight.NET (`http://bit.ly/pyy2ho`). It contains two pages, one with a list of people, and the other with the details about every person (their identifier passes through query string). But, in this case, thanks to the MVVM pattern, we can view it the way we prefer (via ViewModel).

   ° Set up a main page
   ° Launch a navigation event from the ViewModel
   ° Process the parameters of the navigation URL

Let's check the entire interaction on a high level:

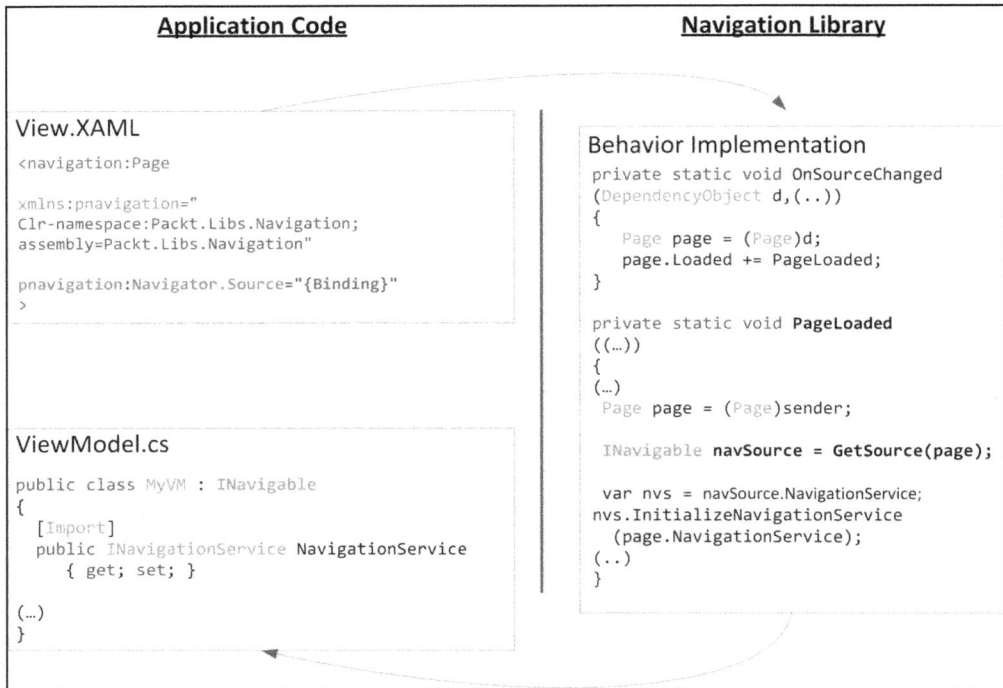

Application Code	**Navigation Library**

View.XAML
 	
`<navigation:Page`
 	
`xmlns:pnavigation="`
`Clr-namespace:Packt.Libs.Navigation;`
`assembly=Packt.Libs.Navigation"`
 	
`pnavigation:Navigator.Source="{Binding}"`
`>`
	Behavior Implementation
	`private static void OnSourceChanged`
	`(DependencyObject d,(..))`
	`{`
	`    Page page = (Page)d;`
	`    page.Loaded += PageLoaded;`
	`}`
	
	`private static void `**`PageLoaded`**
	`((...))`
	`{`
	`(...)`
	` Page page = (Page)sender;`
	
	` INavigable navSource = GetSource(page);`
	
	` var nvs = navSource.NavigationService;`
	`nvs.InitializeNavigationService`
	`  (page.NavigationService);`
	`(..)`
	`}`

ViewModel.cs
 	
`public class MyVM : INavigable`
`{`
`  [Import]`
`  public INavigationService NavigationService`
`    { get; set; }`
 	
`(...)`
`}`	

Let's go step by step:

1. First, add the DLL of the projects, both contract (**Packt.Libs.Navigation. Contracts**) and implementation (**Packt.Libs.Navigation**):

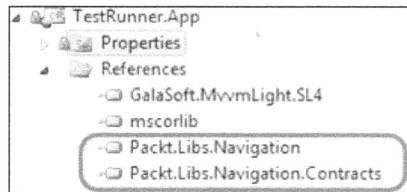

2. In our first ViewModel, in the people list, implement the `Inavigable` interface, defined in `Packt.Libs.Navigation.Contracts`. It exposes a `NavigationService` (so as to navigate to other pages), the URL parameters (that we will see next), as well as two methods, which will allow us to cancel the navigation to a different page and detect when the page has been loaded:

```
public class CustomerListVM : ViewModelBase, INavigable, IHomePage
{
  (...)
  #region INavigable

  public IDictionary<string, string> QueryString { get; set; }

  [Import]
  public INavigationService NavigationService { get; set; }

  public bool CanNavigateAway(Uri DestinationPage)
  {
    return true;
  }

  public void NavigatedToThisPage()
  {

  }

  #endregion INavigable

  (...)
}
```

3. As this ViewModel is also our home page, the interface IHomePage must be
    implemented and, in the function it exposes, we will return "true" indicating
    it is the home page:

```
public class CustomerListVM : ViewModelBase, INavigable, IHomePage
{
  (...)
  #region IHomePage

  /// <summary>
  public bool IsHomePage
  {
    get { return true;}
  }

  #endregion

}
```

4. `NavigationService` is initialized via MEF (import). Therefore, we must add `SatisfyImport` in the ViewModel constructor (we could as well call the `SatisfyImports` from the view):

```
public CustomerListVM()
{
  CompositionInitializer.SatisfyImports(this);
}
```

5. Now, in the `CustomerListPage.xaml`, the namespace of our library must be added. Then, assign the ViewModel to the browser. (This behavior is internally bound to the page event `loaded` to ensure the `DataContext` is available. At this point, the ViewModel is assigned the navigation instance):

```
<navigation:Page
  x:Class="TestRunner.App.Views.CustomerListPage"
  xmlns:pnavigation="clr-namespace:Packt.Libs.Navigation;
  assembly=Packt.Libs.Navigation"
  pnavigation:Navigator.Source="{Binding}"
  (...)

>
```

6. Now, if we want to navigate from the ViewModel to a different page (that is, if the user clicks on a customer link), we only have to use the property we have implemented:

```
string url = NavigationHelper.CustomerURL(idparam);

NavigationService.Navigate(url);
```

7. The page and the `CustomerDetailVM` ViewModel work in a similar way, except if we do not implement the `IHomePage` interface (it is not the home page) and we expect a query string parameter (identifier of the people whose details we want to see). It can be processed as follows:

```
public void NavigatedToThisPage()
{
  // 1. Check the parameters
  // 2. extract the id
  // 3. Perform the load and the binding
  if
    (QueryString.ContainsKey(NavigationHelper.
      CustomerDetailVMParams.idParam))
    {
```

```
        string idvalue =
        QueryString
        [NavigationHelper.CustomerDetailVMParams.idParam];
        int id = Convert.ToInt32(idvalue);

        CurrentCustomer = _model.GetCustomer(id);
    }
}
```

8. To make URL management easier, a static class has been implemented. It maps the addresses to constant value and implements functions to return those URLs containing parameters:

```
public static class NavigationHelper
{

  public static string CustomerListURL()
  {
    return "Customers";
  }

  public static string CustomerURL(int customerID)
  {
    return string.Format("Customer/{0}", customerID);
  }

  public static class CustomerDetailVMParams
  {
    public static string idParam = "myid";
  }

}
```

Packt.Libs.Threading

As our reservations project is momentarily going to use a mock model (sample data), real asynchronous calls are not going to be made. From a developer's point of view, this can be really difficult, since it can abuse calls without noticing the impact it may have on the application usability (for example, timeout).

To solve this, the `AsyncCallSimulator` has been implemented. It adds a random timeout to every call.

Packt.Libs.Utils

In this library, we include those help classes which either do not match any particular .NET namespace or for whom it is not worth creating a project. In our sample, we have included a class to compare date ranges. Two implementations are offered. The first one is for Silverlight applications and the other one is for applications and code at server-side.

This functionality is used to check if a room is available or if it is possible to make a reservation.

Utils library will grow over time, incorporating more help classes.

Packt.Libs.Windows

In this class, we include those controls and classes related to the UI. We have the following:

- `ComboRebindable`: Silverlight ComboBox poses a problem if the collection to which it is assigned changes (that is, when choosing a city and changing the edition list). This class inherits from ComboBox and solves this issue.

- `ProgressBar`: It is the substitute for the BusyIndicator in Silverlight Toolkit. The reason why we use it is that, at the time of the writing of this book, the Silverlight Toolkit version does not work properly with Silverlight 5.

- `IDialogService`: It allows us to show notification and confirmation messages from the ViewModel in a simple way (without coupling). There is a more advanced solution, which permits us to perform the same operation with ChildWindows (`http://bit.ly/54tFcn`).

Summary

Establishing an architecture is a time-consuming task and adds complexity to our project. In exchange, we get some benefits as follows:

- We can give access of the code repository to a graphic designer so that he can create or modify a window without any knowledge about development

- It gives us a possibility for our business logic to be tested via automatic unit tests

- It is easier to make modifications since, for instance, a change in the UI does not have to affect the business logic

- It permits reuse of some functionalities in different parts of the app, or even in other apps

Talking in "ilities" terms, we get improvements in testability, productivity, maintainability, and readability.

Focusing in Silverlight, we have seen how the MVVM pattern allows us to declare the presentation logic in a declarative way, and how libraries and frameworks such as MVVM Light Toolkit and MEF are perfect travelmates.

Additional resources

The area of applications architecture is very exciting, more so if it is backed by a powerful technology, such as Silverlight. However, it requires a lot of study and practice time, to assimilate concepts and check the approaches that best fit your application type and development ring. There is no universal solution. To learn more, refer to the following links:

- Introduction to the MVVM pattern (`http://bit.ly/JYJEL`): Even though this article refers to Silverlight 2 and does not include commands, it is a good starting point to understand certain concepts

- Mix10 MVVM (`http://bit.ly/h2Qdz5`): Session on introduction to MVVM by Laurent Bugniong

- Introduction to MEF (`http://bit.ly/9Izl6b`): A good article to understand the basics

- GalaSoft - MVVM Light Toolkit (`http://bit.ly/TkVcM`): Here you can find these libraries, as well as links to videos and articles

- Mix 11 MVVM Deep Dive (`http://bit.ly/fVTxcV`)

- Firestarter – Silverlight RIA Services and MVVM (`http://bit.ly/hWleiP`): Interesting introduction to MVVM and RIA Services including a downloadable simple application

5

RIA Services Data Access

Most **Line of Business** (**LOB**) applications have to interact with a database. The recommended technology in order to cover this interaction is **RIA Services**. In this chapter, we will learn how it works both in basic and more advanced scenarios. Later, in *Chapter 11, Testing*, you will learn how to implement security with this technology.

Accessing data

Data displayed or updated by a user is stored in a database. In our case, as we are oriented towards Microsoft technologies, it is stored in the SQL Server database.

If you are a veteran, you will remember how connections opened in Windows developments via databases from the application itself, and queries were executed. This was possible as these applications were in the same local network as our server.

When web technologies and globalization came in, things got more complicated. Our database server, due to security reasons, is located behind a firewall, so only certain users/servers can access it. Moreover, our application is executed in environments and languages which do not allow direct access to data, for instance, a web browser and JavaScript language. In order to solve this issue, there were two common options:

- Legacy web applications used to make a post of the page on the server, accessing the database (no AJAX calls), at that stage. This was an easy approach, although it had a limited usability. In order to perform any operations related to database interaction, the user had to wait for the page to be fully sent to the server and come back to their browser.

- For modern websites, an added option was to build a web services layout which implemented the most common operations to access data. Our web application could make asynchronous calls via AJAX, against those web services and access data. Thanks to all this, the broadband consumption is now reduced and the user is allowed to work without having to wait for the answer.

This sort of solution poses a few challenges that need to be highlighted:

- **Validations**: It doesn't make sense to perform all validations on the server side. Hence a few are implemented (namely, figures related to a role, client side, and so on). What happens if the information gets to the server? The process has to be repeated, as we cannot trust the information which comes from the client side (a malicious user could prepare a packet and send it, pretending it is the application in execution).

- **Context**: Nowadays, UIs are rich. By using a single window, it is possible to access different data entities, and working with this can get complex.

- **Configuration**: Configuring a service's layout is not trivial at all. In the case of Microsoft technologies, we have to know about **Windows Communication Foundation (WCF)**.

- **Security**: How can we be sure about the identity of a user? How can we be sure about the information channel? We will deal with this in *Chapter 11, Consuming Web Services*.

Microsoft is best to solve these kinds of challenges in RIA Services. Let us see how it works.

RIA Services pieces

Let us begin by defining RIA Services.

Formal definition (http://bit.ly/nmrOA9):

> *Microsoft WCF RIA Services simplifies the traditional n-tier application pattern by bringing together the ASP.NET and Silverlight platforms. RIA Services provides a pattern to write application logic that runs on the mid-tier and controls access to data for queries, changes and custom operations. It also provides end-to-end support for common tasks such as data validation, authentication and roles by integrating with Silverlight components on the client and ASP.NET on the mid-tier.*

Now, we will define it more informally, according to our experience. The most usual case is that we have a database, probably running under SQL Server, and we create an Entity Framework model. If we limit ourselves to the server, it could be possible to throw queries from here and everything will be ready. What happens when using Silverlight? These are executed in a client machine within a sandbox, and are not able to make those queries. The most common solution is to create a services layer implementing the most common operations, as mentioned in the previous section. This requires a lot of effort from us.

From the implementation point of view, it will be necessary to define all the CRUD operations manually and configure our web services layer. Regarding the client-side implementation, we must take into account that, when generating a proxy against our services, the entities are obtained. But what happens to validations? Normally, they have to be manually replicated in the client layer.

It would be great to have a services layer generator capable of doing the following:

- Generate a code base, taking the model that has been created as the original source. This code base should make use of CRUD methods that could be invoked from the Silverlight application; extract the entities structure manually, and infer validations based upon the model (for instance, no nullable fields, required field validations, varchar [XX], maximum length, and so on).

- Let us customize and add new validations in a straightforward and easy manner.

- Automatically copy entities and validations to the client side of the Silverlight applications, which saves time and effort, as it will not be necessary to copy these validations manually.

- Give the possibility to implement the concept of DataContext in the client side. This allows us to extract *a piece of the database*, including its relations, and manage it only as a *Unit for work*. This means we can navigate using different elements, modify those we consider appropriate, and, later, submit all the changes.

- Avoid the complexity of configuring our services layer, generating the most common case on our behalf.

All this and much more can be obtained with RIA Services.

> RIA Services is not only limited to the ADO.NET Entity Framework. It can also be configured to work with other technologies (for instance, NHibernate), although it requires additional effort. If you are interested in knowing more about this topic, you can go to `http://bit.ly/jkdgtu`.

Let us now define the basic pieces of our jigsaw and, in the next section, we will implement our first sample. In an analogy with a classic development, note the following:

- **Domain Service**: It can be placed at the same level as the web service implemented to show our data layer. RIA Services generate an initial Domain Service with basic operations that we will expand to fulfill all our needs.

- **Entities**: Class structure the entities and validations of our model. These entities are available on both server side and client side.

- **DomainContext**: It is the stateful client-side representation of a Domain Service. It includes data and relationships and operations to load/update entities.

Creating a Domain Service and consuming it from a Silverlight application

Let us get into practice so as to understand all that we have learnt in the previous sections. We will create a new project from scratch, based upon the Silverlight Application template. Why not use a template which is more oriented to RIA Services, such as Business Application? The goal is to clarify all the necessary steps to create an RIA Services project.

Let us begin from the Database First approach, using a simple database. The following image shows a simple database:

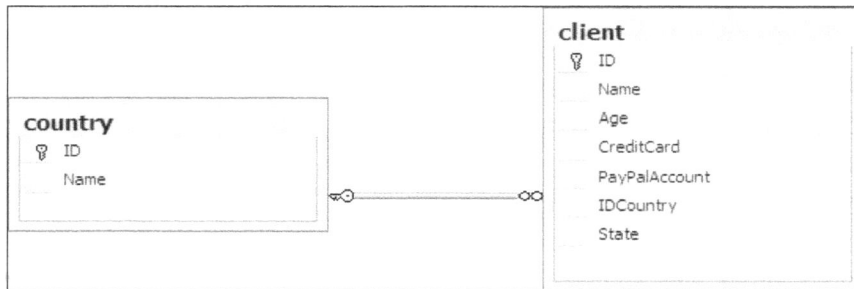

As a summary, these will be the steps to follow: First, the project will be created. Second, the Entity Framework model will be added. Later, the Domain Service will be added, and, to finish, this will be bound to our Silverlight project.

Let us begin by creating the project and adding the Entity Framework model:

1. First, click on **Create new project**. Then, choose **Silverlight application**. Name the project SimpleDB and point out that an associated web project must be created.

2. Create the Entity Framework model, which will work against the database, defined previously. Right-click on the web project and select **Add New Item**. Choose **ADO.NET Entity Model** and name it MyModel, as shown in the following screenshot:

> If you don't see the option of creating a ADO.NET Entity Data Model, download the ADO.NET Entity Framework in the Package Manager Console using the command
> `install-package EntityFramework`

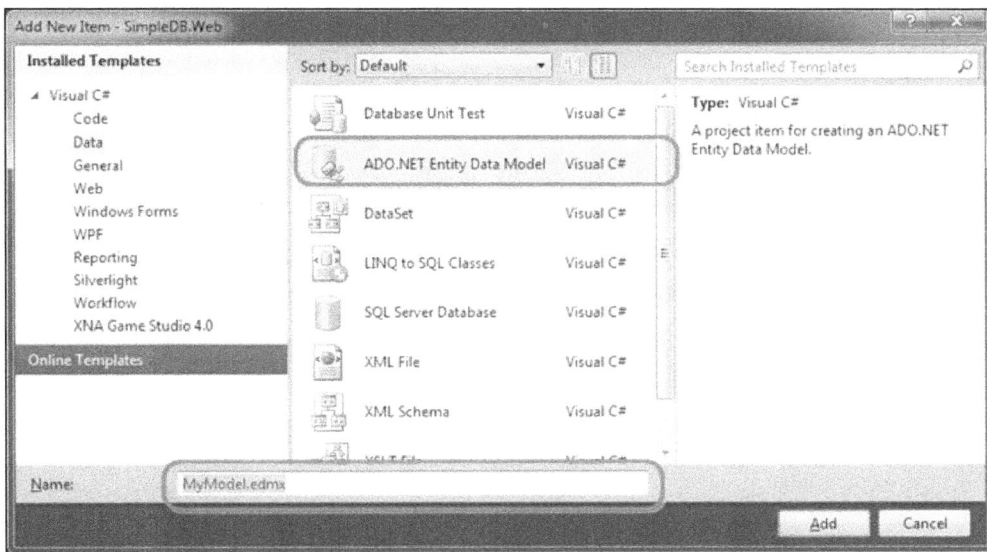

3. Now, a wizard appears and asks us if we can begin from an empty model, or rather, generate it from an existing database. Choose **Generate from database**, as shown in the following screenshot:

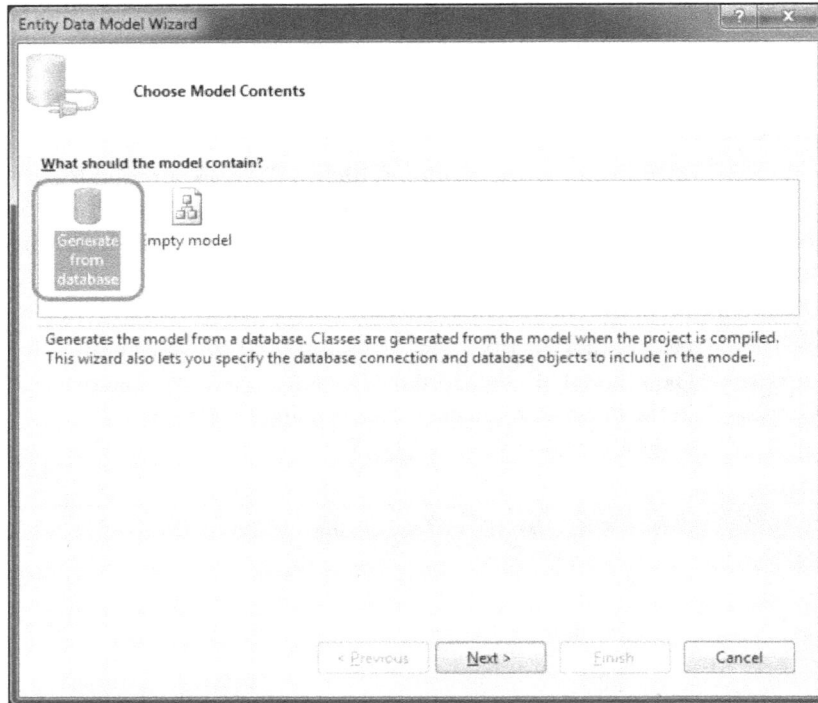

4. The next page in the wizard allows us to configure the connection to the databases we choose. Here, the last connections that we have used are displayed. In our case, we want to create a new connection. Click on **New Connection**, as shown in the next screenshot:

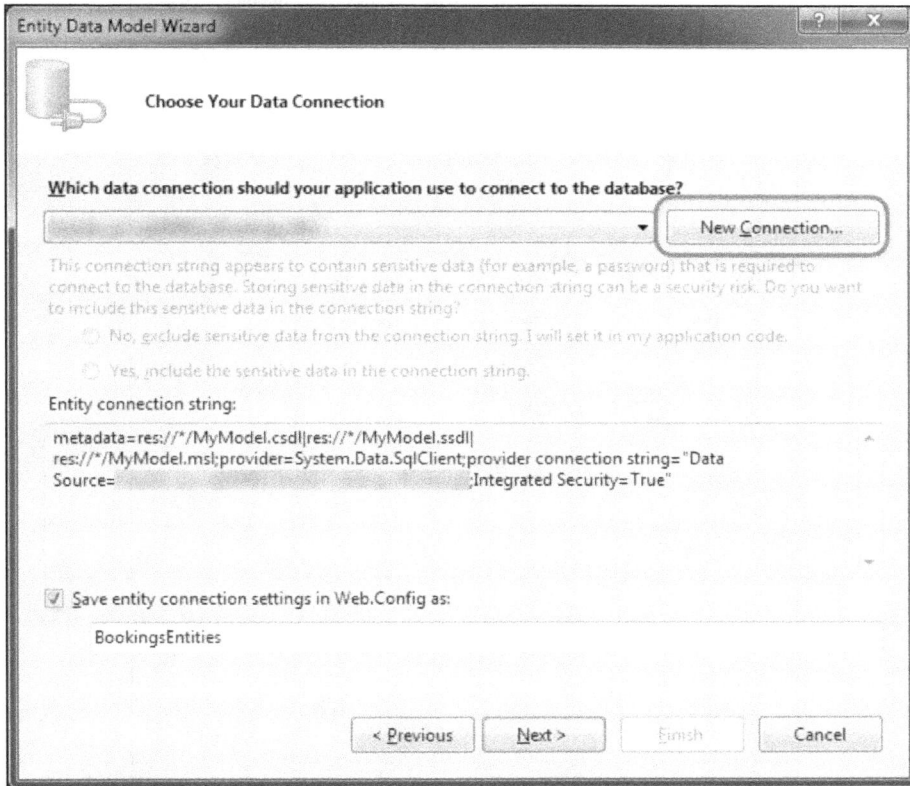

5. In the modal dialog that appears now, choose the connection to the server, as well as to the database, as shown in the following screenshot. Once picked, click **Next**.

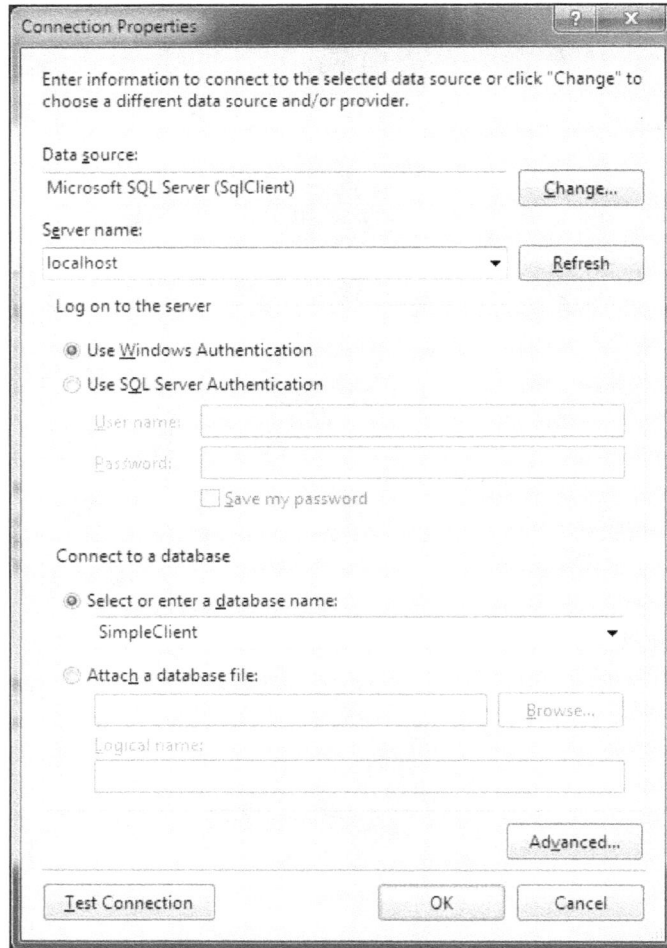

6. As for the last step, choose the tables that will be included in the model and tick the checkbox **Pluralize or singularize generated object names**, as shown in the following screenshot. This will make the entities singular and the entity groups in plural.

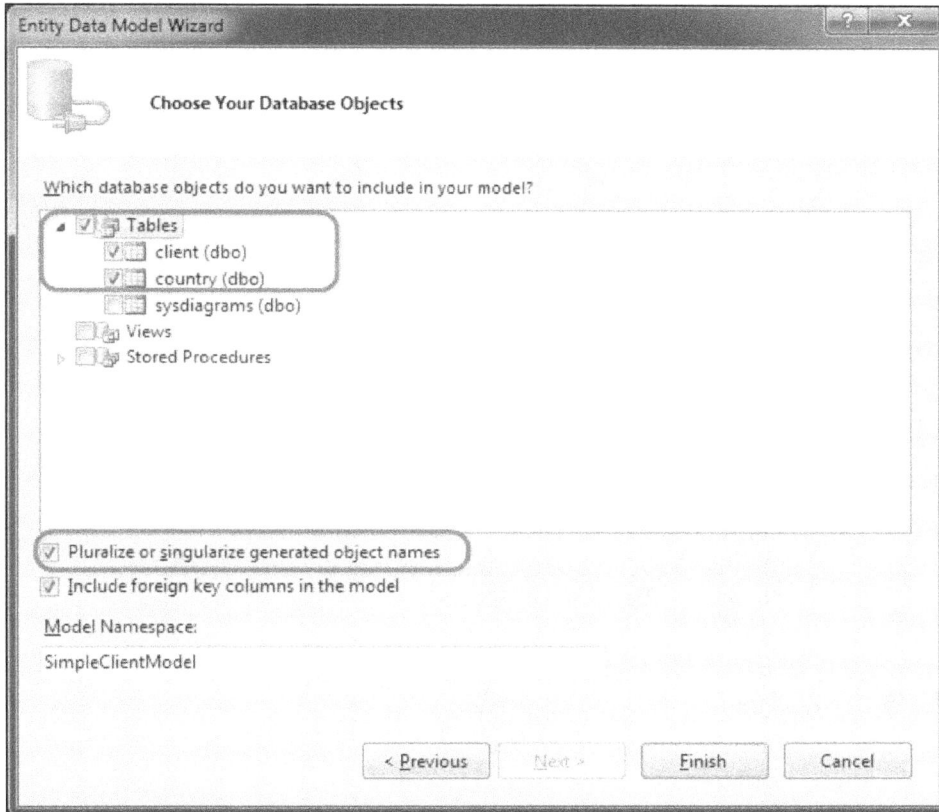

7. When pressing the button **Finish**, the model is generated and looks similar to the following screenshot:

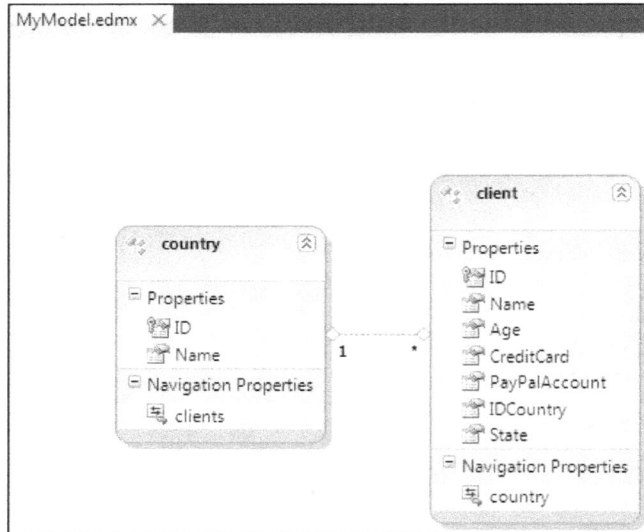

> **What if we want it to point to a different server?**
> In the web.config file, the entry defining the connection to the database can be modified.

The next step is to create the Domain Service. Now that we have the model, let us expose it through a service for our Silverlight application to consume it.

1. First, build the application.

2. Right-click on the web project and select **Add New Item**. Choose **Domain Service Class** and name it MyDomainService, similar to the following screenshot:

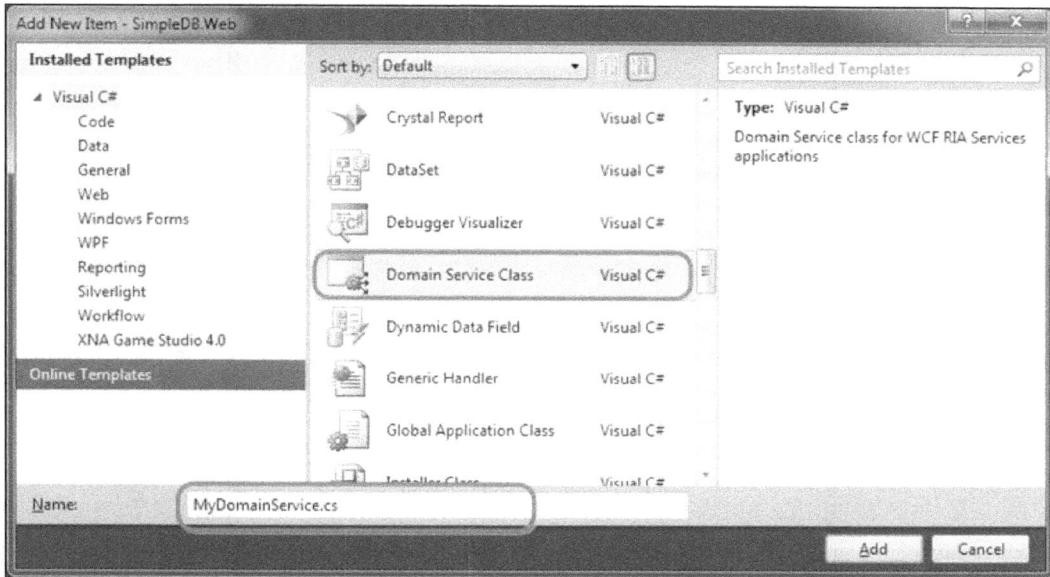

3. A dialog appears where we must indicate from which model the Domain Service must be generated. If there is no entry in that ComboBox, please cancel the operation, build the project, and try again. Specify the entries to be exposed in the Domain Service (both in this case), as well as if we want them to be editable (that is, in some instances, certain data must not be modified).

Add the `MyDomainService` class as shown in the following screenshot:

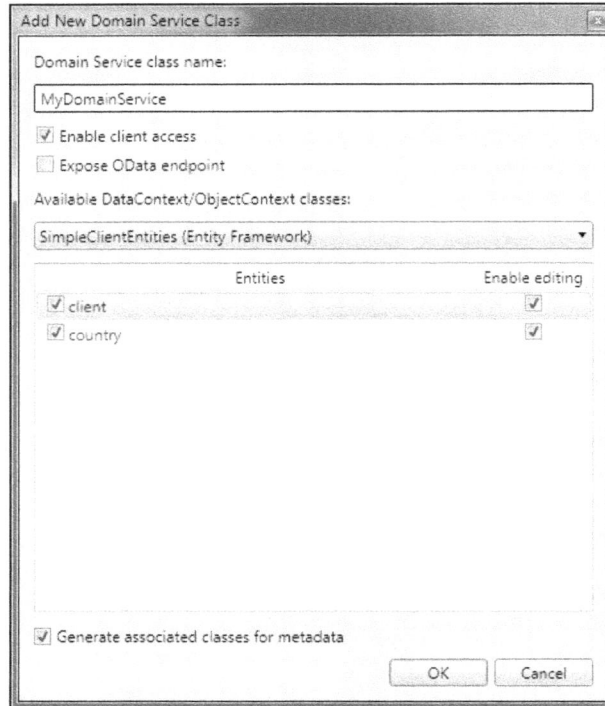

4. The two new files (`MyDomainService.cs` and `MyDomainSerice.metadata.cs`) are displayed, as shown in the following screenshot:

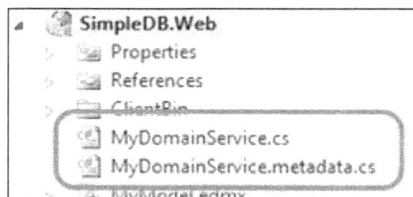

° The first of them, `MyDomainService.cs`, includes the basic operations (Select, Insert, Update, and Delete) against the entities generated. It includes the following lines of code:

```
[EnableClientAccess()]
public class MyDomainService :
  LinqToEntitiesDomainService<SimpleClientEntities>
{
  public IQueryable<client> GetClients()
  {
    return this.ObjectContext.clients;
  }
  public void InsertClient(client client)
  {
    if ((client.EntityState != EntityState.Detached))
    {
(...)
```

> The generated Domain Service has to be understood as a starting point and expanded to fulfill our needs.

- ° The second one, MyDomainService.metadata.cs, contains the entities, including both the validations inferred from the data model, and status tracking (tracking changes, insertion, modification, deleted entity, and so on). It includes the following lines of code:

```
[MetadataTypeAttribute(typeof(client.clientMetadata))]
public partial class client
{
  internal sealed class clientMetadata
  {
    private clientMetadata()
    {
    }
    public int Age { get; set; }
    public country country { get; set; }
(...)
```

The service is ready. Now, how do we consume it from our Silverlight application? Thus the next step will be to bind the service to our Silverlight project. This is also the easiest part.

5. Right-click on the Silverlight project and choose **Properties**.

6. Go to the **Silverlight** tab and select the web project containing the Domain Service in **WCF RIA Services Link** in the ComboBox. If the combo cannot be found at first sight, scroll down. Then build it as shown in the following screenshot:

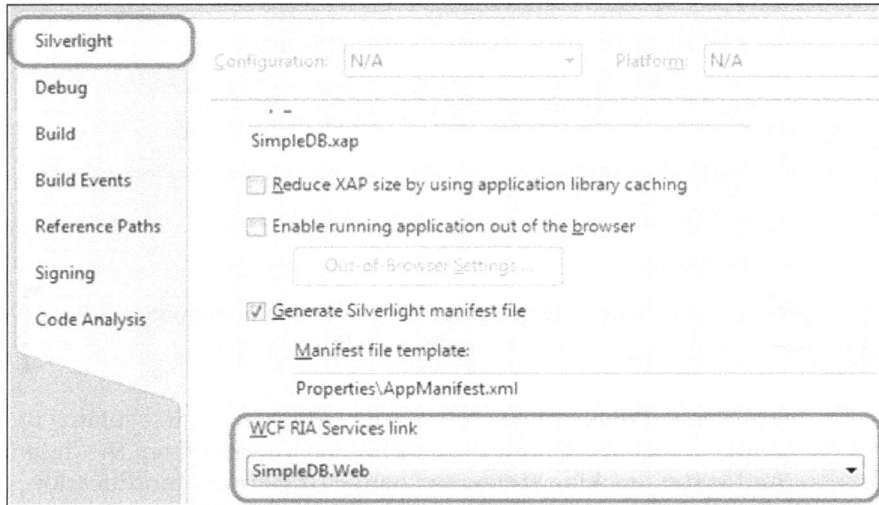

7. Go to the **Solution** window and click on the icon that shows all files, as shown in the following screenshot:

○ See how a file containing the entities and the Domain Context has been generated in our Silverlight application.

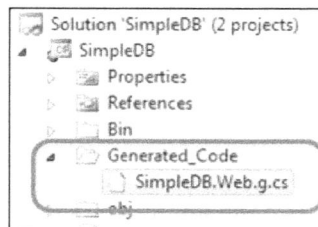

Below is an example of the generated entities:

```
[DataContract(Namespace=
"http://schemas.datacontract.org/2004/07/SimpleDB.Web")]
public sealed partial class client : Entity
{
  (...)
  /// </summary>
  [DataMember()]
  public int Age
  {
    get
    {
      return this._age;
    }
    set
    {
      if ((this._age != value))
      {
        this.OnAgeChanging(value);
        this.RaiseDataMemberChanging("Age");
        this.ValidateProperty("Age", value);
        this._age = value;
        this.RaiseDataMemberChanged("Age");
        this.OnAgeChanged();
      }
    }
  }
(...)
```

And also an example of the generated context:

```
public sealed partial class MyDomainContext : DomainContext
{
  (...)
  /// </summary>
  public EntitySet<client> clients
  {
    get
    {
      return base.EntityContainer.GetEntitySet<client>();
    }
  }
  (...)
```

```
public EntityQuery<client> GetClientsQuery()
{
  this.ValidateMethod("GetClientsQuery", null);
  return base.CreateQuery<client>("GetClients", null, false,
    true);
}
(...)
```

> How can this code be refreshed? Every time the project is compiled, these files are refreshed.

The next section will show how to perform basic operations such as Select, Insert, Update, and Delete on the database.

CRUD

On the sample built in the previous section, let us implement the basic operations (Read, Create, Update, and Delete). You will also learn how to link the results to particular elements of the UI, as well as a succinct introduction to error control.

Read

Let us see how to read data. In this case, we will focus on the necessary code to perform this operation and leave aside things such as linking information to controls. This sample reads from the database and shows a series of message boxes, one for every read message.

1. Let us begin by opening the Code-Behind Mainpage.cs file. Add the using namespace containing our context. When searching in the file SilmpleDB.Web.g.cs, under the hidden folder **Generated_Code**, it can be seen that the space is **SimpleDB.Web** (In the following section, you will see how to get this out of the web project). It is also necessary to add an RIA Services reference, namely, System.ServiceModel.DomainServices.Client using the following code:

   ```
   using System.ServiceModel.DomainServices.Client;
   using SimpleDB.Web;
   ```

2. Define a member variable with our Data Context. It will allow us to perform queries and will contain the data groups obtained as a result of these operations.

```
public partial class MainPage : UserControl
{
    MyDomainContext _context;
```

3. Make a query to obtain a client's list. To do so, we have the `GetClients` query defined in the Domain Service. As it is an asynchronous execution, define a method to be executed when the query is finished.

```
public MainPage()
{
    InitializeComponent();
    // Let us instantiate the DomainContext
    _context = new MyDomainContext();
    // Let us execute the query to extract the clients
    EntityQuery<client> clientQuery = _context.GetClientsQuery();
    OperationBase operation = _context.Load(clientQuery);
    // Hook to the completed event of that query
    operation.Completed += new EventHandler(operation_Completed);
}
```

4. In the callback method, the data we needed is already loaded in our context variable. Iterate according to the client list of the context and display a message with every client's name.

```
void operation_Completed(object sender, EventArgs e)
{
    // Now that the operation has been completed
    // We have information of the list of clients available in the
Context
    // Let us iterate and display a MessageBox showing each item
    foreach (var client in _context.clients)
    {
        MessageBox.Show(client.Name);
    }
}
```

Create

To make an insertion, it is only necessary to create a new instance we want and attach it to the corresponding collection in our context.

The most straightforward way is by using the following code:

```
public MainPage()
{
  InitializeComponent();
  // Let us instantiate the DomainContext
  _context = new MyDomainContext();
  // Let us create the new client entry
  // and fill it with data
  client myClient = new client();
  myClient.Name = "Mark Temp";
  myClient.IDCountry = 2;
  myClient.Age = 20;
  myClient.PayPalAccount = "test@temp.com";
  // Let us add it to the client's context list
  _context.clients.Add(myClient);
  // Let us submit the changes to the server
  _context.SubmitChanges();
}
```

Update

In order to update an entity, it must be loaded and then we will make the changes we intend to and submit them.

To implement it from the first sample, load the clients' list using the following code:

```
public MainPage()
{
  InitializeComponent();
  // Let us instantiate the DomainContext
  _context = new MyDomainContext();
  // Let us execute the query to extract the clients
  EntityQuery<client> clientQuery = _context.GetClientsQuery();
  OperationBase operation = _context.Load(clientQuery);
  // Hook to the completed event of that query
  operation.Completed += new EventHandler(operation_Completed);
}
```

Once loaded, select the client with `ID=5`, update its name, and submit the changes.

```
void operation_Completed(object sender, EventArgs e)
{
  // Let us search for the client in the loaded list
  client myClient = _context.clients.FirstOrDefault((c) => c.ID == 1);
  if (myClient != null)
  {
    // Let us make the desired updates
    myClient.Name = "John Doe Up";
  }
  // Let us submit the changes to the server
  _context.SubmitChanges();
}
```

Delete

For deleting entities, load the necessary data, delete them from the context, and submit changes to the server.

First, load the data, as seen in previous sections. Once loaded, delete the entry with the value `ID=4`, as done in the following code:

```
void operation_Completed(object sender, EventArgs e)
{
  // Let us search for the client in the loaded list
  client myClient = _context.clients.FirstOrDefault((c) => c.ID == 4);
  if (myClient != null)
  {
    // Let us remove it from the context list
    _context.clients.Remove(myClient);
  }
  // Let us submit the changes to the server
  _context.SubmitChanges();
}
```

Error control

In the real world, errors also occur. Two types can be distinguished:

- Those which are within our business logic: These can be expected and are treated as validation errors (these will be dealt with in the next section).

- Unexpected errors: These include those cases that have not been controlled in our business logic, or other kinds of errors, when database servers are down. These will be dealt in *Chapter 8, Security*.

The first type will be covered in the following section. Let's see how to detect if there have been errors when making an insertion. In this case, let us check if the field Name which is to be submitted, has been skipped in our business logic.

```
public MainPage()
{
  InitializeComponent();
  // Let us instantiate the DomainContext
  _context = new MyDomainContext();
  // Let us create the new client entry
  // and fill it with data
   client myClient = new client();
  // This will cause an error, Name cannot be null
  myClient.Name = string.Empty;
  myClient.IDCountry = 2;
  myClient.Age = 20;
  myClient.PayPalAccount = "test@temp.com";
  // Let us add it to the client's context list
  _context.clients.Add(myClient);
  // Let us submit the changes to the server
  // and check for errors
  _context.SubmitChanges(s =>
  {
    if (s.HasError)
      {
        string strError = string.Format("Failed to Insert: {0}",
          s.Error);
        MessageBox.Show(strError);
        // Mark as handled
        s.MarkErrorAsHandled();
      }
    }, null
  );
}
```

> Refer to the following link to find a guide on handling errors:
> http://bit.ly/nFZNdV.

Simple data binding

You already know how to perform basic operations against RIA Services. The next question is how to link that data to our UI controls? The answer is easy—by applying data binding techniques that have been shown in previous chapters.

> There is a way to work with RIA Services where the context is directly exposed in the UI as a DataSource. This approach won't be covered in this book, since it is not advised as it generates severe maintainability issues, except for a few applications or demos.

Now, you will learn to create a clients' list and show details about the current clients. Let us see how:

- First, add a ViewModel file and define two properties, one of them will contain the clients' list and the second one will contain the selected one.

- Choose the first one in the list and display details. This is also bound to the selected element in the DataGrid, so if we change the selected one in the DataGrid, it will also change in the detailed view.

To create the example, take the base sample previously defined in this chapter as a starting point and create a class called MainPageVM, where the clients' list will be loaded. Expose two properties, the list itself and the currently selected element, as shown in the following code:

```
public class MainPageVM : INotifyPropertyChanged
{
  ObservableCollection<client> _clients;
  public ObservableCollection<client> Clients
  {
    get { return _clients; }
    set { _clients = value;
      RaisePropertyChanged("Clients");
    }
  }
  private client _currentSelectedClient;
  public client CurrentSelectedClient
  {
    get { return _currentSelectedClient; }
    set { _currentSelectedClient = value;
      RaisePropertyChanged("CurrentSelectedClient");
    }
  }
}
```

[This sample can be taken as an initial contact. In this chapter, we will show you how to integrate RIA Services with MVVM.]

Define the context and load the asynchronous data. Once loaded, assign data to the properties Clients and CurrentSelectedClient using the following code:

```
MyDomainContext _context;
public MainPageVM()
{
  // Let us instantiate the DomainContext
  _context = new MyDomainContext();
  // Let us execute the query to extract the clients
  EntityQuery<client> clientQuery = _context.GetClientsQuery();
  OperationBase operation = _context.Load(clientQuery);
  // Hook to the completed event of that query
  operation.Completed += new EventHandler(operation_Completed);
}
void operation_Completed(object sender, EventArgs e)
{
  // Let us assign the Clients and CurrentSelectedClient properties
  Clients = new ObservableCollection<client>(_context.clients);
  CurrentSelectedClient = (Clients.Count > 0) ? Clients[0] : null;
}
```

In the view Code-Behind, MainPage.cs, associate an instance of MainPageVM as DataContext, as shown in the following code:

```
public MainPage()
{
  InitializeComponent();
  this.DataContext = new MainPageVM();
}
```

In the interface, define a DataGrid and a details form.

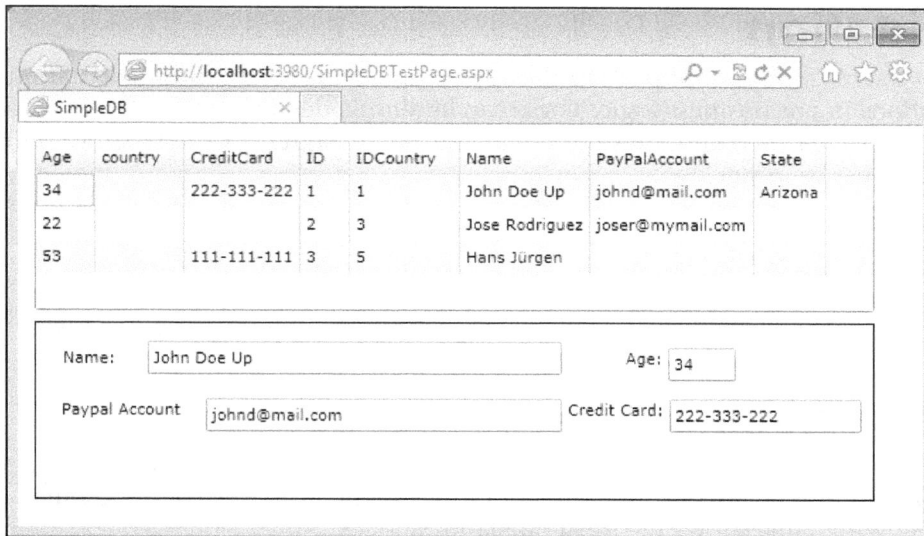

In this form, the `ItemSource` property of the DataGrid is bound to the `Clients` property in our ViewModel. Also, the `SelectedItem` property is assigned to `CurrentSelectedClient`, as shown in the following code:

```
<sdk:DataGrid
  ItemsSource="{Binding Path=Clients}"
  SelectedItem="{Binding Path=CurrentSelectedClient, Mode=TwoWay}"
  (…)
/>
```

Make the same with the details fields and the `CurrentSelectedClient` property, as shown in the following code:

```
<TextBox
  Text="{Binding CurrentSelectedClient.Name, Mode=TwoWay}"
  (…)
/>
```

When we run the application, our DataGrid will show the clients stored in the database. If the selection is modified, the detailed view is updated with the selected client.

Validation

One of the most important parts of the application is the correct implementation of validations in our business logic. These can be simple details, such as the fact that the client must provide their name and e-mail address to sign up, or that before selling a book, it must be in stock.

In RIA Services, validations can be defined on two levels:

- In entities, via DataAnnotations.
- In our Domain Service, server or asynchronous validations via Invoke.

DataAnnotations

The space named `System.ComponentModel.DataAnnotations` implements a series of attributes allowing us to add validation rules to the properties of our entities. The following table shows the most outstanding ones:

Validation Attribute	Description
DataTypeAttribute	Specifies a particular type of data such as date or an e-mail
EnumDataTypeAttribute	Ensures that the value exists in an enumeration
RangeAttribute	Designates minimum and maximum constraints
RegularExpressionAttribute	Uses a regular expression to determine valid values
RequiredAttribute	Specifies that a value must be provided
StringLengthAttribute	Designates a maximum and minimum number of characters
CustomValidationAttribute	Uses a custom method for validation

The following code shows us how to add a field as "required":

```
[Required()]
public string Name
{
  get
  {
    return this._name;
  }
  set
  {
    (...)
  }
}
```

In the UI layer, the control linked to this field (a TextBox, in this case), automatically detects and displays the error. It can be customized as follows:

These validations are based on the launch of exceptions. They are captured by user controls and bound to data elements. If there are errors, these are shown in a friendly way. When executing the application in debug mode with Visual Studio, it is possible to find that IDE captures exceptions. To avoid this, refer to the following link, where the IDE configuration is explained: http://bit.ly/riNdmp.

Where can validations be added? The answer is in the metadata definition, entities, in our Domain Service, within the server project. Going back to our example, the server project is SimpleDB.Web and the Domain Service is MyDomainService.medatada.cs. These validations are automatically copied to the entities definition file and the context found on the client side.

In the Simple.DB.Web.g.cs file, when the hidden folder Generated Code is opened, you will be surprised to find that some validations are already implemented. For example, the required field, field length, and so on. These are inferred from the Entity Framework model.

Simple validations

For validations that are already generated, let's see a simple example on how to implement those of the "required" field and "maximum length":

```
[Required()]
[StringLength(60)]
public string Name
{
  get
  {
    return this._name;
  }
  set
  {
    (...)
  }
}
```

Now, we will implement the syntactic validation for credit cards (format dddd-dddd-dddd-dddd). To do so, use the regular expression validator and add the server file `MyDomainService.metadata.cs`, as shown in the following code:

```
[RegularExpression(@"\d{4}-\d{4}-\d{4}-\d{4}",
ErrorMessage="Credit card not valid format should be: 9999-9999-9999-
9999")]
public string CreditCard { get; set; }
```

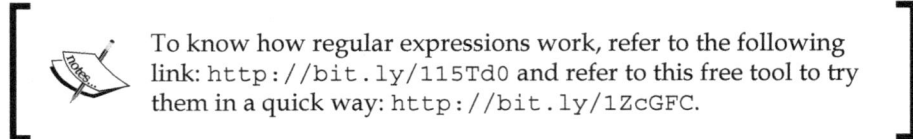

> To know how regular expressions work, refer to the following link: http://bit.ly/115Td0 and refer to this free tool to try them in a quick way: http://bit.ly/1ZcGFC.

Custom and shared validations

Basic validations are acceptable for 70 percent of validation scenarios, but there are still 30 percent of validations which do not fit in these patterns. What do you do then? RIA Services offers `CustomValidatorAttribute`. It permits the creation of a method which makes a validation defined by the developer. The benefits are listed below:

- Its code: The necessary logic can be implemented to make validations.
- It can be oriented for validations to be viable in other modules (for instance, the validation of an IBAN [International Bank Account]).
- It can be chosen if a validation is executed on only the server side (for example, a validation requiring data base readings) or if it is also copied to the client.

To validate the checksum of the `CreditCard` field, follow these steps:

1. Add to the `SimpleDB.Web` project, the class named `ClientCustomValidation`. Within this class, define a static model, `ValidationResult`, which accepts the value of the field to evaluate as a parameter and returns the validation result.

```
public class ClientCustomValidation
{
  public static ValidationResult ValidMasterCard(string
    strcardNumber)
}
```

2. Implement the summarized validation method (the part related to the result call back is returned).

```
public static ValidationResult ValidMasterCard(string
   strcardNumber)
{
  // Let us remove the "-" separator
  string cardNumber = strcardNumber.Replace("-", "");
  // We need to keep track of the entity fields that are
  // affected, so the UI controls that have this property
  // bound can display the error message when applies
  List<string> AffectedMembers = new List<string>();
  AffectedMembers.Add("CreditCard");
  (...)
  // Validation succeeded returns success
  // Validation failed provides error message and indicates
  // the entity fields that are affected
  return (sum % 10 == 0) ? ValidationResult.Success :
  new ValidationResult("Failed to validate", AffectedMembers);
}
```

> To make validation simpler, only the MasterCard has been covered. To know more and cover more card types, refer to the page http://bit.ly/aYx39u. In order to find examples of valid numbers, go to http://bit.ly/gZpBj.

3. Go to the file MyDomainService.metadata.cs and, in the Client entity, add the following to the CreditCard field:

```
[CustomValidation(typeof(ClientCustomValidation),
"ValidMasterCard")]
public string CreditCard { get; set; }
```

If it is executed now and you try to enter an invalid field in the CreditCard field, it won't be marked as an error. What happens? Validation is only executed on the server side. If it is intended to be executed on the client side as well, rename the file called ClientCustomValidation.cs to ClientCustomValidation.shared.cs. In this way, the validation will be copied to the Generated_code folder and the validation will be launched.

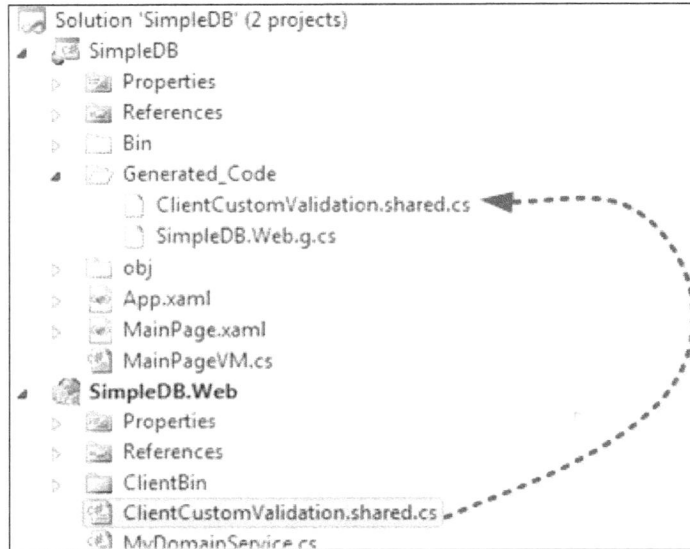

In the code generated on the client side, the entity validation is associated.

```
/// <summary>
/// Gets or sets the 'CreditCard' value.
/// </summary>
[CustomValidation(typeof(ClientCustomValidation), "ValidMasterCard")]
[DataMember()]
[RegularExpression("\\d{4}-\\d{4}-\\d{4}-\\d{4}", ErrorMessage="Credit
card not valid format should be: 9999-9999-9999-9999")]
[StringLength(30)]
public string CreditCard
{
```

This is quite interesting. However, what happens if more than one field has to be checked in the validation? In this case, one more parameter is added to the validation method. It is `ValidationContext`, and through this parameter, the instance of the entity we are dealing with can be accessed.

```
public static ValidationResult ValidMasterCard( string strcardNumber,
  ValidationContext validationContext)
{
  client currentClient = (client)validationContext.ObjectInstance;
```

Entity-level validations

Fields validation is quite interesting, but sometimes, rules have to be applied in a higher level, that is, entity level. RIA Services implements some machinery to perform this kind of validation. Only a custom validation has to be defined in the appropriate entity class declaration.

Following the sample we're working upon, let us implement one validation which checks that at least one of the two payment methods (PayPal or credit card) is informed. To do so, go to the `ClientCustomValidation.shared.cs` (`SimpleDB` web project) and add the following static function to the `ClientCustomValidation` class:

```
public static ValidationResult ValidatePaymentInformed(client
CurrentClient)
{
  bool atLeastOnePaymentInformed = ((CurrentClient.PayPalAccount !=
    null
    && CurrentClient.PayPalAccount != string.Empty) ||
    (CurrentClient.CreditCard != null && CurrentClient.CreditCard !=
    string.Empty));
  return (atLeastOnePaymentInformed) ?
  ValidationResult.Success : new ValidationResult("One payment method
    must be informed at least");
}
```

Next, open the `MyDomainService.metadata` file and add, in the class level, the following annotation to enable that validation:

```
[CustomValidation(typeof(ClientCustomValidation),
  ValidatePaymentInformed")]
[MetadataTypeAttribute(typeof(client.clientMetadata))]
public partial class client
```

When executing and trying the application, it will be realized that the validation is not performed. This is due to the fact that, unlike validations in the field level, the entity validations are only launched client-side when calling `EndEdit` or `TryValidateObject`. The logic is to first check if the fields are well informed and then make the appropriate validations.

In this case, a button will be added, making the validation and forcing it to entity level.

> To know more about validation on entities, go to
> `http://bit.ly/qTr9hz`.

Define the command launching the validation on the current entity in the `ViewModel` as the following code:

```
private RelayCommand _validateCommand;
public RelayCommand ValidateCommand
{
  get
  {
    if (_validateCommand == null)
    {
      _validateCommand = new RelayCommand(() =>
      {
        // Let us clear the current validation list
        CurrentSelectedClient.ValidationErrors.Clear();
        var validationResults = new List<ValidationResult>();
        ValidationContext vcontext = new
          ValidationContext(CurrentSelectedClient, null, null);
        // Let us run the validation
        Validator.TryValidateObject(CurrentSelectedClient, vcontext,
          validationResults);
        // Add the errors to the entities validation error
        // list
        foreach (var res in validationResults)
        {
          CurrentSelectedClient.ValidationErrors.Add(res);
        }
      }, (() => (CurrentSelectedClient != null)) );
    }
    return _validateCommand;
  }
}
```

Define the button in the window and bind it to the command:

```
<Button
  Content="Validate"
  Command="{Binding Path=ValidateCommand}"
/>
```

While executing, it will be appreciated that the fields be blank, even if we click the button. Nonetheless, when adding a breaking point, the validation is shown. What happens is, there is a missing element showing the result of that validation. In this case, the choice will be to add a header whose DataContext points to the current entity. If entity validations fail, they will be shown in this element.

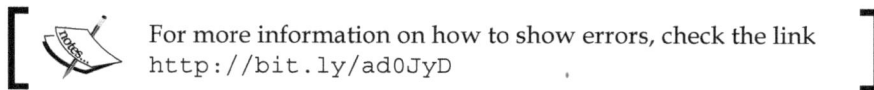

> For more information on how to show errors, check the link
> http://bit.ly/ad0JyD

The TextBox added will show the entity validation errors. The final result will look as shown in the following screenshot:

Client Information	One payment method must be informed at least		
Name:	John Doe Up	Age:	34
Paypal Account		Credit Card:	

Domain Services validations

All validations made so far could be replicated on the client side. However, there are scenarios where validation must only be executed on the server side, either because it needs to access local resources, such as a database lookup, or because intermediate data used for validations cannot be exposed on the client side due to security reasons.

Let us see how to execute validations on the server side only and how to perform, from our Silverlight application, calls to asynchronous validations.

Server validations

In order to implement a server-side validation, we have the option to define a custom validation (as previously seen) without modifying the name of the file from .cs to .shared.cs. In this way, the validation won't be copied to the client side and will only be executed on the server side. This approach is not wrong, but sometimes it is advisable to be more explicit, that is, before making an insertion or an update, it may be adequate to execute some validations.

RIA Services allows us to launch validation exceptions from an operation in our Domain Service. To see how this works, add the following validation to the UpdateClients method to check whether the credit card number is not used by another user.

The following are the steps:

1. Define a server-side function to check if the card number is doubled as the following code:

```
public bool CreditCardNumberAlreadyExists(client currentclient)
{
  List<client> cliensWithSameCreditCard = null;
  if (currentclient.CreditCard != null && currentclient.CreditCard
    != string.Empty)
  {
    cliensWithSameCreditCard = (from c in
      this.ObjectContext.clients where c.CreditCard ==
      currentclient.CreditCard && c.ID != currentclient.ID select
      c).ToList<client>();
  }
  return (cliensWithSameCreditCard != null &&
    cliensWithSameCreditCard.Count > 0);
}
```

2. Update the update server-side method. To do so, it is necessary to read the database, check it and, if there is a clash, launch an exception using the following code:

```
public void UpdateClient(client currentclient)
{
  // Is there a collision? Throw the exception
  if (CreditCardNumberAlreadyExists(currentclient))
  {
    // Let us mark the field affected (it will show up the
    // error on the UI binded element)
    ValidationResult error = new ValidationResult("Credit card
      already exists for another account", new string[] {
      "CreditCard" });
    throw new ValidationException(error, null, currentclient);
  }
  // if no error just perform the update
  this.ObjectContext.clients.AttachAsModified(currentclient,
    this.ChangeSet.GetOriginal(currentclient));
}
```

3. Control the client-side error, when the call is made to `SubmitChanges`. Moreover, it will show an error message if the error occurs (in *Chapter 8, Security*, we shall see how to deal with errors in detail).

```
_context.SubmitChanges(s =>
{
  if (s.HasError)
  {
    foreach (var validationError in
      CurrentSelectedClient.ValidationErrors)
    {
      MessageBox.Show(validationError.ErrorMessage);
    }
    s.MarkErrorAsHandled();
  }
}
, null);
```

> To keep the sample as easy as possible, the message is being shown from the ViewModel. If automatic Unit Testing is going to be added later, or if the ViewModel is reused in a WP7 application, you should use one of the mechanisms described in the previous chapter (IDialogService or Messenger) and decouple the UI from the ViewModel.

Asynchronous validations

Server validation, defined in the previous section, is very interesting. Nevertheless, wouldn't it be interesting to make the validation without submitting changes? Yes, it would. The method previously defined, `CreditCardNumberAlreadyExists`, can be reused and invoked in an asynchronous way.

In this case, add to the validation command, the invoke to the validation itself. When you get the result, check it and, if an error occurs, it is included in the notification to be displayed in the UI.

```
// Let us perform as well the server invoke (credit card
// validation)
InvokeOperation<bool> inv;
// we will use this to get the result of the operation
inv = _context.CreditCardNumberAlreadyExists(CurrentSelectedClient);
_context.CreditCardNumberAlreadyExists(CurrentSelectedClient).
Completed
  += ((s, e) =>
```

```
{
  if (inv.Value == true)
  {
    ValidationResult creditcardExists =
    new ValidationResult(
    "Credit Card already registered",
    new string[] { "CreditCard" });
    CurrentSelectedClient.ValidationErrors.Add(creditcardExists);
  }
}
);
```

Advanced topics

Now that we have covered the basics, let's check some advanced topics that we
will come across in live project developments.

Cancelling changes

When working with RIA Services, something of a data *island* is brought client side.
We can work with it and, once we are ready, send it to the server. What happens
if we want to cancel changes and start again? For instance, a user is modifying a
client file and realizes that they are working on the wrong client, so they want to
cancel the changes made. The entities with which we are working implement the
IRrevertibleChangeTracking. This interface defines a method named Reject,
which restores the affected entity and the associated ones (if applicable) to the
original value.

In this case, if changes are to be cancelled, it will only be necessary to implement
the following code lines (to see it working, press the button **Cancel Changes** in
the sample application):

```
// Let us clear the current validation list
CurrentSelectedClient.ValidationErrors.Clear();
// Let us cast the entity IRevertibleChange
IRevertibleChangeTracking revertible = CurrentSelectedClient as
  IRevertibleChangeTracking;
// Reject Changes
revertible.RejectChanges();
```

> The entity also implements a method called GetOriginal. Why shouldn't it be used? Because it returns a disconnected entity. If the entity had data associated from other entities, they will not be reflected (see association later).

Transactions

Also, it may happen that one of the entities returned an error when trying to save it. In this case, WCF RIA Services calls the function SaveChanges, which internally wraps all those changes (Unit of work) in a transaction. That is, if any of them fail, none of them will be saved.

What if we want to configure the transaction in detail? What if we are not using the ADO.NET Entity Framework? We can override the Submit method and configure the transaction at our convenience (see http://bit.ly/nTv5yb). For more information in this area, refer to the link http://bit.ly/6G0xp4.

> Another interesting topic is to add audit and save a changes log. For more information, check the link.

Domain Service and partial classes

At the beginning of this chapter, we pointed out that Visual Studio wizards generate a Domain Service class, which was to be taken as a starting point and customized according to our needs.

What happens if changes are entered in the ADO.NET Entity Framework model? For instance, when adding a new table or changing a field type, is it necessary to regenerate the Domain Service and manually enter customizations again? No, it is not. Partial classes can be used to implement our customized methods. Therefore, we can refresh our Domain Service without the fear of losing all our changes made. Let us now see, step by step, how to add a partial class to the sample.

1. Go to the server project, Packt.Booking.Server.Web, open the MyDomainService.cs file and add Partial to the class definition.

   ```
   public partial class MyDomainService : LinqToEntitiesDomainService
   <SimpleClientEntities>
   ```

2. Add a new class called MyDomainServicep (**Add | New Class**).

3. Change the header defining that class by the same one placed previously to create an extension of it:

```
public partial class MyDomainService : LinqToEntitiesDomainService
<SimpleClientEntities>
```

4. Add the `using` namespace as the following code:

```
using System.ServiceModel.DomainServices.EntityFramework;
using System.ComponentModel.DataAnnotations;
```

5. Now, open the `MyDomainService.cs` file and cut the customized methods to paste them in the new file, `MyDomainServiceP.cs`:

```
public partial class MyDomainService : LinqToEntitiesDomainService
<SimpleClientEntities>
{
  public bool CreditCardNumberAlreadyExists(client currentclient)
  {
    (...)
```

> What about the entities file? If changes are not many, it is worthwhile to enter changes manually so as to avoid losing the information we have manually entered (that is, validations).

Include

When having a look at the entities that have been created so far, it is seen that they have links to other related entities. For instance, in the client entity, apart from the country number identifier, we can find a property of the `country` type. If a breaking point is added when loading these data, the property will be `null`. What is happening then? By default, the queries generated by RIA Services do not include those bound entities. The bad use of this technique could make our application consume too much bandwidth, as well as resources. What to do then? In the cases where it is justified (for instance, when loading the entity of the associated country or a master-detail association), these entities can be added to our queries.

> What if queries return a lot of registers? Associating more entities means more load. The ideal thing to do here is to use pagination (bear in mind that a few users are capable of processing more than 100 registers at one time). To see pagination solutions, check these two links, http://bit.ly/90ZNtA and http://bit.ly/87REa4 (server paging).

Let us see how to include the `country` entity when loading every client record:

1. First, edit the Domain Service in the server project and include the entity in the query, bringing the clients as the following code:

```
public IQueryable<client> GetClients()
{
    return this.ObjectContext.clients.Include("country");
}
```

2. Still in the server project, open the file containing the entities, `MyDomainService.metadata.cs` and search for the client entity. In the nested class, the `country` property will be found. Add the annotation `include` to it using the following code:

```
public partial class client
{
    internal sealed class clientMetadata
    {
        (...)
[Include]
public country country { get; set; }
```

3. Doing so, the `country` entity of each client will be brought when loading. In the sample, the `DataGrid` can be modified to add the column indicating the `Name` field.

```
<sdk:DataGrid.Columns>
<sdk:DataGridTextColumn
    Binding="{Binding Path=country.Name, Mode=OneWay}"/>
```

Composition

RIA Services also knows a special type of association. In a hierarchy of entities, one entity is referred to as the parent entity and the other related entities are referred to as descendant entities. The child entities cannot exist without the master entity and usually these entities are always displayed or modified together. A typical example is a shop system where we have one entity for each order. This entity also has a list of items; each one has a reference to a product and a quantity. In our sample application, we decided to make a composition between a floor and the rooms of this floor.

Most of the readers probably know compositions from UML class diagrams as the following figure:

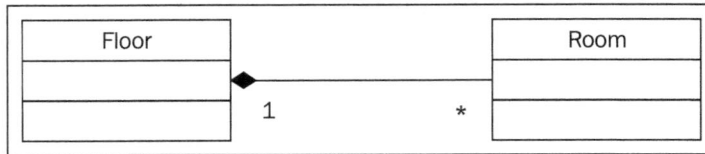

These data classes typically have the following characteristics:

- The relationship between the entities can be represented as a tree with the descendant entities connected to a single parent entity. The descendant entities can extend for any number of levels. This means that we can also decide to configure a composition between a building and the relating floors. This can be a suitable approach in case that, for instance, if we develop a graphic designer, where all the information is needed to render a map of a given building.

- The lifetime of a descendant entity is contained within the lifetime of the parent entity. This means if you delete the floor, all rooms will be deleted as well.

- The descendant entity does not have a meaningful identity outside of the context of the parent entity.

- Data operations on the entities require the entities to be treated as a single unit. For example, adding, deleting, or updating a record in the descendant entity requires a corresponding change in the parent entity.

Let us move from theory to practical work. Defining a composition with RIA Services is very simple, Just apply the `CompositionAttribute` attribute to the property that defines the association in the metadata of the entity, as in the following code:

```
[MetadataTypeAttribute(typeof(Floor.FloorMetadata))]
public partial class Floor
{
internal sealed class FloorMetadata
  {
    [Include]
    [Composition]
    public EntityCollection<Room> Rooms { get; set; }
  }
}
```

When applying the `CompositionAttribute` attribute to a property, the data from the descendant entity is not automatically retrieved with the parent entity. To include the descendent entity in the query results, you must apply the `IncludeAttribute` attribute, as previously described.

Compositions in RIA Services gain the following behaviors:

- Hierarchical change tracking: When a child entity is modified, the parent also transitions to the Modified state. When a parent is in the Modified state, all of its children are included in the change-set that is sent to the server, including any unmodified children. Therefore, our update method must be modified, which will be seen later.

- Public entity sets for child Types are not generated on the code-generated DomainContext. Children are only accessible via their parent relationship.

Effectively, this means that you do not have to manage your child entities manually. Just create a new room, add this room to the floor where it belongs and call the `SaveChanges` method of the DomainContext. The client will send all entities, including the child entities, to the server, which updates them in the correct order, for example, first updating the master entity and next an insertion for the child entities.

In addition to this code, our update method must also be changed for the `Floor`. The problem is that the Entity Framework makes a so called deep-attach, which means that it also adds all child entities of this composition to the DataContext object. If more than one room is added at one Unit of Work to your client context, the system will send all the entities to the server, but two of them have the same primary key.

Therefore, if you do not change the update method, an exception will be thrown with the following message: **InValidOperationException was unhandled by user code: An entity with the same identity already exists in this EntitySet.**

```
public void UpdateFloor(Floor currentFloor)
{
  currentFloor.Rooms.Clear();
  if (currentFloor.EntityState == EntityState.Detached)
  {
    Floor original = ChangeSet.GetOriginal(currentFloor);
    if (original != null)
    {
      ObjectContext.Floors.AttachAsModified(currentFloor,
        original);
    }
    else
```

```
        {
          ObjectContext.Floors.Attach(currentFloor);
        }
      }
      foreach (Room change in ChangeSet.
        GetAssociatedChanges(currentFloor, p => p.Rooms))
      {
        ChangeOperation changeOperation =
          ChangeSet.GetChangeOperation(change);
        switch (changeOperation)
        {
          case ChangeOperation.Insert:
            if (change.EntityState == EntityState.Added) break;
          if (change.EntityState != EntityState.Detached)
          {
            ObjectContext.ObjectStateManager.
              ChangeObjectState(change, EntityState.Added);
          }
          else
          {
            ObjectContext.Rooms.AddObject(change);
          }
          break;
          case ChangeOperation.Update:
            ObjectContext.Rooms.AttachAsModified(change,
            ChangeSet.GetOriginal(change));
          break;
          case ChangeOperation.Delete:
            if (change.EntityState == EntityState.Detached)
            {
              ObjectContext.Rooms.AttachAsModified(change);
            }
          ObjectContext.DeleteObject(change);
          break;
        }
      }
    }
```

The code is not as complicated as it probably seems. The following steps must be followed:

1. Remove all child entities from the collection. Do not worry, the changes do not get lost, because the Entity Framework tracks all changes and they will be taken care of later.

2. If the parent entity is detached, attach it. It is important to check if the original entity is not null. If any property has not been changed directly, but only added, removed, or changed some of its child entities, the original entity will be null and the method `AttachAsModified` fails.

3. Get all changed child entities from the change tracker and handle them, depending on their change operation.

You probably recognized that this code snippet will look the same for all compositions you may have in your application and that it is not a good idea to just copy and paste it.

> It is good practice to follow the DRY principle (Don't Repeat Yourself), and then provide a generic solution in the demo application, which can be found in the `UpdateFloor` method of the `BookingDomainService`.

> More information about composition in general can be found at the MSDN website: `http://msdn.microsoft.com/ en-us/library/ee707346%28v=VS.91%29.aspx`. Some information about why a custom update method is required can be found at `http://blogs.msdn.com/b/digital_ ruminations/archive/2009/11/18/composition- support-in-ria-services.aspx`.

Solving the many-to-many relationship issue

A limitation of RIA Services is that it does not support many-to-many relationships (for more information, refer to `http://bit.ly/p8O8IE`). What workarounds are available?

- The easiest one consists of adding a `dummy` field to our table and regenerating the model. The linked table will be shown correctly. Once the update has been made, the additional column can be deleted.

- Another option, although a little more complicated, consists of adding the entity to the model yourself, mapping it to the linking table, and then adding the foreign key relationships to the other two tables.

- As a third option, there is a Codeplex project, solving the problem of many-to-many in RIA Services (`http://bit.ly/g2WrUJ`).

RIA Services and MVVM

RIA Services is a great technology, but how does it fit into the MVVM pattern? Can we easily encapsulate it in a Model? How can we isolate RIA Services in the model definition in order to allow developers to implement automated unit testing?

Encapsulating RIA Services in a model

When RIA Services came into the market, its pros were highlighted as a RAD (Rapid Application Development) technology. It was praised so much that most members of the community have the wrong perception that it cannot be used with applications building an architecture (that is, based on the MVVM pattern).

On the contrary, RIA Services can be encapsulated in a model by using one of the following approaches:

- Database first: get advantage of the entities extracted from the database and use them as the transport layer.
- Use objects POCO and T4 templates to generate the code. This means hard work (`http://bit.ly/eFwcJ2`).
- Use CodeFirst and POCO objects (at the time of printing, the RTM version of the RIA Services SP2 was not available yet).

> Another wrong perception is that RIA Services only works with ADO.NET Entity Framework. In fact, it can be combined with NHibernate and other technologies, although it means more work on our behalf (`http://bit.ly/c7zvxN`).

Which approach should be taken to implement our model layer?

Define the operations in a contract (interface). The contract will only expose the entities we are dealing with (nothing about context or RIA Services particularities).

Implement a model which inherits from this contract, so that:

- We will work internally with RIA Services and instantiate a context to work with.
- For it to be consumed by one or several ViewModels, we will only deal with the contract previously defined (make sure the RIA Services part is present).

- The model which will be created, unlike other models, will have a status. That is to say, it will bear the record of the elements that have been modified or inserted, for instance. It will track the 'island' of objects or, as in Unit of Work say, anything we have brought from the server. As it has a status, it must be decided how to instantiate it. A singleton for the whole application? A model instance for every ViewModel? In the following section, this issue will be dealt in depth and we will provide a solution based on the Factory pattern.

As in the previous chapter, a contract and a model were defined. In this one, we will see how, except for refactoring and using RIA Services entities, we will be able to use it almost entirely and replace the Model Mock implementation with the real one based on RIA Services.

Two interesting entries about it can be found on the Internet, by Shawn Wildermuth—RIA Services and MVVM (http://bit.ly/bhoap2), and by John Papa—MVVM why and how (http://bit.ly/hWleiP).

Context lifetime discussion and model factory

The RIA Services context is inspired by the Entity Framework and other O/R Mapping Tools. Most of them implement the Unit of Work pattern, which is described by Martin Fowler under his site, http://martinfowler.com/eaaCatalog/unitOfWork.html.

> Martin Fowler, a well-known author and software architect, published a list of patterns for Enterprise Applications on his side as a short summary of his book *Patterns of Enterprise Application Architecture* http://bit.ly/2gSwXH

This is how it works:

1. A Unit of Work is started, typically the first time when data is retrieved or queried from the database. The entities itself will be stored in the session object and the changes are tracked by framework. In RIA Services, you start it by instantiating a new context object.

2. The user manipulates the data and the entities will be added or removed from this context and single properties or even complex relationships are updated and changed. Often, there is also an in-memory caching system to ensure that only one entity exists for one record of the database.

3. The job is done and when it's time to commit, the framework decides what to do. It can open a new transaction, handle concurrency, and write all changes to the database. In RIA, a commit is done by the SaveChanges method.

This pattern is great and provides a lot of advantages. For example, by writing changes to the database at one point of the time, the system is able to make optimizations, for example, when a lot of entities are added to the session object, it is more efficient to make a bulk insert than a lot of single insert operations. The change tracking system also allows to only update the changed fields, instead of sending the whole entity to the database.

Furthermore, we are free to define what a Unit of Work, in our context, is. For a normal web application, it is very easy. Typically, you define that one request is a Unit of Work. In a desktop or RIA application, it is more complicated and we have multiple options. For the sake of simplicity, we decided to use one domain context in our sample application only and to avoid losing the changes that have to be asked to the user. Whenever we start editing another context, the changes are lost when they do not save it.

But this is not the best approach, especially when we have some background progresses (the Domain Context is not thread-safe) and also for scenarios where the user should be able to modify multiple entities in parallel, for example, when they edit their notes or other documents.

Because **Managed Extensibility Framework (MEF)** is being used, there is the option to configure our model implementation without using shared instances, which means that each view model gets its own model object. Because this means that the smallest Unit of Work is equal to the lifetime of a view model, a better approach is necessary. Therefore, a model factory that has a method to create a new model must be defined as the following code:

```
public interface IModelFactory
{
  IModel CreateModel();
}
```

This factory is injected as a shared instance to each view model, and whenever they want to start a Unit of Work, they can use the factory to create a new model object.

In our test scenario, person entities must be edited. The main requirement is that each person can be edited and saved without affecting the other items in our list.

Therefore, implement the following approach:

1. Use a main model to load all person objects from the RIA service.

2. Whenever a person is changed, create a new object for this person only to start a new Unit of Work. Now we must detach this person from its old model and attach it to the new model, but because of the fact that the changes are lost if we do so, we have to get a copy of the person from the new model and copy the changes from the old person to the new person.

3. Replace the old person in the list with the new person object. When it is changed we do not have to do anything because there is already a separate model for this person.

4. If the user wants to save the person, the SaveChanges method of our model can be used to finish the Unit of Work. This domain context can still be reused in case the person is edited again.

We provide a full example for a very simple scenario, which can be extended following the same approach for more advanced applications.

LOB application case study: applying what we have learned

In this chapter, the Model Mock implementation has been replaced by the real one (based on RIA Services). As the entities have not been generated from RIA Services, some tweaks have to be performed on the contracts so that they return the entities defined by RIA Services. The application is also to be implemented and, when completed, refactored a little bit.

- First, all the operations to be performed in the model were defined.
- Second, the logic of all the windows in the application was implemented.
- To use the Unit of Work concept, the model factory was created. This will allow a new model instance, without having to share context.

Let us explore the changes that have been introduced by navigating the project structure.

Server

In the simple sample that has been implemented in this chapter, the Entity Framework model and Domain Services were generated directly in the web project. When talking about modularity or encapsulation, this does not make much sense. For our real application, we have created a project of the type library called Packt. Booking.Server.Data. The model and the Domain Services have been defined in it.

How to bind the project to our web project?

- Add the `Packt.Booking.Server.Data` reference to our web project (**Add Reference**).

- The `server.Data` project contains an `app.config` file with a series of configuration entries. These must be copied to the `web.config` file. In the source code of the application, they are marked with the literal, `server.data.configuration`.

The process requires a little patience. An error in an entry will cause the project not to be bound correctly. How can we check if everything is OK? The `server.data` project must be already built and bound to the Silverlight application. We would have to check if the code is generated including the entities (a sample project can also be created; this will be seen in the following section).

Apart from the project structure, some interesting points can be found, regarding implementation of the Domain Services.

- Use of a partial class to implement the methods we have customized such as `DomainServiceP.cs`.

  ```
  public partial class BookingDomainService :

  LinqToEntitiesDomainService<BookingsEntities>
  ```

- Methods not returning entities such as `Invoke`.

- Use of `Include` in the `Booking` entity, for instance:

  ◦ `DomainServiceP.cs`

    ```
    public IQueryable<Building> GetBuildingsPlusLocation()
    {
    return this.ObjectContext.Buildings.Include("Location");
    }
    ```

  ◦ `BookingDomainService.metadata.cs`

    ```
    internal sealed class BuildingMetadata
    {
        (...)
    [Include]
    public Location Location { get; set; }
    ```

- Use of composition to define the relation between `Floors` and `Rooms` (master/detail), in the `BookingDomainService.metadata.cs` file.

  ```
  [Composition]
  public EntityCollection<Room> Rooms { get; set; }
  ```

Test

Two kinds of project will be distinguished in this folder:

- **TestRunner**: It will be used to manually test different modules. In this case, it contains a test application to check whether the link to RIA Services is correct or not (it loads a list of database rooms in a grid).

- **UnitTest**: In this folder, our Unit Test projects are added. This will be dealt with in *Chapter 7, Out of Browser Applications*. If we had followed TDD, first, the interfaces would have been defined, followed by the tests, and finally the implementation.

Model

Two kinds of projects can be found in the model folder:

- **Contracts**: Apart from updates in the model contract, to cover all the functionality of the application, we have implemented a new IModelFactory contract, which will allow us to instantiate a new model every time we need it. Why is this useful? Because it allows us to create a new Unit of Work when necessary, avoiding conflicts when submitting and sharing a context (more information can be found in the *Context lifetime discussion and model factory* section in this chapter).

- **Real**: This is the implementation of the model based on RIA Services. As seen in the *Encapsulating RIA Services in a model* section, it is an implementation of the model with a status.

Modules

Regarding modules, apart from the implementation of the logic of all windows, we must remark that now, when initializing the ViewModel, instead of importing an IModel from the constructor, an IModelFactory is imported. Therefore, the initialization looks as follows:

```
[ImportingConstructor]
public MyBookingsVM(IModelFactory ModelFactory)
{
_model = ModelFactory.CreateModel();
```

In this way, the `ModelFactory` instance can be stored in a member variable and a new one can be created when needed. Let us see the advantages it brings. Imagine that the user is allowed to insert a new room from the page **MyBookings** and the following happens:

- The user is updating a new booking.
- The user realizes there is a missing room in the system. Next to the combo, there is a **+** button, which allows us to add a new room without switching windows.
- The user clicks on **Save** and all the data will be sent, as well as the booking in progress. This one, at this point, can contain wrong data. Consequently, two Units of Work are needed to perform this operation.

If `IModelFactory` is used, the scenario will be the following:

- The user is updating a new booking.
- The user realizes there is a missing room in the system. Next to the combo, there is a **+** button, which allows us to add a new room without switching windows.
- A new Unit of Work is created. With the Factory model, we create a new instance of the model and a new data context will be obtained internally.
- The user clicks on **Save** and now, as they are working with a different context, only the new room data is submitted.
- Once it has been satisfactorily saved, there are two options:
  - First, in the new context, detach the new entity `Room` and attach it to the older one. In this way, we will have it in our entity `Room` (beware of the fact that **Attach** does not bring the entity status).
  - Refresh the list of rooms in the old context.

Summary

At last, we got to the chapter devoted to data access. Here we have covered the technology that is recommended to build this access in Silverlight. Besides, we have seen how to integrate it in the MVVM architecture pattern. Are we now ready to develop a full application? There are still some important topics, such as security and automatic Unit Testing. Anyhow, we encourage you to begin codifying and playing with the technology. Go for it!

Additional resources

For more information on RIA Services, check the following readings:

- Silverlight Show introduction to RIA Services at `http://bit.ly/9oPae3`.
- Nikhil Kothari—RIA Services and Validation at `http://bit.ly/9IngnA`.
- Jeff Handley—RIA Services Validations at `http://bit.ly/aqpJNx`

6
Out of Browser (OOB) Applications

LOB (Line of Business) applications executing within a web browser are fine, but if we think from the perspective of a final user, it is not the option that they would choose first. This is due to the fact that:

- Having a desktop application is easy. It can be directly accessed by double-clicking so that it is launched quickly.

- Most of the time, it is necessary to leave Silverlight sandbox application. This happens, for example, when we need to access the filesystem, or with a special hardware via COM (such as an ATM).

- It is also crucial that, when executing an application, it allows us to work offline.

Similarly, from the point of view of the user, there are certain restrictions which are normally not well accepted, even though they are 100 percent desktop (namely WPF). It would be great to have the possibility of eliminating them:

- Installing a desktop application can carry problems, depending on the OS and installation details. It would be fantastic if they could run under a standard, which is independent from those details.

- In order to update a version already installed, it must be uninstalled and installed again. Wouldn't it be preferable that the application itself detected if there is a new version and updated automatically (even though this process is not dramatic)?

- Usually, desktop applications only work on a particular OS (that is, Windows). We would love to execute it in different platforms (for example, Mac).

- A desktop application normally has quite relaxed permissions. Hence, we dream of an application having restricted access to the hardware and software of our machine. It would only have permissions if allowed.

- A desktop application needs a given version of the .NET Framework installed on the machine.

In this chapter, you will learn how to install and execute our applications as Out of Browser (OOB), work with elevated permissions in and out of the browser, support cross domain calls, and work with the WebBrowser control.

Out of Browser (OOB)

Out of Browser (OOB) applications are executed out of the web browser, or that is the impression they give.

Regarding the final user, an OOB application is similar to a desktop application; the user installs it, gets a direct access icon to it, and when executed, it runs under a standard window, as shown in the following screenshot. It can even be uninstalled through the **Control Panel**.

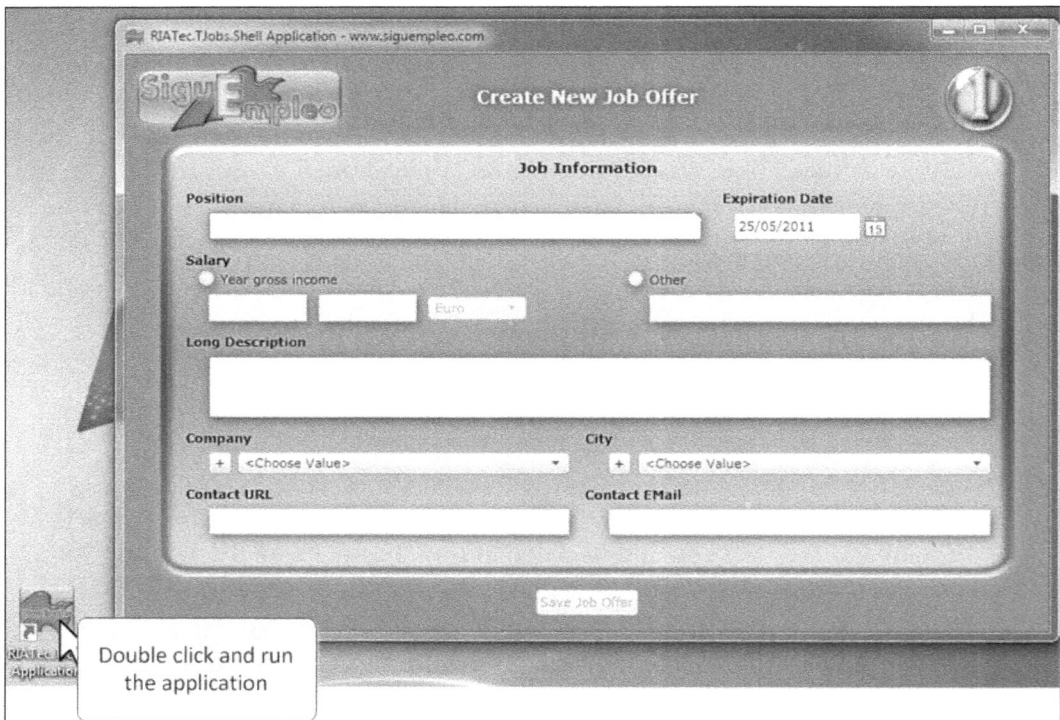

From the point of view of the Software Developer, an OOB application still runs under a *hidden* browser, that is, it is a Silverlight application with the same features as an application running under a browser.

Until the arrival of Silverlight 5, the main difference with an application executing in the browser was the fact that it could work with trusted permissions and perform operations, which the sandbox normally does not allow (accessing the filesystem, executing commands via COM+, and so on).

Executing an application in OOB mode

Allowing a Silverlight application to be executed as an OOB is very easy. We just need to tick a checkbox in the project settings. Let's see how to do it.

First, create a new Silverlight application called `01_Simple_OOB_App`. In the `MainPage`, a text block must be added displaying the message **Simple OOB App**. When you execute it, it will look as a standard in-browser application, as shown in the following screenshot:

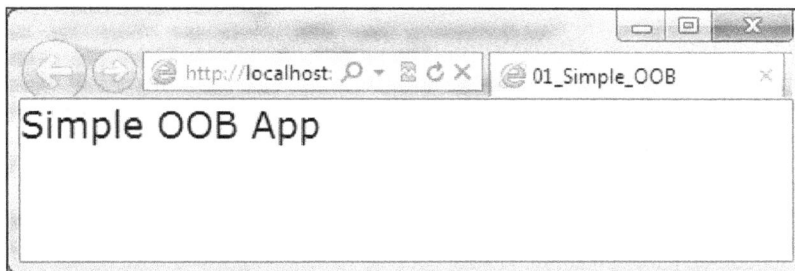

In order to enable OOB mode, follow these steps:

1. Right-click on the Silverlight project `root`. When the context menu is displayed, click on **Properties**:

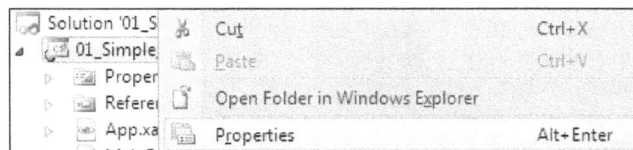

2. Select the **Silverlight** tab and tick the checkbox with the message **Enable running application out of the browser**:

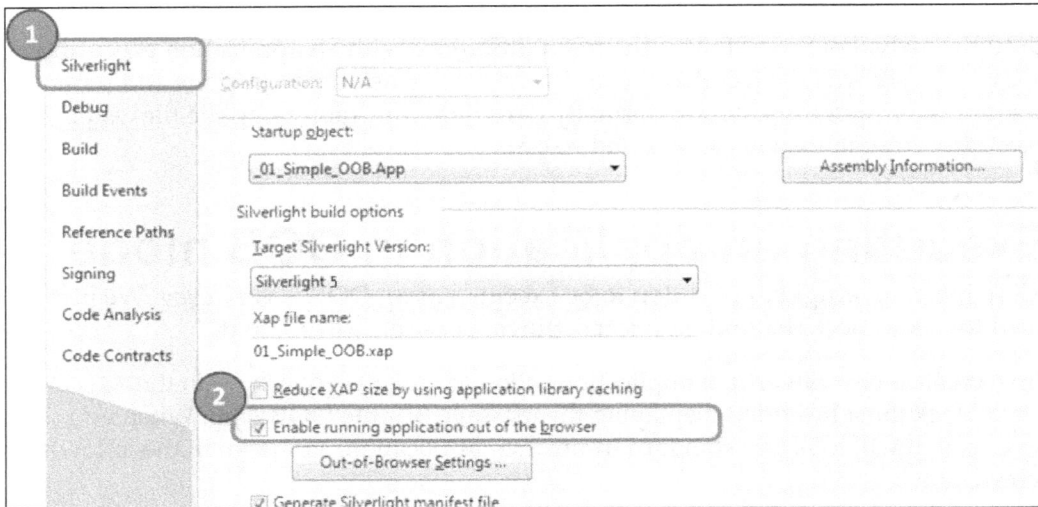

3. When executing the application, it still runs in the browser but, if we right-click on it, there will be a new option **Install 01_Simple_OOB Application onto this computer...** in the context menu, as shown in the following screenshot:

4. If we click on that option, we get a message prompt asking to install the app, as shown in the following screenshot:

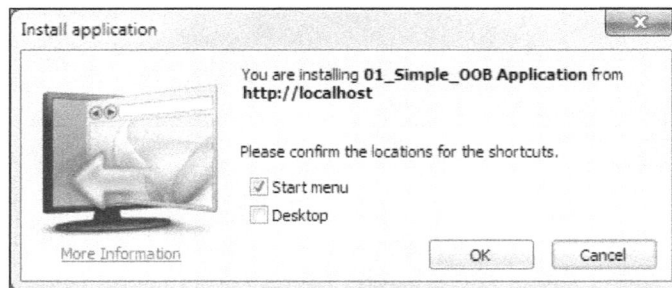

5. Once we click **OK**, the application is installed and ready to be used as OOB.

It is great to use apps as a final user, but what happens with developers? In case we want to debug our OOB application, will we have to install it every time we run the environment? Of course not. In the project properties (**Context menu | Properties**), the **Debug** tab allows us to choose that the application starts up straight in OOB mode (the Silverlight project will have to be chosen as a start-up project):

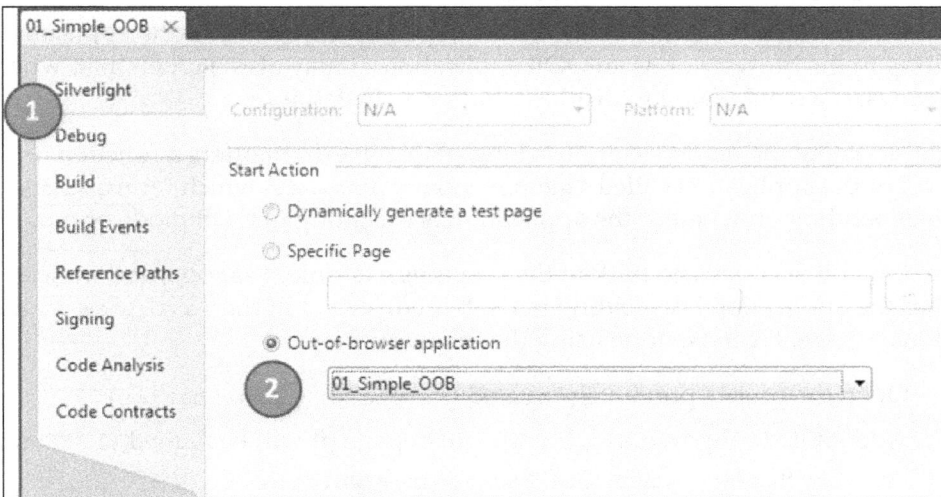

Enhancing the experience—tooling up and updating

As we have already seen, enabling the OOB mode in our application is something quite straightforward. Nevertheless, the following doubts may have arisen:

- In some cases, I want to know if my application is running in normal or OOB mode to, for instance, show one UI or another. How can I do that?

- How can I know if the application is already installed?

- When installing from a not very intuitive contextual menu, is there any way to display our own UI in order to allow the user to install the application?

- How do I uninstall an OOB application?

- I would like to let the users install my application from a CD, eliminating the need to be connected to the Web. Is that possible?

- When a new version of my application is uploaded to the production server, is there any way to detect updates and install new versions automatically?

In-browser/OOB detection

Sometimes, the UI we want to show differs depending on whether the application is executing in the browser or as an OOB application. It may also happen that, when it is in-browser, we only want to display a button to install it.

In order to know the mode we are working with, Silverlight offers a function on the level of the application called `IsRunningOutOfBrowser`, which returns `true` or `false` depending on whether the application is executing in OOB mode or not.

To see how it works, let's go back to the previous example, `TestOOB`, and indicate whether the application is executing in OOB mode or not in the `TextBlock` we use in the main page. It can be done using the following steps:

1. Open the project previously created (`Simple_OOB_Application`).

2. Add an ID to the `TextBlock` of the main page (it will be named `tbStatus`):

```
<Grid x:Name="LayoutRoot" Background="White">
  <TextBlock x:Name="tbStatus" Text="Simple OOB App"
    FontSize="16"/>
</Grid>
```

3. In the constructor of the page, check the value of the application variable
   `IsRunningOutOfBrowser`, which will display one of two messages
   depending on the state.

```
public MainPage()
{
  InitializeComponent();

  if (App.Current.IsRunningOutOfBrowser == true)
  {
    tbStatus.Text = "I'm running out of browser";
  }
  else
  {
    tbStatus.Text = "I'm running in browser";
  }
}
```

4. Therefore, in case we are executing in OOB mode, the following message
   will be displayed:

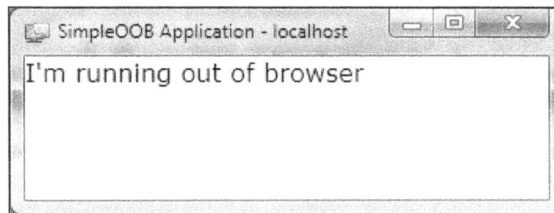

Detecting the application installed

Another common scenario arises when the application is being executed in the
browser and we need to know if it has already been installed as OOB. For instance,
a common example of this is when we want to display a message asking the user
whether to install the application or not. We can make use of the application variable
`InstallState`, which returns a type enumerated with one of the following values:
`NotInstalled`, `Installed`, `Installing`, or `InstallFailed`.

Thus, in the sample application that has been created, it could be checked whether the application is installed or not in the following way:

```
public MainPage()
{
  InitializeComponent();

  if (App.Current.InstallState == InstallState.Installed)
  {
    tbStatus.Text = "Application Installed";
  }
  else
  {
    tbStatus.Text = "Application not installed";
  }
}
```

Installing the custom interface

As mentioned previously, installing the application from the contextual menu of our Silverlight application was not intuitive at all. Perhaps it could be possible to place a button so that the user could begin the installation. Up to what point can we customize the installation process of our Silverlight application? Silverlight allows us to launch the installation process by code, as long as it comes from a user petition (such as a click on a button). The dialog which asks if we want to install the application cannot be customized.

To install the application, the method Install of Application must be called. Let's add this functionality to our basic sample:

1. Add a button to the main window:

```
<Grid x:Name="LayoutRoot" Background="White">
  <TextBlock x:Name="tbStatus" Text="Simple OOB App"
    FontSize="16"/>
  <Button Content="Install" Height="23"
    HorizontalAlignment="Left" Margin="142,55,0,0"
    Name="button1" VerticalAlignment="Top" Width="75" />
</Grid>
```

2. Subscribe to the Click event:

```
<Button Content="Install" Height="23" HorizontalAlignment="Left"
  Margin="142,55,0,0" Name="button1" VerticalAlignment="Top"
  Width="75" Click="button1_Click" />
```

3. Check if the application has already been installed in the handler of the button and add the call to `Install`:

```
private void button1_Click(object sender, RoutedEventArgs e)
{
  if (Application.Current.InstallState ==
    InstallState.NotInstalled)
  {
    Application.Current.Install();
  }
  else
  {
    MessageBox.Show("Application already installed");
  }

}
```

4. Execute the application. When you click on the new button, the dialog box asking you if you want to install the application will be displayed, as shown in the following screenshot:

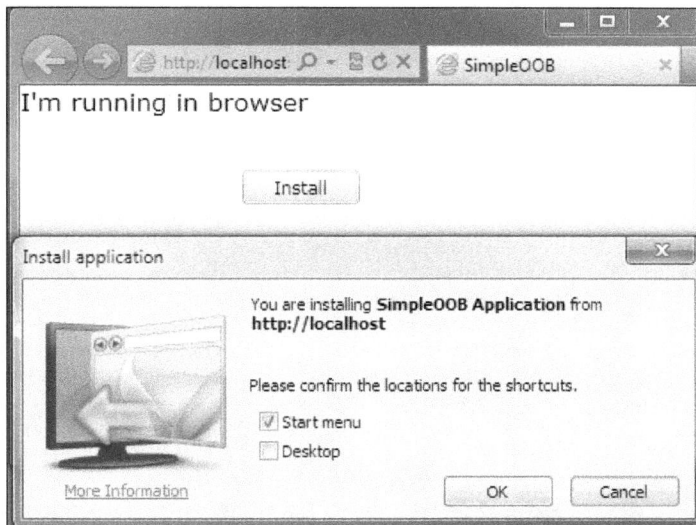

Uninstalling an OOB application

To uninstall a Silverlight application, the user can choose among several options:

- They can right-click on the application and, in the contextual menu, choose the **Remove this application...** option, as shown in the following screenshot:

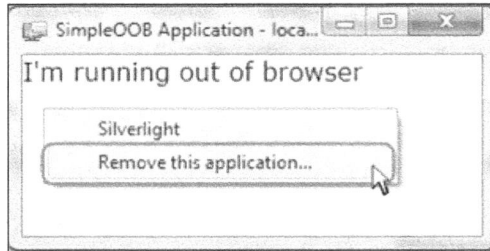

- It can be uninstalled right from the Windows **Control Panel**:

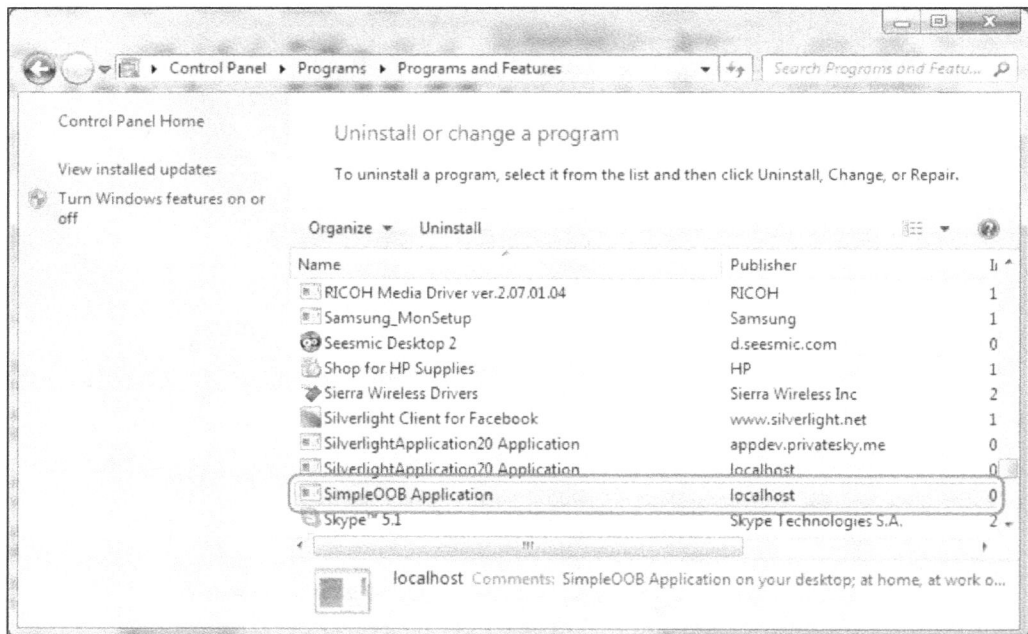

The customization of the installation is an improvement that is pending to be added to Silverlight.

Offline installation

Sometimes, we face scenarios where it is necessary for the user to be able to install the application from a CD, or that an administrator can make an implementation. This scenario is not ideal for Silverlight applications (normally, the user downloads them from a URL, either intranet or extranet and, moreover, benefits from automatic updates).

If you face this situation, you may wonder whether it is more convenient to orient development to WPF-Click once, or use the method explained by Tim Heuer in his blog: Installing Silverlight Offline (`http://timheuer.com/blog/archive/2008/09/29/install-silverlight-2-rc0-offline.aspx`).

Even though this method allows us to install our OOB application in a silent mode, it has certain limitations:

- If the user does not have the Silverlight plug-in installed, they will need to be connected to the Internet to download it from the Microsoft website

- The installation in silent mode is not valid for trusted OOB applications

Updates

OOB applications are installed on our own machine, which means there are a lot of advantages, such as fast boot, offline work mode, and so on. Nonetheless, what happens if we upload an update to the server? Is there a way to update our local application? Of course there is. What's more? It is possible in an easy and powerful way. Let's see it in action:

In the `app.cs` file, subscribe to the event named `CheckAndDownloadUpdateCompleted` and, later, make the asynchronous petition to check if there is a new update and, if so, download it automatically. The following is the source code:

```
private void Application_Startup(object sender, StartupEventArgs e)
{

  CheckAndDownloadUpdateCompleted +=
  new CheckAndDownloadUpdateCompletedEventHandle
  r(Application_CheckAndDownloadUpdateCompleted);
  CheckAndDownloadUpdateAsync();
  (...)
}
```

```
private void Application_CheckAndDownloadUpdateCompleted(object
  sender, CheckAndDownloadUpdateCompletedEventArgs e)
{
  MessageBox.Show("Application updated, please restart.");
}
```

> Updates will work as long as our XAP is not in a file that needs security.

Offline work

An advantage of working with OOB applications is that, once they have been installed, it is not necessary to have an Internet connection to execute them (they are downloaded locally). What does this mean? It is possible to implement an offline work method for our applications, which permits, for example, that a user on a flight can work with the application and, later, when they have an Internet connection, they can synchronize the data with the server.

To work offline, it is necessary to have a repository to store reference data, as well as changes or new creations. If our Silverlight applications normally work within a sandbox and we do not have access to the HDD of the local machine, what can we make use of? In such cases, we have two options: either requiring elevated permissions for our application to execute (this will be dealt with later) or making use of the Silverlight Isolated Storage.

Isolated Storage is a virtual filesystem that allows a Silverlight application to store data in an invisible folder in the machine. By default, a Silverlight application can use 2 MB of storage. Isolated Storage is a 10 MB OOB application, but the user can be asked to increase the quota.

Let's see a simple sample of how to read and write data in the Isolated Storage. This example is available in the online material on `http://bit.ly/5gEwuM`.

You can create a file in the Isolated Storage using the following code:

```
using System.IO.IsolatedStorage;
using System.IO;

(...)

private void WriteContentToIsoStorage(string content,
  string filename)
```

```
{
  using (IsolatedStorageFile isf =
    IsolatedStorageFile.GetUserStoreForApplication())
  {
    using (IsolatedStorageFileStream isfs = new
      IsolatedStorageFileStream(filename, FileMode.Create, isf))
    {
      using (StreamWriter sw = new StreamWriter(isfs))
      {
        sw.Write(content);
        sw.Close();
      }
    }
  }
}
```

You can read the information using the following code:

```
using System.IO.IsolatedStorage;
using System.IO;

(...)
private string LoadContentFromIsoStorage(string filename)
{
  string data = String.Empty;
  using (IsolatedStorageFile isf =
    IsolatedStorageFile.GetUserStoreForApplication())
  {
    using (IsolatedStorageFileStream isfs = new
      IsolatedStorageFileStream(filename, FileMode.Open, isf))
    {
      using (StreamReader sr = new StreamReader(isfs))
      {
        string lineOfData = String.Empty;
        while ((lineOfData = sr.ReadLine()) != null)
          data += lineOfData;
      }
    }
  }
  return data;
}
```

> To continue learning how this works, you can follow this link: http://bit.ly/qkY9UM.

How it works

Normally, when data have to be obtained or updated, we communicate with the server via a web service to get or modify this information.

To avoid this connection, we can do the following: first, get the most commonly read data and store them in a cache; second, the user creates his/her own entries, which are stored in the local repository (Isolated Storage). Once the user has an Internet connection again, offline data is sent to be synchronised in the repository.

Offline work is not as easy as it may sound. Another book could be written only on this! If you want further information about this, we can recommend the following session by Steve Lasker, Offline Microsoft Silverlight Applications (`http://bit.ly/1tIxNt`).

Breaking the sandbox—trusted applications

Up to now, we have seen how an OOB Silverlight application runs within a sandbox. That is to say, its access to certain resources is limited or restricted. What happens if we need to perform operations that the sandbox has restricted due to safety reasons? To solve this issue, there are applications with elevated permissions:

- A trusted OOB application is a program the user trusts (similar to when a desktop application is installed on our machine).
- Its XAP file is signed with a certificate, which ensures its trustworthy origin.
- It has elevated permissions, which makes it possible, for example, to make calls to COM components, P/Invoke calls, or access the local filesystem.
- For the application to be installed/executed, it needs the express authorization of the user.

Enabling trusted mode

How can an OOB application be enabled to require elevated permissions? To configure a Silverlight program that already exists, follow these steps:

1. Go to the **Properties** tab of the Silverlight Project (contextual menu of the project, **Silverlight | Properties**) and click on the button **Out-of-Browser Settings...**:

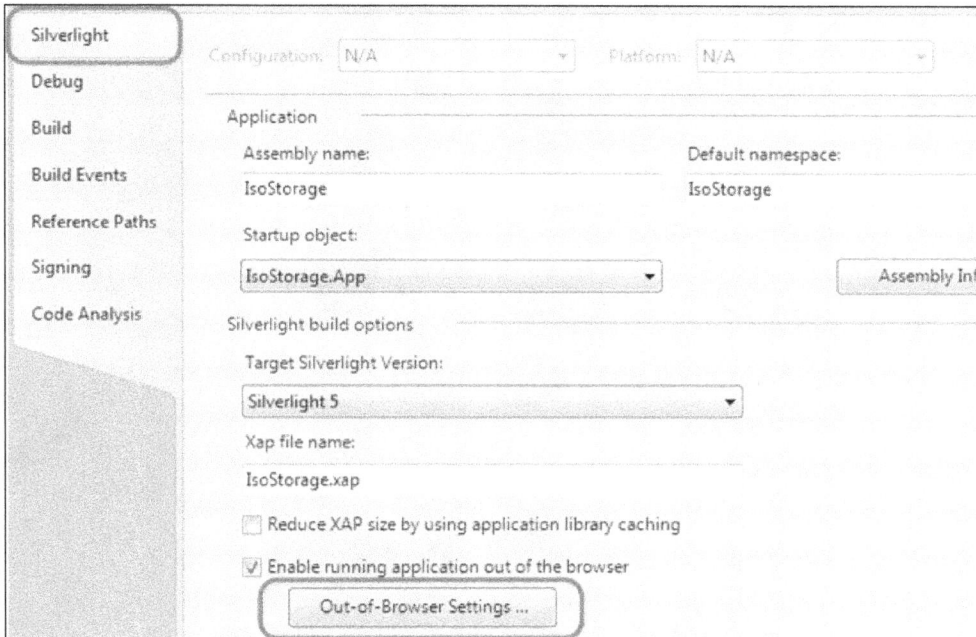

2. A dialog is displayed, where the option **Require elevated trust when running outside the browser** must be checked, as shown in the following screenshot:

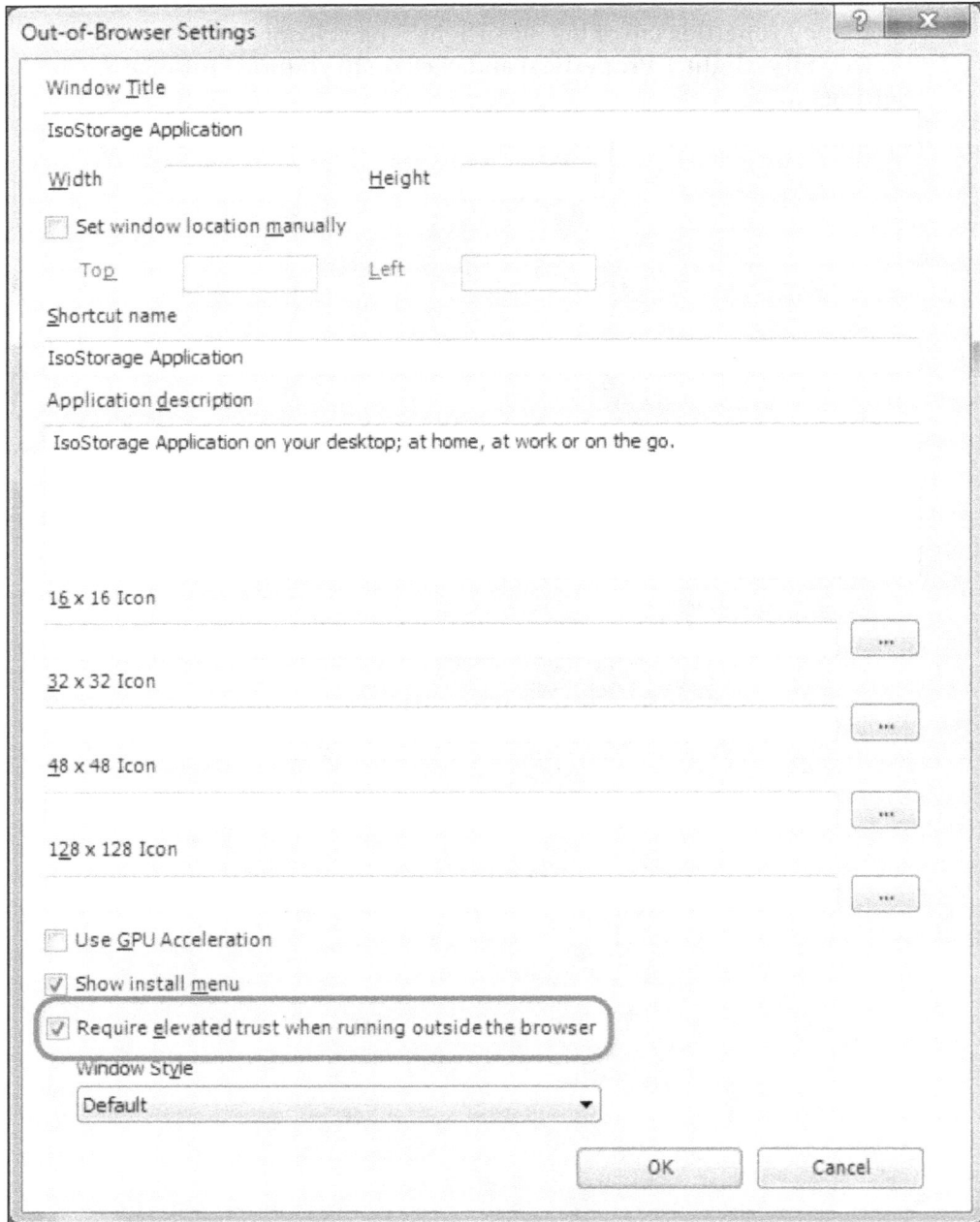

Out-of-Browser Settings

Window Title

IsoStorage Application

Width   Height

☐ Set window location manually

   Top [   ]   Left [   ]

Shortcut name

IsoStorage Application

Application description

  IsoStorage Application on your desktop; at home, at work or on the go.

16 x 16 Icon

  [...]

32 x 32 Icon

  [...]

48 x 48 Icon

  [...]

128 x 128 Icon

  [...]

☐ Use GPU Acceleration

☑ Show install menu

☑ Require elevated trust when running outside the browser

Window Style

[Default   ▼]

[OK]   [Cancel]

After these steps, our application will be enabled as OOB trusted. However, if a user tries to install it, they will receive a warning indicating the source that published the application cannot be trusted. To eliminate this message, we will have to use our enterprise's certificate or acquire a new one (we can buy one or, if it is an intranet, our IT administrator can generate a new one). This operation can be performed from the **Signing** tab in the project's properties (right-click on **Silverlight project** | **Properties** | **Signing**).

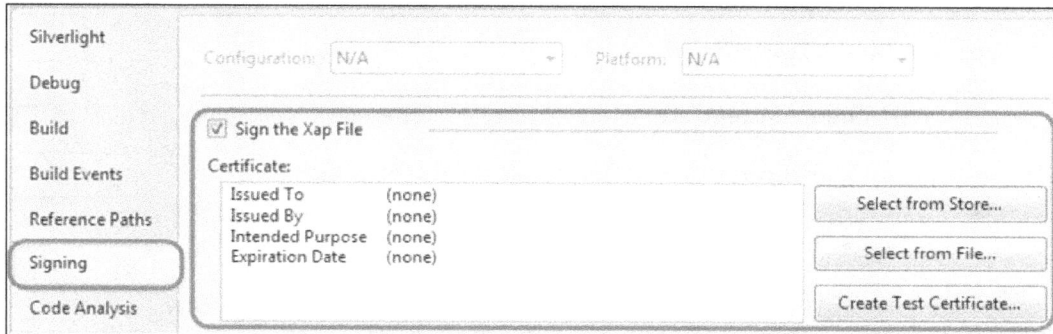

Advantages of trusted applications

Now we have our trusted application, which has the following additional advantages:

- We can access the filesystem of the machine (from the Silverlight 5 version).

- We can make calls to COM components. We can read or write to the registry (only current user entry), call other executable files, and so on.

- It is possible to make P/Invoke calls.

- We can make petitions to a URL, even if they are cross domain. It is not necessary that the server has a cross-domain policy enabled.

- It is possible to integrate a WebBrowser control in our application. That is, we can display HTML in our Silverlight application and interact with it.

- Real windows can be created. Normally, when new windows are created in a Silverlight application, they are a fantasy; that is to say, they are not physical windows, but they are displayed within the main one. If our application is trusted (only SL version 5), we can create floating windows and, for instance, they can be displayed on several monitors.

Accessing files

Our trusted application has access to the local filesystem (if it is Silverlight 5; in case it is Silverlight 4, it can only access folders, such as My Documents and via COM calls it's possible to gain additional access). The operations on System.IO, which previously returned safety errors, will now be executed flawlessly.

As a sample, let's see how the content of the Program Files file can be listed in our trusted Silverlight application:

```
public class ViewModel
{
    public ObservableCollection<string> DirNames { get; set; }

  public ViewModel()
  {
    DirNames = new ObservableCollection<string>();

    // Let's try to enumerate the directories that are
    // under Program Files, this operation would throw an
    // exception if the application is not a trusted one.
    DirectoryInfo di = new DirectoryInfo("C:\\Program Files");

    foreach (var info in di.EnumerateDirectories())
    {
      DirNames.Add(info.FullName);
    }
  }
}
```

Making calls to COM+

We can make calls to COM components, which open plenty of doors, such as reading and (partially) writing on the registry, communicating with devices, launching apps, and even using Excel Automation.

However, the main disadvantage of this approach is that it only works in Windows. So if our application needs to run in Mac, this code must be isolated and will not offer this functionality for that platform.

> If you need to detect under which OS a Silverlight application is running, you can use Environment.OSVersion.

Let's see a couple of examples of how to make these calls.

Writing an entry on the registry

In order to do so, create a new Silverlight Application project and tick the checkboxes (**Enable Running application out of the browser, Out-of-Browser Settings | Require elevated trust when running outside the browser**).

Add the reference to the **Microsoft.CSharp** DLL (**Add Reference | .NET | Microsoft.CSharp**):

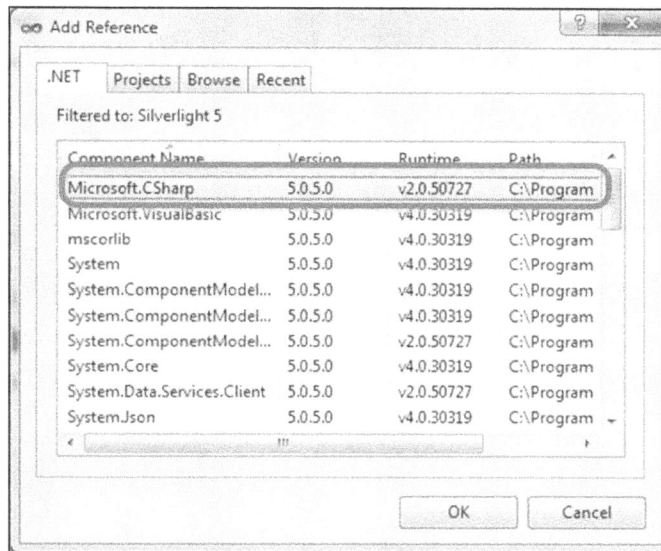

Make sure this DLL and **System.Core** are referenced:

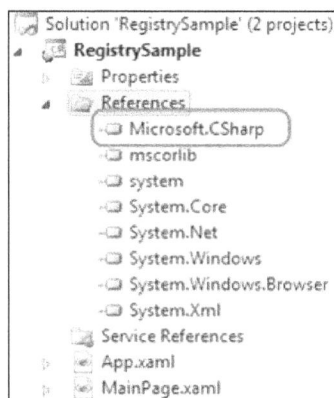

You can write the entry on the registry using the following code:

```
using System.Runtime.InteropServices.Automation;

(...)
private void button1_Click(object sender, RoutedEventArgs e)
{
  using (dynamic shell =
    AutomationFactory.CreateObject("WScript.Shell"))
  {
    shell.RegWrite(@"HKCU\Software\MyTest", "");
  }
}
```

The result is as shown in the following screenshot:

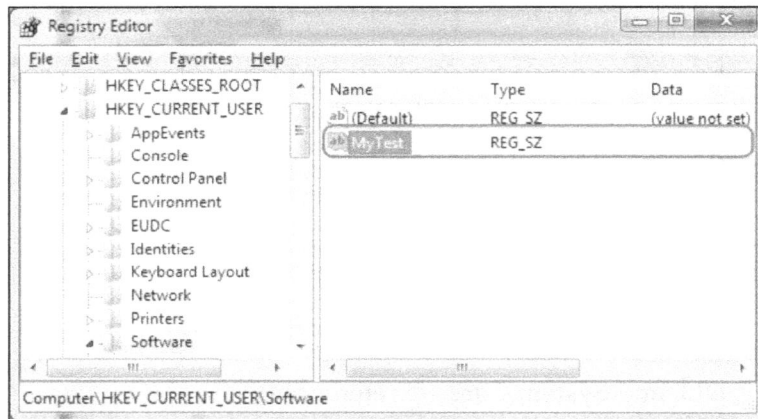

Executing notepad from our application

Another interesting feature is the ability of launching other applications from our trusted application. In the following code we will launch a Notepad.

```
using System.Runtime.InteropServices.Automation;
(...)
private void button1_Click(object sender, RoutedEventArgs e)
{
  dynamic cmd = AutomationFactory.CreateObject("WScript.Shell");

  cmd.Run(@"c:\Windows\notepad.exe", 1, true);
}
```

P/Invoke

As an innovation, Silverlight 5 includes call support via P/Invoke. Platform Invocation Services allows managed code to call unmanaged functions that are implemented in a DLL. This is only allowed for full-trust applications.

Let's see how this works by creating a sample, which calls a `kernel32.dll` method reproducing system beeps. Follow the steps mentioned next:

1. Create a new Silverlight project (application) and configure it to be an OOB application with trusted permissions.

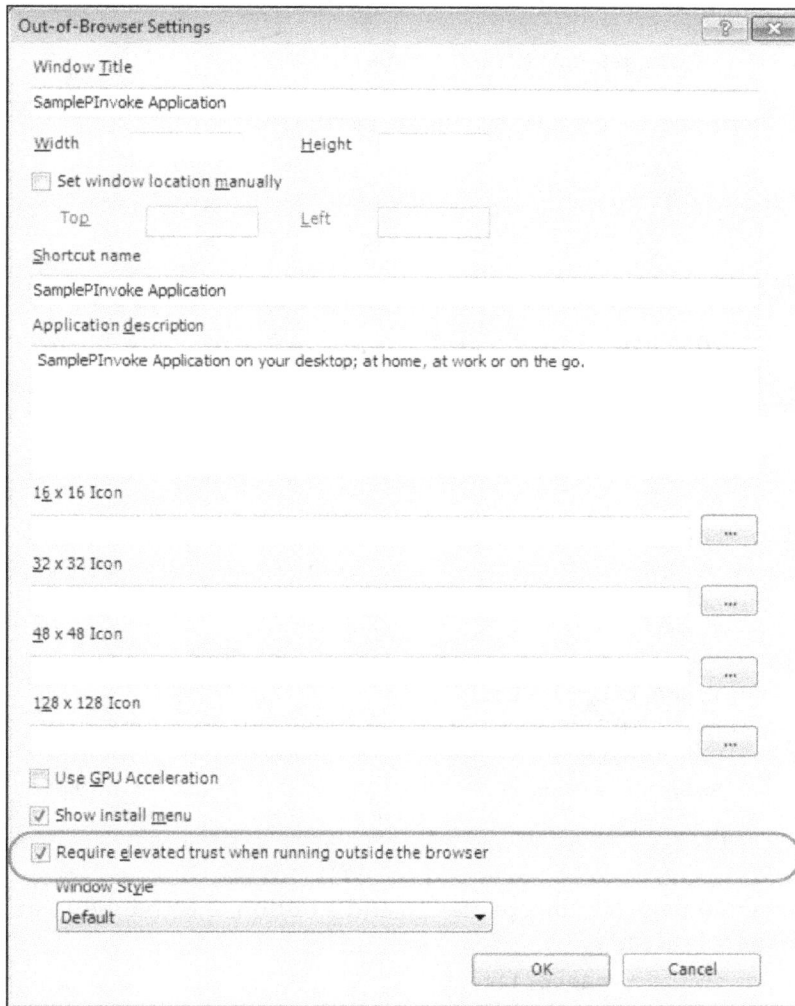

2. Add a new class (by means of **Add New Class**) called `MyBeep`. Implement the `Beep` method of the Kernel 32 DLL.

```
using System.Runtime.InteropServices;

public class MyBeep
{
  [DllImport("User32.dll")]
  private static extern Boolean MessageBeep(UInt32
    beepType);

  public void PlaySound(BeepTypes type)
  {
    if (!MessageBeep((UInt32)type))
    {
      throw new Exception("Beep failed!");
    }
  }
}

public enum BeepTypes : uint
{
  Ok = 0x00000000,
  Error = 0x00000010,
  Warning = 0x00000030,
  Information = 0x00000040
}

public static class BeepTypeExtensions
{
  public static BeepTypes AsBeepTypeEnum(this string
    beepType)
  {
    BeepTypes beepTypeEnum;
    return Enum.TryParse(beepType,true,out beepTypeEnum)
      ? beepTypeEnum
      : BeepTypes.Error;
  }
}
```

3. In the main page (`mainpage.xaml`), add a button to be bound to the `Click` event as follows:

```
<Button Content="Beep !!"

  Click="button1_Click" />
```

4. In the Code-Behind (`MainPage.cs`), make the call to the method defined in the `MyBeep` class.

```
private void button1_Click(object sender,
  RoutedEventArgs e)
{
  MyBeep myBeep = new MyBeep();
  myBeep.PlaySound(BeepTypes.Information);
}
```

> If an exception appears when executing the action, check the application settings and make sure that it is running in OOB trusted mode.

Cross-domain calls

When executing our Silverlight application within the sandbox, we can make calls to services, or ask for resources, which are in our domain. However, if we try to access resources in a different domain (namely a feed of Apple's film trailers) this call can return an error since, due to safety reasons, these calls are restricted unless the web service authorizes them explicitly. The following are the solutions we have within sandbox:

- The server may have an XML file with the cross-domain policy indicating we have access to these resources. It can be checked by launching a query to the Apple feed and using the Fiddler packages sniffer. We will then realize if this server exposes a cross-domain policy.

- It is possible to implement a service in our server acting as a proxy. The bad thing about this approach is that we overload the server and the response to the client is slower.

If our application is executed as trusted, this restriction does not exist. We can make the petition to a cross domain without having the cross-domain policy enabled. For instance, we can make a query to the Apple feed to check new cinema openings.

```
private void button1_Click(object sender, RoutedEventArgs e)
{
  WebClient wc = new WebClient();

  wc.DownloadStringCompleted += new
    DownloadStringCompletedEventHandler(wc_DownloadStringCompleted);
  wc.DownloadStringAsync(new
    Uri("http://www.apple.com/trailers/home/xml/current.xml",
    UriKind.Absolute));
}
```

```
void wc_DownloadStringCompleted(object sender,
    DownloadStringCompletedEventArgs e)
{
    MessageBox.Show(e.Result);
}
```

WebBrowser control

Another interesting control we can only use in trusted OOB applications is the WebBrowser control. This allows us to view HTML pages within our Silverlight application. Besides, if the page is in the same domain, we can even interact with it via **Silverlight | JavaScript**.

How it works

Let's check how this control works by creating a simple example:

1. Create a new Silverlight project (application) and configure it so that it is executed as an OOB application with trusted permissions.

2. In the XAML, add the namespace `System.Windows.Controls` and instantiate the control:

```
<UserControl x:Class="WebBrowser.MainPage"
    xmlns="http://schemas.microsoft.com/winfx/2006/xaml/presentation"
    xmlns:x="http://schemas.microsoft.com/winfx/2006/xaml"
    xmlns:d="http://schemas.microsoft.com/expression/blend/2008"
    xmlns:mc="http://schemas.openxmlformats.org/
        markup-compatibility/2006"
    xmlns:controls="clr-namespace:System.Windows.Controls;
        assembly=System.Windows"
    mc:Ignorable="d"
    d:DesignHeight="300" d:DesignWidth="400">

    <Grid x:Name="LayoutRoot" Background="White">
        <controls:WebBrowser Source="http://www.bing.com"/>
    </Grid>
</UserControl>
```

3. The result we obtain is shown in the following screenshot:

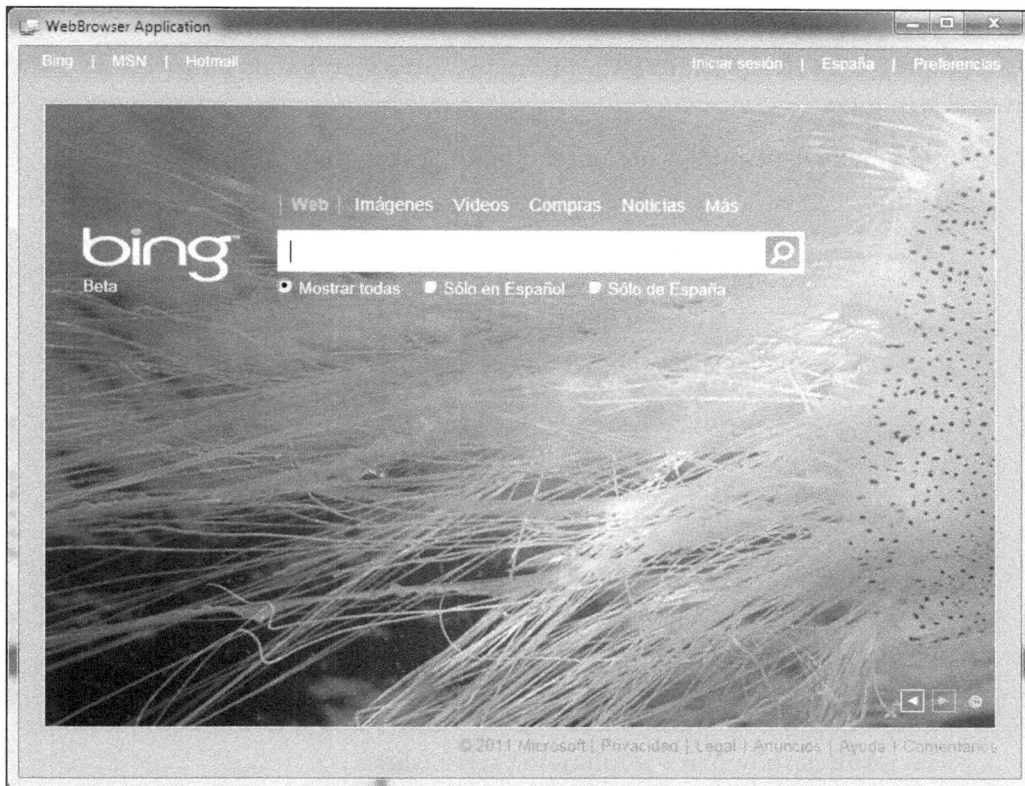

Limitations to take into account:

- Control is placed on top of the ZOrder. In case we want to show a ChildWindow, for example, this will not be visible at first. To give it visibility, we need to create a rectangle using a WebBrowser Brush, make a static picture to the WebBrowser Control content and, when the dialog box is shown, hide the WebBrowser showing our rectangle.

- For safety reasons, we cannot capture the moment when the user navigates from one page to another; neither can we make JavaScript calls from Silverlight if the page belongs to a different domain.

- It is a heavy control, so it is not a good idea to create and destroy it dynamically quite often.

Real windows

Another advantage of trusted OOB applications is the fact that they can show physical windows.

At the moment, these windows are not modal in Silverlight 5. The following is how it works:

1. Create a `Windows` object and assign the `content` property of this control to a given UserControl.

2. Then, we see how this sort of window can be displayed:

```
private void button1_Click(object sender, RoutedEventArgs e)
{
  Window wnd = new Window();

  wnd.Width = 500;
  wnd.Height = 350;
  wnd.Title = "This is a test window";
  //We indicate here a custom user control to display in the
  //new window
  wnd.Content = new MyControl();
  wnd.Visibility = Visibility.Visible;
}
```

3. The result is shown in the following screenshot:

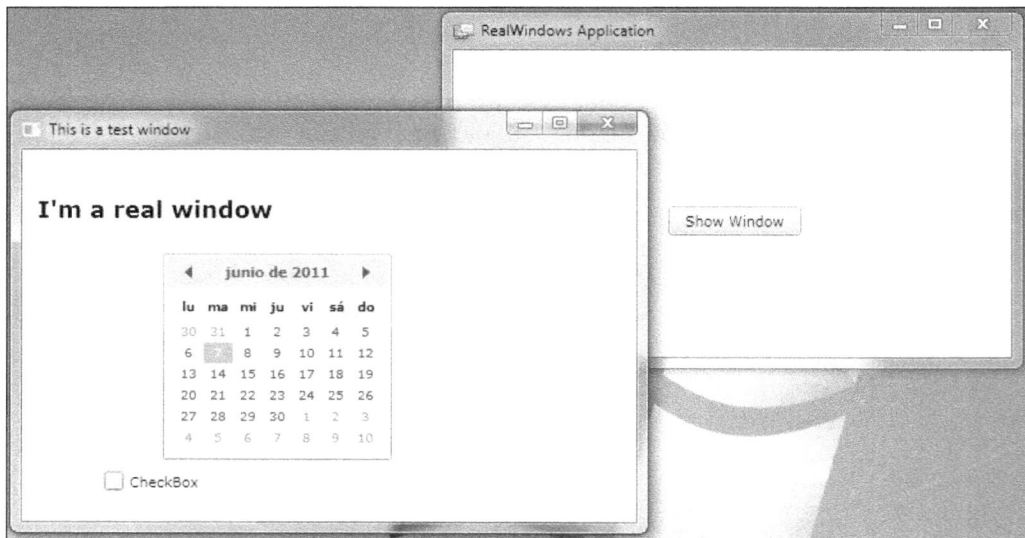

In-browser trusted applications

Having trusted applications, which are executed as if they were desktop applications, is a powerful and interesting idea, but what happens if we need to have elevated permissions for applications running in the browser? For instance, a bank's intranet.

Silverlight 5 incorporates **in-browser trusted** applications, whose main features are as follows:

- It is a specific functionality for enterprise applications.
- The administrator controls which applications can be executed via group policy.
- The user is not asked and neither is the application installed. It is marked as valid, so it will be executed by the administrator.
- It can be integrated as part of an HTML website, without the need to give elevated permissions to the entire site.

On the other hand, the doubt arises, when developing, shall we create our own test certificate? The answer is no. If we execute from localhost, the restriction is not applied.

Thus, in the example that was previously implemented (getting the content of C:\Program Files), we only need to select the properties of our Silverlight project (right-click on **Silverlight | Properties**) and select the option **Require elevated trust when running in-browser**, as shown in the following screenshot:

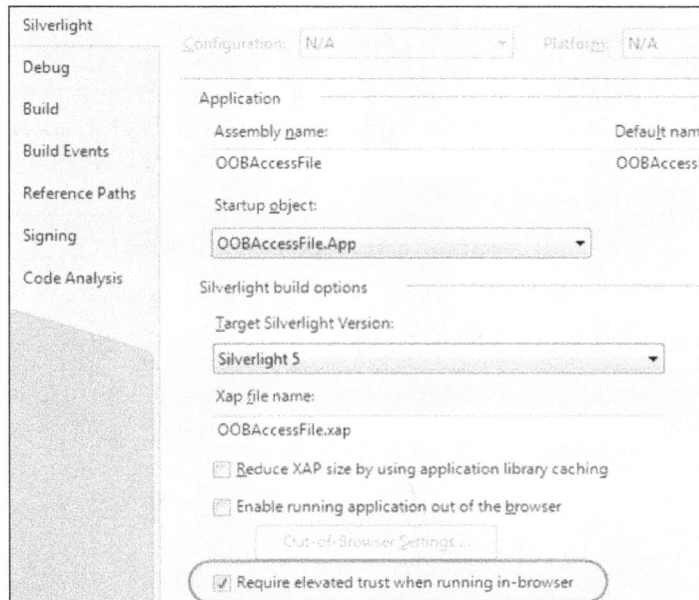

When executing the application, it can be seen running flawlessly within the browser.

As we pointed out earlier, if the application in production is displayed, it will fail as it is not executed from localhost. The following are the necessary steps to avoid it:

- The XAP file has to be signed with a certificate (this can be seen in depth in *Chapter 11, Security*).

- The network administrator has to specify a setting for the trusted in-browser applications to be executed in all machines. Particularly, the flag of the registry entry `HKEY_LOCAL_MACHINE\SOFTWARE\Microsoft\Silverlight\AllowElevatedTrustAppsInBrowser` must have the value of 1.

- The network administrator has to add the certificate in which the XAP has been signed with as a trusted certificate (`CurrentUser\Trusted Publishers`).

For more information about the display process, please visit the link `http://bit.ly/kKbdpl`.

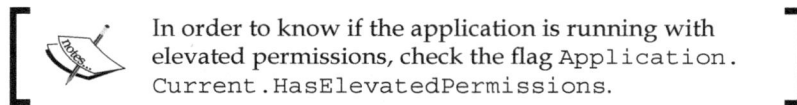

> In order to know if the application is running with elevated permissions, check the flag `Application.Current.HasElevatedPermissions`.

LOB application case study: applying what we have learned

As final users, one of the disadvantages of using web applications is the fact that we have to remember URLs, open the browser, and so on. Isn't it easier to double-click on a desktop icon and run an application? That is what has been added to our booking application:

- We detect whether it is running or not within the browser
- If so, an option is shown to install the application as OOB
- Then, we install the application as OOB

Thus, when executing the application within the browser, a new option is added in the navigation menu, as shown in the following screenshot:

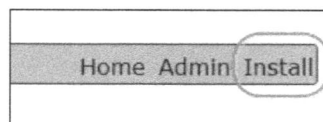

When clicking the **Install** button, the confirmation dialog appears and the application gets installed (then, go to the desktop icon and execute it).

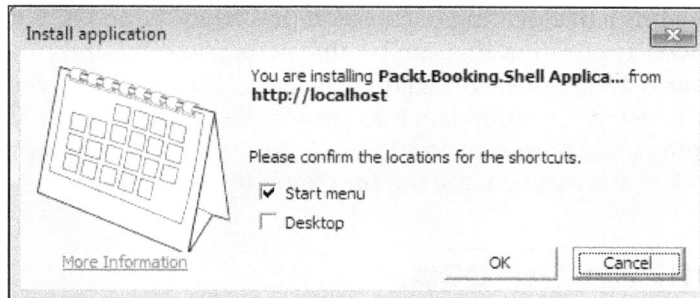

It is necessary to bear in mind that the application item has been customized. This can be set up in the project properties, **Out-of-Browser Settings**.

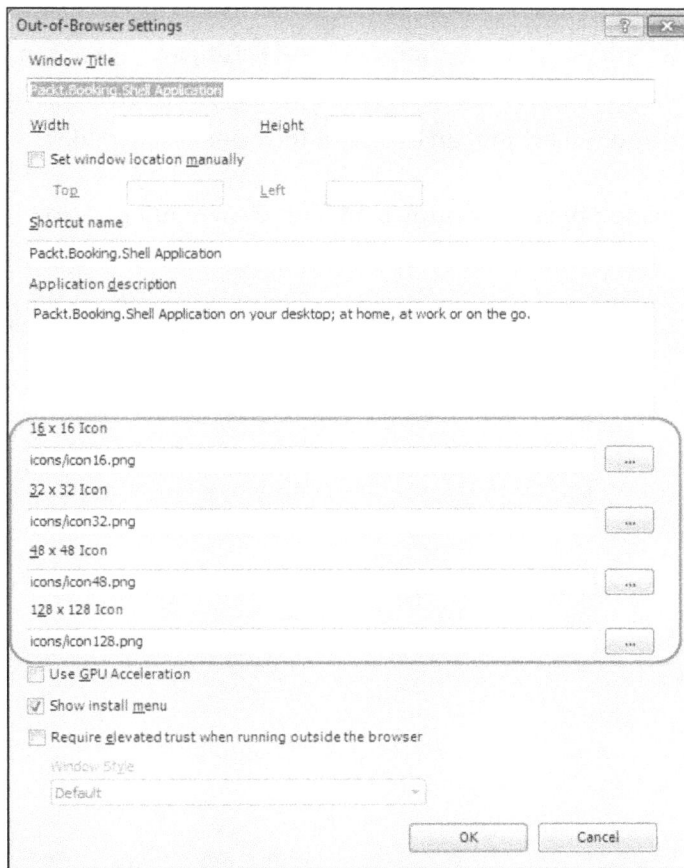

Summary

The capabilities offered by Out of Browser (OOB) applications are amazing. If we also add the possibility of elevating permission (in-browser and OOB trusted), the result is a light web application that can be almost as powerful and functional as a desktop application. Remember this chapter when a client indicates non-standard requirements of a web application (such as the integration of the application in an ATM, accessing the local filesystem, and so on). Anyway, before accepting, make the possible concept tests and ensure the functionality is covered.

Additional resources

If you need to dive deeper into any of the features presented in this chapter, you can check the following links:

- How far can I get using COM+? This post by Justin Angels summarizes it nicely at `http://bit.ly/4Ama4H`

- In-browser `http://bit.ly/kKbdpl` and settings `http://bit.ly/oKFbzG`

- P/Invoke, how does it work? `http://bit.ly/r2DTQF`

- P/Invoke and Silverlight, an excellent introduction by Vikram Pendse `http://bit.ly/qI3XhN`

- How to create physical windows, by Pete Brown `http://bit.ly/gZ4w7S`

Testing your LOB Application

7

It is always crucial with software to ensure that applications do exactly what they are intended to. Despite its importance, this question has not been paid the necessary attention due to the difficulty of the task, except for certain sectors where reliability is critical (*mission critical*),such as sanitary environments, flight control, factory software, the military industry, and so on. However, nowadays we bear witness to a dramatic change in this sense, and every project must have a test strategy.

In this chapter, we will start by covering current testing techniques, and then we will move from standard .NET testing to specific Silverlight testing procedures. In brief we will cover:

- Introducing a bit of theory
- Testing server code
- Testing client code using general-purpose tooling
- Testing client code using Silverlight-specific tooling
- Adding testing to our trunk project sample, using the **Moq** framework

Types of testing

The different ways to test software can be divided into two groups:

- **Static analysis**: This inspects the application code.
- **Dynamic analysis**: This considers the results of the application execution.

In static analysis, we first have the result of the compiler, either in the form of errors or warnings. Second, we find the semantic analysis based on best practices, such as those provided by ReSharper, StyleCop, or FxCop. Finally, we have the formal verification of programs, a branch with a deep theoretical base that is used above all, in protocol verification. Its effectiveness is very high as it checks all possibilities, but at the same time, it needs plenty of resources and specific languages for its execution.

On the other hand, dynamic analysis needs code execution and is able to focus either on isolated parts, or on the whole application. In the first case, we mainly refer to unit testing, where results are executed and verified individually, in an isolated way. Another program is in charge of execution and verification, so these tests can be automated and repeated as many times as necessary, such as in a process of continuous integration. We have to point out that the concept of unit testing is also related to those of integration tests (testing the behavior of different modules working together), regression tests (set of tests used to ensure that the behavior of the application is not altered by any maintenance change), and system tests (testing the behavior of the entire system). But going deep into these and other types of tests is out of the scope of this book.

Tests can be performed if we execute the application. In this case, we can count on test engineers who manually follow a script, or use tools allowing us to automate or record user actions, so as to repeat them in the future. In this case, tests are known as **Automated UI Testing**.

Before going on with this topic, we need to have an understanding of two concepts, **white-box testing** and **black-box testing**. White-box tests assume that the testers know the source code of the program being tested. Therefore, they are at the level of the developer, so they know the cases where tests are more appropriate. In black-box tests, the tester only has access to the results of the code execution. They are at user-level, and their goal is that their expectations about the application are fulfilled. Both types of tests are complementary to achieve a correct test plan.

Methodologies

Consider the classic cycle of software development, the **Waterfall model**. It includes analysis, design, implementation, and testing, roughly speaking. The testing stage was usually pushed into the end, and in projects with tight deadlines, it was probable that the tests weren't done properly. The adoption of new architectures in applications, which make testing easier, as well as their own current prominence in those architectures may be helped by the boom of quality assurance processes (such as ISO standards, see www.iso.org). All these factors applied to software, have given more importance to testing in this process.

To these factors, we can add methodologies such as **Test-Driven Development (TDD)**, derived from **Extreme Programming** (or **XP**) and related to the **Agile Movement**. TDD proposes that tests guide development, so tests are the first thing to be developed. This test definition will act later as a cast of the code to be developed. We also obtain a particular shape following that cast; if we base development on tests, the application will be developed to fit into that cast, accomplishing the requisites previously established by them.

Now, we will show how to apply these concepts to a Silverlight LOB application. We will distinguish the types of tests we can do (synchronous, asynchronous, or user interface), and the technologies we have for doing this. Later, we will discover how the correct class design will make test implementation easier.

Tests will be done using **MSTest,** the tool included in Visual Studio. There are many others, such as **NUnit** and **XUnit**, whose basic operation is similar.

Unit testing with Silverlight

As we already know, in a Silverlight business application, we will have code on both client-side and server-side. The first one will be based on the .NET Framework, and the second one, on Silverlight. To make concept assimilation easier, we will first talk about testing on .NET 4.0, then, we will deal with particular cases in Silverlight where we will apply the concepts previously seen.

Testing server code

Tests will have to be grouped into a **test project**, which is a special kind of project Visual Studio executes to check test results (or **MSBuild**, if we are in a context of continuous integration). In order to generate this project, we have to select **Test** as the template from the **Installed Templates** list, and then **Test Project**, as shown in the following screenshot:

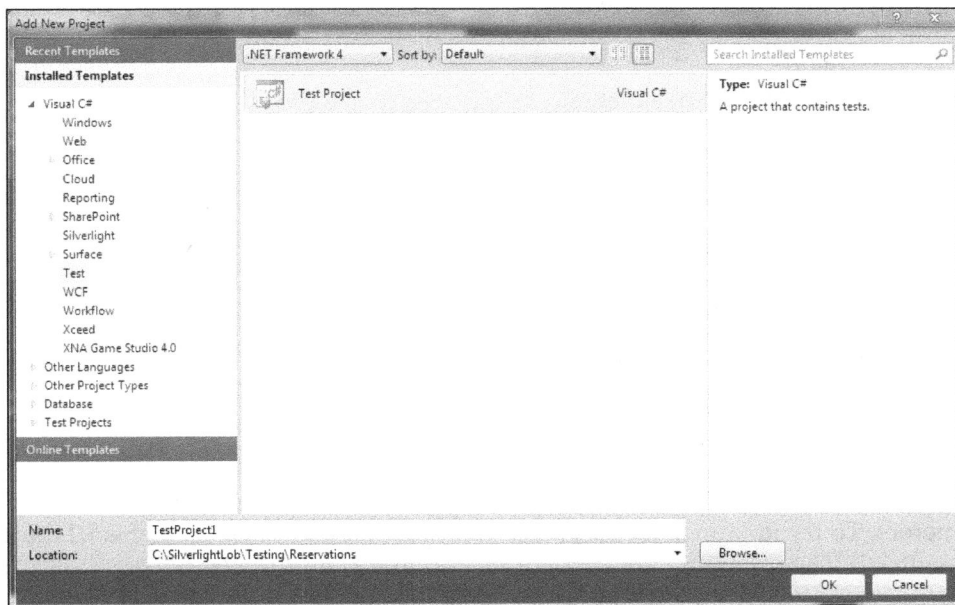

Give a name to the project (in this example, **ReservationsTest**) and it will generate a simple structure similar to the following screenshot:

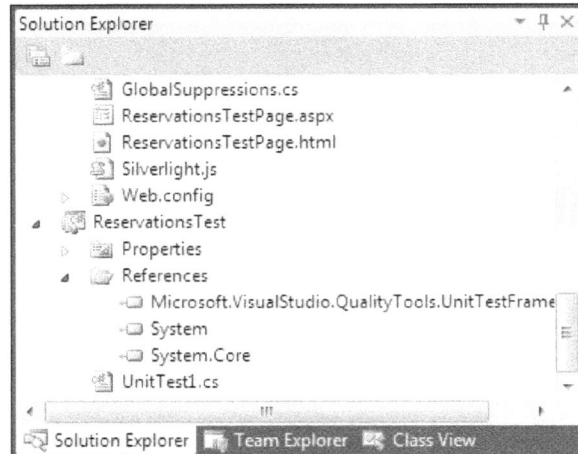

This includes the reference to the MSTest test library, as well as a first **UnitTest1.cs** file with an empty test class. Change its name to CalculusTest.cs and modify its content with our own test class:

```
using Microsoft.VisualStudio.TestTools.UnitTesting;
using Reservations.Web;
namespace ReservationsTest
{
  [TestClass]
  public class CalculusTest
{
    [TestMethod]
    public void Add3And2Test()
{
var target = new Calculus();
      int expected = 5;
      int actual = target.Add(3, 2);
      Assert.AreEqual(expected, actual);
    }
  }
}
```

The expected behavior of the Calculus.Add method is trivial to sum the two given parameters. To try it, launch an execution with parameters 3 and 2, to check later that the result is 5. The following are some other comments on this class:

- The `TestClass` attributes indicate that this class contains test methods. It is compulsory for it to be taken into account when tests are executed.

- It is recommended to finish the names of the test classes with the suffix `Test`, as many test runners will search them using this convention.

- The `TestMethod` attribute indicates that the method is a test in itself. It is compulsory.

- It is also recommended that the suffix `Test` is added to the names of methods, which need to be as descriptive of the test as possible.

- In a test class, there can be other support methods. They will not have the `TestMethod` attribute or the `Test` suffix.

- The names of variables `target`, `expected`, and `actual` are a general convention. They indicate the tested object (`target`), the expected value (`expected`), and the actual value obtained (`actual`).

- MSTest offers the `Assert` class with a lot of methods for checking, such as `AreEqual` that is used in this case.

- In `AreEqual`, as well as in other methods, we first have to indicate the expected value and then the actual one. Therefore, in case the conditions are not fulfilled, the error message will be correct.

Tests are usually structured in three stages, **Arrange**, **Act**, and **Assert(AAA)**. This can be appreciated in the previous sample. First, the target is created, the method is then called, and finally, the results are verified. You can learn a bit more about this pattern in a brief article using the link, `http://bit.ly/v0aoGU`.

Now, we will only have to add the reference to the project we are going to test, as well as the `Calculus` class. This can be done via Visual Studio Intellisense, which will suggest (thanks to a red line under the unidentified nouns) creating the `Calculus` class and the `Add` method with its two parameters and its type of return. This new functionality of Visual Studio 2010 helps apply the TDD methodology, first testing and then code generation. After that, we will only have to move the class to the web project (updating the references in the test project) and implement it. As a result, we will have something similar to the following:

```
namespace Reservations.Web
{
  public class Calculus
  {
    public int Add(int a, int b)
    {
      return a + b;
    }
  }
}
```

The easiest way to execute the previous test on this method is to place the cursor in the `AddTest` method and press the button **Run Tests in Current Context** in the **Test tools** toolbar, which appears automatically when we are on a test project class. We can also make use of that command in the **Test | Run** submenu. Visual Studio will build the involved projects and will show the execution process of the tests in a window, as follows:

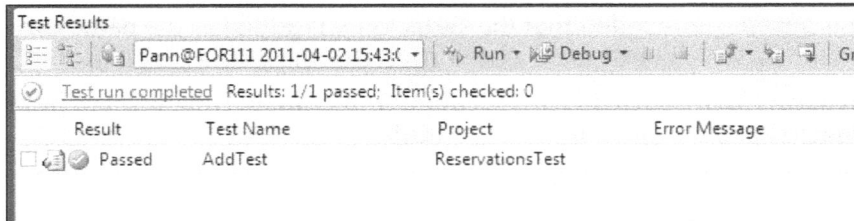

If the test fails, it is possible to check the error message from this window, navigate to the unaccomplished assert sentence, or see the particular exception. The same command allows us to try all the methods in a test class if we place the cursor on the class name. Visual Studio permits other ways to select the tests which have to be executed, even by creating batches of tests that can be saved. There are also third-party tools, which provide different functionalities for running tests.

Now, we will see how this approach to try server code can be used to try Silverlight client code.

Testing client code with MSTest

There is a certain difficulty in the fact that the MSTest test project we have created runs on the whole .NET Framework, not just on Silverlight. Therefore, there are other specific libraries to test Silverlight code that will be dealt with later, but these libraries make it difficult to automatically execute tests, which becomes a decisive factor in continuous integration environments. So, before we look at those libraries, we will describe a simple way to test classes included in our Silverlight project via MSTest.

> Warning! This technique is not applicable in all classes, as will be shown soon, but its advantages make it the recommended method to use as long as the class to be tested permits it.

You will see that Visual Studio will mark the reference as wrong (yellow warning triangle), if it is necessary to add a reference to the Silverlight project in the previous test project. From now on, the situation differs depending on the .NET version we're working with (4.0 or previous).

If the test project uses .NET 4.0, you will be able to add a reference to the Silverlight project of an MSTest project. Despite the error displayed in the reference (yellow warning triangle), the project will run without issues. For instance, the `Calculus` class previously mentioned could be copied to the Silverlight project (it could be renamed as `CalculusSL`) and, modifying the references properly, the test will work. This is possible thanks to the new **Assembly Portability** feature added in .NET 4.0, which only works if the Silverlight class we're testing uses the following libraries:

- `Mscorlib`
- `System`
- `System.Core`
- `System.ComponentModel.Composition`
- `Microsoft.VisualBasic`

This is the first restriction to the classes that can be tested in this way. For example, any class working with a visual interface, with access to web services or data via WCF RIA Services cannot be tested with this method. On the contrary, those business classes or utilities, which contain plenty of logic, but few references, are ideal. This invites us to decompose classes as much as possible, following principles such as the **Single Responsibility Principle (SRP)**, one of the five **SOLID** principles. Moreover, it would also be good decomposing these classes to different .NET or Silverlight assemblies.

> It is not necessary for the web project to be a .NET 4.0 one, a previous version can also be used. Nevertheless, it is required that the test project be a .NET 4.0 one in order to accept the direct reference to a Silverlight project.

This method can be seen in action in the second sample of this chapter, where both classes `CalculusTest` and `CalculusSLTest` have been implemented. Although, the reader should be aware that the best practices recommend the client and server code should be tested in separate test projects.

On the other hand, in case we cannot use .NET 4.0, there is an alternate strategy, which we can briefly describe. Instead of adding a reference to the Silverlight project in the test project, a link will be added to those files we want to test (as it was pointed out previously, not every class is valid). To add the link:

1. Right-click on the test project.
2. Select **Add Existing Item.**
3. Find and select the class, or several of them.
4. Now, in the dialog box, select **Add Existing Item**, expand the options of the **Add** button and select **Add as Link.**

Doing this, the file is not copied (it remains in its original folder), but its code is compiled again in the test project. Thus, we can develop tests on this class, and there are no sync issues since it consists of only one file.

> This technique can be also used in .NET 4.0 with those classes not supporting portability. Even so, there are other classes which cannot be tested either, as we will see in the next section.

Libraries to test Silverlight code

As we have already commented, there are specific features in Silverlight, which make certain classes unable to be tested with the technique mentioned previously, due to particular dependencies of their framework, or because of the use of asynchronous features or visual elements. To solve this issue, there are specific libraries for testing in Silverlight, as follows:

- **Silverlight Unit Testing (SilverlightUT)**: This was originally developed by Microsoft to try the Silverlight Toolkit, which also includes it. When the Toolkit is installed, the templates are integrated with Visual Studio 2010. Tests are executed on the browser, within Silverlight.

- **SilverUnit**: With a higher level of isolation, this library does not require a browser. So it is more automatable, yet allows the testing of visual elements.

- **Selenium-Silverlight**: This is an automation web library extended to support Silverlight.

- **AgUnit**: This is a plugin for ReSharper that allows you to run and debug Silverlight unit tests from within Visual Studio.

- **StatLight**: This is a command-line tool developed for automating the setup, execution, and gathering results of Silverlight unit tests.

These are representative samples of the types of existing libraries of isolated execution, unit tests, or visual interface. As was shown previously, we have an integrated solution at our disposal in Visual Studio 2010, which we will see now. It is important to remark that this library, developed by Jeff Wilcox, supports tests for asynchronous operations, so we will study it with the help of two examples, one synchronous and the other asynchronous.

Testing synchronous client code with Silverlight Unit Testing

First of all, you need to get Silverlight Toolkit installed on your computer. This is a very complete piece of software distributed by Microsoft through Codeplex under **Microsoft Public License (MS-PL)**, so you can download it from `http://silverlight.codeplex.com/releases`. Please be careful not to choose the Windows Phone version instead of the Silverlight one.

> If you try to open a test project of this type on a computer, which does not have Silverlight Toolkit previously installed, you will get an error similar to:
>
> **Unable to read the project file 'x.csproj'. The imported project "...\Microsoft.Silverlight.Toolkit.Build.targets" was not found. Confirm that the path in the <Import> declaration is correct, and that the file exists on disk.**
>
> After installing Silverlight Toolkit, you will be able to open that project.

After installing Silverlight Toolkit, Visual Studio 2010 incorporates a new type of project called **Silverlight Unit Test Application** in the Silverlight templates, as shown in the following screenshot. This generates a SilverlightUT application, which is actually in charge of testing our Silverlight application or library.

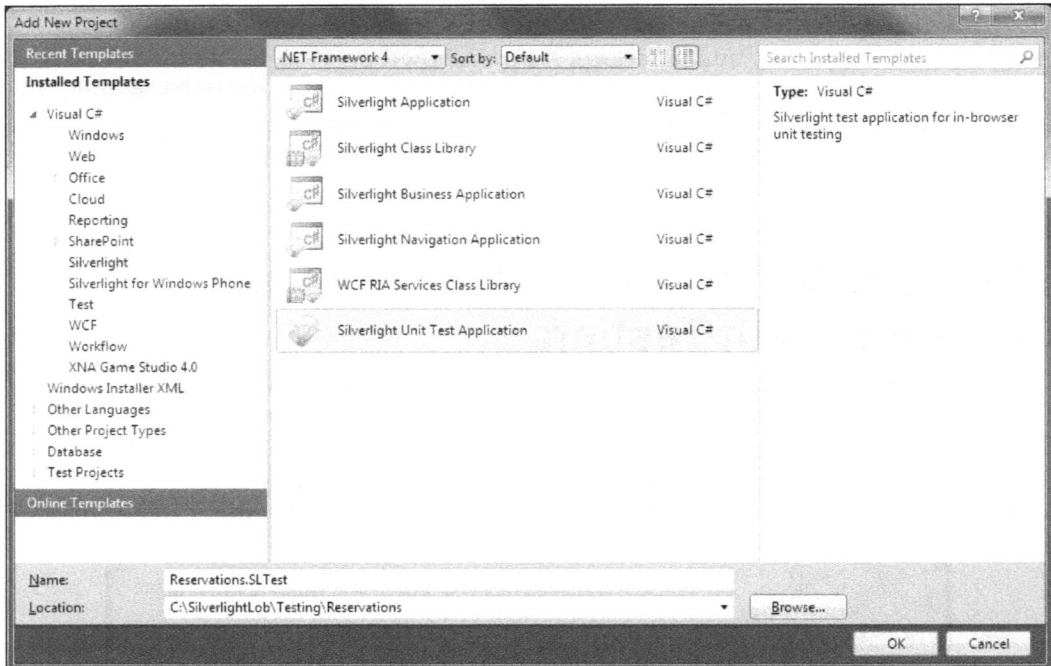

When we add a project of this kind, Visual Studio shows us the **Options** window of any Silverlight application:

New Silverlight Application

Click the checkbox below to host this Silverlight application in a Web site. Otherwise, a test page will be generated during build.

☑ Host the Silverlight application in a new or existing Web site in the solution

Reservations.Web

New Web project name:

Reservations.SLTest.Web

New Web project type:

ASP.NET Web Application Project

Options
Silverlight Version:

Silverlight 4

☐ Enable WCF RIA Services

☑ Add a test page that references the application

☑ Make it the start page

☑ Enable Silverlight debugging (disables javascript debugging)

OK   Cancel

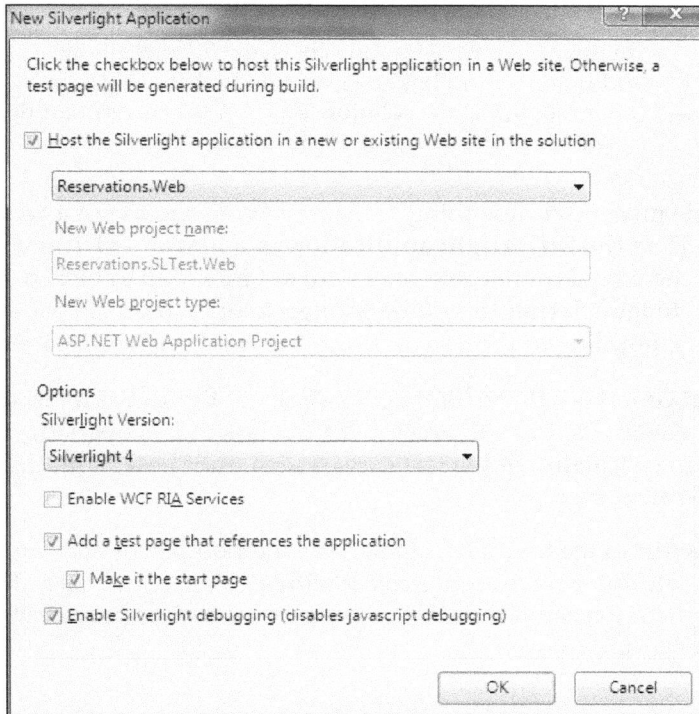

The same web project of the application can be used, as it suggests. In this case, it is advisable to uncheck the checkbox **Make it the start page** as shown in the previous screenshot, so that our web project keeps on launching the application and not the tests (although this can be changed later in the project web properties). A new page will be generated in the web project, with which tests will be launched (navigating to their URL when in execution). Of course, we will have to be careful with this page when putting the application into production.

> In this case, Visual Studio is in charge of everything. Adding a second link to Silverlight in the web project, after rebuilding the solution, will add the corresponding .xap file to the ClientBin file of the web project.

Nevertheless, the most advisable thing to do is to avoid the use of a web project, unchecking the **Host the Silverlight application in a new or existing Web site in the solution** checkbox, so that references are not included in tests from the code. Therefore, to launch tests, it will be enough to open the TestPage.html file generated when compiling in the bin\Debug folder of the Silverlight test project.

This new project contains a Silverlight application configured as a test application, together with a Tests.cs file with an empty test class. If it is opened, you can see that it has the same structure of the test classes seen until now, with the TestClass and TestMethod attributes.

Lets modify this test to try the CalculusSL.Add method. From now on, you need to have in your solution a Silverlight project with a CalculusSL class. If not, it will suffice to add it with the same code of the Calculus class we previously used. The changes to do in Tests.cs are:

1. Rename the class as CalculusSLTest.
2. Rename the TestMethod1 method as AddTest.
3. Include the same content of the AddTest method as previous.
4. Add to the test project a reference to the Silverlight project we are to try.
5. Add at the beginning the necessary usage instructions.

There are great similarities with MSTest tests seen that we have examined in the previous section. The only difference lies in the type of test project used. However, this difference is crucial:

- While in MSTest, tests run on .NET 4.0 (via compatibility mode); in SilverlightUT, they run on the real Silverlight engine. So we can access all the features, as well as get more reliable and accurate data.
- Consequently, references to other Silverlight projects will not be marked as warnings.
- Tests are executed on the browser and not *within* Visual Studio. This feature in SilverlightUT allows us to use the actual Silverlight engine.

The execution on the browser makes test automation difficult, and it also makes it hard to integrate results collection into a Continuous Integration (CI) environment.

As we have already anticipated, in order to execute SilverlightUT tests, commands in the **Test** menu are not used because this project is not exactly a test project, but just another Silverlight application. Thus, to assess tests, the test project must be executed. The following are two ways to do it, depending on how the test project has been integrated into the solution:

- If we include a test page for this project in the web application, the solution will have to be executed and then we will have to navigate to the page URL

- On the contrary, if we did not do so, we will have to build the test project and open the `TestPage.html` static page, which should be in `\bin\Debug\`

The test project execution, whatever the chosen method, will open a Silverlight application in the browser, which will list the existing tests and assess them. Before that, the **Tag Expressions** window allows us to select the tests we want to execute, as shown in the following screenshot:

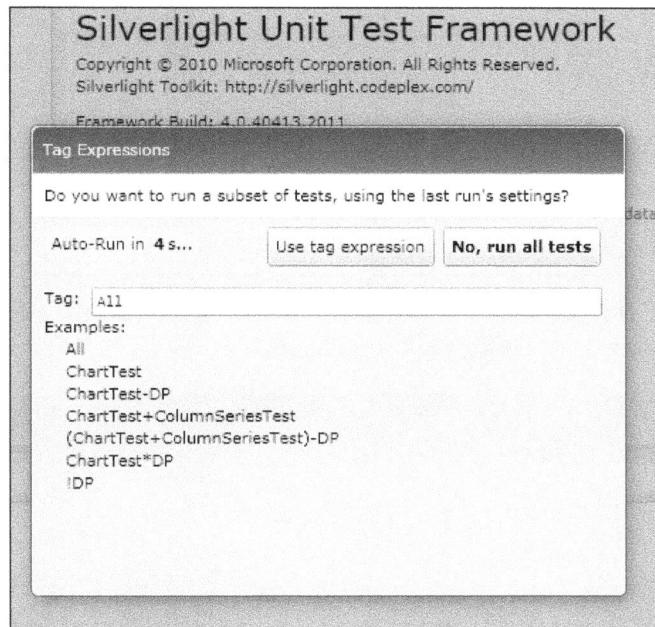

The window shown in the previous screenshot is shown for five seconds and, if no action is performed, the assessment of all tests will begin. In order to execute a subset of tests, we can enter an expression that filters the desired tests.

Now the tests are executed. The progress will be shown until it displays the global result. In our case, we will see a page similar to the following:

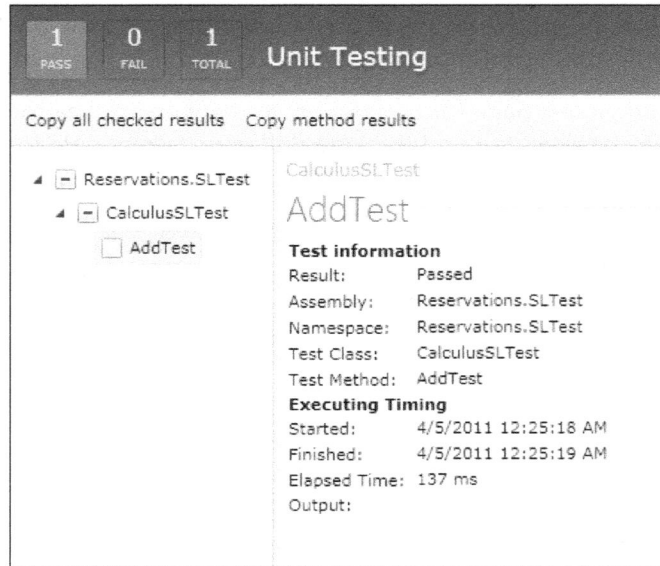

We can have complete information on the execution of the tests, and their result with an initial summary of the number of tests that have passed or failed. When clicking on one of the test methods in the tree placed on the left, we can see particular details of their execution. If it has failed, information on the error and the stack trace will be shown, as we can see in the following screenshot:

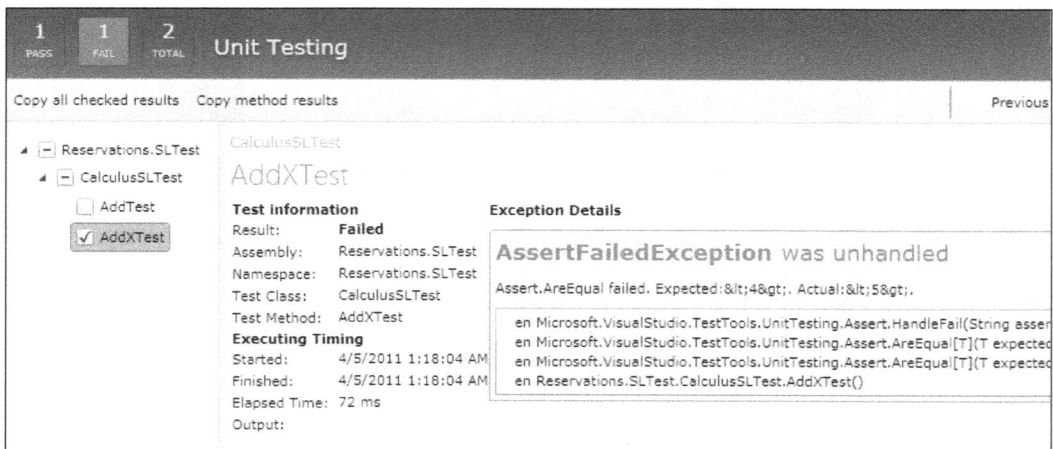

As shown in the previous screenshot, we can achieve the same results as in the previous method, but on a more complex and artificial infrastructure. Nevertheless, this infrastructure will allow us to test code that makes use of the advanced Silverlight features, even debugging it by executing the tests in a step-by-step mode.

Testing asynchronous client code with Silverlight Unit Testing

Now we will see an example of where to test two of these features in action, visual elements and asynchronism. To do so, let us create a page with a public property called `Message`. This property will be initialized in the `Loaded` event of the Page, simulating a typical data load in a simple way.

> This load can be carried out on a visual element, but to test them, we would have to make them public (using `x:FieldModifier` in the XAML notation), which is not recommended. Besides, even this practice is unable to simulate certain behaviors, such as a button press. For this, a framework such as Selenium can be used. However, the suggested method is to test the View Model, as we will see in the next section.

1. Locate the Silverlight project (you can use a new one if you want to).
2. In the **Solution Explorer** window, right-click on it to open the context menu.
3. Select **Add | New item...**
4. In the **Add New Item** dialog, select **SilverlightPage** and write `MessagePage.xaml` as its name.
5. Create a handler for the `Loaded` event of the page, with the following code:
   ```
   Message = "Hi";
   ```
6. Also in the Code-Behind file, create the property:
   ```
   public string Message { get; set; }
   ```
   Now, we will create a test of this load behavior.
7. Locate the test project of SilverlightUT (you can also create a new one).
8. In the **Solution Explorer**, right-click on that project.
9. Select **Add | Class...**.
10. Name it **MessagePageTest.cs**.

11. Replace the class code with the following:

```
[TestClass]
public class MessagePageTest{
  [TestMethod]
  public void MessageLoadedTest() {
var target = new MessagePage();
Assert.AreEqual("Hi", target.Message);
  }
}
```

Try to compile the project. It is possible to find errors due to lack of references (such as `System.Windows.Controls.Navigation`). In this case, it is enough to add these references to the test project, or also the `using` lines on the file. This will be normal when adding elements, which make use of new libraries, especially of the UI.

When executing the test (through `bin\Debug\TestPage.html`), you will realize it has not passed.

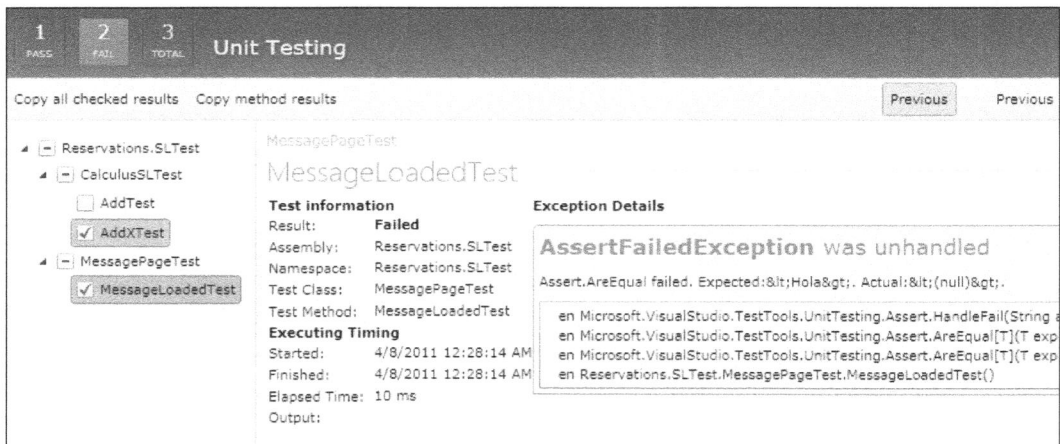

We can see the reason in the previous screenshot. The assert statement which established that the result message had to be `Hi` has not been passed. The message is still `null`. Why? Because, although the page has been created, it has not been loaded. For this, we have to display it. To avoid having to actually display it, let us make the most of SilverlightUT, which offers a special test class called `SilverlightTest` from which we have to inherit (it will be necessary `using` the namespace `Microsoft.Silverlight.Testing`). This class provides a `TestPanel` property, a visual element to which we can add the elements we want to visualize (or whose visualization we want to simulate). We will do it with the following sentence before the assertion:

```
TestPanel.Children.Add(target);
```

But this is not enough. There is another crucial feature for the test to be passed, the management of the asynchronous flow. In fact, the page is not loaded immediately when it is added to TestPanel, nor is the Loaded event associated with it called. If we want to pass it, we need to *give it time*. Add the assertion to an asynchronous execution queue that provides the SilverlightTest class via the Enqueue methods. Eventually, the test class will look as follows:

```
[TestClass]
public class MessagePageTest : SilverlightTest {
  [TestMethod]
  [Asynchronous]
  public void MessageLoadedTest() {
    var target = new MessagePage();
    TestPanel.Children.Add(target);
    EnqueueCallback(() =>Assert.AreEqual("Hi", target.Message));
    EnqueueTestComplete();
  }
}
```

Let's dive into the details:

- The class inherits from SilverlightTest base class.
- The method incorporates the [Asynchronous] attribute to indicate this is an asynchronous test, that is, it will make use of the Enqueue methods.
- The EnqueueCallback method adds the message checking to the queue. So it will be executed when the previous target visualization instruction has ended completely, including the call to the Loaded event.
- This sort of test normally ends with a call to EnqueueTestComplete, in order to finalize the test, when all the calls in the queue are processed.

If we execute the test now, it will be passed. This mechanism is really powerful, and allows us to make tests of asynchronous behaviors in an easy way.

> In a SilverlightUT project, normal tests mixed with other tests which inherit from SilverlightTest can be found. Also, in a single test class, there can be asynchronous methods mixed with others which are not asynchronous.

Isolating unit tests via substitutes

As we have seen, checking individual elements through unit tests is relatively easy. However, in many instances, the complexity lies in being able to deal with methods and classes separately, as they usually contain dependencies of other elements, which are not subjected to test and, what is more, this can make it difficult or impossible.

Let's pose an example, a ViewModel loading a collection of clients via access to a web service. If we want to test that ViewModel, it is necessary to dispense with the actual access to the web service. Nevertheless, as the call is in the code, we must replace the web service client with another object having the same interface, which does not perform its task, but appears to do so. It is possible to make use of several substitute strategies:

- **Fake**: Using classes specifically created for a task that returns the values we need (usually sample data).
- **Stubs**: Configurable classes that can be useful for several tests.
- **Mocks**: Objects which are normally dynamically created. Apart from configuring their behavior, we can later consult how it has been used. This is usually known as **Mocking**, but sometimes this word is used to mean any type of substitute.

One of the pre-requisites to apply any of these strategies is to use a **Dependency Injection (DI) pattern,** so that we can substitute the actual object for a fictitious one. In brief, this pattern uses an abstract factory that allows redefining what concrete type of instance is going to be created for any required type (usually an interface). Some popular frameworks for DI are Unity, Castle Windsor, .NET, StructureMap, and MEF among others.

To produce these substitutes, there are also many libraries at our disposal, such as Moq, Rhino Mocks, and Moles. In the following section, we will see an example of using Moq.

LOB application case study: applying what we have learned

As we have mentioned earlier, testing could be applied in different ways. We could have written the tests before the code, following a TDD methodology for development, or **Behavior-Driven Development (BDD)**. But we can also write the tests afterwards, as part of a quality assurance process, or to be included in a battery of regression tests. Also tests are a great tool in order to discover the behavior of a system, even more if it is a legacy system, or a subsystem that is not properly documented. As the code has already been written before introducing the tests, we could use these as a tool for discovering or checking that the application runs properly.

Now we are going to write, configure, and run a couple of unit tests, and in the full sample of this chapter you can find many more of them.

We choose `MyBookingsVM` as an interesting piece of code for testing:

- It has some business logic related to UI.
- It is decoupled from external sources (server and database).
- It is Silverlight code (no server code, which would be easier to test).
- If you have complex code that does not satisfy these conditions, you should refactor it in order to be properly tested. As a bonus, subsequent maintenance will be easier.

As we have seen before, even though we are going to test Silverlight code, we might have written tests on standard .NET. However, in this case, we need to reference some Silverlight libraries, as `System.Windows 2.0.5.0`, which are not included in the compatibility list we provided previously. Therefore, we ought to use SilverlightUT.

In our sample, we find the next problem. We are using SL5 libraries and also SL4 ones. This is not a problem for Silverlight, but when referencing from .NET, compatibility is not properly applied, that is, after referencing `System.Windows 5.0.5.0`, the compiler still produces an error, as it does not find `System. Windows 2.0.5.0`.

Besides, we cannot upgrade every library to SL5, because we are using third-party libraries such as MVVM Light, which have no SL5 version at the time of writing.

Some test environments, such as **ReSharper**, are sometimes able to run these tests successfully without using SilverlightUT, as they compile them with different references. Standard Visual Studio test execution engine cannot do so (it cannot even build it). The recommendation is to try, firstly if you can run the test in an automatic way (using a standard .NET 4.0 test project), and use SilverlightUT or an other Silverlight-specific test framework only when the first approach does not work.

We start by opening the current trunk solution from the previous chapter, and then creating a new **Silverlight Unit Test Application** project (remember, Silverlight Toolkit should be installed already). Test the project and name it **Packt.Booking. Modules.MyBookings.SLTest**. Select SL5 as the version, and host it in our web project, but uncheck **Make it the start page.** Remember that you should remove this testing page before moving to production.

You should get the following screenshot:

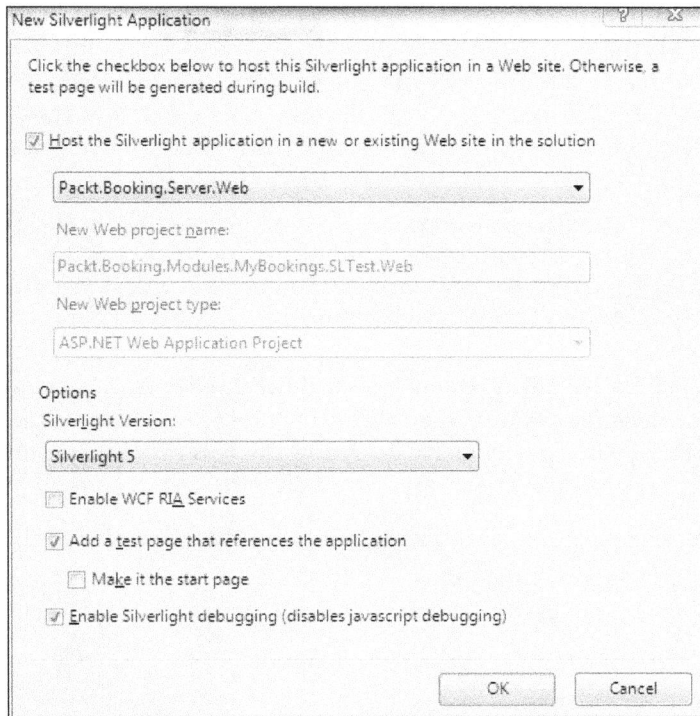

Now, rename `Tests` as `MyBookingsVMCommandsTest`, and replace the empty test method with the following code:

```
[TestMethod]
public void CancelChangesCommand_MustBeDisabledIfThereIsNoSelection_
Test()
{
  //Arrange
  var target = new MyBookingsVM();
  target.CurrentBooking = null;
  //Act
  var value = target.CancelChangesCommand.CanExecute(null);
  //Assert
  Assert.IsFalse(value);
}
```

Please note that you are going to write the names of these methods only once, because they will be automatically executed. Thus, we recommend using a fully descriptive name that will help you when supervising the test's execution. Moreover, in this case, the intention of the test is pretty clear, and the **Cancel Changes** command must be disabled when there is no booking selected.

> Note that we use the test convention called AAA, which divides the tests into three areas, Arrange, Act, and Assert, as we introduced earlier. In the next test, the comment titles must be omitted.

To get the test project compiling, the required library references have to be added. You can discover missing libraries by building the test project and checking the box, **You can discover missing libraries by building the test project** and checking the errors in the output window. In our case, the following are the list of references:

- `Packt.Booking.Modules.MyBookings` (the library under testing)
- `Packt.Booking.Common`
- `Packt.Libs.Navigation.Contracts`
- `System.ServiceModel.DomainServices.Client`
- `GalaSoft.MvvmLight.SL4`

You should also add the required using statements. Visual Studio 2010 can help you in this task with their smart tips.

The test can be run by executing our solution (remember that the start project must be the Web one), and navigating to the new page that has been created for testing this project, which must be called **Packt.Booking.Modules.MyBookings. SLTestTestPage.html** (there is also an `aspx` version). You can shorten it to ease the URL navigation. I prefer to use **MyBookingsTestPage.html**.

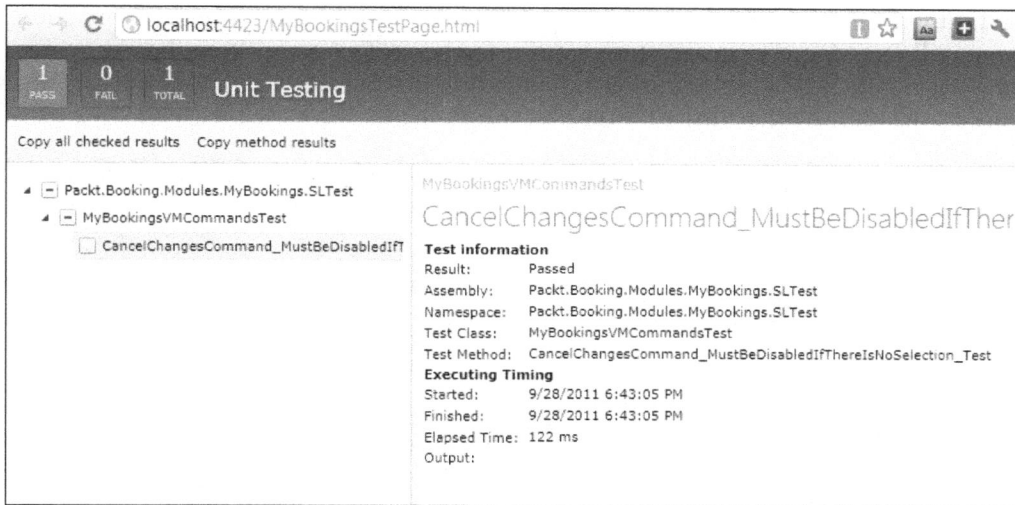

Perfect! The test was passed, but it is incomplete if we do not test other cases, so let's write a new test called CancelChangesCommand_ MustBeEnabledIfSelectionHasChanges_Test.It is a pretty clear name, you should agree. Consequently, we can copy the previous test, remove the null assignment (thus keeping the default fake Reservation created on the no-arguments constructor), and change Assert to true. Nevertheless, we have to force some changes, and that is a big problem, because the empty constructor creates a fake Reservation not linked with any context, and context keeps tracking changes. Therefore, we might also have to deal with a DomainContext for this unit test, and then it would not be a unit test but an integration test, and it will also have a lot more complexity.

This can be avoided by mocking the Reservation object, that is, by using a fake instance that returns the changes when we want it, and is not dependent on a DomainContext. Any object can be mocked in two ways:

- Creating a new fake class with the same interface as the real class
- Using a mocking framework, such as Moq

The first way is easier to understand, but it is more tedious and requires more code. So we will use Moq. There are other similar frameworks for mocking, but Moq gets along especially well with Silverlight, thereby all that we are going to learn can be easily translated to other frameworks.

First, we need a fake `Reservation` instance, which always returns true when `HasChanged` is called:

```
varreservationMock = new Mock<Reservation>();
reservationMock.Setup(r =>r.HasChanges).Returns(true);
//Now we can use reservationMock.Object
```

The previous code generates a mock object for the `Reservation` class. This object can be configured to return any value as a response to any call, as it is done with a `Setup` call for the `HasChanges` property, which defines that `true` should be returned always. Finally, the mock object is not a `Reservation`, but it publishes a reservation instance through its `Object` property, so that is the object we will use.

Anyhow, before going further with Moq, one important aspect must be underlined. Both the ways described earlier for mocking objects, are based on supplanting the object, so we need to create a class, which passes for a `Reservation`. In order to accomplish this, we must extend from the `Reservation` class and override the `HasChanges` property, which requires:

- `Reservation` class not sealed
- `HasChanges` member is marked as virtual

None of them are satisfied by our `Reservation` class, and we cannot change it as it is a self-generated code. Even more, we cannot make `HasChanges` virtual because it is defined in the `Entity` class, which belongs to a compiled library.

Don't worry. This is a great chance to learn more about testing and refactoring. In order to mock a `Reservation` object, we should extract an interface for its class, let's call it `IReservationEntity` interface. It should declare every public method, property, and event of `Reservation`, and it must be used in place of the entity class everywhere. We must also declare that the `Reservation` class implements the `IReservationEntity` interface, which can be done in an extension file (as `Reservation` is partial). You can see the full `IReservationEntity` code in the sample.

After this refactoring task is performed, now we can write our test dealing with an `IReservationEntity` instance rather than with the `Reservation` class:

```
[TestMethod]
public void
  CancelChangesCommand_MustBeEnabledIfSelectionHasChanges_Test()
{
  varreservationMock = new Mock<IReservationEntity>();
  reservationMock.Setup(r =>r.HasChanges).Returns(true);
  var target = new MyBookingsVM();
  target.CurrentBooking = reservationMock.Object;
  Assert.IsNotNull(target.CurrentBooking);
  Assert.IsTrue(target.CurrentBooking.HasChanges);
  var value =target.CancelChangesCommand.CanExecute(null);
  Assert.IsTrue(value);
}
```

As we can see, the interface is implemented by the fake object, by creating a new Mock generic instance. We then setup the `HasChanges` property to return `true`. Besides, we use the object published by the Mock instance. The rest of the methods and properties are not mocked up, but we do not care about that while they are not being called.

We can add the Moq library to the test project in two ways:

- Downloading it from its site (see references at the end of the chapter)
- Using NuGet, looking for Moq or installing a package called Moq

NuGet (`nuget.org`) is a package manager developed by Microsoft that integrates with Visual Studio. It offers a public repository of third-party libraries that can be added easily to your projects. It gives you two ways of doing that:

1. Using a visual interface, selecting **Add Package Reference...** in the project Context menu of the **Solution Explorer**.

2. Using the **Package Manager Console** window, that can be opened in the **View** menu, change the target project selected in this window, and then type the command:

   `install-package Moq`

3. After installing Moq, now the code will compile and the two tests will be passed.

4. If you are interested, you have more tests to read in the sample code of this chapter.

Summary

We have seen that testing a complete Silverlight application is different depending on the part of the application we are testing, but it follows some general best practices and recommendations for other technologies. Fortunately, we can choose between different utilities, from integrated Visual Studio support to Silverlight-based framework. Always keep in mind that the easier the test to be executed, the more useful and more used it will be by us or by our team mates.

We have discovered that asynchronous behaviors require a special approach, and we have also learned how to test single units of code by isolating them through refactoring, interfaces, dependency injection, and mocking of external objects. Testing is a matter of a big extension and of main importance nowadays, but we have tried to give an introduction so that you can start using it in your LOB applications with Silverlight. Now you can learn more by reading the additional resources.

In the next chapter, you will learn how to manage errors and other exceptional situations in your application. There's no perfect program, so even though we develop a complete set of tests, it will probably be the case where the application crashes or, moreover, cases where we must manage exceptions. We must even consider in our tests the exceptions which are thrown or which are caught. Thereafter, we will learn how to add logging to our application in order to store errors and status execution of our application.

Additional resources

- Test-driven development (TDD): http://en.wikipedia.org/wiki/Test-driven_development

- Behavior-driven development (BDD): http://en.wikipedia.org/wiki/Behavior_Driven_Development

- ExtremeProgramming or XP: http://en.wikipedia.org/wiki/Extreme_programming

- Agile Movement: http://en.wikipedia.org/wiki/Agile_software_development

- SilverlightUnitTesting (SilverlightUT): http://archive.msdn.microsoft.com/silverlightut

- SilverUnit: http://www.codeplex.com/CThru/Wiki/View.aspx?title=SilverUnit

- Selenium-Silverlight: `http://code.google.com/p/silverlight-selenium/`
- AgUnit for ReSharper: `http://agunit.codeplex.com/`
- StatLight: `http://statlight.codeplex.com/`
- Arrange-Act-Assert test pattern: `http://c2.com/cgi/wiki?ArrangeActAssert`
- Mocks Aren't Stubs, by Martin Fowler: `http://martinfowler.com/articles/mocksArentStubs.html`
- Moq Framework: `http://code.google.com/p/moq/`

8
Error Control

As an advanced developer, you probably spend a lot of time handling errors and catch the exceptions in your application. You try to keep all scenarios in mind where something can go wrong, but nevertheless, suddenly your application stops working when one of your most important customers is testing your product. The hardware may be faulty or the service may not be available due to maintenance. Your job is to locate this error and to ensure that it will never occur in a future version.

In this chapter, you will learn how to be prepared for such situations and to collect all necessary information for your software testers. You will learn something about logging in Silverlight, exception handling, and how you can send this information to your bug report system. Furthermore, we will discuss how to separate these aspects from your domain logic.

Following best practices

Exception handling and error control is a complicated topic. You can do it in the wrong way very easily. Therefore, there are a lot of best practices and coding guidelines to help you to avoid mistakes. If you have Visual Studio 2010 Premium or Ultimate, you can directly use the static code analysis tool integrated in Visual Studio that can also be enabled in the project settings. If you have another version of Visual Studio, you can use FxCop, which is free and checks your assemblies with the same rules. These rules are documented and explained in MSDN (Static code analysis at `http://bit.ly/knvNkf`).

Exception handling

Many software development communities have a very large thread in the forum about coding styles horror. Most of the posted code snippets are about exception handling, which shows how difficult this topic is. Therefore, we must talk about exception handling first, along with what to do and what not to do.

Getting started

This part gives you an initial introduction to exception handling in Silverlight and a warm up for all developers who are familiar with this topic.

Try and catch

Let's have a look at the syntax of the easiest expression in exception handling:

```
try
{
   // Statement
}
catch (FileNotFoundException e)
{
   // Statement
}
catch (IOException)
{
   // Statement
}
catch
{
   // Statement
}
```

The `try` block contains the statements that might throw an exception. If no runtime exception occurs, all statements in the `try` block will be executed; otherwise the flow of control immediately jumps to an associated exception handler, if one is present.

You can specify any type that derives from the `Exception` class in the `catch` expression to handle the exception of the appropriate type. Do not catch general exception types because this can hide runtime problems and complicate debugging.

If no exception handler for a given exception is present, the program stops executing with an error message. This exception can be handled using a global exception handler.

If a `catch` block defines an exception variable, you can use it to get more information on the type of exception that occurred.

The "finally" expression

If you use classes that allocate unmanaged resources and implement the
`IDisposable` interface, you should call the `Dispose` method if an exception occurs.

```
FileStream fileStream = null;
try
{
  fileStream = new FileStream("MyFile.txt", FileMode.Open);
  // Statement
}
catch (IOException)
{
  // Statement
}
finally
{
  if (fileStream != null)
  {
    fileStream.Dispose();
  }
}
```

The statements in the `finally` block are always executed even if an exception occurs
that has not been handled before. This is the perfect place to clean up all unmanaged
resources.

You can also use the `using` statement, which guarantees that resources are released
when a runtime exception occurs.

```
using (FileStream fileStream =
new FileStream("MyFile.txt", FileMode.Open))
{
  // Statement
}
```

> Nesting `using` statements can induce exceptions when an object
> that has already been disposed is disposed of again. Therefore,
> it is recommended not to use a `using` statement inside another
> `using` statement. Only use a `using` block for the inner part and
> use `finally` to release the other resources. More information is
> provided at Rule CA2202 (`http://bit.ly/iCmLw0`).

Strategies

Sometimes you cannot do more than just catch the exceptions, but there are no suitable solutions to solve the problem that caused the error. There are three strategies you can make use of in this situation:

- **Caller beware**: The first option is not to handle the exception at all. This might lead to problems when the class is in an undefined state and the method is invoked at a later point. Furthermore, the user will not be provided sufficient information about the exception.

  You can use the `finally` block without a `catch` block to release the resources and stay in a defined state.

- **Caller confuse:** The second option is the worst. The caller catches the exception, executes some clean-up operations, and throws the same exception again. But this does not provide additional information about the exception.

- **Caller inform**: The caller catches the exception, wraps into another exception with additional information recorded, and throws it. The stack trace of the new exception starts at this point, but the original source of the exception is still available by the wrapped exception object.

```
public string LoadConfiguration(string file)
{
  Stream stream = null;
  try
  {
    stream = new FileStream(file, FileMode.Open);
    // Read from configuration file.
  }
  catch (FileNotFoundException)
  {
    // Don't handle the exception.
    throw;
  }
  catch (IOException e)
  {
    throw new IOException("Cannot read config file.", e);
  }
  finally
  {
    if (stream != null)
```

```
        {
          stream.Dispose();
        }
      }
    }
  }
```

We do not catch the `FileNotFoundException`, because we do not have any additional information, but handle the `IOException` to inform the caller that we could not read the configuration file.

> Whenever a new exception is thrown, part of the information it carries is the stack trace. If you rethrow an exception, a new stack trace will be created and you will not have the information where the exception comes from.
>
> You can take a look at Rule CA2200 (`http://bit.ly/j9ouo5`) for more details.

Asynchronous patterns

Normal exception handling does not work if you start operations that work asynchronously in the background. Typical examples are the `WebClient` and the `Image` class from Silverlight. When an exception is raised in the background thread, you can often get information about this from an event.

AsyncCompletedEventArgs

The `AsyncCompletedEventArgs` class is used in Silverlight for the `WebClient` class and when you add a service reference using Visual Studio and `svcutil.exe`, using it is very easy:

```
static void WebClientExample()
{
  WebClient webClient = new WebClient();
  webClient.DownloadStringCompleted += new
    DownloadStringCompletedEventHandler
    (webClient_DownloadStringCompleted);
  webClient.DownloadStringAsync(address);
}

static void webClient_DownloadStringCompleted
  (object sender, DownloadStringCompletedEventArgs e)
{
  if (e.Cancelled)
```

```
      {
        // Notify the user.
      }
      else if (e.Error != null)
      {
        // Notify the user.
      }
      else
      {
        // Do something with the string
      }
    }
```

Only one event is used to get the notification that the operation has been completed. The event argument has two properties named `Cancelled` and `Error` that should be checked before reading the result of the operation.

Keep in mind that this event is raised in the background thread. You must use the Dispatcher to change the status of your View, for example, if you want to show an error text or a message box.

Read the class reference in MSDN to get more information about the Dispatcher at `http://bit.ly/tEtJM3`.

ExceptionRoutedEventArgs/ UnhandledExceptionEventHandler

The `Image` class uses a different approach. Two events exist, where one is used to get the notification that the image has been opened and the other is used to notify that the image could not be loaded.

```
    static void ImageExample()
    {
      Image image = new Image();
      image.ImageOpened +=
        newEventHandler<RoutedEventArgs>(image_ImageOpened);
      image.ImageFailed += new
        EventHandler<ExceptionRoutedEventArgs>(image_ImageFailed);
      image.Source = source;
    }

    static void image_ImageOpened(object sender, RoutedEventArgs e)
    {
      // Image has been loaded.
    }
```

```
static void image_ImageFailed
  (object sender, ExceptionRoutedEventArgs e)
{
  // Image could not be loaded.
}
```

In this case, the code for both scenarios is strictly separated and you do not have to check the state of the event arguments.

The UnhandledExceptionEventHandler is used in the same way but provides some more information.

Global exception handling

You have learned how to handle all the exceptions so far, but you always have to keep in mind all edge cases and situations where an exception can occur, which is more or less impossible. Therefore, the Application object has an event that you can use to treat the unhandled exceptions.

When you create a new Silverlight application, Visual Studio automatically registers a method to this event and reports the exception to the browser:

```
public App()
{
  // More Code
  UnhandledException += this.Application_UnhandledException;
}

private void Application_UnhandledException
  (object sender, ApplicationUnhandledExceptionEventArgs e)
{
  // Dont stop working
  e.Handled = true;
}
```

The Handled property can be set to true, if you want to continue, but recognizes that you will probably leave the application in an undefined state.

Understanding the exception types

Eric Lippert made a very good summary about the different kinds of exceptions that can occur, at his blog http://bit.ly/d2cOZ4. We think this a good starting point for this part of the chapter.

Fatal exception

Fatal exceptions cannot be handled by the developer. You cannot catch them or release your resources. They are raised from the system because your machine or process is out of memory or your hardware is defective. Do not think too much about these exceptions. Show an error message to the user and try to close your application in a safe way if possible. Use the global error event handler for this scenario.

Boneheaded exceptions

These exceptions are your own fault and you should be able to prevent or at least handle them. They are thrown because of a bug in your program code. Try to reproduce the exception and fix the bug, but do not just catch the exceptions and show an error message. Typically, such an exception is thrown when you pass a null reference to a method that requires a valid reference or if you divide a real number by zero.

It really helps to follow the coding guidelines that are documented by Microsoft and other developers. Another very useful tool that can help you to avoid these failures is Code Contracts. It is a static analyzer that follows the different paths in your application and detects the code lines where an error can occur. You can describe the contracts in the form of preconditions, postconditions, and object invariants. This also helps to think about the input and output of methods to prevent vexing exceptions. (Code Contracts at `http://bit.ly/MePem`).

Vexing exceptions

Wrong design decisions can cause vexing exceptions. For example, let's suppose you only expect a number from the user, but the user can enter any string. Therefore, your parsing routine fails and throws an exception.

Think about the input and output carefully and do not expect that the user will see how to use your application at the beginning. They may also follow paths through the dialogs which are unusual.

Exogenous exceptions

These exceptions appear to be somewhat similar to vexing exceptions, but they are not the result of unfortunate design choices or something that happens inside your application. Rather, they are the result of external dependencies that cause an error.

Think about the previous sample where we try to read from a file. Always catching the `FileNotFoundException` seems to be a bad solution. We can try to eliminate the `catch` block:

```
if (File.Exists(file))
{
  using (Stream stream = new FileStream(file, FileMode.Open))
  {
    // Load the config
  }
}
```

If you compare the code with the previous example where we need a `finally` block to close the final stream, you will recognize that the code is shorter and easier to understand. Unfortunately, it does not work. This code can cause a race condition in some situations. Another process could have deleted, locked, or moved the file between the first line of code where the file is checked and the second line where it is finally opened.

Does it help to lock the file? No because probably the storage has been removed or the network drive is not available anymore. You have to catch exogenous exceptions because it could always happen no matter what you do, but use additional methods and checks to control the flow of your application.

Logging

We are able to catch all exceptions and handle them, if possible. Sometimes it is not possible to deal with all scenarios and therefore, we must introduce a logging mechanism to our application in order to collect information that can help to fix a bug.

Logging is more complicated in Silverlight than in a normal client or web application:

- We cannot write to files directly
- The isolated storage has only limited space, but we can ask the user for more
- The application is running client side, the connection to a logging server can fail, or the server might not be available
- The logging information must be persistent
- Only a few frameworks for logging exist that also work together with Silverlight

At the moment, there is only one open source library for logging, which is the Silverlight port of the Enterprise Application Framework.

Enterprise application framework

The **Microsoft Enterprise Library** is a collection of reusable software components (application blocks) designed to assist software developers with common enterprise development challenges. Application blocks are provided as source code plus documentation that can be used "as is," extended, or modified by developers to use on complex, enterprise-level line-of-business development projects (description from the codeplex site). Enterprise Library is made up of a series of blocks. Each one is designed to manage a specific cross-cutting concern. In case this concept is unfamiliar, a cross-cutting concern is a task that you have to perform at different places in your application and which can be found in more or less any application. Accomplishing those tasks usually does not fulfill any functional requirement.

The blocks can be used independently from each other and you can decide to use the `logging` block only and use other frameworks for caching and validation. This is very helpful, especially in Silverlight because you can mix different libraries and reduce the size of your binaries.

Furthermore, the documentation is very good and it is open source — these are the two advantages of using this library.

Architecture

The `logging` block decouples two different aspects. First, the domain-specific code where you decide what to log and which information you want to save in the logging targets and, second, the more general process where you store the logged information.

There are many objects involved in this multistep logging process and it is important to understand how this flow works:

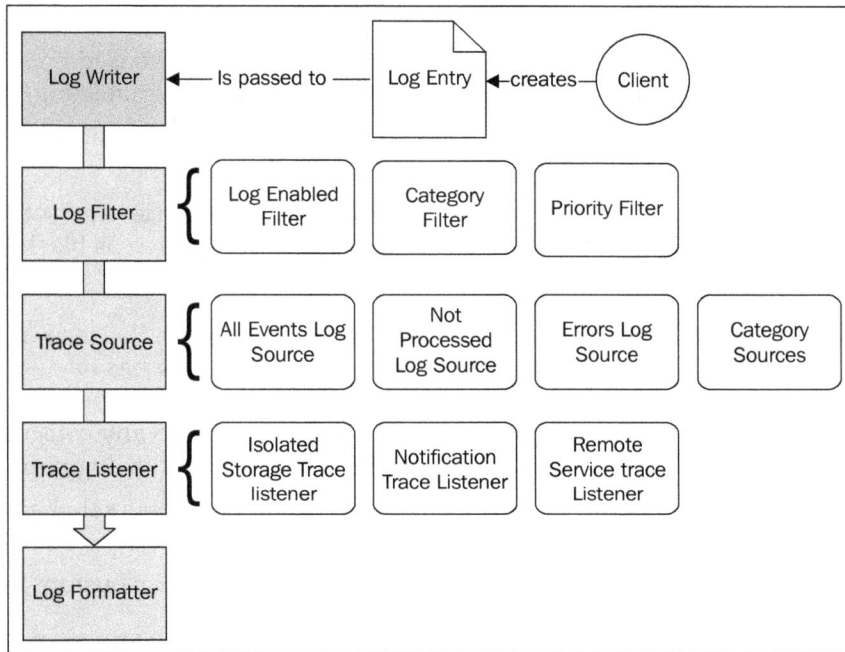

The following steps are executed for each log item:

1. **Creating the LogEntry:** The user creates a new log entry by using an instance of the `LogWriter` class or by creating a new `LogEntry` explicitly and passing it to the `logging` block.

2. **Filtering the LogEntry:** The `logging` block filters the log entry depending on the configured filters in the settings file. These filters prevent any further processing and are useful, for instance, when you want to temporarily disable logging because of performance issues.

The following filters are provided and you can define your customer filter:

- ○ `LogEnabledFilter`: All log entries can be filtered based on a property. Use this filter to temporarily disable or enable logging.
- ○ `PriorityFilter`: Only log entries whose priority is between minimum and maximum are passed through the next step.
- ○ `CategoryFilter`: You can specify a list of categories and set a property to define if these categories are interpreted as blacklist or whitelist.

3. **Selecting trace sources:** The right trace source is selected. It acts as a link between the log entries and the log targets. Each category has its own trace source and there also exist some built-in trace sources for all log entries—the entries that have not been processed and do not belong to any category and the entries that could not be processed due to an error while logging.

4. **Selecting trace listeners:** In the fourth step, the trace listeners that are associated with the current trace source are selected.

   Only three listeners exist, but you can also define your own custom listener:

   - ○ `IsolatedStorageTraceListener`: The entries are stored in the isolated storage. There are also some classes that can be used to read the log entries.
   - ○ `RemoteServiceTraceListener`: The entries will be passed to a storage that also writes the log entries to the isolated storage. After a given period of time, the messages from the storage will be sent to the service. If this service is not available, the listener tries to send the log entries later. Therefore, log entries cannot be lost.
   - ○ `NotificationTraceListener`: It is the most simple trace listener that just invokes an event. This can be useful when you want to trigger custom code.

5. **Formatting the log entry:** In the final step, the log entry is formatted and finally written to the log destination. By default, a text formatter is used, which uses a text template with placeholders.

Practice

We have already learned enough about the theory and the concept of the Enterprise Library and also about exception handling a few pages back. Now it is time to start with some practice and build a sample application where we can test the concepts.

First, download and install the installer for the Microsoft Enterprise Library 5.0 Silverlight Integration Pack, which can be found at `http://bit.ly/11topI`.

Now, create a new Silverlight application project and add the references to the following assemblies, which have been installed in the global assembly cache:

- **Microsoft.Practices.EnterpriseLibrary.Common.Silverlight**, which can be found by the name **Enterprise Library Shared Library**

- **Microsoft.Practices.EnterpriseLibrary.Logging.Silverlight**, which can be found by the name **Enterprise Library Logging Application Block**

- **Microsoft.Practices.ServiceLocation**

- **Microsoft.Practices.Unity.Silverlight**

```
Solution 'SilverlightLoggingDemo' (1 project)
  SilverlightLoggingDemo
    Properties
    References
      Microsoft.Practices.EnterpriseLibrary.Common.Silverlight
      Microsoft.Practices.EnterpriseLibrary.Logging.Silverlight
      Microsoft.Practices.ServiceLocation
      Microsoft.Practices.Unity.Silverlight
      mscorlib
      system
      System.Core
      System.Net
      System.Windows
      System.Windows.Browser
      System.Xml
    App.xaml
    MainPage.xaml
```

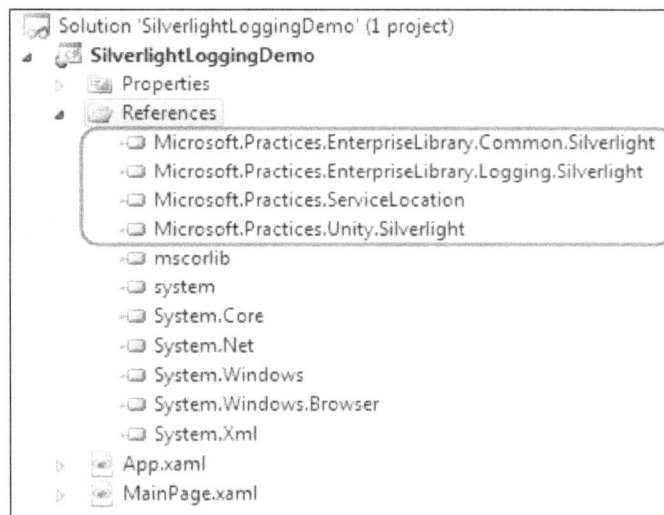

The next step is to initialize the logging system. Enterprise Library is using Unity Application Block to resolve all dependencies for a component.

Unity is a lightweight extensible dependency injection container that is also available at **Codeplex**. At some points, it can be compared with **Microsoft Extensibility Framework**. It injects other components by the constructor or properties, but has no mechanisms to load and manage your components with catalogs. Instead you have to register the types explicitly by code.

The core system of the Enterprise Library registers the components and you can use unity to create a new instance of the main `UserControl` and inject the dependencies by the constructor.

At the moment, we will only need the `LogWriter`, which is our main entry point to create log messages.

```
public partial class MainPage : UserControl
{
  public LogWriter LogWriter { get; private set; }
  public MainPage(LogWriter logWriter)
  {
    LogWriter = logWriter;
    InitializeComponent();
  }
}
```

We will also replace the new statement in `App.xaml.cs` where we create our main view to resolve the dependencies with Unity.

```
private void Application_Startup(object sender, StartupEventArgs e)
{
  this.RootVisual =
    EnterpriseLibraryContainer.Current.GetInstance<MainPage>();
}
```

When the application is debugged, an exception will be thrown, which is a little bit obtrusive, but implies that the `logging` block has to be configured before using it.

Configuring the Enterprise Library in old versions was very hard, which is probably one of the main reasons why most developers do not use it in real-world applications. In Silverlight, it is much easier. The configuration is an XAML file and you have all the same helpers that you also have when views are created manually, such as auto completion.

```
<ResourceDictionary>
  <el:LoggingSettings DefaultCategory="default"
    x:Key="loggingConfiguration"
    LogWarningWhenNoCategoriesMatch="True">
    <el:LoggingSettings.TraceListeners>
      <el:NotificationTraceListenerData Name="event"/>
    </el:LoggingSettings.TraceListeners>
    <el:LoggingSettings.TraceSources>
      <el:TraceSourceData Name="default" DefaultLevel="Error">
        <el:TraceSourceData.TraceListeners>
        <el:TraceListenerReferenceData Name="event"/>
        </el:TraceSourceData.TraceListeners>
      </el:TraceSourceData>
    </el:LoggingSettings.TraceSources>
  </el:LoggingSettings>
</ResourceDictionary>
```

To reduce the size, the previous code snippet does not contain the declarations of the XML namespaces. You can find this in the code bundle of this chapter.

What we do here is to define a trace source named "default" and link this trace source with the trace listener named "event". Whenever we log a new message with level `Error` or lower, this log entry is passed to the trace listener that we defined (`Values` for the enumerations range from the lowest for `Critical` to the highest value for `Verbose`). All other log entries will be discarded.

We said before that the **NotificationTraceListener** sends the log entries to another class that provides access to an event. This class implements the `ITraceDispatcher` interface, which can also be injected by the constructor.

```
public MainPage(LogWriter logWriter, ITraceDispatcher dispatcher)
{
  LogWriter = logWriter;
  dispatcher.TraceReceived +=
  (sender, e) =>
  {
    MessageBox.Show(((LogEntry)e.Data).ToString());
  };

  InitializeComponent();
}
```

It can be tested by adding two buttons to our view. One of them writes to the `LogWriter` with level set to `Verbose`, the other uses the `Error` level. A message box will only be seen when the first button is clicked.

Changing requirements do not affect our code. You only have to modify the configuration to use another listener, for example, if you want to write the log entries to the isolated storage.

Exception handling

Let's now combine error logging with exception handling. The same scenario as previously will be used. We want to open a file:

```
public void OpenFile(string fileName)
{
  LogWriter.Write("Start: OpenFile");
  try
  {
    using (FileStream fileStream =
    new FileStream(fileName, FileMode.Open))
```

```
      {
        // Do something
      }
    }
    catch (FileNotFoundException)
    {
      LogWriter.Write("File not found");
      throw;
    }
    finally
    {
      LogWriter.Write("Completed: OpenFile");
    }
  }
```

We do not handle the exception but need a lot of additional code that does not belong to our business logic and the functional requirements. This code is repeated very often and therefore does not follow the DRY (Don't Repeat Yourself) principle.

The first idea leads to integrate a helper method, which accepts the name of the method and an action that is invoked inside the try block.

```
public static class LogHelper
{
  public static void LogOperation
    (this LogWriter writer, string name, Action action)
  {
    try
    {
      writer.Write("Started: " + name);
      action();
    }
    catch
    {
      writer.Write("Failed: " + name);
      throw;
    }
    finally
    {
      writer.Write("Completed " + name);
    }
  }
}
```

Our code is much simpler now:

```
public void OpenFile(string fileName)
{
  LogWriter.LogOperation("OpenFile",
  () =>
  {
    using (FileStream fileStream =
    new FileStream(fileName, FileMode.Open))
    {
      // Do something
    }
  });
}
```

It looks better, but logging has not been separated from the business logic and this is exactly the situation which PostSharp is perfect for.

PostSharp

PostSharp is a framework that allows developers to use **Aspect-oriented programming** (AOP). AOP is a paradigm to separate cross-cutting concerns from the core-level concerns. Typical scenarios are logging, tracing, exception handling, and transaction management. But PostSharp can also be used to implement the INotifyPropertyChanged interface for every property of your ViewModel with one line of code.

PostSharp is not only a class library but also provides some post-build steps, which will be triggered automatically when the references are added to the assemblies. It provides a wide range of base attributes, which can be used to define custom code that is injected into the members and classes where you assigned them. It is easier to understand by looking at a simple example.

First, we download the free community edition of PostSharp from the website (http://bit.ly/dDppYP).

The next step is to add a reference to the PostSharp assembly and create a new class named LoggingAttribute. This is a custom attribute that can only be applied to methods and extends the OnMethodBoundaryAspect that comes with PostSharp.

```
[AttributeUsage(AttributeTargets.Method)]
public class LoggingAttribute : OnMethodBoundaryAspect
{

}
```

The OnMethodBoundaryAspect is an attribute, which when applied to a method defined in the current assembly, inserts a piece of code before and after it. This is perfect for our needs, because we want to add some log messages before and after the method.

Before doing some logging, we need a reference to the LogWriter. This can be done in the same way as the main view was created. We just ask Unity for the right instance.

```
protected LogWriter LogWriter { get; set; }
public LoggingAttribute()
{
  LogWriter =
    EnterpriseLibraryContainer.Current.GetInstance<LogWriter>();
}
```

Finally, some methods can be overwritten and our log entries posted. PostSharp provides all the information we need, like the name of the method or parameters that have been passed to it.

The final code will look similar to the following:

```
[AttributeUsage(AttributeTargets.Method)]
public class LoggingAttribute : OnMethodBoundaryAspect
{
  private LogWriter LogWriter { get; set; }
  public LoggingAttribute()
  {
    LogWriter =
EnterpriseLibraryContainer.Current.GetInstance<LogWriter>();
  }

public override void OnEntry(MethodExecutionArgs args)
  {
    LogWriter.Write("Entry: " + args.Method.Name);
    base.OnEntry(args);
  }

  public override void OnExit(MethodExecutionArgs args)
```

```
  {
    LogWriter.Write("Completed: " + args.Method.Name);
    base.OnExit(args);
  }

  public override void OnException(MethodExecutionArgs args)
  {
    LogWriter.Write("Failed: " + args.Method.Name);
    base.OnException(args);
  }
}
```

The code in the OnEntry method is called before the body of the method is invoked, the OnExit method is called at the end of the method in a finally block and the OnException method is called when an exception occurs by injecting a catch block to our method.

We only have to assign the attribute to our method and when this method is called, the log entries will be created before and after the method.

```
[Logging]
public void OpenFile(string fileName)
{
  using (FileStream fileStream =
  new FileStream(fileName, FileMode.Open))
  {
    // Do something
  }
}
```

If this version is compared to the method with the other solutions, we will see that it is definitely easier to read and understand.

Our assembly can be opened now with Reflector to see what PostSharp did to inject our code. Reflector is a tool to browse, analyze, and debug the .NET code. It is available for a very low fee, but there are also some similar tools that are free to use. You can download the trial version from the website http://bit.ly/gNzOuK.

As a free alternative, I recommend ILSpy (`http://wiki.sharpdevelop.net/ILSpy.ashx`).

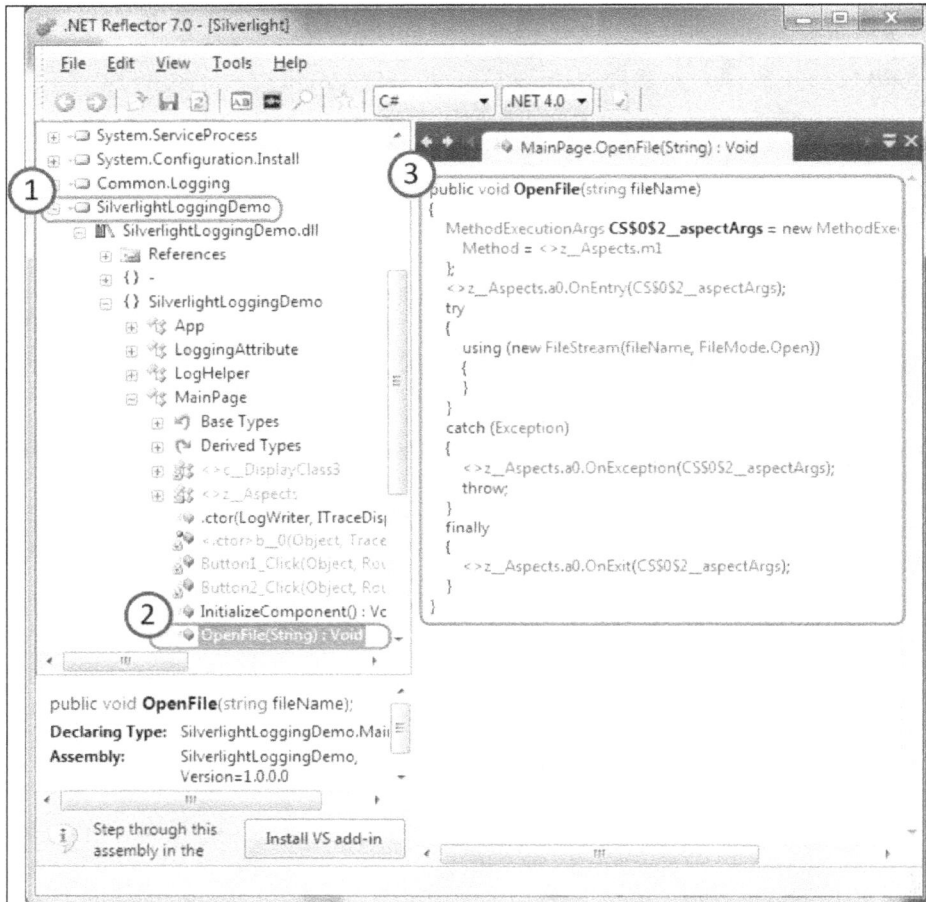

Just open the assembly, select your assembly, and then select any member. You can see the decompiled source code at the right side now. This is also very helpful for taking a look at the implementation of the Silverlight Framework to understand how some classes work.

Now, you can see that the generated code is not much different from our first version of this method, but our code looks very nice and only contains the business logic, without cross-cutting concerns.

The combination of Enterprise Library and PostSharp is very powerful. There is a very strict separation between your code and the logging aspect, but you can still use the advanced features of the `logging` block like listeners and XAML configuration files.

Using PostSharp usually brings a lot of ideas to our minds. The product page also shows a lot of examples and there are quite a lot of additional open source libraries that contain more aspects.

We would like to finish this part of the chapter with a last example. Our goal is to trace the performance of some methods. Imagine you get a request from your customer, who states that sometimes the application is very slow. A profiler was used, but at your powerful machine everything is fine and you do not see any issues. You become suspicious that one of the ten methods is very slow at the machine of your customer and, therefore, it would be good to log how long they need for execution. The methods can be changed, but it is easier to make an aspect that measures the time.

```
[AttributeUsage(AttributeTargets.Method)]
public class TracePerformanceAttribute : OnMethodBoundaryAspect
{
  private Stopwatch Stopwatch { get; set; }
  private LogWriter LogWriter { get; set; }
  public TracePerformanceAttribute()
  {
    LogWriter =
      EnterpriseLibraryContainer.Current.GetInstance<LogWriter>();
  }

public override void OnEntry(MethodExecutionArgs args)
  {
    _watch = Stopwatch.StartNew();
  }

  public override void OnExit(MethodExecutionArgs args)
  {
    _watch.Stop();
    string message =
    string.Format("Time for execution {0}: {1}",
    args.Method.Name,
    _watch.Elapsed);

    LogWriter.Write(message);
  }
}
```

Before the body of our method is executed, the `OnEntry()` method of our aspect is called. Create and start a new stopwatch and stop this after the body in the `finally` block. The elapsed time is reported to our logging system.

This aspect can be assigned in the same way as the `logging` attribute:

```
[Logging]
[TracePerformance]
public void OpenFile(string fileName)
{
  using (FileStream fileStream =
  new FileStream(fileName, FileMode.Open))
  {
  // Do something
  }
}
```

Reporting bugs

We are now able to log exception and debug information, but finally the developers and testers must get this information.

One option is to use the service logger from the Entity Library. However, this is too much information and our customers will probably not be happy when they notice that we are collecting information about the usage of the application.

Therefore, it is a better idea to show a dialog when the application is crashing and display a button with which the user can send a report to our service.

This report must be sent to different targets. We want to send an e-mail to the head of the testing team and also want to create a new work item in our bug report system.

Architecture

The system is implemented using WCF. The server provides multiple services, which implements the same interface. The Silverlight application creates a new bug report and sends it to one of these services, so that the service forwards this item as an e-mail to a mail box of one our developers, or creates a new work item in our Team Foundation Server.

The **Composite Bug Report Service** forwards the item to a list of registered services and can be used if we want to inform several people through different channels, but the **Mail Bug Report Service** or **TFS Bug Report Service** can also be used directly in the application, if you think this feature is not necessary.

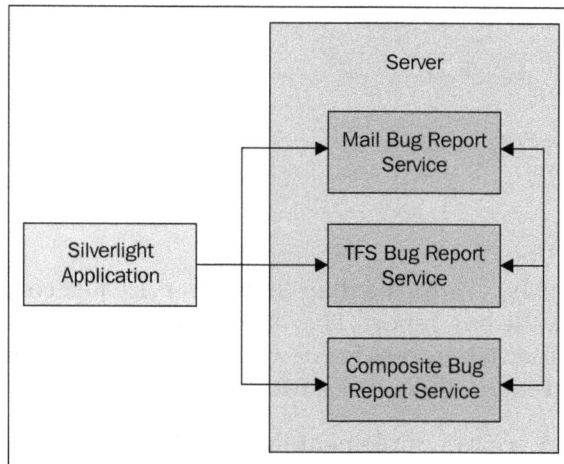

This service implements the IBugReportService interface:

```
[ServiceContract]
public interface IBugReportService
{
  [OperationContract]
  void Notify(BugReport bugReport);
}
```

The BugReport class is a data contract with several properties that stores the information that is interesting for us.

Service implementation

The Composite Bug Report Service is very simple:

```
public class CompositeBugReportService : IBugReportService
{
  public List<IBugReportService> Services = new
    List<IBugReportService>();
  public CompositeBugReportService()
  {
    Services = new List<IBugReportService>();
    Services.Add(new TfsBugReportService());
    Services.Add(new MailBugReportService("testers@company.de"));
    Services.Add(new MailBugReportService("architect@company.de"));
  }
```

```
public void Notify(BugReport bugReport)
{
  foreach (IBugReportService service in Services)
  {
    service.Notify(bugReport);
  }
}
}
```

As mentioned previously, Composite Bug Report Service just contains a list of other services and forwards the bug report. This is very powerful, because it can be used as an adapter to our internal process for new bugs. The system can be extended by reading the configuration for this service from a configuration file.

As another illustration, we can implement the TFS Bug Report Service. This decision was made because the Team Foundation Server is used for our daily work and also because it has a very good API and an SDK that is shipped with Visual Studio to get access to almost any information.

If you use another Bug Tracker, you can move to the next part of the chapter, but probably the next site can convince you to change your infrastructure.

Usually, a Client Access License is necessary to work with the Team Foundation Server, but if somebody only posts new work items and views the work items he has created, they do not need such a license.

First, add some reference to the following assemblies:

- `Microsoft.TeamFoundation.dll`
- `Microsoft.TeamFoundation.Client.dll`
- `Microsoft.TeamFoundation.WorkItemTracking.Client.dll`

It is also a good idea to set up a new user for our service that has access to our project in the Team Foundation Server, but you can also use an existing user.

The next step is to establish a connection to our project:

```
NetworkCredential credential = new
NetworkCredential("ServiceUser", "Password");
TfsTeamProjectCollection collection
= new TfsTeamProjectCollection(new
    Uri("http://localhost:8080/Tfs/Collection"), credential);
```

Let's create a `NetworkCredential` object with the name and password of our user. Now, establish a connection to the team project collection to get access to the different services of the Team Foundation Services.

The service that is responsible for our items like Tasks and Bugs is the `WorkItemStore`, which also has a reference to an object that can be used to post new `WorkItems` to our project.

```
WorkItemStore workItemStore = collection.GetService<WorkItemStore>();
Project project = workItemStore.Projects["My Project"];
```

This object can now be used to create new work items.

We only instantiate a new object of the `WorkItem` class and copy all the information from our bug report to this object. Finally, we can send this work item to the Team Foundation Server.

```
public void Notify(BugReport bugReport)
{
  WorkItem workItem = new WorkItem(project.WorkItemTypes["Bug"]);
  workItem.Title = bugReport.Title;
  workItem.Description = bugReport.Text;
  // Other properties
  project.Store.BatchSave(new WorkItem[] { workItem },
    SaveFlags.None);
}
```

It is very easy to get it running, but if you plan to use a similar system, it is advisable to secure your service and also use the configuration file to store the credentials, the name of the project, and some other settings. If required, this service can be reused for different applications.

Client implementation

The last step is to use this service in our application. Therefore, two concepts are used from the previous parts of the chapter. For instance, we use the global exception handler to send a new bug report when an unhandled exception occurs and we use the Enterprise Library in combination with the isolated storage to save our log items.

First, change the configuration a little bit to send all log entries to an `IsolatedStorageTraceListener`:

```
<el:LoggingSettings DefaultCategory="default"
  x:Key="loggingConfiguration"
  LogWarningWhenNoCategoriesMatch="True">
  <el:LoggingSettings.TraceListeners>
    <el:IsolatedStorageTraceListenerData Name="defaultListener"
      RepositoryName="defaultRepos" />
  </el:LoggingSettings.TraceListeners>
  <el:LoggingSettings.TraceSources>
```

```
    <el:TraceSourceData Name="default" DefaultLevel="All">
      <el:TraceSourceData.TraceListeners>
        <el:TraceListenerReferenceData Name="defaultListener"/>
      </el:TraceSourceData.TraceListeners>
    </el:TraceSourceData>
  </el:LoggingSettings.TraceSources>
</el:LoggingSettings>
```

Then, add a service reference to our TFS Bug Report service and subscribe to the global exception handler, as shown in the first part of this chapter, to handle all unhandled exceptions.

The Enterprise Library exposed an interface of the IsolatedStorageLogEntryRepository class with the same name that was specified in the configuration as the repository name using Unity. Resolve a reference to this object to get the stored work items.

```
private void Application_UnhandledException
  (object sender, ApplicationUnhandledExceptionEventArgs e)
{
  IsolatedStorageLogEntryRepository repository =
  EnterpriseLibraryContainer.Current.GetInstance
    <IsolatedStorageLogEntryRepository>("defaultRepos");
  IEnumerable<LogEntry> logEntries =
  repository.RetrieveEntries();
  // Send report to service.
}
```

Finally, create a new ErrorReport that also contains information about the LogEntry and send this report to our service using the classes that have been generated by Visual Studio when we added the service reference.

Do not forget to ask the user before hand and have a look at the code for this chapter in order to get an impression of how this will look in your application.

LOB application case study: applying what we have learned

The last step for this chapter is to extend our sample application with some error handling mechanisms. We will use the following approach:

Server side

At the server side, a new table is introduced where we store all the messages. Whenever a new exception is raised, we query if such a record already exists in the database. If not, we generate and fill a new entity. We also use a category value, which identifies if it is a server-side or client-side error.

```
private static int StoreError(ErrorItem errorItem, int category)
{
  int errorCode = -1;

  using (BookingsEntities entities = new BookingsEntities())
  {
    // Query if a record exists.
    Error error = QueryErrorItem(errorItem, category, entities);

    if (error == null)
    {
      // If no record exists,
      // create new one.
      AddErrorItem(errorItem, category, entities);
    }

    // Combine the category with error id to
    // create the error code.
    errorCode = category * 1000 + error.ID;
  }

  return errorCode;
}
```

The error code is a combination of the category value and the identity of the entity. I also added a new value object, the `ErrorItem` class, which contains all the information not managed by this code.

By overloading the `OnError` method of the `DomainContext` class, we can catch all exceptions on the server side. The method described previously is used to generate the error code and send this error code only to the client using the `DomainException` class. In this way, we ensure that no sensitive data is exposed. Furthermore, the error code is used for bug fixing and support.

```
protected override void OnError(
DomainServiceErrorInfo errorInfo)
{
  Exception exceptionObject = errorInfo.Error;
```

```
ErrorItem errorItem =
new ErrorItem
{
   ExceptionType = exceptionObject.GetType().FullName, Message =
exceptionObject.Message, Details = exceptionObject.StackTrace
};

int errorCode = StoreError(errorItem, CategoryServer);

errorInfo.Error =
new DomainException
{
   ErrorCode = errorCode
};

base.OnError(errorInfo);
}
```

Now, the `ErrorItem` class comes into the picture again. We use this class as a data contract for a custom method in the `DomainService` to send details about unhandled client exceptions to the server. This follows the approach in the part where we discussed bug reporting.

```
public int StoreMessage(ErrorItem errorItem)
{
  try
  {
    int errorCode =
    StoreError(errorItem, CategoryClient);

    return errorCode;
  }
  catch
  {
    return LoggingErrorCode;
  }
}
```

What is special about this method is that we use a custom error code that indicates that an exception occurred during error handling and that we just use a catch operation without doing something with the exception. Generally speaking, it is not a good idea, but in this case it is fine, because if we try to handle or log the exception, we might end up in an infinite loop.

Client side

Although we are talking about the Silverlight part of our application now, we must also handle the server-side exceptions at the Client.

The flow of server-side exceptions is described by the following figure:

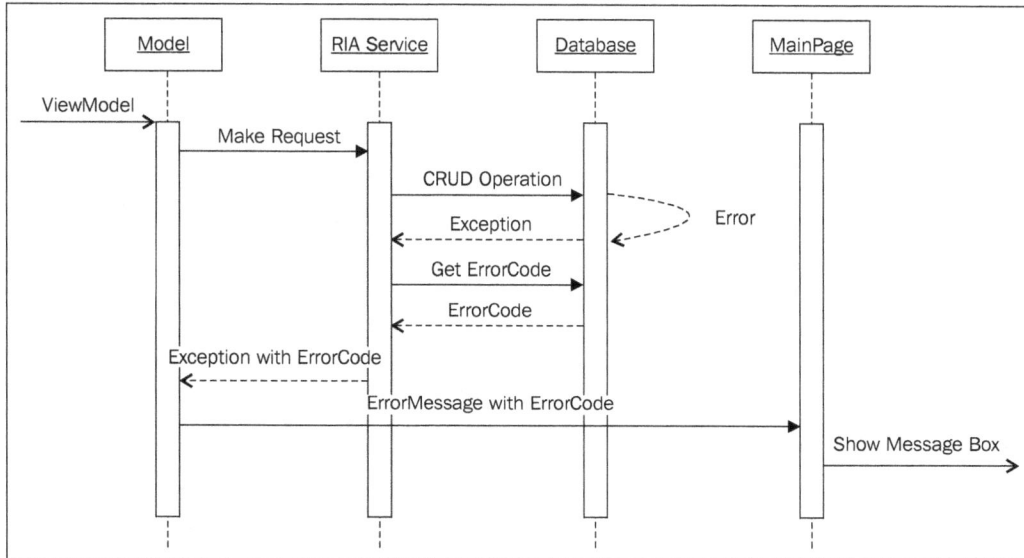

A **ViewModel** makes calls to a method of the model, which makes a request to the RIA Service, which in turn forwards this request as CRUD (Create, Read, Update, and Delete) operation to the database using Entity Framework. An error occurs and an exception is thrown. We handle this exception using the `OnError` method in the RIA Service and make another request to the database to get the error code.

We transport this error code to the client using the `DomainException` class, which is handled in a model. We can identify whether it is such an exception or not, because exceptions that are raised from the server-side validations usually do not have an error code. If the error code is not zero, we format a string and send the text to the `MainPage` using an MVVM Light message. The `MainPage` is responsible for showing a dialog; in this case, we just use a message box. You should design a custom dialog that explains in the friendliest way that something is broken.

For unhandled client-side exceptions, a logging system is also introduced. The main goal is not to log at too many places but to be able to maintain and extend the application. Therefore, only the model itself, which provides all available business operations, produces error items.

The methods are changed in the following way:

```
public void AddFloor(Floor floor)
{
  Trace("Floor Adding");

  Context.Floors.Add(floor);

  SubmitChangesAsync();

  Trace("Floor Added");
}
```

As discussed earlier, this adds a lot of noise to the code. Only half of the lines are domain-specific code. So it is a better idea to use some functional programming or, better still, to use PostSharp to separate these cross-domain concerns. However, we wanted to keep it simple and not to force you to install PostSharp, so we decided to use the simplest approach.

We use the `EnterpriseLibrary` and store all `LogItem` objects in the isolated storage. The settings are similar to what we saw in this chapter earlier.

Whenever an unhandled exception occurs, we collect all log items from the isolated storage and create an error item.

```
private static ErrorItem BuildErrorItem(Exception exception)
{
  IsolatedStorageLogEntryRepository repository =
  GetRepository();

  StringBuilder stringBuilder = new StringBuilder();

  foreach (LogEntry entries in repository.RetrieveEntries())
  {
    stringBuilder.AppendLine(entries.Message);
  }

  string details = stringBuilder.ToString();

  ErrorItem errorItem = new ErrorItem();
  errorItem.ExceptionType = exception.GetType().ToString();
  errorItem.Message = "Unhandled exception occured";
  errorItem.Details = details;

  return errorItem;
}
```

We instantiate a new object of our RIA Services Domain Context and send this error item to the service. As a result, the error code is received and our message is used to show a dialog with this code.

```
private void Application_UnhandledException(object sender,
    ApplicationUnhandledExceptionEventArgs e)
{
  ErrorItem errorItem = BuildErrorItem(e.ExceptionObject);

  SendMessage(errorItem,
      errorCode =>
  {
    string errorMessage = CreateMessage(errorCode);

    Messenger.Default.
    Send(new ErrorMessage(errorMessage));
  });
}

private static void SendMessage(ErrorItem errorItem,
Action<int> callback)
{
  BookingDomainContext domainContext =
  new BookingDomainContext();

  InvokeOperation<int> result =
  domainContext.StoreMessage(errorItem);

  result.Completed += (sender, e) =>
  callback(result.Value);
}
```

This process is summarized by the following figure:

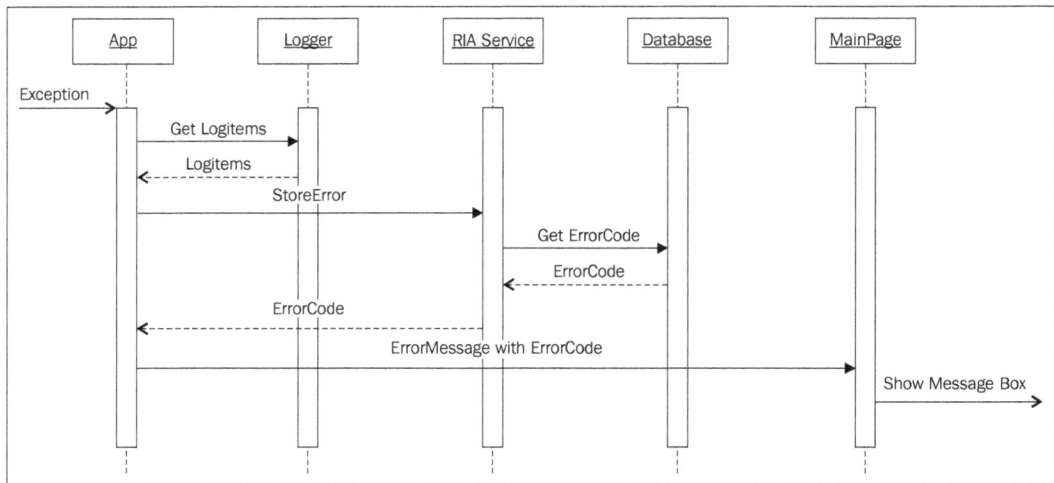

We handled both types of exceptions, server-side as well as client-side, but there are still a number of tasks to perform to improve the system:

- Use a separate database for the errors, so that when the normal database gets broken there is still a second system for logging. Use a bug reporting system, such as a work item system of the Team Foundation Server, to manage your bugs and exceptions and automatically send the errors to this system.

- Identify critical errors and design more categories to provide more information to the user. Design a notification system for these kind of bugs to notify your support team that something very critical has happened.

- Use a normal logging system, such as NLog or Log4net, for the server to trace and write the information to a file. This way, you still have some information in the log when your database crashes.

Summary

In this chapter, we have learned a lot about error control. Do the best you can to write an application that is very stable. The previous chapter about Architecture and Unit Testing can help you to design your system for changing requirements and to test it using automated tests.

For all situations out of your control, you now have the tools to get the best out of it. Try to avoid these situations and design a nice dialog with some details about the exception to give your customers and users the feeling that this will be fixed soon.

Additional resources

There are a lot of free materials about error handling on the Web, especially discussions about clean code, in blogs of members of the .NET community. It is well worth reading them, but it is most important to go through your code and to think about what can go wrong and how you can improve it. The materials that are most important in this process are as follows:

- Static code analysis: `http://bit.ly/knvNkf`
- Code Contracts: `http://bit.ly/MePem`
- Introduction to Exceptions and Exception Handling at MSDN: `http://bit.ly/jKJmpb`
- Vexing exceptions, Eric Lippert: `http://bit.ly/d2cOZ4`
- Enterprise Library at Codeplex: `http://bit.ly/diZrXW`
- Installer for Enterprise Library 5.0 Silverlight Integration Pack: `http://bit.ly/lltopI`

9
Integration with other Web Applications

Although the main aim of this book is to give instructions for the development of an LOB application in Silverlight from scratch, there are two important details that cannot be forgotten. First of all, Silverlight is intended for web development; secondly (but not less relevant), Silverlight is just a newborn in the web world. Thus, web development with Silverlight should not be regarded as something exclusive, but as complementary to traditional web development.

On the other hand, given the fact that we create RIA applications with Silverlight and the term *application* could be changed with *widget*, Silverlight can be understood as an extension for applications that already exist. Thanks to Silverlight, great interactive and visual value is added to applications, reducing complexity and time for development.

That's the reason why Microsoft wanted to offer a communication channel between Silverlight and the outer world, understanding outer world as a combination of HTML and JavaScript (the traditional Web).

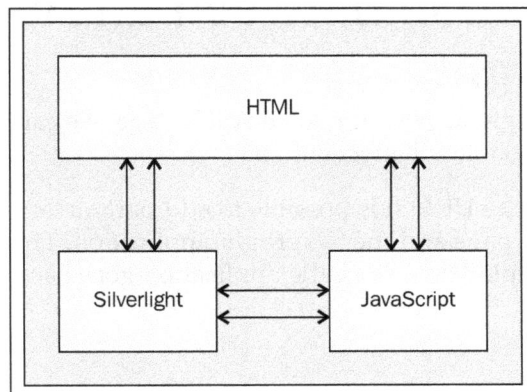

Page architecture

If an HTML page containing a Silverlight application is dissected, it can be seen that the application is contained in an object, which is part of the page **Document Object Model** (DOM). Consequently, an HTML page (or web application) can hold HTML forms, JavaScript code and, in our case, one or more Silverlight components.

> A Document Object Model (DOM) is essentially an Application Programming Interface (API), which provides a standard object collection to represent HTML documents, a standard model of how these objects can be combined, and a standard interface to access and handle them. Through DOM, applications can access and modify the content, structure, and style of HTML documents.

An HTML page can suffer alterations both in content and in style. JavaScript is in charge of them. If we had a typical RIA application developed in JavaScript and Ajax, JavaScript could be considered as an HTML page engine, since it is in charge of handling and loading the page elements. Someone could think this is not entirely true, as an ASP.NET web form application does not need JavaScript in order to interact with the elements of the page. But this is a completely different scenario and, as we have already seen in previous chapters, we would lose the application status in every postback this way, being necessary to establish it again in every post to the server. The case we are contemplating, where Silverlight is placed, consists of HTML, JavaScript, and Ajax.

Silverlight could be seen as a liberation from the JavaScript world but, even without noticing, there still remains a little trace of it. When adding a Silverlight object to an HTML page, everything begins with the initialization of an element type `Object`, which, of course, is done via JavaScript.

Communication between an ASPX page and Silverlight

When adding a Silverlight application to an ASPX page, we can establish different paths for the information flow between them:

- **Parameters in the URL**: It is possible to add parameters to the URL both from the ASPX page and the Silverlight application. This is a way to initialize a Silverlight application, since the application goes back to a starting point in every postback.

- **Cookies**: As with any website, we can access the browser cookies. This access can be used as a way to authenticate a user in the Silverlight application and for the initial configuration.

- **Session**: Instead of transferring the information in the URL, it can be stored in the session of the .NET application. Data is accessed from Silverlight via a call to a web service.

- **Initparams**: Use the initparams of the Silverlight `Object` tag initialization. This can allow us to inject some startup values and collect them when our Silverlight app is instantiated.

As an example, let's see how the URL can be used to transfer information from an ASPX page to a Silverlight application. In the example, we will create a web form with a couple of textboxes and a button, which will send the information to the server. The Silverlight application will have the same content, that is, a pair of textbox controls and a button. However, although the result does not make much sense, it will show that it is a postback for a Silverlight application. This is a great example for understanding the postback behavior in a .NET application and its effect on an embedded Silverlight application hands on!

Create a new Silverlight project with the name `SilverlightURL` in the same way as you did in previous chapters of the book. As usual, be sure that you have created the associated web project. Unlike the rest of the examples we've dealt with, in this case, the content will be added to the ASPX page and the associated Code-Behind file. The aim of this example is to achieve something similar to the following screenshot:

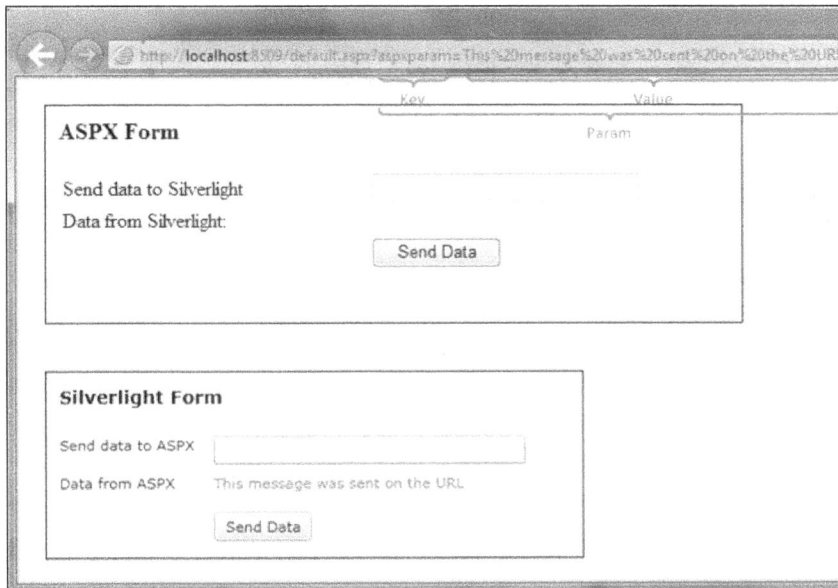

As can be seen, there are two forms. The **ASPX Form** is a web form with the following .NET controls:

- **TextBox**: This will contain the text that will be sent to the Silverlight application
- **Label**: This will show the message received from the Silverlight application
- **Button**: This will postback on the form

The **Silverlight Form** is actually the Silverlight application and consists of similar controls to those seen in the **ASPX Form**. Once both applications have been laid out, we can begin to give content to the initialization events (Page_Load and MainPage) and the buttons of both applications.

For the web form application, the Code-Behind of the Default.aspx page will be as follows:

```
public partial class _default : System.Web.UI.Page
{
  protected void Page_Load(object sender, EventArgs e)
  {
    // Check if the URL has parameters
    if (Request.QueryString.Count > 0)
    //and check if one of them is what we are waiting for
    lblReceivedValue.Text =
      Request.QueryString["silverlightparam"];
  }

  protected void btnSendData_Click(object sender, EventArgs e)
  {
    // Reload the page adding to the URL a parameter
    // with the text entered by the user
    Response.Redirect("default.aspx?aspxparam=" +
      txtData.Text );
  }
}
```

Check if we have the parameter sent from Silverlight in the Page_Load of the page. If so, show it in a label object.

The handler of the Click event of the button reloads the page, but altering the URL, since it adds the text the user has been able to add in the form.

The Silverlight application code is practically identical. The only detail to highlight now is the use of the HtmlPage object, which gives us an interface to handle the elements of the page DOM. This class will be dealt with in more depth later in this chapter.

```
public partial class MainPage : UserControl
{
  public MainPage()
  {
    InitializeComponent();

    IDictionary<string, string> qString =
      HtmlPage.Document.QueryString;
    string queryParam ="";
    // Check if the URL has parameters
    if (qString.Count > 0)
    //and check if one of them is what we are waiting for
    if (qString.Keys.Contains("aspxparam"))
      queryParam = qString["aspxparam"];

      lblDataFromASPX.Text = queryParam;
  }

  private void btnSendData_Click(object sender, RoutedEventArgs e)
  {
    // Reload the page adding to the URL a parameter
    // with the text entered by the user
    HtmlPage.Window.Navigate(new
      Uri("http://localhost:8509/default.aspx?silverlightparam="
      + txtDataToSend.Text));
  }
}
```

When initializing the Silverlight application, the parameters of the URL are checked, showing a message if the parameter aspxparam was provided. The event of the **Send Data** button forces a new load of the page.

What we have seen so far could be considered as an introduction to remind us of the fact that Silverlight is still on the Web and is part of a website (including the pros and cons of using querystring). Next, we will show how it is actually possible to interact with the page elements.

Accessing Silverlight from JavaScript

Here's where many web developers really feel at home. They love JavaScript! The reader may wonder what JavaScript lovers are doing with Silverlight. There are a few reasons for this. Both JavaScript and Silverlight complement each other. On the other hand, the architecture we can build with JavaScript, even if we are extremely organized, cannot match the tidiness we can achieve with Silverlight.

The access to a Silverlight object from JavaScript code is quite easy. It is only necessary to have the Silverlight object instantiated and specify which methods will be accessed from JavaScript in Silverlight.

To register a Silverlight object, we will use the event onLoad of the element of the type Object, which contains the Silverlight application in the HTML page, to obtain an instance of the Silverlight application as soon as it is loaded.

```
<object data="data:application/x-silverlight-2,"
  type="application/x-silverlight-2" width="100%"
  height="100%" id="silverlightApp">
.  . .
  <param name="onLoad" value="pluginLoaded" />
.  . .
.  . .
</object>
```

What is shown in the previous HTML code is the way to show the host Silverlight object the name of the JavaScript function, which it has to execute when the Silverlight object has been loaded. Now, as it can be grasped from the following source code, the pluginLoaded function obtains it and stores a reference to the Silverlight object.

```
// Silverlight Object Reference
var slCtl = null;

// Silverlight Loaded Event Handler
function pluginLoaded(sender, args) {

  slCtl = sender.getHost();
}
```

> Inside the object tag, we can specify initparams that can be processed by the Silverlight application once it is launched.

Exposing methods and functions

From now on, we have a door (still closed) towards objects and methods defined in the Silverlight application. The next step will be to open that door and declare which methods will be available from Silverlight. To do so, we will simply define methods or functions. The only special feature of these methods is the attribute that is added to the header [ScriptableMember]. Let's walk through an example:

```
[ScriptableMember]
public void LoadContact(string s)
{
  int param = Int32.Parse(s);
  _theViewModel.GetContactById(param);
  DisableAddContactButton(true);
}
```

Returning complex data

From the functions defined in Silverlight, we can return data to JavaScript (both simple and complex data, even JSON serialized objects). To let JavaScript call a Silverlight function that returns a custom type, the ScriptableType attribute has to be added to the class defining it and all its public properties should be defined as a ScriptableMember.

```
[ScriptableMember]
public Contact GetContact()
{
  Contact o = new Contact();
  o.Name = "Jose";
  return o;
}

[ScriptableType]
public class Contact
{
  [ScriptableMember]
  public string Name { get; set; }

  [ScriptableMember]
  public string GetName()
  {
    return this.Name;
  }
}
```

Registering a Silverlight object

As a final step, before trying to access the methods defined in the JavaScript code, the object containing these methods has to be registered as accessible. In our example, we will make the object showing the view of the Silverlight application accessible. The `HtmlPage` and its method `RegisterScriptableObject` will be used here. This method receives two parameters:

- The first one is the name with which the object will be later identified from JavaScript
- The second one contains a reference to the exposed object

```
public ContactFormView()
{
  InitializeComponent();
  this.DataContext = _theViewModel;

  // Create and register a scriptable object.
  HtmlPage.RegisterScriptableObject("SessionSL_JS", this);
}
```

Now the Silverlight object and the methods are defined as accessible, so we only have to invoke them from Silverlight.

```
/// Call to Silverlight Method to edit the selected contact
function EditContact(row) {

  // Get Silverlight Object
  var SLPlugin = slCtl;

  // Call Silverlight method
  SLPlugin.Content.SessionSL_JS.LoadContact(
  row.attr('id').split('_')[1]);

  ShowContactForm();
}
```

In order to access the functions defined in Silverlight:

1. Access the object containing the reference to the Silverlight object.
2. Get the object defined as `ScriptableMember` through the name we gave it before, `SessionSL_JS`.
3. Specify the function to be executed, `LoadContact`.

Accessing JavaScript from Silverlight

It is now time to perform the reverse process. We will access the functions defined in JavaScript from our Silverlight application. In this sense, the working is a little bit simpler, since we do not have to do anything special to define functions in JavaScript. They only have to be accessible for the page in general.

HtmlPage object

Before continuing, let's look in detail at the **HtmlPage** object. This class offers functionality to access and handle the DOM of the page. Through the **HtmlPage** object, it is possible to:

- Access/Invoke JavaScript functions
- Register a Silverlight object in the HTML page, making it accessible from JavaScript
- Obtain an **HtmlDocument** object to manipulate the page DOM

From the **HtmlPage** object, an object of the type **HtmlWindow** is obtained via the **Window** property on which JavaScript functions will be invoked.

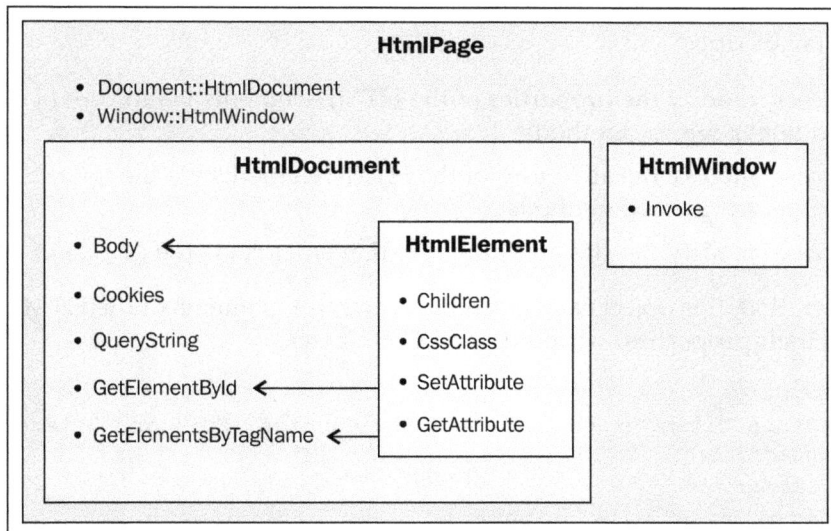

DOM handling from Silverlight

Now, let's check how to go deeper and handle the DOM object and access the properties of a given HTML element.

HtmlDocument

From the `HtmlPage` object, an instance of the `HtmlDocument` object can also be obtained. With the `HtmlDocument` object, it is possible to:

- Search for page elements (by name, class, or type), via the `GetElementById` and `GetElementByTagName` methods
- Access the list of the URL parameters
- Obtain the cookies

HtmlElement

When we search for a page element via the `HtmlDocument` object, we obtain an `HtmlElement` object. This class provides a series of methods which make it possible to handle the DOM objects. Nevertheless, unless it is strictly necessary, it would be more advisable to modify the HTML objects of the page making use of its own language, JavaScript:

- Access/modify the properties of the HTML elements via the `GetProperty` and `SetProperty` methods
- Access/modify the attributes of the HTML elements via the `GetAttribute` and `SetAttribute` methods
- Access/modify the classes of the HTML elements via the `CssClass` method

As an illustration, this object can be used to search for elements of the HTML page and access their properties, attributes, and CSS classes.

```
/// <summary>
/// Disable Client's Buttons (Add New Contact, Edit and Delete
/// Contact)
/// </summary>
/// <param name="value"></param>
private void DisableAddContactButton(bool value)
{
  // Get HtmlDocument object of the Page
  HtmlDocument htmlDoc = HtmlPage.Document;
```

```
// Search an element
HtmlElement htmlEl = htmlDoc.GetElementById("btnAddNewContact");

// Search an element's collection
ScriptObjectCollection htmlEls =
  htmlDoc.GetElementsByTagName("IMG");

foreach (HtmlElement item  in htmlEls)
{
  // Check DOM object class
  if (item.CssClass == "editRow"
    || item.CssClass == "deleteRow")
  // Add property
  item.SetProperty("disabled", value);
}

htmlEl.SetProperty("disabled", value);
if (value)
// Modify attribute
  htmlEl.SetAttribute("value",
    "The Button was disabled From Silverlight.");
Else
  htmlEl.SetAttribute("value", "Add New Contact");
}
```

Interaction between Silverlight and JavaScript

Now that we know the possibilities that Silverlight offers us in order to handle the DOM, invoke JavaScript functions, as well as defining objects and methods accessible from JavaScript, we will work upon a sample—a little more complex—which shows all these features working together.

Address book

Our goal is to create an application to store our friends' contact data. To do so, we will create two applications, one in HTML and JavaScript and the other one in Silverlight. Each of them will make reciprocal calls between them. The HTML application is functional on its own and the Silverlight application is an extension of the first one. The HTML application will show a contact list, whereas the Silverlight application will offer a form to edit them, as shown in the following screenshot:

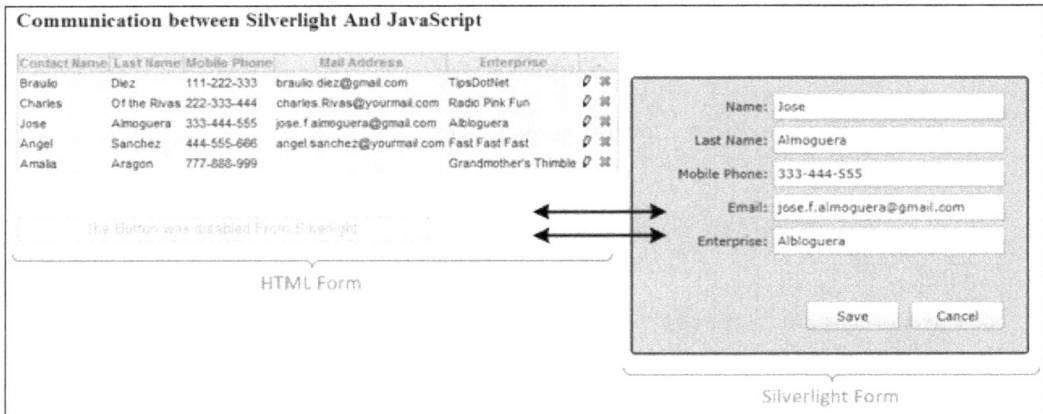

The sample can begin in a web application, which will only show the contact list. Later on, the functionality of this application is extended, allowing the contacts to be edited, for which a couple of buttons are added to the contact grid (**Edit** and **Delete**), as well as a third button, in order to add new contacts. For this new functionality, a new Silverlight application is built, containing a contact edition form.

Therefore, the new actions will begin with the traditional web application, but the application flow will continue in the Silverlight application and then end again in the HTML application, refreshing the contact grid. The events associated with the **Edit** or **Add** buttons will be controlled by the Silverlight application.

On the other hand, the HTML application will be in charge of showing/hiding the edition form via operations on the DOM object containing the Silverlight application.

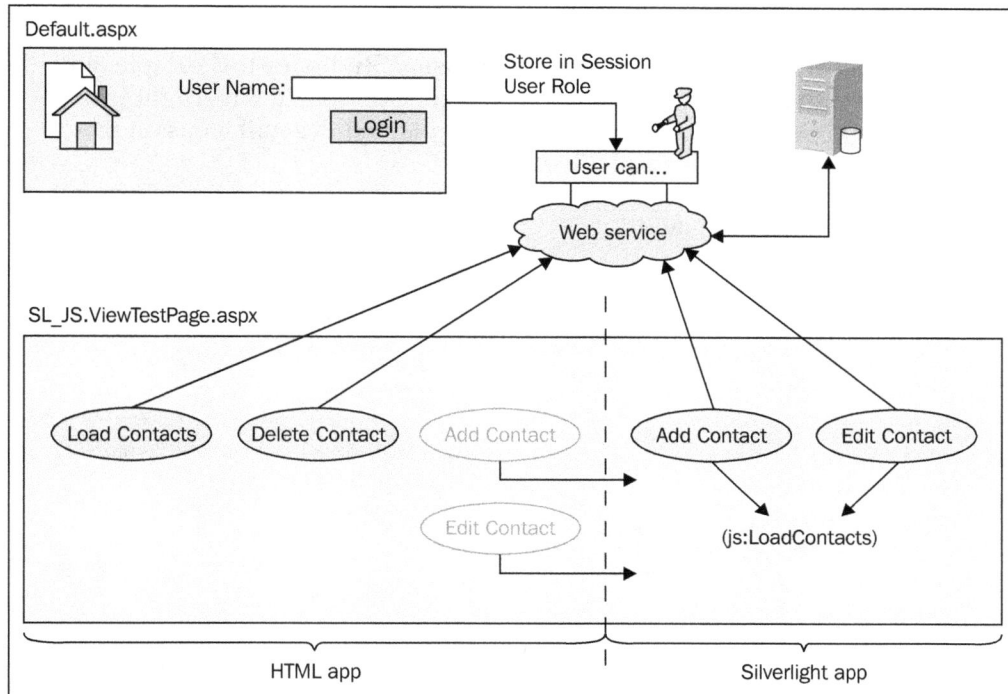

As you can see from the previous figure, two pages can be found, the first being the
`Default.aspx` main page, which will ask for the **User Name,** and a second page
with the web application. The default page will store the name of the logged user
in the `Session` object of the web application, to check it later both in the HTML
form and in the Silverlight application. Depending on its value, it will be allowed
to perform different actions. For the development of this sample, we will base it on
a single table database. (The creation script for this database can be found, together
with the complete code for this sample, in the sample source code for this chapter.)

Visual Studio solution

Let's have a look at the structure generated in Visual Studio for this sample, with the different projects that form the solution. As the generation of a Silverlight project applying the MVVM pattern has already been explained, we will focus on the interaction between JavaScript and Silverlight.

```
Solution 'SL_Javascript' (7 projects)
  SL_JS.Client                              Silverlight application(MVVM pattern)
    SL_JS.Entities
    SL_JS.Model
    SL_JS.View
    SL_JS.ViewModel
  SL_JS.Server                              Data Access layer: These projects are common for the
    SL_JS.Server.DataLayer                  Silverlight and HTML applications
    SL_JS.Server.Entities
    SL_JS.WebHost
      Properties
      References
      Classes
      ClientBin
      Javascript
        _sessionSLJS.js
        jquery-1.4.2.js
        jquery-1.4.2.min.js
      Services                              Web applications
        Ijs_Service.cs                       - Login page (default.aspx)
        js_Service.svc                       - Contact list page (SL_KS.ViewTestPage.aspx)
        SLJS_Service.svc                     - [Silverlight instance]  (SL_KS.ViewTestPage.aspx)
      Styles                                 - Web services
      Default.aspx
      Silverlight.js
      SL_JS.ViewTestPage.aspx
      SL_JS.ViewTestPage.html
      Web.config
```

Once the Visual Studio solution is created, let's describe the content shown in the previous screenshot. (The implementation of the MVVM pattern is up to you. It should be possible to simplify the Silverlight application in one single project, which includes the interface for the edition of the contact form and access to the web service for the operations).

Silverlight:

- **SL_JS.Entities**: Silverlight project which contains the reference to the web service of the Silverlight application. It contains the web application entities.
- **SL_JS.Model**: Silverlight project which contains the access methods to the web services for loading and handling of contacts.
- **SL.JS.ViewModel**: Silverlight project in charge of preparing data to be consumed by the View.
- **SL_JS.View**: Silverlight project containing UIs. In our sample, it will have the form to edit contacts.

In these projects, it must be taken into account that the following three operations will be implemented:

- Load a contact from a (numeric) identifier
- Enter a new contact
- Modify the data of an existing contact

Server:

- **SL_JS.Server.DataLayer**: A .NET project with methods for the database access of the CRUD operation on the contacts.
- **SL_JS.Server.Entities**: A .NET project with the entities definition. For this application, we only need **ContactEntity** with the properties that can be identified, as shown in the following screenshot:

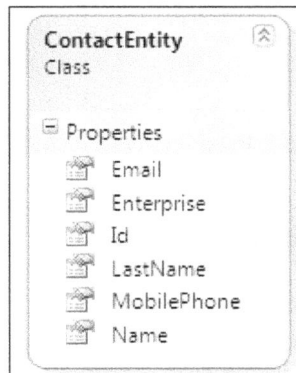

Web services: At first sight, two web services can be distinguished, the first one is for the Silverlight application and the second one is for the HTML application. This is due to the fact that a WCF service for Silverlight is somewhat special (more information about this is given in the next chapter).

ASPX pages: One for the login and the second one for the address book application.

Login page

Let's begin by analyzing the **Login** page. The `Default.aspx` page has been added to the solution. This page contains a web form with a textbox (to enter the username) and a button to complete the login process. As shown in the following source code, when pressing the **Login** button, the application stores the username in the `Session` object of the application and redirects it to the page containing the contact list:

```
public void btnLogin_click(Object sender, EventArgs e)
{

  if (txtUserName.Text == "jose.f.almoguera")
    Session["ROLE"] = "FULLACCESS";
  else if (txtUserName.Text == "braulio.diez")
    Session["ROLE"] = "ONLYUPDATE";
  else if (txtUserName.Text == "miguel.fernandez")
    Session["ROLE"] = "ONLYINSERT";
  else
    Session["ROLE"] = "";

  Response.Redirect("SL_JS.ViewTestPage.aspx");
}
```

Contact list

The `SL_JS.ViewTestPage.aspx` added by Visual Studio has also been used when creating our web project for Silverlight in order to add the grid with the contact list. The grid load is made via JavaScript operations and Ajax calls. (You can see the complete code in the sample source code for this chapter.) Bearing in mind that just when loading the page, the grid with the contact list is initialized, let's see how the JavaScript functions are executed when pressing the grid (**Delete** and **Edit** contacts) and page (**Add** contacts) buttons.

```
/// Call to Silverlight Method to edit the selected contact
function EditContact(row) {

  // Get Silverlight Object
  var SLPlugin = slCtl;
```

```
// Call Silverlight method
SLPlugin.Content.SessionSL_JS.LoadContact
  (row.attr('id').split('_')[1]);

ShowContactForm();
}

///Call to Silverlight Method to insert a new contact
function AddNewContact() {
  slCtl.Content.SessionSL_JS.InsertNewContact();
  ShowContactForm();
}
```

As shown in the previous code snippet, in both the functions — apart from calling another JavaScript function in order to show the Silverlight object — the action (editing or adding) is derived from the Silverlight object. If the deletion of a contact is requested, the action is performed directly from JavaScript via a call to a web service.

```
///Call to web service to remove the selected contact
function DeleteContact(row) {
  var value = row.attr('id').split('_')[1];
  $.ajax({
    type: "post",
    mode: "abort",
    contentType: "application/json; charset=utf-8",
    url: "./services/JS_Service.svc/DeleteContact",
    data: '{"id":"' + value + '"}',
    success: function (data) {
      if (data.d == false)
        alert("Action not allowed");
      else
        //Refresh the Contact Grid
        LoadContactList();
    }
  });
}
```

The rest of the JavaScript code is beyond the scope of this book, but it can be reviewed in the sample source code for this chapter.

Contact edition

We have seen where the flow of the operations on the grid goes; so let's see what Silverlight does in response to those events.

```
[ScriptableMember]
public void LoadContact(string s)
{
  int param = Int32.Parse(s);
  // Call the viewModel to search the contact
  _theViewModel.GetContactById(param);
  // Disable the AddContactButton
  DisableAddContactButton(true);
}

[ScriptableMember]
public void InsertNewContact()
{
  // Disable the AddContactButton
  DisableAddContactButton(true);
  // Tell the ViewModel to clear the form
  _theViewModel.NewContact();
}
```

Both functions call the `DisableAddContactButton` function. This function accesses the page DOM and searches for the **Add New Contact** button by its name. Apart from enabling or disabling it, it changes its value attribute, displaying **The Button was disabled From Silverlight** on the button. Check the following source code:

```
/// <summary>
/// Disable Client's Buttons (Add New Contact, Edit and Delete
/// Contact)
/// </summary>
/// <param name="value"></param>
private void DisableAddContactButton(bool value)
{
  // Get HtmlDocument object of the Page
  HtmlDocument htmlDoc = HtmlPage.Document;

  // Search an element
  HtmlElement htmlEl =
    htmlDoc.GetElementById("btnAddNewContact");

  // Search an element's collection
  ScriptObjectCollection htmlEls =
```

```
        htmlDoc.GetElementsByTagName("IMG");

    foreach (HtmlElement item  in htmlEls)
    {
      // Check DOM object class
      if (item.CssClass == "editRow" ||
        item.CssClass == "deleteRow")
        // Add property
        item.SetProperty("disabled", value);
    }

    htmlEl.SetProperty("disabled", value);

    if (value)
      // Modify attribute
      htmlEl.SetAttribute(
        "value",
        "The Button was Disabled from Silverlight.");
    else
      htmlEl.SetAttribute("value", "Add New Contact");
    }
```

Apart from acting on the **Add New Contact** button, it also disables the grid buttons (**Edit** and **Delete**), preventing the user from clicking on them while the form for contact edition is displayed. To do so, it scouts the list with all the IMG elements of the form and acts on those containing the CSS class editRow or deleteRow, establishing the disabled property of the HTML object to true (or false).

Calling JavaScript code

When the user clicks on the **Save** button, the handler of the Click event is executed. It makes the appropriate call to the ViewModel to enter or modify data for a contact, and also invokes a call to the CloseContactForm JavaScript function to hide the Silverlight application or form.

```
    //Save or Insert Contact and Close the PopUp
    private void btnSave_Click(object sender, RoutedEventArgs e)
    {
      _theViewModel.UpdateContact();
      DisableAddContactButton(false);

      //Call to JavaScript function to close (hide) the Silverlight App
      HtmlPage.Window.Invoke("CloseContactForm");
    }
```

Thus, all the operations to enter or edit a contact receive a response from the server, which indicates whether the user is authorized to perform that action or not. If the operation has been performed, the call is made on the LoadContactList JavaScript function for it to make all the necessary changes in order to update the grid content. If it hasn't, the user is informed through an alert message in JavaScript, invoking the Alert function with the message **Action not allowed**.

```
void _theViewModel_evActionCompleted(object sender,
ActionCompletedEventArgs e)
{
  if (e == null)
    HtmlPage.Window.Invoke("alert", "Action not allowed");
    //If Insert or Update succeeds, invoke
    //client Ajax in action to retrieve the Contact List
  else if (e.IsCompleted)
    HtmlPage.Window.Invoke("LoadContactList");
}
```

Finally, to make it work, the Silverlight object has to be accessible from Silverlight, so the object must be registered as accessible.

```
public ContactFormView()
{
  InitializeComponent();
  this.DataContext = _theViewModel;
  _theViewModel.evActionCompleted += new
  EventHandler<ActionCompletedEventArgs>(
    _theViewModel_evActionCompleted);

  // Create and register a scriptable object.
  HtmlPage.RegisterScriptableObject("SessionSL_JS", this);
}
```

LOB application case study: applying what we have learned

Let's investigate the following scenario. Our Bookings app is going to be integrated into the company intranet. Depending on the branch of the company, the employee belonging to the intranet will be displayed using different corporate colors. Is there any way for the current page hosting the bookings app to notify the application to change the colors/theme to the current valid corporate colors?

To simulate this, we have added two HTML buttons to the main hosting page. By clicking on these buttons, a JavaScript function will fire a call to a Silverlight method indicating the new set of colors to use (in our case, we will simulate this by changing the background of the menu bar, however, a real app would update the theme being used).

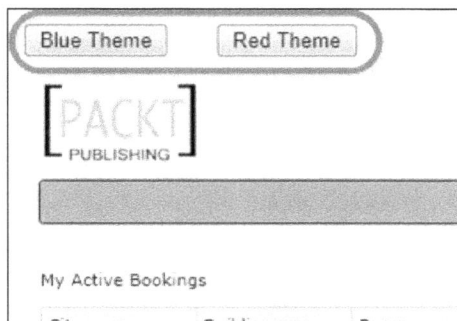

On the Silverlight side, we will go through the following steps:

1. Define a message to notify a theme change has been requested.

2. In the `MainPage.cs`, we will register a method to be called by JavaScript (entry point theme change request). This method will send the message indicating the theme change.

```
public MainPage()
{
  InitializeComponent();
  (...)
  // Create and register a scriptable object.
  HtmlPage.RegisterScriptableObject("SLThemeManager", this);

}

[ScriptableMember]
public void ChangeTheme(string strTheme)
{
  Messenger.Default.Send(new
    ChangeThemeMessage(strTheme)
  );
}
```

3. The menu bar will be registered to that event and will change the background of the menu bar to the newly selected one (we could just change the theme, or register other controls to the ChangeThemeMessage).

```
public Menu()
{
  InitializeComponent();

  (...)

  Messenger.Default.Register<ChangeThemeMessage>(this,
    (strTheme) => {
      switch (strTheme.Content)
      {
        case "blue":
          bdMenuContainer.Background =
          new SolidColorBrush(Colors.Blue);
          break;

        case "red":
          bdMenuContainer.Background =
            new SolidColorBrush(Colors.Red);
          break;
      }
    }
  );
}
```

On the JavaScript side, we will go through the following steps:

1. We add a parameter to register to the loaded event.

```
<object data="data:application/x-silverlight-2,"
  (...)
  >

  <param name="source"
    value="ClientBin/Packt.Booking.Shell.xap"/>
  <param name="onLoad"
    value="pluginLoaded" />
```

2. Get the Silverlight control instance.

```
// Silverlight Object
var slCtl = null;

// Silverlight Loaded Event Handler
function pluginLoaded(sender, args) {
  slCtl = sender.getHost();
}
```

3. Implement a method that will perform the call to the SL app to change the theme.

```
function changeToTheme(strtheme) {
  slCtl.Content.SLThemeManager.ChangeTheme(strtheme);
}
```

4. We define the two buttons and subscribe to the OnClick event.

```
<button type="button"
  onclick="changeToTheme('blue');"
  >Blue Theme</button>
```

Summary

In this chapter, we have learned how a Silverlight application can be seamlessly integrated inside an HTML web-based app (HTML 4 or 5) and how we can establish communication in both ways (HTML to Silverlight app and Silverlight app to HTML). This lets us easily integrate Silverlight-based islands into existing classic web ecosystems.

In the next chapter, we will continue integrating Silverlight with other technologies and systems. We will learn how to consume standard web services.

Additional resources

For more information about JavaScript/Silverlight integration you can check the following links:

- **MSDN**: Reference guide for the objects implied in the communications between Silverlight and HTML: http://msdn.microsoft.com/en-us/library/cc645076(v=vs.95).aspx

- **jLight**: Interesting library about DOM access from Silverlight through a syntax similar to that used with jQuery: http://jlight.codeplex.com/

10
Consuming Web Services

Web services have become a basic part of the architecture of any modern software application, not only regarding Line of Business (LOB) applications but all types. With the generalization of the Internet and devices connected 24/7, applications need a continuous way to communicate with client and server sides. Even though in the entire book we have been working with web services in the form of WCF RIA Services, this is a very specialized way of remotely accessing databases through an automatic layer of services. Even though these services can be customized in several ways, they can't reach the level of flexibility that web services can offer us, as we will see in this chapter.

Therefore, web services get into the picture for solving two different kinds of problems:

- We need to establish communication between client and server but WCF RIA Services doesn't fit into our implementation scenarios. Maybe we could make use of a custom service for a bundle of data to be transferred just by one call, or some other special operation or optimization.
- It is also essential to connect with an existing web service, whether it is our own (it could be another department system or a legacy service) or a public API (such as Google, Facebook, Twitter, and so on).

In this chapter, we will begin with an overview of what web services are, and then investigate what kind of web services we can find or use. Then, we will learn how to implement and consume a simple WCF service, and also how to consume a public API via a REST protocol. Finally, we will apply all this new knowledge on our trunk application.

Definitions

The W3C defines a **web service** as:

> *A software system designed to support interoperable machine-to-machine interaction over a network. It has an interface described in a machine-processable format (specifically Web Services Description Language, known by the acronym WSDL). Other systems interact with the Web service in a manner prescribed by its description using SOAP messages, typically conveyed using HTTP with an XML serialization in conjunction with other Web-related standards* (http://en.wikipedia.org/wiki/Web_service#cite_note-0).

This is a good starting point, which allows us to extract some ideas, to elaborate on them further:

- Machine-to-machine communication
- Described in WSDL
- HTTP (or HTTPS) with an XML serialization (or at least formatted in XML, as data could be binary serialized)

What we call *web services* have in common that they are HTTP-based, so we can see them as an evolution of RPC, sockets, CORBA, and the like, being migrated to the Internet era with a brand new architecture called Service-Oriented Architecture (SOA).

> Service-Oriented Architecture (SOA), http://en.wikipedia.org/wiki/Service-oriented_architecture) is not exclusive for web services even though its design principles can be built especially well on these protocols.

It is important to note the point described by machine-to-machine communication. These services use HTTP and all the Internet stack of protocols (IP, TCP, DNS, and so on), which are primarily designed for a machine-to-human purpose, and apply them for communication between systems.

Before going ahead with subsequent ideas, it is necessary to distinguish between two main classes of web services:

- SOAP based, which fit the definition of the W3C:
    - WSDL for services definition (readable by machines)
    - UDDI for services discovery
    - XML format
    - Wrapped with standard SOAP headers

- REST based, a back-to-sources approach taking the best of the HTTP protocol and reducing the amount of message data:

   ° JSON (JavaScript Object Notation) format

   ° Commands through HTTP verbs plus URI info

Although the verbosity of SOAP-based services makes them cumbersome, modern libraries allow ease of dealing with them. In the following section, we will use WCF for building a standard SOAP-based web service, and after that, we will see how to do the same with a simpler REST service, which paradoxically will require more code.

Implementing and consuming a WCF service

Windows Communication Foundation (WCF) (`http://msdn.microsoft.com/en-us/library/ms735119(v=vs.90).aspx`) is Microsoft's unified programming model for building service-oriented applications.

As we have seen, WCF is not specific to web services, but it offers a more general purpose model. It uses high-level abstractions as its constructing elements:

- **Messages**: Data units are sent from one point to another.
- **Endpoints**: These are sources or targets for the communication. They can be clients or services (modelling typical client-server architecture), and can have a unique address associated with them (URI format).
- **Protocols**: The way in which data will travel from one endpoint to another.
- **Binding**: This defines the protocols and parameters used by an endpoint.
- **Service**: This refers to a set of functionality composed by operations.
- **Operations**: Access methods to the functionality provided by services.

WCF offers several concrete implementations of these concepts, for example, for binding we have:

- `basicHttpBinding`: A basic binding for using HTTP protocol
- `wsHttpBinding`: A more elaborate HTTP binding, which allows you to control all aspects of WS-*, addressing security, authentication, and so on

There are more predefined binding types, such as `ws2007HttpBinding` or `mexHttpBinding`. Moreover, WCF can be extended to implement your own bindings, by implementing them from scratch or composing existing elements. For example, you can use binary format by declaring a custom binding which uses a `binaryMessageEncoding` over an `httpTransport`:

```
<bindings>
  <customBinding>
    <binding name="binaryHttpBinding">
      <binaryMessageEncoding />
      <httpTransport />
    </binding>
  </customBinding>
</bindings>
```

> An important point about WCF and Silverlight 4 is that the default WCF binding is currently `wsHttpBinding`, so it is going to be defined when we create a new WCF service. However, Silverlight 4 does not support this binding; it only supports `basicHttpBinding`. Therefore, it has to be changed in our WCF service in order to be consumed from Silverlight (we will see how to achieve this in the next section). Please note that this is a temporary issue, because Silverlight 5 does currently support `wsHttpBinding`.

Proposal for sample projects

We are going to build from scratch a simple solution with two projects, a web server and a Silverlight client. The responsibility of the web server will be to provide a WCF service (plus host our Silverlight client). That service could do whatever we want, such as retrieve data, access a database, and so on. But for the sake of simplicity, we are only going to get and set a public message. Think of it as a management system for a traffic display similar to those on highways where a message can be sent, and the display will check for it in order to show it to the drivers. It is a simple example, but at least you cannot say it is useless.

Thus, our service will have two methods, namely, `SetMessage` and `GetMessage`. The message will be kept in memory on a server-level variable, just for simplicity.

Building the server

Let's start by creating a Silverlight solution, as it will also create an ASP.NET web project:

1. Create a new **Silverlight Application** project, as shown in the following screenshot:

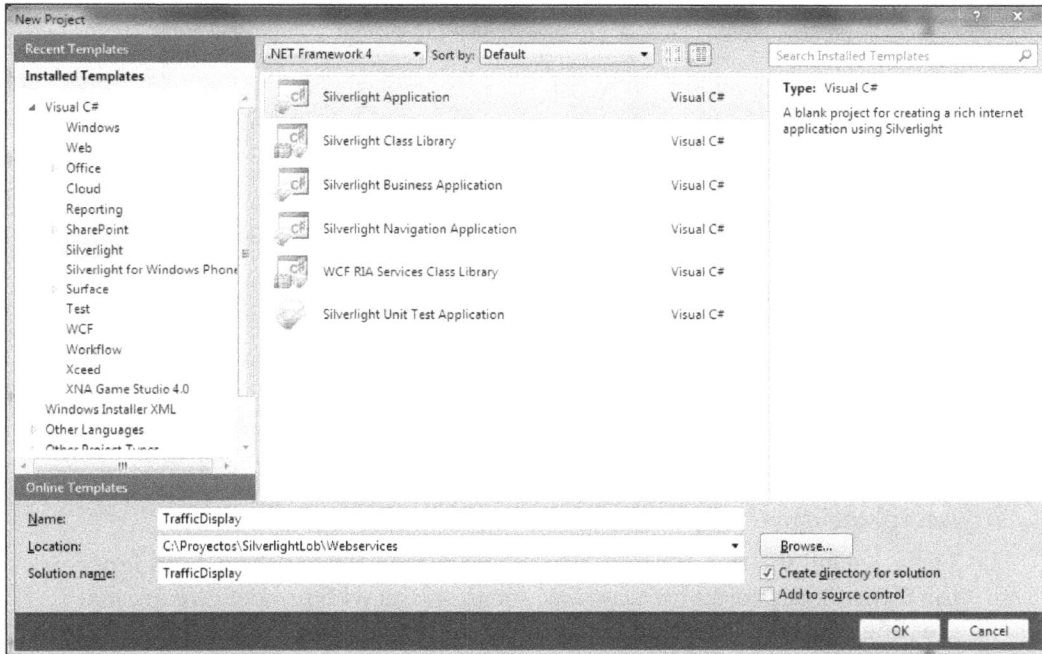

2. Select your preferred folder, use `TrafficDisplay` as **Name** and click on **OK**.

3. We can host a WCF service in our application either in a classic **ASP. NET Web Application Project** or in an **ASP.NET MVC Web Project**. It's your choice, but for this sample, we will run it with an **ASP.NET Web Application Project**.

There is no need to check the option **Enable WCF RIA Services** in this sample, but you can do it if you want it. One project can host both WCF Services and WCF RIA Services simultaneously.

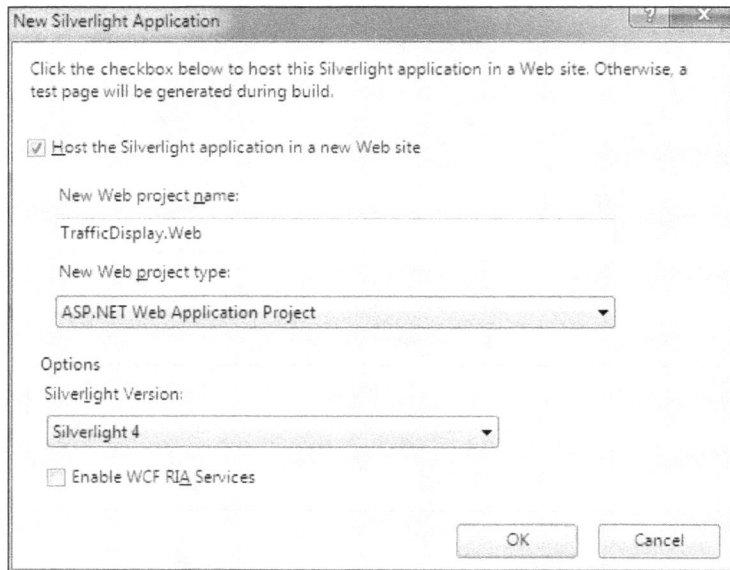

4. Accept the name proposed and click on **OK**.

    Then, we get the two projects already known in the solution. Let's ignore the Silverlight project for now and focus on the web project. We are just creating our WCF service.

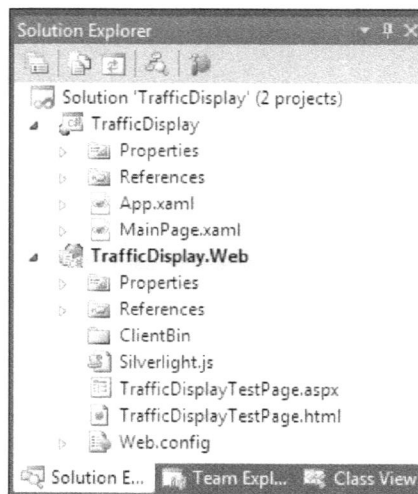

5. Right-click on the **TrafficDisplay.Web** project node and select **Add |
New item...**.

6. On the top right **Search Installed Templates** box, write `wcf`, as shown in
the following screenshot:

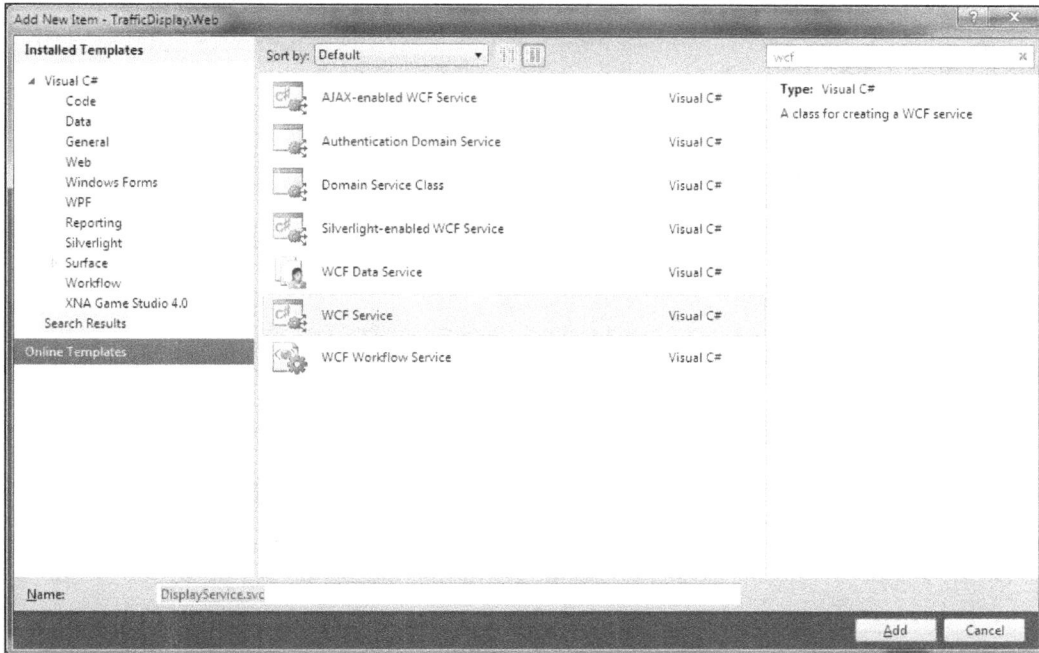

7. Select **WCF Service**, and write **DisplayService** as the **Name**. As you can
see, there are several more specific WCF service types. Some of them are
different types, and others are just standard WCF Services with a concrete
configuration.

That's the case of Silverlight-enabled WCF Service. The WCF service
generated is a standard one with a configuration adapted to Silverlight.
But for a matter of completeness, we are going to use a plain WCF service
and change its configuration manually.

8. Two new files are obtained in our web project, namely, an interface
(**IDisplayService.cs**) and an implementation (**DisplayService.svc**).

Let's learn a bit more about how WCF works. Every WCF service is defined by two parts, **interface** and **implementation**. Interface is the contract you agree to comply with, and it is labeled with the [ServiceContract] attribute (the whole interface) and with the [OperationContract] method, as you will see in following code listing. This is the public part, which every client will be able to discover, to reference and consume, and this will also be the entry point for our server. On the other hand, you must have a class that implements that interface. This is the execution we really get when the service is called.

Both new files we created previously included some sample code to help start with our service. They include a DoWork method that we will replace. First consider the following code for IDisplayService:

```
[ServiceContract]
public interface IDisplayService {
  [OperationContract]
  string GetMessage();

  [OperationContract]
  void SetMessage(string newMessage);
}
```

We have defined the two methods we mentioned previously. In order to implement them, apply the following code to the DisplayService class:

```
public class DisplayService : IDisplayService {
  public static string CurrentMessage;

  public string GetMessage() {
    return CurrentMessage;
  }

  public void SetMessage(string newMessage) {
    CurrentMessage = newMessage;
  }
}
```

Of course, this is probably the worst way of implementing this functionality, but it is also the simplest. Static variables have concurrency issues, a very severe matter for a web project. Besides, you could be interested in using an application variable rather than a static one, but then it should be enabled as aspNetCompatibilityEnabled and defined as AspNetCompatibilityRequirementsMode.Allowed in the service. This WCF content is out of the scope of this book, so we will keep it simple.

We will now try out our WCF service at **Solution Explorer**, by right-clicking on the **DisplayService.svc** file and selecting **View in browser**. A help page appears in the web browser, allowing us to see even the WSDL definition of our service.

Enabling WCF service for Silverlight 4

As we have previously said, this WCF service has been configured by default with `wsHttpBinding`, which is not supported by Silverlight 4. If you are using Silverlight 5, you can use this binding, so you can pass this section.

To consume this WCF service from Silverlight 4, its configuration has to be changed to `basicHttpBinding` in the web project `web.config` file. Currently, you should have something similar to the following inside the `<configuration>` tag of your `web.config`:

```
<system.serviceModel>
  <behaviors>
    <serviceBehaviors>
      <behavior name="DisplayServiceBehavior">
        <serviceMetadata httpGetEnabled="true" />
        <serviceDebug includeExceptionDetailInFaults="false" />
      </behavior>
    </serviceBehaviors>
  </behaviors>
  <services>
    <service behaviorConfiguration="DisplayServiceBehavior"
      name="DisplayService">
      <endpoint address="" binding="wsHttpBinding"
        contract="IDisplayService">
        <identity>
          <dns value="localhost"/>
        </identity>
      </endpoint>
      <endpoint address="mex" binding="mexHttpBinding"
        contract="IMetadataExchange"/>
    </service>
  </services>
</system.serviceModel>
```

As shown in the previous code, binding is defined as `wsHttpBinding`. This should be changed to `basicHttpBinding` in order to be consumed from Silverlight 4.

If such services configuration cannot be found in your `web.config`—it depends on your Visual Studio version and tooling installed—maybe you do not need to make any change, that is, in case the configuration generated by default looks similar to the following when the WCF service was added:

```
<system.serviceModel>
  <serviceHostingEnvironment multipleSiteBindingsEnabled="true" />
  <behaviors>
    <serviceBehaviors>
```

```
        <behavior name="">
          <serviceMetadata httpGetEnabled="true" />
          <serviceDebug includeExceptionDetailInFaults="false" />
        </behavior>
      </serviceBehaviors>
    </behaviors>
  </system.serviceModel>
```

If so, the service should be working properly from Silverlight 4 without having to change any configuration, as the generic configuration was applied.

Now that we are done with server side, let's deal with the Silverlight client.

Designing the client UI

Let's draw a simple visual interface for our simple service. Just two columns, a TextBox and a Button in the first one, and a TextBlock and another Button in the second one. It is similar to the following screenshot:

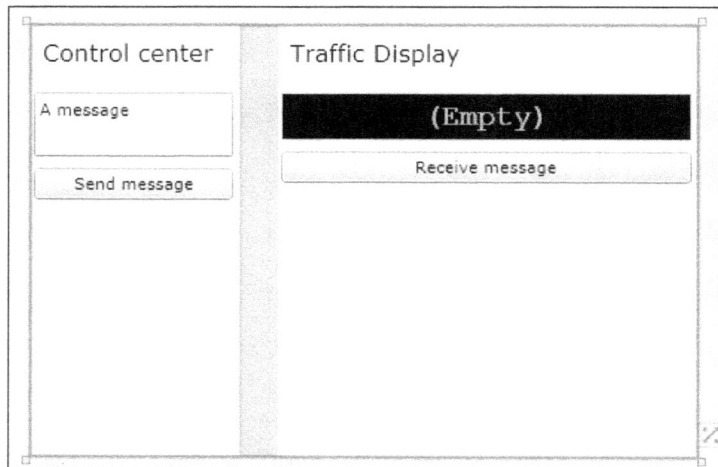

You can get this with the following simple XAML markup on MainPage.xaml:

```
<Grid x:Name="LayoutRoot" Background="White">
  <Grid.ColumnDefinitions>
    <ColumnDefinition Width="*"/>
    <ColumnDefinition Width="24" />
    <ColumnDefinition Width="2*"/>
  </Grid.ColumnDefinitions>
```

```xml
<StackPanel Grid.Column="0" Orientation="Vertical">
  <TextBlock FontSize="16" Margin="10"
    Text="Control center"/>
  <TextBox x:Name="sendTextBox" Margin="4"
    Text="A message" Height="45"/>

  <Button Margin="4" Content="Send message"
    Click="sendButtonClick"/>
</StackPanel>

<Border Grid.Column="1" Background="LightBlue"/>

<StackPanel Grid.Column="2" Orientation="Vertical">
  <TextBlock FontSize="16" Margin="10"
    Text="Traffic Display"/>
  <Border Background="Black" Margin="4">
    <TextBlock x:Name="receiveTextBlock"
      FontFamily="Courier New" FontSize="20"
      Foreground="YellowGreen" Margin="4"
      TextAlignment="Center" Text="(Empty)"/>
  </Border>
  <Button Margin="4" Content="Receive message"
    Click="receiveButtonClick"/>
</StackPanel>
</Grid>
```

Before we can implement the handlers for the events, the service needs to
be referenced.

Referencing a WCF service from client

In order to proceed, our web project has to be compiled. Let's see how to add
a reference in Silverlight to the new DisplayService:

1. Compile the solution.
2. Right-click on the **References** folder of the **TrafficDisplay** Silverlight
   project and select **Add Service Reference...**.
3. Visual Studio shows you the **Add Service Reference** dialog.
4. Click on the **Discover** button to look for **Services in solution**.

> You can also write a well-known URL and reference it for a public or intranet service.

5. We should get just one service **DisplayService.svc**.

6. Expand this node, which takes some time, as Visual Studio has to start this web service in order to ask about their operations. At this point, we are using WSDL to get method names and signatures in a fully transparent way.

7. Expand the next node one more time, till you can select the **IDisplayService** node.

8. Then you can see our two operations, **GetMessage** and **SetMessage**. Click **OK**.

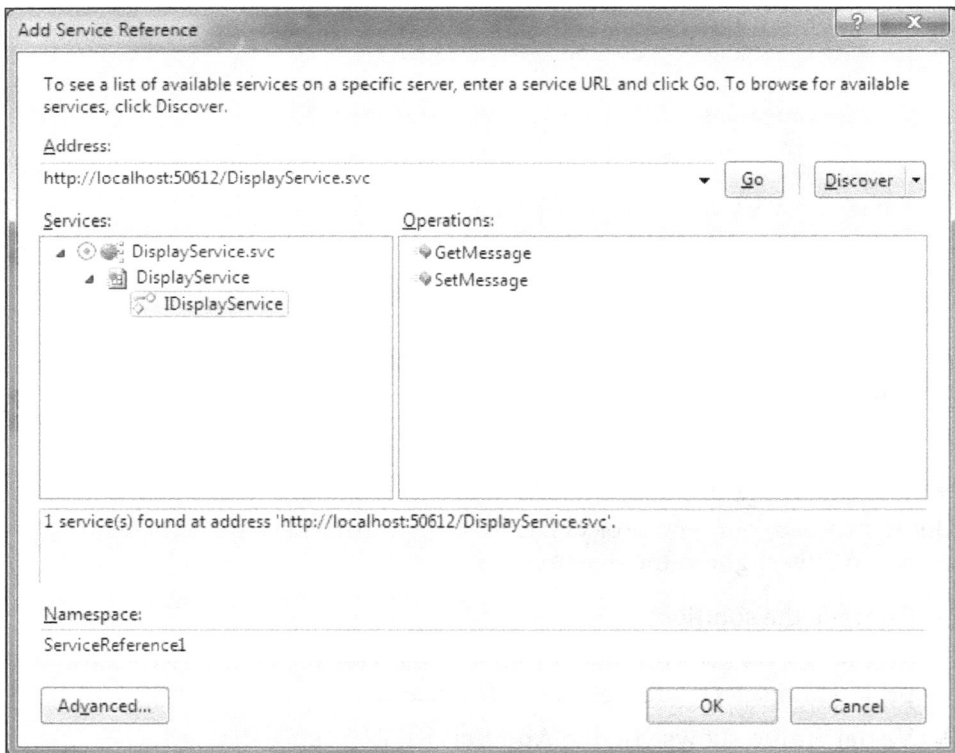

Add Service Reference

To see a list of available services on a specific server, enter a service URL and click Go. To browse for available services, click Discover.

Address:

http://localhost:50612/DisplayService.svc ▾ | Go | | Discover ▾

Services:
- ▲ ⊙ DisplayService.svc
  - ▲ DisplayService
    - IDisplayService

Operations:
- GetMessage
- SetMessage

1 service(s) found at address 'http://localhost:50612/DisplayService.svc'.

Namespace:

ServiceReference1

Advanced... | OK | Cancel

This action has created a **ServiceReference1** (you could have named it in another way in the previous dialog) inside the `Service References` folder, and a configuration file named `ServiceReferences.ClientConfig` with arguments to bind the service. Here, we can change the connection parameters when you publish the application to a production environment, for example, the URL associated with the service, but it can also be done through **Configure Service Reference...** from the context menu of **ServiceReference1**.

If we open **ServiceReference1** by double-clicking it on **Solution Explorer**, **Object Browser** shows the classes that have been generated for consuming the service. We are going to use **DisplayServiceClient**, which is the proxy class that allows us to call the service transparently from Silverlight, just as you would call any local class.

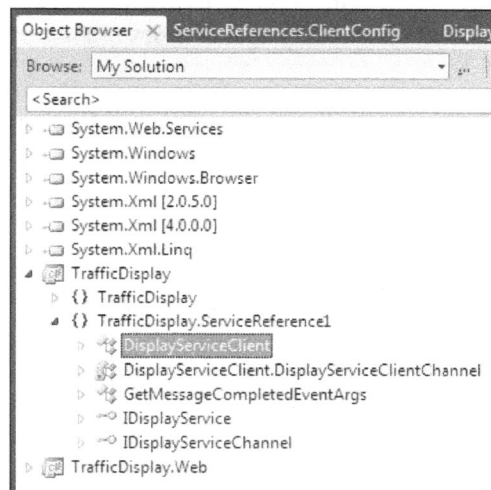

All these self-generated classes can be updated when the original service is modified by adding or editing operations. There is no need to update when its implementation is changed. It could, however, be necessary if we change the public interface of operations. You only have to right-click on **ServiceReference1** and select **Update Service Reference**.

This service reference procedure can also be applied to an **ASMX service**, with the only difference being the `SoapClient` suffix. ASMX services are previous versions of the .NET web service protocol SOAP 1.1, which in WCF is called `basicHttpBinding`.

Consuming a WCF service from Silverlight

Now, **Send** and **Receive** buttons can be implemented. `DisplayServiceClient` class publishes an asynchronous method to call every operation published in the contract of the WCF service plus an event to be notified when this asynchronous call has finished. There is no alternative; you cannot apply a synchronous approach because of the Silverlight philosophy that pretends the user interface was never blocked. Some frameworks such as PRISM or MVVM Light try to give a synchronous facade wrapping the use of web services, but this is only a mask.

Consequently, if you want to retrieve data, or just know if a service call was successful, you have to listen to the appropriate event and then call the method.

Now, let's see how to implement both handlers (in `MainPage.xaml.cs`):

```
using TrafficDisplay.ServiceReference1;
[...]
private void SendButtonClick(object sender, RoutedEventArgs e)
{
  var service = new DisplayServiceClient();
  service.SetMessageAsync(sendTextBox.Text);
}

private void ReceiveButtonClick(object sender,
  RoutedEventArgs e) {
  var service = new DisplayServiceClient();
  service.GetMessageCompleted += ReceiveCompleted;
  service.GetMessageAsync(sendTextBox.Text);
  //Nothing else. Just wait for Completed Event
}

private void ReceiveCompleted(object sender,
  GetMessageCompletedEventArgs e) {
  if(e.Error != null)
    receiveTextBlock.Text = "Error: " + e.Error.Message;
  else
    receiveTextBlock.Text = e.Result;
}
```

If no parameter is defined when creating the `DisplayServiceClient` instance, it reads them from the configuration file. This is the preferred way.

You should always wait for the `Completed` event, to check if any errors occurred, due to the fact that the only way to know whether the operation call was successful is to check the `e.Error` property, as it could be seen previously. For the operations returning void, this is not necessary if you do not need confirmation of success, as it is assumed via the `SetMessage` operation (please note that, even in this operation, you should notify the user about the possible error).

Now, you can execute the solution and test it by sending messages from the Control Center and receiving them from the Display.

Using complex types via WCF

So far, we have implemented two WCF operations only using the `string` type. Most built-in types can also be used in the operation signature, but you can use your own types too, if you define them properly:

1. Create a brand new class in the server for this purpose.
2. Label it with `[DataContract]` for the class and `[DataMember]` for the fields being sent (no labeled fields will be omitted).
3. Use this new class as an argument or as a return value in operations.
4. In the client, creating the service reference will generate a local version of this `DataContract` labeled class. Also, the client service can be updated to get the new changes, which include the new `DataContract` classes.

Then, we can consume a service with a complex type as an argument or as a return type, just as we did with the previous operations, and just as any other local method, in a transparent fashion. Please note that if some list type is included, such as `IEnumerable` or `IList`, it would be transformed to an Array type on the client side. You can change this behavior on the web service configuration in order to use any more powerful structures such as `ObservableCollection`.

For example, a new operation can be added to our service, called `GetAllMessages`, which must retrieve a list of messages plus their publication time. So let's start by creating a new class `Message` to keep the text of a message and its publishing time. This class will be tagged with `DataContract` and `DataMember` to be considered on the WCF service. Use a code similar to the following for the `Message` class:

```
using System;
using System.Runtime.Serialization;

namespace TrafficDisplay.Web {
  [DataContract]
  public class Message {
```

```
    [DataMember]
    public string Text { get; set; }

    [DataMember]
    public DateTime PublishingTime { get; set; }
  }
}
```

Next, add the new method to the service, first to the interface and then to the implementation; something similar to the following code to `IDisplayService` interface:

```
[OperationContract]
IEnumerable<Message> GetAllMessages();
```

And then complete `DisplayService.svc` class with a list of messages:

```
public class DisplayService : IDisplayService {
  public static IList<Message> Messages =
    new List<Message>();

  public string GetMessage() {
    if(Messages.Count == 0)
      return null;
      return Messages.Last().Text;
  }

  public void SetMessage(string newMessage) {
    Messages.Add(new Message {
      Text = newMessage,
      PublishingTime = DateTime.Now
    });
  }

  public IEnumerable<Message> GetAllMessages() {
    return Messages;
  }
}
```

Our server project can now be compiled. Before moving to the client Silverlight project, the first thing to do is to update our **ServiceReference1** in the client, selecting **Update Service Reference** in its context menu. After that, the reference can be inspected in **Object Browser** (by double-clicking). You will then see a new `Message` class and the new method and `Completed` event for `GetAllMessage` in `DisplayServiceClient`.

Next, the UI has to be improved in order to show the result of this method, and consume it as we did with `GetMessage`.

You can find the bits about how to do so in sample 02 of the code sample of this chapter. When you open it, the web project must be selected as the StartUp Project (in the context menu of the project). If the Silverlight client is not served by the web project, you can get into a cross-domain problem, which is covered in more detail in *Chapter 11, Security*. Visual Studio warns about that case with this dialog:

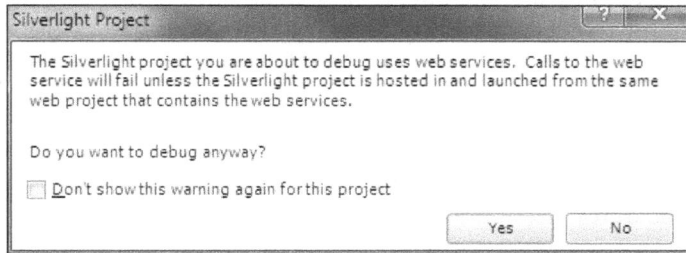

Now, let's move on to consume an external service.

Consuming a public API web service

The second part of this chapter is devoted to the other main type of web services, that is, the **REST services**. As mentioned previously, we can briefly define them as the creation of web services over HTTP protocol with minimum overload. REST (Representational State Transfer) is a complete architecture for building software defined in 2000 by Roy Fielding `http://en.wikipedia.org/wiki/Representational_State_Transfer` (`http://bit.ly/nnTsYp`). We are not covering it, but we will learn how to consume a public REST service.

Typically, most of modern public API web services rely on:

- Defining requests via URL parameters (both path and query string)
- Simplifying response complexity and weight using formats as JSON (JavaScript Object Notation) instead of XML
- Making use of HTTP verbs with full semantic, such as `GET` for reading, `PUT` for adding or updating, and `DELETE` for erasing

These are also common principles in the REST architecture, but they should not be confused. Here, we are only taking care of the first two of those ideas, accessing the Twitter public API via URL for querying, and JSON as a format for retrieving data. This is part of a general trend of moving presentation logic and data consuming on client, either JavaScript and HTML5 or Silverlight.

[We use the Twitter API as a standard web service.]

Twitter API

Whereas the Twitter API publishes a lot of functionality such as querying, publishing, advanced and specific querying, and so on. We are only using one feature, querying for tweets containing certain words. This can be done using the following URL: `http://search.twitter.com/search.json?q=SL5`.

You can see how all the information about the method call is present on that URL:

- Global service: `search.twitter.com`
- Method: search
- Format of retrieved data: JSON
- Query words: SL5

If you navigate to this URL, you should get a JSON-formatted response with the latest tweets containing that word. Now we are going to process that response.

Please note that the Twitter API also allows getting data in XML format, but as an exercise, we will request it in JSON format. So to work with XML, `atom` can be used as a keyword instead of `json` in the URL request, and it could be processed later with XML to LINQ (for more information on this, refer to Pete Brown's article available at `http://bit.ly/pDOKC3`).

Starting the Twitter project

Let's start by implementing a call to the Twitter API using the `WebClient` class. `WebClient` is a generic proxy class, which allows us to connect with any web service regardless of its interface. But this simplicity comes at a cost, and you will have to deal with the service manually, without a specific proxy and the specific data classes generated via registration as we get before registering the service as a service reference.

First, a user interface (UI) will be designed, then raw data will be retrieved with a call to the service, and finally the response will be parsed with a data class, which we have to implement. Let's start with the UI:

1. Start Visual Studio and select **File | New | Project...**.
2. Select **Silverlight | Silverlight Application** and name it `TwitterSearchApi`.
3. In the next dialog, it is not necessary to create a new website, so uncheck it and click **OK**. In this sample, we are making no use of web project, as we are consuming an external service.
4. Design the UI on the `MainPage` with a `TextBox`, a `Search` button and a `ListBox`, using the following code:

```
<Grid x:Name="LayoutRoot" Background="White">
  <Grid.RowDefinitions>
    <RowDefinition Height="Auto"/>
    <RowDefinition Height="*"/>
  </Grid.RowDefinitions>
  <StackPanel Orientation="Horizontal">
    <TextBox x:Name="searchTextBox" Text="SL5"
      Width="120" Margin="4"/>
    <Button Grid.Row="0" HorizontalAlignment="Right"
      Margin="4" Content="Search"
      Click="SearchButtonClick"/>
  </StackPanel>
  <ListBox Grid.Row="1" x:Name="listBox" Margin="4">
    <ListBox.ItemTemplate>
      <DataTemplate>
        <StackPanel Margin="4">
          <TextBlock Text="{Binding from_user}"
            FontSize="16"/>
          <TextBlock Text="{Binding text}"/>
          <TextBlock Text="{Binding created_at}"
            HorizontalAlignment="Right"/>
        </StackPanel>
      </DataTemplate>
    </ListBox.ItemTemplate>
  </ListBox>
</Grid>
```

Calling the Twitter API

Now it is crucial to implement a handler called `RefreshButtonClick` in order to start a service call in an asynchronous manner. Again, there are two steps involved. Firstly, an asynchronous method must be called, and secondly, an event must be listened to for the finished signal. But as `WebClient` is a generic proxy, we do not have a `SearchAsync` method; instead of that, we have to use one of the generic methods it supplies, in this case, `OpenReadAsync` to call an HTTP GET and a `Stream` returned through its `OpenReadCompleted` event.

The code for our **Click** event handler should be similar to the following (in `MainPage.xaml.cs`):

```
private void SearchButtonClick(object sender,
  RoutedEventArgs e) {
  var client = new WebClient();
  client.OpenReadCompleted += RefreshCompleted;
  client.OpenReadAsync(CreateUri(searchTextBox.Text));
}

private static Uri CreateUri(string searchText) {
  return new Uri("http://search.twitter.com/search.json?q="
    + searchText);
}
```

Therefore, by using `WebClient`, any URL and its contents can be called, so firstly we need to compose the custom URL for our arguments. After that, we only need to parse the response content. We will cover this in the next section.

Remember you have to validate `searchText` before calling `CreateUri`. Moreover, it is a best practice to use an application setting to save the Twitter search URI.

Processing JSON format

We can parse the JSON object manually, but Silverlight includes a power class to help us. With `DataContractJsonSerializer` it is possible to parse a JSON string and generate an object of a given type, even considering nested objects. This requires that we previously define the defined target class, which should have the same fields as the JSON object, exactly the same names and the appropriate types, even child classes. You can achieve this by analyzing the JSON object or by reading its API documentation. In our case, the search service returns a JSON object with a property called `results`, which contains an array of instances, one per tweet. Let's see how to parse it step by step:

1. Firstly, create target classes in Silverlight. In this case, the classes have been called `SearchResult` and `Tweet`, but you can use any names you want. Anyway, the properties must have these exactly identical names (even lowercase). Note that it was not necessary to declare every JSON-existing property, just those that we want to read.

```
public class SearchResult {
  public Tweet[] results { get; set; }
}

public class Tweet {
  public string text { get; set; }
  public string from_user { get; set; }
  public string created_at { get; set; }
}
```

2. In order to use `DataContractJsonSerializer`, it is important to add a reference to `System.ServiceModel.Web` in our Silverlight project. Just select **References | Add Reference...** and you can find the assembly in the **.NET** tab.

3. Now, this generic serializer can be used to parse the JSON object and generate .NET instances, and then these instances will be assigned to the listbox items source. The code for the remaining `RefreshCompleted` handler is as simple as the following code:

```
private void RefreshCompleted(object sender,
  OpenReadCompletedEventArgs e) {
  var serializer =
    new DataContractJsonSerializer(typeof(SearchResult));
    var r = (SearchResult)serializer.ReadObject(e.Result);
    listBox.ItemsSource = r.results;
}
```

> Bear in mind that our `SearchResult` object should be viewed as a local version of a **Data Transfer Object** (DTO), so it is not a best practice to pass it through a different layer. It is only targeted to keep data from Twitter API, so you should populate your independent business entities instead, if you need to use it further.

4. Finally, the application can be tested. Run the project, write some text, and select the **Search** button, as shown in the following screenshot:

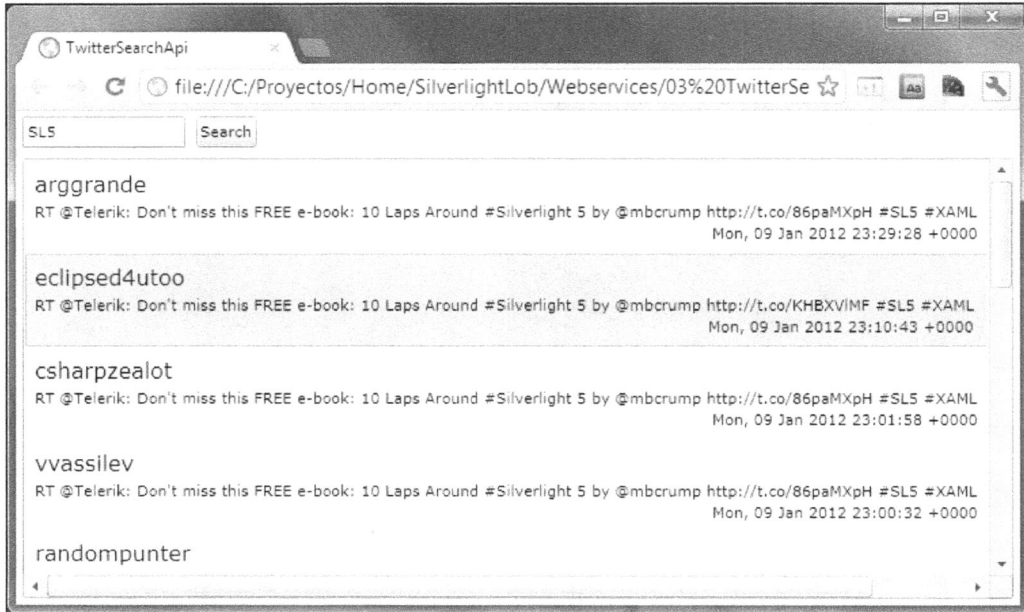

LOB application case study: applying what we have learned

Now we are going to add a new feature to our trunk application. A simple and useful one could be to display weather information while editing a booking. To get the weather information, we are using a public web service from WebServiceX hosted on `http://www.webservicex.net/globalweather.asmx`.

When you click on this URL, you will find two methods in this service:

- `GetCitiesByCountry`: This method gets a list of cities and countries to help pass the arguments to the other method

- `GetWeather`: This method returns complete weather information for a given city in a country

The service seems to be implemented using an ASP.NET service (ASMX), and has published its WSDL (which you can display by opening the Service Description link). This will allow us to automatically reference the service in our project and generate the client proxy objects ready to make calls to the service, which will also deserialize the answer for us. Nonetheless, after studying the service signature, we found that WSDL doesn't provide the result in a structured way, but as an XML string. Thus, we should study some sample results and then deserialize it manually. Thereby our steps will be as follows:

1. Adding a Service Reference to this web service in our `MyBookings` project. When done, we will get a `GlobalWeatherSoapClient` proxy class.

2. Adding a deserializer class, named `GlobalWeatherGetWeatherDeserializer`, which will generate a structured result in a `WeatherInfo` instance from the XML string returned by the service.

3. Adding a new `ViewModel` class, named `WeatherQueryVM`, to obtain and provide this information to the user.

4. Adding some controls to the `MyBookings.xaml` page to show the information from the ViewModel.

5. Including an instance of `WeatherQueryVM` in `MyBookingsVM` and getting it synchronized with the current booking selected.

6. Setting up the service configuration at the main level, the `Shell` project.

The following is a simple figure to help understand the affected classes:

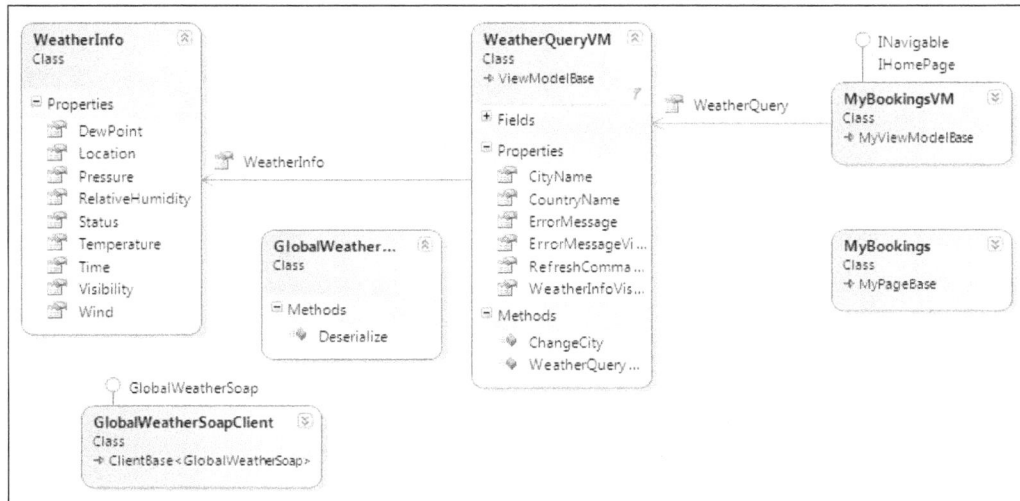

The following are some important points to take into consideration about the auto-generated code:

- We are consuming this service directly from the client and not from the server. Silverlight is powerful in doing that, and this decision reduces the load of our server, improving the scalability of the application.

- We are not extracting a new project for this feature, but are creating a new isolated set of classes that implement it, with reduced coupling with the rest of the system.

- Adding a service reference to a project generates a new configuration file called ServiceReferences.ClientConfig, but this file is not used if it is not in the main project of the solution. Consequently, we should copy this file to the main project—Shell in our application—even merging it with the previous file if it already exists.

Implementation of the service client

Let's go through the following steps:

1. **Adding the Service Reference**: Right-click on the **MyBooking** project and select **Add Service Reference**:

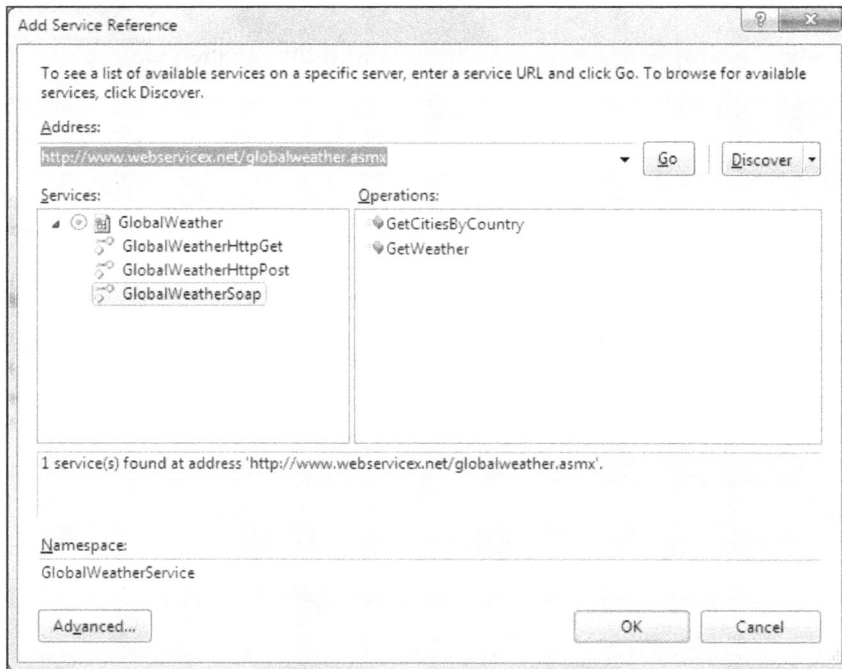

After pasting the service URL and clicking **Go**, we get three versions of the service. Choose **GlobalWeatherSoap**, and rename the service as `GlobalWeatherService`. Any of the three versions should work. As we mentioned previously, **ASMX** is the old .NET web services infrastructure, before WCF was born. It matches with WCF basicHttpBinding SOAP 1.1, so it will be consumed through a WCF client.

2. **Deserialize support**: As we have seen earlier, the ASMX definition does not detail the content of the response of the service. The information provided by WSDL just declares a plain XML text, so we need to deserialize the data contained in the XML body. This is due to a deficient service declaration, as XML deserialization could be done by WCF if it was properly specified in the web service. If that were the case, deserialize support would not be necessary.

   In order to facilitate the use of the service, we should implement a `WeatherInfo` class (with no logic, just a **DTO** object with the properties shown in the figure under the section *LOB application case study: applying what we have learned* earlier in this chapter), and a `deserializer` class with a unique `Deserialize` method making use of LINQ to XML to create a new `WeatherInfo` instance from the string returned by the service:

```
public WeatherInfo Deserialize(string xml)
{
   if (xml == "Data Not Found")
      return null;
   var xRoot = XDocument.Parse(xml);
   var xWeather = xRoot.Element("CurrentWeather");

   return new WeatherInfo {
      Location = (string) xWeather.Element("Location"),
      Time = (string) xWeather.Element("Time"),
```

   These classes have been included in a new `Services` folder and some sample responses for future reference are stored in a subfolder.

   Also, we are trapping the `city not found` error, which only returned a string in place of the expected XML.

3. **Building the ViewModel class**: This is an important step. It is responsible for getting the service information, by using the proxy client. It is also responsible for deserializing our class, and for publishing it. The implementation of the `WeatherQueryVM` class is organized into a few areas:

   ° **Weather service**: The code responsible for getting the response from the service

- ○ **Input properties**: The values needed to call the service (`CityName` and `CountryName`)

- ○ **Output properties**: The values returned from the service (the whole `WeatherInfo` object, and also some error information)

- ○ **Methods**: `ChangeCity` method propagates the city from the booking to this instance to be used in the request to the service

- ○ **Commands**: `RefreshCommand` command is used for executing the query to the service.

There is no complex logic in this class. You can read it in detail in the code sample.

4. **Drawing the UI:** In order to show these properties' values to the user, we should add some controls to the view along with the booking info. We will use data binding for both showing the values and managing the visibility of the visual elements. The root container, a `Grid`, is bound to the new property called `WeatherQuery`, so all nested elements can be bound using relative paths.

5. **Changing existing MyBookingsVM:** In the `MyBookingsVM` class, we should add a new property `WeatherQuery` (so we include it in the `MyBookingsVM. properties.cs` file):

```
public WeatherQueryVM WeatherQuery { get; set; }
```

We initialize it on the constructors' code with a new instance (with sample input properties' values). Also, the code is written to get it synchronized with the city in the booking, when changing both `CurrentBooking` and `SelectedIDCity`, with the help of a new property `SelectedCityName`, which looks up in the `Cities` collection.

6. **Service configuration**: The last step is the easiest one, as it is just necessary to copy the `ServiceReferences.ClientConfig` file from the **MyBookings** project to the **Shell** project because there is no such file present there. We keep the original file for documentation purposes, since it is useless within the library project.

When running the application, a weather information area appears, where the city name is filled as the current booking is changed. However, in order to make it work, you must introduce the right country name. We have not used the `GetCitiesByCountry` method, which might help us in correctly writing the name of the city. It's an open exercise to improve the current feature, such as including the country name in our database schema.

Summary

In this chapter, we have learned how to create a simple WCF web service and how to consume it from a Silverlight client. You can explore all the power of WCF, but keep in mind that the Silverlight WCF client can set some limitations to this power, as sometimes only some bindings and channels are supported. Anyway, it is being improved in every new version.

We have seen how easily Visual Studio generates all proxy classes (`Client` classes) in Silverlight from the WDSL definition of a web service. We have also learned how to consume an existing web service without WSDL facilities, passing parameters on URL and receiving and parsing the JSON response, close to REST principles. You can also apply this model with your own web services when it doesn't fit the WCF standard, that is, not publishing a WSDL guide to the service. For instance, those services created as actions in ASP.NET MVC, or those implemented using other platforms such as PHP, Java, and so on.

Finally, we have implemented a new feature in the trunk application that lets the user get weather information for the booking city from a public web service, and even though the service publishes its WSDL definition, the content response was not structured, so we ended up deserializing it manually.

11
Security

Security is a crucial and complex aspect which can fill several books in itself. It must be considered from the very beginning of a project, as well as taken into account for all decisions to be made. Nevertheless, in our case, for the sake of didacticism, it has been postponed to the final chapter so that we have all the pieces in the jigsaw of which our application consists. Two application areas can be distinguished:

- **Client-side security**: Applications run in a client machine, with all the derived risks of this practice. Basically, it exposes our code to its analysis and possible exploits.

- **Server-side and communication security**: Our applications communicate with a backend located in the server to retrieve and store data. In this case, security must be added for the data not to be exposed to unauthorized users or operations.

Even though this is a comprehensive topic, in this chapter, we will try to cover the basics about what can affect a business application, both on the client side and the server side.

Client-side security

In this case, let's suppose that our web application will be downloaded and executed in a remote machine, something that can be considered as a *hostile environment*. We have just provided an alleged malicious user with a perfect laboratory with which he/she can try to manipulate our application since:

- He/she will be able to see the binary code and resources (for example, binary XAML) by simply renaming the XAP file to ZIP

- It will be possible for him/her to access its source code by using a tool, such as a reflector (http://bit.ly/apbHRB)

- The original libraries could be replaced in the XAP content by others with he same interface, but containing malware
- It is also feasible to extract any critical data in the client code or configuration files

It cannot be forgotten that these issues are also found in different development technologies, such as HTML and JavaScript (where the code is directly exposed) or in a desktop application.

Consequently, our server must never trust the client, as it is more exposed and can be altered without our consent. That is, everything which is validated or verified at the client side must be validated again by the server. Despite this second filter, we will see how to mitigate these threats from the client as follows.

Critical information

In LOB applications, we can be tempted to store information about configuration in an XML file, or in the application code itself, including such data as users and passwords to access third-party systems. This should be avoided because any malicious user could consult the XAP as we mentioned earlier, or with more sophisticated approaches (such as a memory dump) getting it from the code or the application in execution.

What should we do then? Should we base security only on the credentials entered by the user? That ought to be enough to communicate and authenticate with the server, both in the application and third-party services. For instance, to send an e-mail, a user would enter his credentials to connect with the server and then send a petition through web service to our server using the previous authentication. Later, the server checks that the user sending the petition has the appropriate permissions and then uses the proper keys (now stored in the server) to send the e-mail via SMTP. The same principle must be applied both to websites based on JavaScript and desktop applications.

Signing assemblies

As we pointed out earlier, a Silverlight application is downloaded and executed in client computers, so a malicious user could be able to substitute a library with malicious code for the clean one.

The solution lies in signing our libraries using a combination of public/private keys. Therefore, if anyone replaces a library with another one containing different code, the application will throw an exception when trying to validate the signature and it will not be executed.

Every single project must be individually signed from the project properties in Visual Studio. The following are the steps to do this:

1.   Create a **Silverlight Class Library** project and name it `MyLib`.

2.   In the project properties, choose the **Signing** tab and check the **Sign the assembly** checkbox, as shown in the following screenshot:

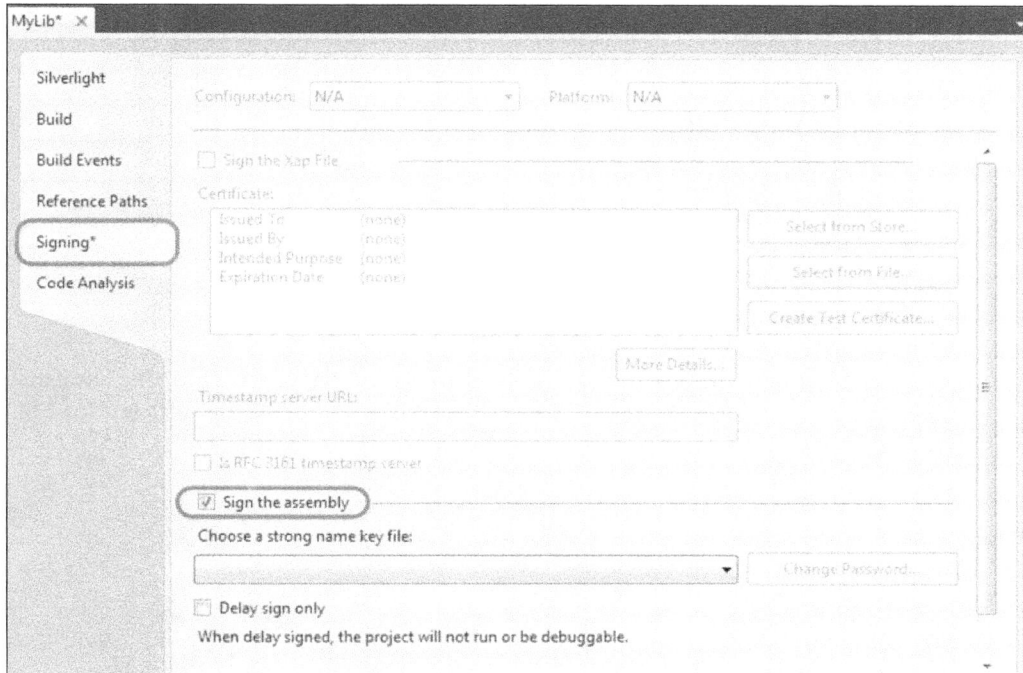

3.   Under that checkbox, there is a ComboBox called **Choose a strong name key file**, which allows us either to create a new key file or to choose an existing one (**Personal Information eXchange (PFX)** or **Strong Name Key File (SNK)**):

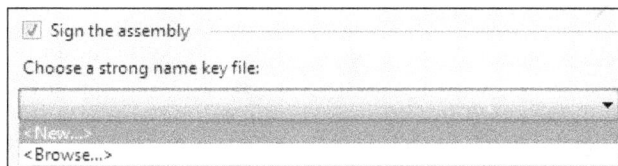

4. Create a new key file, give it a name and, in this case, do not protect it with a password (**Protect my key file with a password** should be unchecked). You could, however, choose to protect it just in case you do not trust the people who can access your source code.

Create Strong Name Key

Key file name:

myKey

☐ Protect my key file with a password

Enter password:

Confirm password:

OK   Cancel

5. Now we have our DLL signed. The key file is available in the project solution (`myKey.snk`). It could be used in some other library projects, which could be added to the solution.

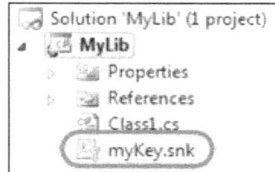

Solution 'MyLib' (1 project)
  MyLib
    Properties
    References
    Class1.cs
    myKey.snk

This has to be done in every project that is part of the solution since, when a project is created in Visual Studio, it will be generated without a signature.

XAP and certificates

Silverlight applications are executed within a sandbox, which means that they are isolated and only have limited access to the hardware and critical data of the machine where they are being executed. In *Chapter 6, Out Of Browser (OOB) Applications*, we dealt with a new type of application, trusted OOB applications, which are able to perform operations that could damage or compromise the user information.

Here, it is important to have reliable knowledge about where the application comes from. For this purpose, it could be signed with a Code Signature Certification (PFX), which has to be acquired from a trustworthy authority (VeriSign, Thawte, GoDaddy, Comodo, and so on). In case the application is not signed, the following issues may arise:

- When installing the OOB trusted application, a security warning pops up, as shown in the following screenshot:

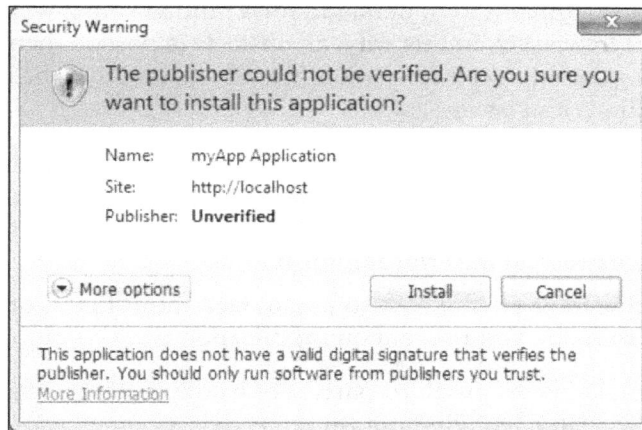

- The auto-update that we saw in *Chapter 6,Out Of Browser (OOB) Applications,* is not operative. This is due to the fact that the application is not signed and there is no guarantee that whatever gets updated is not malware.

In our Silverlight application, we could go to the **Signing** tab and select the PFX file intended to be used to sign the whole XAP (**Select from File...**), but if we do not already have one (**Select from Store...**) you need to create a test certificate (not trustworthy, **Create Test Certificate...**).

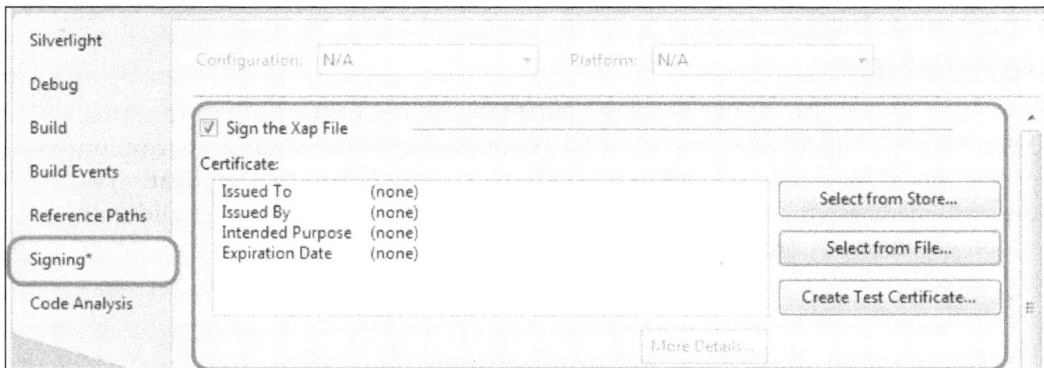

In this case, it is crucial to use a strong keyword with a password and put our PFX file in a safe place. If a third party could access and discover the code, they could create malware and sign it, indicating that the source is our company.

XAP and obfuscation

Preventing someone from disassembling our code is actually impossible, although we can make things more difficult for them by obfuscating it, that is, generating an assembly that is more difficult to understand for a human being, whereas a computer is able to execute it flawlessly. In this way, an obstacle is posed when practising inverse engineering so as to get information from the assembly. The following are the derived limitations and issues:

- Obfuscated code does not offer absolute security, so we cannot be overconfident and include critical data in our source code. In this case, an advanced attacker, or an attacker with a little more time, would be able to eventually extract all the critical information.
- The available tools are not easy to use; in fact, the obfuscation process itself can break the code and prevent our application from continuing to work.

The tools we can make use of are third party. For example, Deep Sea Obfuscator (`http://bit.ly/jTTfH6`), Dot Fuscator (`http://bit.ly/982bJp`), Codefort (`http://bit.ly/yOWjYh`), and .NET Reactor (`http://bit.ly/gUz8e`).

Server-side and communication security

In the previous section, we learned how to try and secure our application on the client side, and that it is nearly impossible to avoid any malicious attack or manipulation.

Now, we are going to learn how to add security on the server side, the last frontier a hacker has to face and the one where we have more control.

Validations

As we saw earlier, the server must not trust the validity of the information that comes from the client, as it can never be guaranteed that the data came from our application. These could come from a pretender, or even another application of ours, which shares the service. Therefore, it may have ignored all the validations implemented in our Silverlight application.

Due to this, the validations of the server must be repeated. To avoid heavy weather, the developer could feel tempted to omit client-side validations, which would not be incorrect nor may suppose a security risk. However, it is essential to recognize the value of these client-side validations and their contribution to the user experience, since the user gets immediate warnings when a piece of data is not correct, or when it is not possible to click on a certain button because it is disabled, avoiding the frustration of performing an action and eventually receiving a server error that rejects data, denies permissions, and so on. Besides, in order to prevent the work from being duplicated, more error-prone architecture should be generated. RIA Services gives the chance to implement validations on the server side that get automatically propagated to the client side (Silverlight application), via restrictions defined in the model with the use of Data Annotations. For more complex questions, we will have to figure out the best way to face validation in every single case, and whether it is beneficial for the user to receive client validation or not.

Cross-domain calls

For security reasons, a non-trusted Silverlight application only permits the making of calls to web services in the same domain. In this way, an application will not be able to send information or execute unauthorized commands to third parties.

Even if this security measure is assumed, sometimes it can be necessary for our application to directly access a third-party service. This can be done with the help of **cross-domain policies**.

What are these policies? They are defined in XML files, which must be at the root of the web server that has to be called. They indicate the third-party domains authorized to make calls to our domain and to what subfolders. For instance, in an image library portal, we could give them access to the public images folder, but not to the user administration folder.

To apply these policies, when a Silverlight application is going to make a petition to a third-party service, the following sequence is automatically executed:

1. The Silverlight application checks if there is a cross-domain policy in the target server that we want to have access to.
2. This checks the policy's file and decides whether to give it permission to access the service we want to call.
3. If we get permission, the call to the web service is made.

This sequence can be seen in action if we execute Fiddler (a famous HTTP packet tracker, more information is available at `http://bit.ly/GLSq7`) and we try to call a web service in a domain, which is not the source of the application.

Silverlight supports two kinds of policy files:

- **ClientAccessPolicy.xml**: The format of this file is defined by the Silverlight team and offers a more detailed control of the authorized domains.

- **Crossdomain.xml**: The format of this file is set by Adobe. It is useful if you are interested in your services being accessed both from Silverlight and Flash.

Let's see, as an illustration, the aspect of a `ClientAccesPolicy.xml` file, but remember not to use it just as it is, since it gives access to every domain and folder:

```xml
<?xml version="1.0" encoding="utf-8"?>
<access-policy>
  <cross-domain-access>
    <policy>
      <allow-from http-request-headers="SOAPAction">
        <domain uri="*"/>
      </allow-from>
      <grant-to>
        <resource path="/" include-subpaths="true"/>
      </grant-to>
    </policy>
  </cross-domain-access>
</access-policy>
```

If you want to customize it, for instance, to restrict access only to certain domains or folders, you can follow the guide available at `http://bit.ly/hhaBMr`.

Security in our communications

We have already seen how applications that are executed on the client side can be secured. However, as explained earlier, information transmitted from client to server can get exposed. So somebody could capture a trace to study it or intercept it and send malicious information instead of the original.

In order to avoid this, we have two entry-level points:

- **Implementing authentication and authorization**: These are two key concepts in computer security. Authentication allows us to identify and verify that a user identity is authentic. Authorization allows us to check that a user (logged in or anonymous) has permission to perform a certain action, normally via roles.

- **Ensuring communications**: To do so, an SSL certification can be acquired to access our services via HTTPS, so that the information is encoded and a spy cannot read our packets.

Now, we will see how to apply the concepts of authentication and authorization in the two main communication channels with the server that has been proposed in this book, namely, data access via RIA or WCF Services.

Authentication and authorization with RIA Services

RIA Services adds a layer on top of WCF to hide the complexity and allows us to focus on performing CRUD operations. It also contains a functionality to allow us to authenticate and authorize, (this functionality is fully integrated with the ASP.NET Membership Provider).

Authentication

So as to identify a user, first the authentication mechanism has to be established on the server since, although the process is initiated on the client side, the server guarantees the identity. We can make use of the authentication mechanisms that ASP.NET offers to use (this is the platform on which our server runs). To do this:

1. Define a Membership Provider, `CustomMembershipProvider`. In this class, implement (at least) the check which will validate if a user defined by their username and password is valid.

2. Register that Membership Provider in the `web.config` of the ASP.NET application.

3. Create an Authentication Domain Services (RIA Services) `MyAuthenticationDomainService`. In this case, it is not necessary to implement additional code.

4. In our Domain Service, we can indicate that it is compulsory for a user to be authenticated to access data. This can also be used for a method.

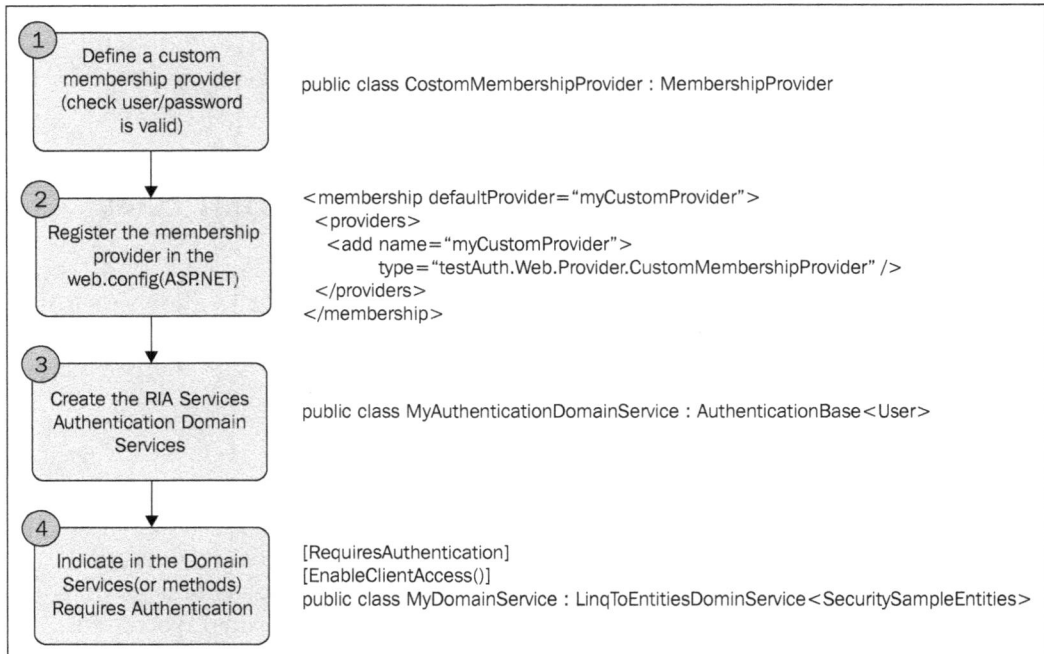

① Define a custom membership provider (check user/password is valid)	`public class CostomMembershipProvider : MembershipProvider`
② Register the membership provider in the web.config(ASP.NET)	```<membership defaultProvider="myCustomProvider">
<providers>
<add name="myCustomProvider">
type="testAuth.Web.Provider.CustomMembershipProvider" />
</providers>
</membership>```
③ Create the RIA Services Authentication Domain Services	`public class MyAuthenticationDomainService : AuthenticationBase<User>`
④ Indicate in the Domain Services(or methods) Requires Authentication	```[RequiresAuthentication]
[EnableClientAccess()]
public class MyDomainService : LinqToEntitiesDominService<SecuritySampleEntities>```

Now, our authentication platform is configured in the server. Using it on the client side involves the following steps:

1. Initialize the security in the context (`WebContext`).

2. Ask the user for their credentials with an interface developed for this purpose, where the user must enter their name and password. Then, make an asynchronous call to the server in order to authenticate the user.

3. The response of the asynchronous operation will show whether it has been successful or not.

4. Later, it could be possible to check if there is an authenticated user and their name, through `WebContext.Current.User`.

```
public App()
{
  (_)
  WebContext context = new WebContext();
  context.Authentication = new FormsAuthentication(),}
  Application LifetimeObjects.Add(context);
}


_loginOp = WebContext.Current.Authentication.Login(
                    new LoginParameters(txName.Text, txPassword.Text)
                                                );
_loginOp.Completed += new EventHandler(loginOp_Completed);


void loginOp_Completed(object sender, EventArgs e)
{
  (...)
  if (!_loginOp.LoginSuccess)
  {
      MessageBox.Show("User Name/Password not valid");
  }
  else
      (...)
MessageBox.Show("Welcome Mr. " +WebContext.Current.User.Name);
```

Steps (left column):

1. Initialize security context (app initialize)

2. Ask for user credentials and validate them(async call)

3. Once async call completed check if login operation has been successfully completed

4. We can extract as well the user information

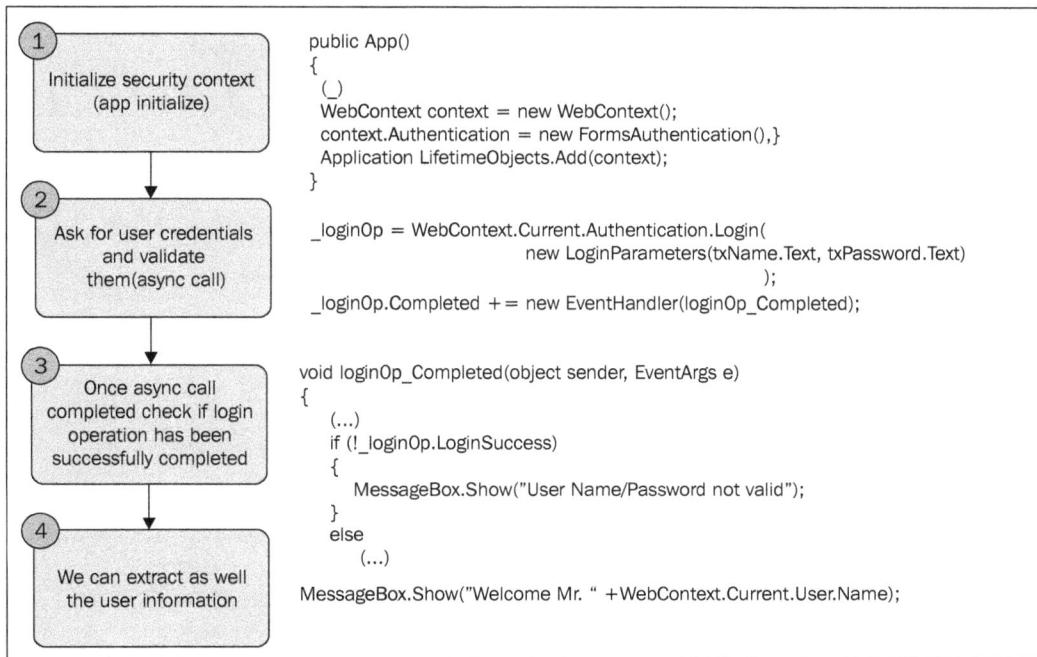

In the Silverlight client, we only have the username, as it has been exposed previously. We recommend performing the essentials of security on the server side. If it is necessary to perform conditional actions on the client side, such as enabling commands or viewing certain data, it should be done by requesting this information from the server, avoiding the risks we have already pointed out.

Authorization

If we want to know the permissions that a user is assigned once authenticated, we establish our own authorization mechanism via roles. Again, it is possible to make the most of the possibilities that ASP.NET gives us by following the steps given next:

1. Define a Role Provider, CustomRoleProvider. This will implement at least one consultation, which will return the roles assigned to a particular user according to their name.

2. Register that Role Provider in the web.config of the ASP.NET application.

3. Annotate the Domain Service calls that require the user to belong to certain roles with the `RequiresRole` attribute for them to be executed.

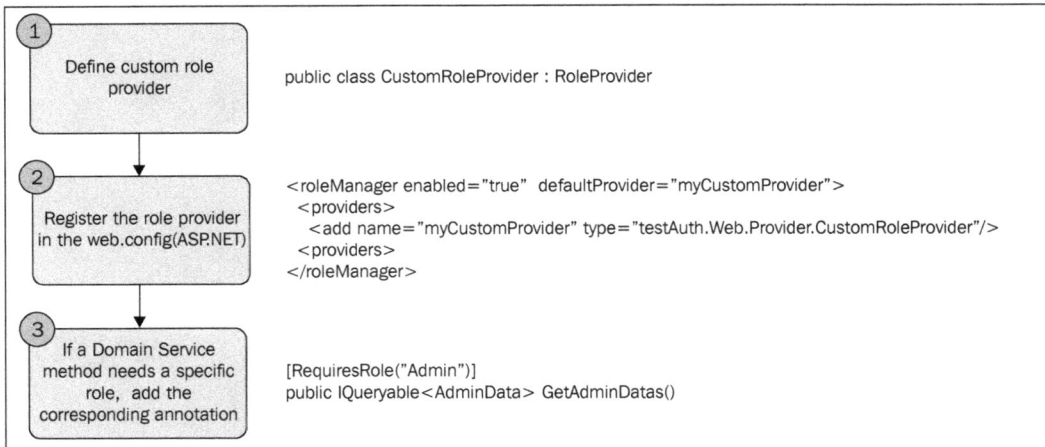

---

① Define custom role provider

```
public class CustomRoleProvider : RoleProvider
```

② Register the role provider in the web.config(ASP.NET)

```
<roleManager enabled="true" defaultProvider="myCustomProvider">
  <providers>
    <add name="myCustomProvider" type="testAuth.Web.Provider.CustomRoleProvider"/>
  <providers>
</roleManager>
```

③ If a Domain Service method needs a specific role, add the corresponding annotation

```
[RequiresRole("Admin")]
public IQueryable<AdminData> GetAdminDatas()
```

It must be noted that, for role assignment to users (that is, for Role Provider implementation), it is possible to use the standard implementation based upon SQL Server and offered for ASP.NET, or a customized one. For further information, please visit `http://bit.ly/L9prf`.

Actually, to have better control of permissions in our model and integrate the users with the rest of the entities, it is advisable to use entities of our own. Probably, a user entity (with access name, encoded password, and the associated role) will suffice, in case our application does not need a user to have more than one role. Doing this, the implementations of the two providers will be simple queries to the data of this entity via Entity Framework Data Context.

Now, our server is configured and the information on the current user and their roles can be accessed. Use the mechanisms which ASP.NET provides for any web application, either with the described attributes or by accessing `HttpContext.Current.User.Identity.Name`. This piece of data is also available with the user property in pages, controls, controllers, and so on. Also, it is possible to access user roles in the same way, consulting individually if a user belongs to a role or not, such as `HttpContext.Current.User.IsInRole("Admin")`.

On the other hand, there are two client-side aspects which have to be considered:

- It is possible to know the roles of a particular user accessing `WebContext.Current.User.IsInRole`. Although this may act as a filter, more oriented to make the application use easier, it must be ratified by the server in every call.

- Manage the possible permission errors that may be received when trying to call a method to which we are not authorized. Even though this could make the UI uglier, it is preferable not to allow the user to perform an action they are not allowed to.

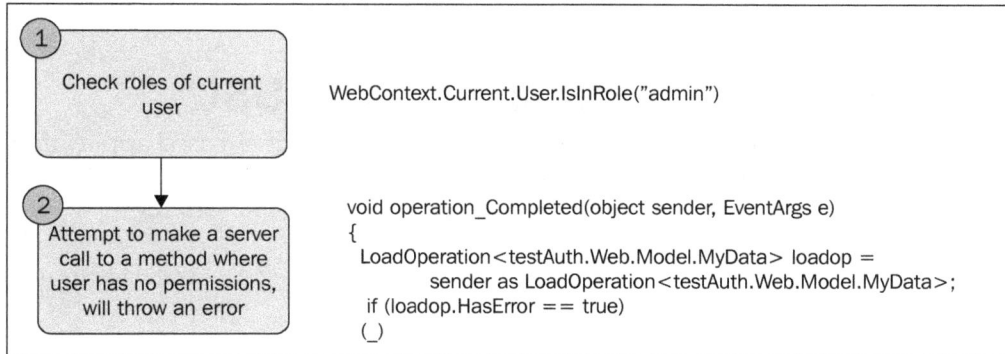

1 Check roles of current user	WebContext.Current.User.IsInRole("admin")

2 Attempt to make a server call to a method where user has no permissions, will throw an error	void operation_Completed(object sender, EventArgs e)
	{
	  LoadOperation<testAuth.Web.Model.MyData> loadop =
	        sender as LoadOperation<testAuth.Web.Model.MyData>;
	  if (loadop.HasError == true)
	  (_)

Authentication and authorization in WCF Services

If we aim to use the authentication and authorization mechanisms configured in ASP.NET from a WCF service, it must be asked that the service is executed in the same ASP.NET context, sharing status and session with it. Thereby, we will have access to the ASP.NET and, consequently, to the user authenticated in the web application from our web service. So as to enable the compatibility in all services, the following section must be added to the web.config service:

```
<system.serviceModel>
  <serviceHostingEnvironment
    aspNetCompatibilityEnabled="true"/>
...
...
</system.serviceModel>
```

Another option implies the establishment of the compatibility individually in the header of the class defining the web service, by means of the attribute AspNetCompatibilityRequirements:

```
[AspNetCompatibilityRequirements(RequirementsMode =
  AspNetCompatibilityRequirementsMode.Allowed)]
  publicclassMyService
```

One way or another, we can now enjoy the possibility of checking the user and the roles they belong to in our WCF service, in the same way as we saw earlier in the chapter:

```
if (HttpContext.Current.User.IsInRole("Admin"))
...
```

Protecting communications with SSL

To enable the use of Secure Sockets Layer (SSL) in a RIA Services-based application, it is just necessary to add the `RequiresSecureEndpoint=true` parameter in the attribute `EnableClientAccess` of the Domain Service, `MyDomainService`:

```
[EnableClientAccess(RequiresSecureEndpoint = true)]
public class MyDomainService :
  LinqToEntitiesDomainService<SecuritySampleEntities>
```

If the aim is to have this secure communication operating, it will be necessary to enable SSL in IIS by registering the corresponding certification, as in `http://bit.ly/nqcnMW`.

Regarding WCF Services, it is essential to perform three modifications in order to enable access via SSL.

The first thing to do is to modify the binding configuration in the server. When entering a context where the user has already passed a security filter, the configuration (in `web.config`) will be as follows:

```
<binding name="MyService.customBinding0">
  <security mode="Transport">
    <transport clientCredentialType="None"/>
  </security>
</binding>
```

Then, it is time to configure the `behavior` in the same file, `MyService.MyServiceBehavior`, where the HTTPS is activated by means of the `httpsGetEnabled` property.

```
<behavior name="MyService.MyServiceBehavior">
  <serviceMetadatahttpsGetEnabled="true" />
</behavior>
```

Finally, change the Silverlight client configuration to establish the appropriate values in the `endpoint`, as can be seen in the following source code:

```
<service
  behaviorConfiguration="MyService.MyServiceBehavior "
  name="MyService">
  <endpoint binding="basicHttpBinding"
    bindingConfiguration=
    "MyService.customBinding0"contract="MyService" />
  <endpoint address="mex" binding="mexHttpsBinding"
    contract="IMetadataExchange" />
</service>
```

LOB application case study: applying what we have learned

For our booking application, the following is necessary:

- The user must identify themselves before starting the application
- The bookings information assigned to the user must be shown
- To detect the user role:
    - **Normal**: Their bookings can be viewed, as well as created and updated
    - **Administrator**: They can also manage the available floors and rooms

In order to do so, we enter a few changes, both on the server side and the client side.

Server side

Regarding the server, we define ASP.NET providers for authentication and authorization in the project named `Packt.Booking.Server.Data`. There, we also define the Authentication Service of RIA Services.

Once defined, we need to modify the web.config of the web project (Packt. Booking.Server.Web), indicating the providers that will be used.

```
<!-- Security-->
<authentication mode="Forms" />
<membership defaultProvider="myCustomProvider">
  <providers>
    <add name="myCustomProvider"
      type="Packt.Booking.Server.
      Data.Providers.CustomMembershipProvider" />
  </providers>
</membership>
<roleManager enabled="true"
  defaultProvider="myCustomProvider">
  <providers>
    <add name="myCustomProvider"
      type="Packt.Booking.Server.
      Data.Providers.CustomRoleProvider" />
  </providers>
</roleManager>
```

Once into the services, the annotation is added so as to ask the user to be authenticated to access the Domain Service. Also, we add the annotation to ask for the administration role in those operations wherever it is necessary.

```
[RequiresAuthentication]
public partial class BookingDomainService :
  LinqToEntitiesDomainService<BookingsEntities>
{
(...)
[RequiresRole("Admin")]
public void UpdateFloor(Floor currentFloor)
{
(...)
```

Regarding the source code, the ID of the user who has logged in must also be checked. For this purpose, we use:

```
reservation.IDUser =
  GetUserIDFromLoginName
  (this.ServiceContext.User.Identity.Name);
```

We have already used this control in the operations named InsertBooking and GetMyReservations. Now, we would only need to check in Update and DeleteBooking (to ensure that malicious users do not modify entries that are not theirs).

Client side

The first surprise we get on the client side is that the code generated by RIA Services does not incorporate a `WebContext`. It is due to the division previously made, that is, isolating the Domain Service and Authentication Service to a data project. Then, we must create our own class. It can be found in `Packt.Booking.Common\Web`, and it can be initialized as we saw at the beginning of the chapter.

```
public sealed partial class WebContext :WebContextBase
{

    #region Extensibility Method Definitions

    /// This method is invoked from the constructor once
    /// initialization is complete and can be used for
    /// further object setup.
    partial void OnCreated();

    #endregion

    /// Initializes a new instance of the WebContext class.
    publicWebContext()
    {
        this.OnCreated();
    }

    /// Gets the context that is registered as a lifetime
    /// object with the current application.
    public new static WebContext Current
    {
        get
        {
            return ((WebContext)(WebContextBase.Current));
        }
    }

    /// Gets a user representing the authenticated
      ///identity.
    public new User User
    {
        get
        {
            return ((User)(base.User));
        }
    }
}
```

As soon as the application is started, it shows a login dialog, as shown in the
following screenshot:

From the ViewModel, we will perform the corresponding calls of the Authorization
Service and will send a message, once successfully authenticated.

```
LoginOperationloginOp =
  WebContext.Current.Authentication.Login(Login,
  Password);

loginOp.Completed += (s, e) =>
{
  if (loginOp.HasError)
  {
    (...)
  }
  Else
  {
    if (loginOp.LoginSuccess)
    {
      Messenger.Default.Send(new
        LoginSuccessfulMessage()); ());
    }
    (...)
```

The following message is used to redirect the user to the main page:

```
Messenger.Default.Register<LoginSuccessfulMessage>(this,
  (p) =>
{
  stringurl = NavigationHelper.MyBookingsURL;
  NavigationService.Navigate(url);
});
```

It is also used to disable the **Administration** option in the menu, if the user does not have the Admin role:

```
Messenger..Default.Register<LoginSuccessfulMessage>(this,
  (p) =>
{
  if (WebContext.Current.User.IsAuthenticated == true
  &&WebContext.Current.User.IsInRole("Admin"))
  {
    UserHasAdminPermissions = true;
  }
});
```

If a malicious user finds a way to access the administration options without having permissions, or they try to send an HTTP petition, they will see that the server rejects the petition, as it has not been authenticated

Summary

In this chapter, we saw how easy it is to add security to our application. It is also possible to create OOB trusted applications and add authentication and authorization levels in an easy way.

Additional resources

For more information on security, check the following links:

- Assemblies signature: `http://bit.ly/abJMfG`
- Signing an XAP with a code certification: `http://bit.ly/liasVl`
- RIA Services and security: `http://bit.ly/991Tjz`

Index

Symbols

[PACKT] PUBLISHING enterprise ⌗
professional expertise distilled

Thank you for buying
Mastering LOB Development for Silverlight 5: A Case Study in Action

About Packt Publishing

Packt, pronounced 'packed', published its first book "Mastering phpMyAdmin for Effective MySQL Management" in April 2004 and subsequently continued to specialize in publishing highly focused books on specific technologies and solutions.

Our books and publications share the experiences of your fellow IT professionals in adapting and customizing today's systems, applications, and frameworks. Our solution based books give you the knowledge and power to customize the software and technologies you're using to get the job done. Packt books are more specific and less general than the IT books you have seen in the past. Our unique business model allows us to bring you more focused information, giving you more of what you need to know, and less of what you don't.

Packt is a modern, yet unique publishing company, which focuses on producing quality, cutting-edge books for communities of developers, administrators, and newbies alike. For more information, please visit our website: www.packtpub.com.

About Packt Enterprise

In 2010, Packt launched two new brands, Packt Enterprise and Packt Open Source, in order to continue its focus on specialization. This book is part of the Packt Enterprise brand, home to books published on enterprise software – software created by major vendors, including (but not limited to) IBM, Microsoft and Oracle, often for use in other corporations. Its titles will offer information relevant to a range of users of this software, including administrators, developers, architects, and end users.

Writing for Packt

We welcome all inquiries from people who are interested in authoring. Book proposals should be sent to author@packtpub.com. If your book idea is still at an early stage and you would like to discuss it first before writing a formal book proposal, contact us; one of our commissioning editors will get in touch with you.

We're not just looking for published authors; if you have strong technical skills but no writing experience, our experienced editors can help you develop a writing career, or simply get some additional reward for your expertise.

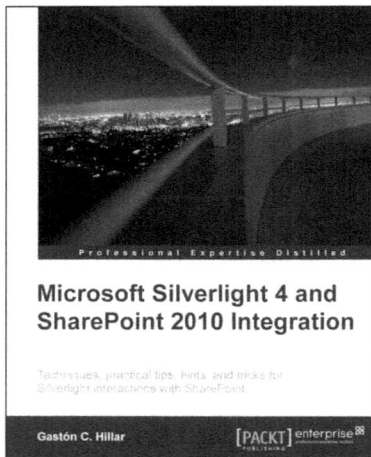

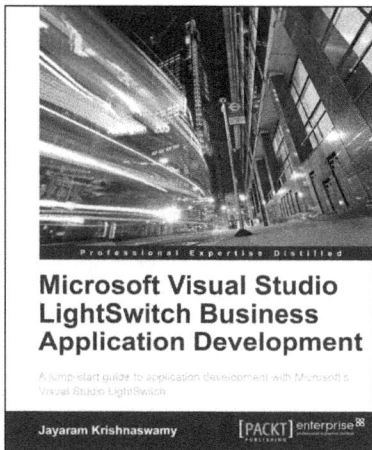